THE NEXT SUPPER

THE NEXT SUPPER

The End of Restaurants as We Knew Them, and What Comes After

COREY MINTZ

PUBLICAFFAIRS
New York

PublicAffairs
Hachette Book Group
1290 Avenue of the Americas, New York, NY 10104
www.publicaffairsbooks.com
@Public_Affairs

Printed in the United States of America.
First Edition: November 2021

Published by PublicAffairs, an imprint of Perseus Books, LLC, a subsidiary of Hachette Book Group, Inc. The PublicAffairs name and logo is a trademark of the Hachette Book Group.

The Hachette Speakers Bureau provides a wide range of authors for speaking events. To find out more, go to www.hachettespeakersbureau.com or call (866) 376-6591.

The publisher is not responsible for websites (or their content) that are not owned by the publisher.

Print book interior design by Linda Mark.

Library of Congress Cataloging-in-Publication Data
Names: Mintz, Corey, 1975– author.
Title: The next supper : the end of restaurants as we knew them, and what comes after / Corey Mintz.
Description: First edition. | New York : PublicAffairs, 2021. | Includes bibliographical references and index.
Identifiers: LCCN 2021012800 | ISBN 9781541758407 (hardcover) | ISBN 9781541758421 (ebook)
Subjects: LCSH: Food service—Moral and ethical aspects. | Restaurants—Moral and ethical aspects.
Classification: LCC TX911.3.E84 M56 2021 | DDC 641.3002—dc23
LC record available at https://lccn.loc.gov/2021012800

ISBNs: 9781541758407 (hardcover), 9781541758421 (ebook)

LSC-C

Printing 1, 2021

For Katie Gillmor Ellis (1944–2016),
who taught me you never throw anything away;
you just save it for later.

Contents

Introduction

"YOU HAVE JOINED THE CALL, BUT YOU ARE THE ONLY ONE here," says the machine. I can't tell if it's a simulated voice meant to sound human or a human voice modulated to sound robotic.

It's Monday, March 16, 2020, the day the restaurants died. Like most people, I've spent the weekend watching the world come to a sudden halt. Just a week before, restaurants had been placating customers with the promise that they were treating the coronavirus with an abundance of caution, that their staff and premises upheld the highest standards of hygiene. That it was safe to dine with them. As the weekend neared, though, diners started canceling reservations. In normal times, restaurateurs don't like to advertise empty dining rooms, but something unprecedented was happening. Early on Wednesday, the eleventh, Ashwin Deshmukh announced his New York restaurant had just hit $100,000 in canceled event business, the number climbing to $385,000 by the afternoon. By Friday, the thirteenth, industry leader Danny Meyer closed all nineteen of his restaurants, followed quickly on Sunday, the fifteenth, by the entire nations of France and Spain.[1]

I'm supposed to be speaking with Janet Zuccarini, who owns a half dozen restaurants in Los Angeles and Toronto—not about impending doom, but regarding legal and cultural distinctions between the two countries in which she operates. Zuccarini's company, Gusto 54, has a great reputation for how they treat, train, compensate, and retain staff, something that in my quest to find restaurants to support, I care about very much. Given her success on both sides of the border, I'm hoping she can shed some light on the differences in working conditions, labor laws, and management styles between the United States and Canada. "You have joined the call, but you are the only one here," I'm reminded.

There are at least five *Twilight Zone* episodes in which the protagonists inexplicably find themselves in a landscape devoid of people—"Time Enough at Last," "King Nine Will Not Return," "Two," "Stopover in a Quiet Town," "Where Is Everybody?" There may be more. In my near-silent basement office, sitting at my ironing board–size desk, wedged between a treadmill, racks of my wife's clothing, my comic books, and piles and piles of baby clothes we're waiting for our five-month-old to grow into, I feel like I'm in one of them. It's hard to be certain that the world outside does exist and I'm not the last person alive. There's no certainty that earth hasn't been eaten by Galactus. If I get off this call and head upstairs, will there be anyone there? Were my family, my life, and all the hours I wasted watching television just an implanted memory, a sensory-deprivation hallucination, a *Jacob's Ladder* near-death fever dream? Am I the last survivor of a nuclear war and my ironic punishment is to be eternally trapped on a conference call with myself?

It's been five minutes. I hang up the video call and try one of the numbers I have for her in my email. Zuccarini picks up on the first ring. I sheepishly explain who I am. "Sorry," she says, as if our phone call is at all important in the context of the catastrophe she's facing. "I'm in crisis mode. I have ten restaurants, nearly a thousand employees."

All weekend, Zuccarini has been glued to her phone and computer, watching the situation unfold in Italy, where the country has been on lockdown but the general population isn't following the rules, and China, where COVID-19 infections have slowed but only after draconian public restrictions. She hasn't slept. I ask if she's going to close her businesses. It's just after nine in the morning in California. This is a few hours before proactive state governments start mandating the closure of nonessential businesses and a few days before the National Restaurant Association predicts five to seven million jobs will be lost.[2] "Yeah. I'm thinking of shutting down. I think it's the right thing to do. We're gonna go today to just takeout and delivery. I'm making plans to close them all down. I don't know how to financially carry on with zero revenue and employees on salary."

It gets worse. She's been in the process of launching five more restaurants this year. One is completed, a ten-thousand-square-foot restaurant that opened just weeks ago; the other four are still under construction. "It's not like I stockpiled cash. I don't have backers. I'm financing everything. And all the cash is out on all these projects. When I go to zero revenue, and a thousand employees . . . ," she repeats, her voice trailing off. Zuccarini is a successful restaurateur. She's leveraged that success to expand. At the worst possible moment, she is way overextended.

My gut falls away. I got into writing through the side door, as a restaurant critic. I came into that position after years as a professional cook; I never went to journalism school. I never formed the instinct to push my way in when people are at their most vulnerable, was never taught how to go about it. So I feel like I'm intruding, and I want to get off the phone. Zuccarini has a talk scheduled with another restaurant group, hoping she can learn how to survive this ordeal. I tell her she'd better take that call. She thanks me and promises to set up a call for later, when things have settled down. Things never do settle down.

After hanging up, I look at my notes. Over the past six months, I'd spoken to restaurateurs, cooks, servers, teachers, economists, activists, and policy makers, asking a lot of variations on one question: Knowing what I know about what goes on in restaurants, how food is produced, who grows it, who cooks it, who profits, and who is exploited, how do I eat out and maintain my values? I'm convinced there's a better way to be a restaurant customer. That's why I wanted to write this book—to find those answers and share them.

And suddenly, there are no more restaurants. In the past five days, the unofficial president of Hollywood Tom Hanks tested positive for COVID-19 and the NBA suspended its season, marking the moment when America started treating the pandemic as a real threat. Today McDonald's ceased dine-in service. And by tomorrow, publicly traded restaurants will have lost half of their value.[3]

There will be restaurants again. Even in this dark moment, I know that. But when? What will they look like? Who will survive and in what form? Was this an unjust, senseless cataclysm? An opportunity to recode the twisted DNA of the dining industry? Both?

WE THINK OF restaurants as places to eat. And they are—in the same way that Tony Soprano would describe his operation as "waste management" or a Japanese feudal lord might have complained about the annual rice tax to Kyoto for their "small family business." A restaurant dining room, in other words, is real but also a theatrical facade. For those on the inside, restaurants are fiefdoms, organized according to their own rules and customs, often apart (though not legally exempt) from the law of the land, with oversize personalities playing a disproportionate role in leadership. Yes, restaurants are where we eat. They are also places where wage theft, tip skimming, and abuse are rampant.

On the outside, for diners, restaurants are our gateway into the modern food system. Food binds us together, but very few of us have any hands-on involvement with its production.

At the dawn of the twentieth century, with 41 percent of America's workforce employed in agriculture, people had a direct relationship with their food source. By the 1950s that had fallen to about 12 percent. In 2017 it was 1.3 percent. Human civilization has urbanized. Because of it we enjoy a lot of conveniences. That massive migration toward urban centers means that most of us don't have any real connection to where food comes from, how it's produced, or who grows it.

Meanwhile, we spend more and more of our food budget for food away from home (that's FAFH, the statistician's umbrella term for money spent at restaurants, bars, hotels, water parks, hot dog stands, Saved by the Bell pop-ups, and the like). In the 1950s, dining out was about a quarter of our grocery budget. It grew to 50 percent by 1992, and it continued to rise, until 2015, when America's dining-out spending exceeded that for home food for the first time. Though it was for only one financial quarter, it was the continuation of a trend that wasn't stopping, with the dining-out numbers overtaking grocery in the warm months of 2018 and 2019.

In the past decade, many of us have uncovered a lot of unpleasant truths about where our food comes from—within the restaurant industry itself and in the entire food chain that supplies both professional kitchens and the kitchens in our homes with raw ingredients. We've switched to fair-trade coffee beans that properly pay growers. We've chosen to eat fruit that's grown locally, in season, rather than accept the environmental toll of flying raspberries from Chile in the winter. We've changed some of our eating habits because of this realization. Mostly those changes are confined to our grocery choices, though: we can pick up that carton of free-range eggs or opt for the organic bananas instead of the conventional ones. Or, at least, we can if we're lucky enough to live in a place with a supermarket that stocks these items and we have the cash to pay for them. As diners, we have a far-wider expanse of options for where and how to spend our money—for what kind of businesses we want to support. But though we have far more options for where to eat, dining out offers even fewer choices if we are concerned about the ethics involved.

Working as a cook, and then as a restaurant critic and food reporter, I've seen this industry from the inside out and back again. I've been on the boats at dawn, where fishers find out if they'll be able to pay their mortgage based on how many pickerel they hauled out of the lake. I've walked over fields of broccoli devastated by swede midges, the risk of growing organic vegetables without spraying pesticides. I've cooked in kitchens alongside young people who started smoking just so they could take a break in their thirteen-hour, sub-minimum-wage workdays.

The restaurant industry, to put it as politely as I can, is fucked up. At best, restaurants are problematic faves. Once you know what Michael Jackson did, it's hard to include "Don't Stop 'til You Get Enough" in your wedding playlist. Once you know how the sausage is made, how a chef treats their employees, or where they get their tomatoes, it's hard to eat that spicy chicken sandwich. With each lesson on the injustices within the system, it becomes more difficult to see only the surface of our dining industry, represented to consumers through top-ten lists and to economists as an untouchable job-creation engine, and to ignore the rusty, unappetizing parts of our broken food system in need of overhauling.

If we learned anything from the 2008 recession, it's that once the economy recovers, people want to forget the pain, sadness, and uncertainty. We want to spend and reclaim our consumer lifestyles. We probably won't want to learn any lessons or change the behaviors that got us into trouble in the first place. Change happens most often out of necessity. When not impelled, we return to the safety and comfort of the familiar status quo, even if it wasn't such a swell deal to begin with. COVID-19 has shaken things up: restaurant spending obviously didn't exceed that for groceries in 2020. But I am worried that, as the pandemic recedes, we will revert to the trajectory we were on before—that in our relief, and as we have done after previous crises, we will snap back into supporting a restaurant industry that is fundamentally broken.

But I believe there is room for improvement and that we eaters can be part of that. In our society, dining out is among the most fundamental of human activities and a source of community that can't be replaced. Even if it seems right now that it's facing extinction.

I'M A STINKER, I know. But I wasn't always such a killjoy. How did I go from being a cheerleader for restaurants and chefs, gorging on pork bellies like they were grapes, to being a scold and a nag, bumming people out with my constant reminders of pay disparity, the unfairness of tipping, slave shrimp, food-media payola, migrant farm labor exploitation, and so on? My conspiracy theory is that I was tricked, by a clever newspaper editor, into developing a conscience.

My first day as a journalist began with denying that I was one. After years of cooking in restaurants, I'd miraculously been hired by Canada's largest newspaper to fill in for their restaurant critic during her maternity leave. Right away I went to the HR Department on what turned out to be a futile mission to tell them they'd made a mistake, that my title should be "critic," and not "reporter," as listed on my contract. I could tell you if an octopus had been sufficiently braised, or if a rich sauce overwhelmed the vibrancy of spring asparagus, but I didn't know the first thing about reporting. There was no such job description as "critic" in this workplace, I was told. Everyone there was considered a journalist and classified as either reporter, editor, or photojournalist.

That afternoon, I found myself in a roomful of editors and writers, most of them at least twenty years older than me. It was the weekly story-pitch session. Though I was shy and didn't know how to dial an outside line (press 9) or where to find spare batteries (in the drawer near the photo assignment editor), when it was my turn I proposed a story about the paradox of cooking wages—the nicer a restaurant is, the less the cooks are paid, sometimes not at all. Half of the room didn't believe me. The other half told me that young people need to pay their dues. These were mostly baby boomers who had worked hard to succeed, and they'd been rewarded with good, secure, well-paying jobs and benefits, at least until the newspaper industry collapsed.

A year in, with the mat leave winding down, my boss, Kim, called me into her office with an idea. I had recently gotten to interview Ruth Reichl, then editor of *Gourmet* magazine, former dining critic for the *New York Times* and the *LA Times*, and pretty much my hero. Instead of taking her to a restaurant, I had cooked for her, a guanciale (spicy, cured pork jowl), lettuce, and tomato sandwich—in my home, where she turned around and grilled me on the provenance of the GLT's ingredients. In addition to writing a standard article about the interview, I also wrote a blog post about getting to meet Reichl, whose memoirs were my blueprint for how to be a critic, the stress of cooking for her, and how I'd chosen that dish. Kim wanted to know if I could do that every week. And for the next five years, that's what I did.

At first it was just one guest or two. From the beginning, the mandate was broad—cook a meal for an interview guest in my home. Fair enough. Very soon I realized that I couldn't cook and interview simultaneously, so the one-on-one turned into a dinner party, often populated by guests who brought their own personalities and questions into the story. During that time, I hosted a thousand people in my home. How could I not think they were teaching me something?

Early in the process Kim told me to stay away from chefs, restaurant owners, farmers, and other food-industry types. At the time I think she was looking to avoid what she knew was a dead end: the column becoming a repetitive platform for restaurant culture. I think she also saw the potential for something more and knew that forcing me to interact with a wider spectrum of humanity would be good for me, or at least the column. I think she knew, as a seasoned journalist, what she was doing: I knew restaurants but needed an education in the world outside.

Soon there were politicians, academics, sex-crime police, architects, competitive eaters, puppeteers, magicians, leather daddies, activists, acupuncturists, arborists, an abortion doctor, high-rise window washers, and a succession of mayors at the table.

Until then, my universe had been very small. Before social media and the trend of open kitchen design, the realm of restaurant cooking, usually in windowless rooms, closed you off from outside influences. Now things were opening up. A dinner with my city councilor, including an unsatisfying answer about why my neighborhood's trash bins were so small, sent me down the rabbit hole of local politics, searching for answers not found in a cookbook. Hours spent eating and drinking with civil rights lawyers, egg farmers, refugees fleeing persecution in Uganda and Russia, and a North Korean travel guide shed light on my city, my country, and my planet. The curricular aspect should have been obvious to me. At one point I was just inviting professors in a transparent exchange of smoked brisket and ceviche for lessons in economics or psychology or whatever I happened to be interested in at the time.

After five years of this, we ended the column and started a new one, "Kitchen Temp" (no one at the paper wanted to gamble that readers would know how to pronounce *stage* or *stagiaire*, the industry term for an unpaid kitchen intern), in which I spent a shift cooking in a different restaurant kitchen every week. My ambition was to use my kitchen skills (even if I was old and they were rusty) to gain the trust of the cooks (a task that took the first half of each shift), in order to observe and describe the complexity of the anthill inside a restaurant and how each one was different.

In a twist anyone could have seen coming, this quickly diverted me to the beat of restaurant labor. At one restaurant, in about 2015, the chef asked me if I knew any good cooks. This was at the starting period of a kitchen labor shortage. When I asked about pay, he told me his day rates. Without a hint of embarrassment he quoted the pay for a twelve-hour shift, with no breaks (they ate staff meals on their feet, while prepping), which worked out to less than minimum wage and was illegal.

At another restaurant, when the dishwasher didn't show up, I jumped into the dish pit for Sunday brunch service. After four hours in a tight, humid space, hundreds of free-range eggs sputtering on the griddle, grease from a mountain of home-smoked bacon mingling with the air, and an endless barrage of dirty dishes slammed down in front of me, each one slicked with yolk residue and customer spittle, I was happy for a breather. The last thing I wanted to do was inhale nicotine. But I remembered, from when I did this for a living, that smoking is often the only excuse, during a long day, for leaving the kitchen or getting off your feet. The alley behind every restaurant is where cooks, in that brief respite from the constant demand to display pain-resistant machismo, are prone to complain.

Though I don't smoke, I went into the alley to ask the cooks for a cigarette. All three of us were sticky from a mixture of sweat and steam, having pumped out a grueling brunch shift. We shared a smoke and started talking about wages.

Over the following months, I spoke with dozens of cooks, in alleys or bars, hearing that nothing had changed since my time in the kitchen. I was finally ready to write the story about how cooks are paid, the one I'd pitched on my first day as a journalist. Only by this time, I knew how to do it.

By then I knew how to investigate, to gain the trust of sources, to be thorough and fair in my research, to present it all to the reader in a palatable form. After publication, I became an enemy to the chefs I had lionized only a few years earlier.

That part didn't bother me. The role of critic had accustomed me to being unpopular. What bothered me was the nagging feeling that I wasn't done; once I'd looked under the rock, I couldn't stop looking. Suddenly, all I could see were the systemic problems in food that I'd spent years ignoring—in our restaurants, fields, oceans, classrooms, hospitals, prisons, boardrooms, and chambers of government. Now I understood why Reichl had been less interested in discussing restaurant reviewing with me than asking about where I'd gotten my tomatoes and meat, how the people and animals involved were treated, if I'd made the mayonnaise myself. Those things matter, in a way that telling people where to get the best tasting menu never can.

※

A DECADE AGO, as food culture began its mission creep into the center of our thoughts and conversations, it came with a message of peace and goodwill. "I love the speed with which the food world moves, ushering forth new taste sensations and better ideas with the let's-top-ourselves alacrity of Apple Computer and the anything's-possible ambition of 1960s NASA," wrote David Kamp in his 2006 book, *The United States of Arugula: How We Became a Gourmet Nation.* "I love the way each new month brings with it some strange, unexpected, or simply delicious new edible to try."[4] Even in prose intended to celebrate our obsession with food, Kamp quickly devalues its importance: food leaves behind the loftiness of reaching the moon and takes on the disposable nature of fast fashion, prized only for newness.

But when Kamp wrote his book, the idea of learning where our food came from was new outside of agricultural and environmental circles; for most people, food originated in the supermarket or the restaurant. It became posh to go to a "farm-to-table" dinner, to eat at a "nose-to-tail" restaurant, to champion the farmer, and to respect the animal and the environment in a way that the previous decade of food television, focused on "dump-and-stir" recipe tutorials, hadn't touched on.

Except none of that has paid off. Average consumers, even ones who call themselves foodies, don't know where food comes from. They have never been to a farm or on a fishing boat, could not tell you the financial hit a grower takes with one poorly timed frost. The family farm continues its march toward the same consolidation that befell railroads, retail, banks, and media. We still eat massive amounts of beef, which is destroying the planet, and shrimp harvested by slaves. We still pay the people cooking the world's fanciest food minimum wage, or less. We haven't done anything about the inherently corrupt system of tipping. We've taken no meaningful action on climate change, which is already starting to displace wildlife in our food systems. If it was cool for a minute to care about these things, that moment has passed (or had, before a pandemic brought it all back into stark relief), without meaningful change for the people, plants, and animals that sustain us with food.

We chat up the latest venture-capital innovations in food production—indoor vertical farming! eating bugs!—as if they will save us. They won't. In place of progress, we have birthed a two-tiered system for food obsessives to accrue social capital while shilling on social media—luxurious temples of gastronomy for those who can afford to dine off handmade porcelain plates and carnival food for everyone else,

Frankenstein mash-ups (ramen burger, cotton-candy burrito) meant to be photographed, not eaten.

Here's a confession: I love hazelnut Snickers. Not since *The Godfather, Part II* has a sequel so successfully played on the strength of its predecessor to evolve into something, against the odds, even more satisfying. I've also learned they're made with palm oil, which contributes to deforestation in Indonesia that will soon drive orangutans to extinction, and chocolate from the Ivory Coast, a region rife with forced child labor. Once you know that, how does that affect your eating choices? "I urge this kind of inquiry for all of you who are reevaluating the ways in which you have moved through the world," advises Nigerian American recipe writer Yewande Komolafe, in an essay explaining the difference between industrially refined palm oil and the red palm oil used in West African cuisine. "Reconsidering cherished beliefs and challenging well-meaning concerns are part of this process."[5]

Having been an unquestioning promoter of food culture for so many years, I am ashamed. Some part of me wants to climb back into that cocoon, to a time when I didn't know or care about the larger ethical conflicts entangled in our diets. I'm not trying to solve the age-old riddle, is it better to know or not know? But speaking for this guy, who used to enjoy a pound of fried shrimp (before learning about forced labor on the oceans) followed by a half jar of Nutella (refined palm oil again), I have to admit I was a lot happier back then.

We learn as we go, about many things. During that period, I also wasn't living on a budget or exercising, until I realized the importance of physical and financial health and started doing those things. But those were comparatively easier than the life change I'm faced with now. There were clear guides, trainers, and YouTube videos to follow. What's the equivalent of learning proper form for a squat when developing ethical purchasing practices for dining out? That's where this book comes from. That's what I hope it can be.

A decade of obsession over the superficial trappings surrounding what we eat has left so many of us more hungry, angry, and cheated than ever. It's a hole dug deeper by the unfair burden placed on the service industry during the COVID-19 pandemic. The great news is that we can do something about it. Abstinence is always a choice. Though personally, I'm not prepared to live by myself in the wilderness or on a commune. I still love restaurants.

When you're having a great restaurant experience, I mean something truly special, it's like every element of the room, every person, every hunk of beef, every salt shaker, is part of one organism. It could be you're eating something you've never had before or something you've eaten a thousand times but never imagined could taste so good. The servers are psychic. They know exactly when to slide in to ask if you're ready to order and when not to interrupt the conversation. Your water glass fills up by magic. The suggestion of another drink doesn't seem like a hard sell but the most brilliant inspiration anybody ever had. The diffused lighting, sconces, chandeliers, and candles all working in concert, flatters you with cheekbones seen only on magazines. You're funnier than usual. Time stands still and speeds up. There's nothing like it, and special doesn't have to mean fancy. Standing in the river of customers at Bergen Bagels, at Flatbush and Sixth in Brooklyn, watching the brutal efficiency of staff taking orders, slicing, toasting, schmearing, and bagging is breathtaking to behold.

My adoration for the restaurant experience is undiminished. I'm just trying to find a way to square that with what I know lies beneath.

For better or worse, I was born into this capitalist culture that values profit over people. I'm just trying to find my way in it, while still pursuing what I love—food, which at the beginning, middle, and end of the day is all I think about and is still the greatest tool I know for bringing people together.

❧

FOR TOO LONG we have applied the "What happens in Vegas stays in Vegas" slogan to restaurants. There's a shockingly common belief that cheating doesn't count when you're on vacation. Even if it makes no practical sense, the feeling is understandable. You've worked hard all year and been fiscally responsible. Haven't you earned the right to start every morning of your Paris trip with a croissant or to sleep with a stranger on the train to Madrid? At home I try to eat a sensible, balanced diet. When I'm traveling, I'm eager to make the most of my time and appetite, so I often eat until I'm sick. Even if most of us don't cheat on our spouses while traveling, we probably cheat on our diets. "When am I going to be here again?" we rhetorically ask before ordering more noodles, more cheese, more everything.

Too often, we make the same mental calculation in restaurants five miles from our home. In this era when we keep learning more about where our food comes from, and adapt our food choices in our grocery shopping and cooking, many of us still suspend those principles when we're dining out.

We can't afford to pause our values that often.

I don't think we do it consciously. We meet friends at a restaurant, look at the menu, and maybe have questions about where these things are coming from or the quality of the ingredients, but we don't want to be that person. We don't want to be the Fred Armisen and Carrie Brownstein characters from their iconic "Is it local?" *Portlandia* sketch, peppering the restaurant's server with questions about where the chicken is from and how it was raised.

That sketch was an instant classic. It landed at a time, 2012, when two streams were starting to run together: ethically conscious eaters who were questioning the sources of their food and postrecession diners who had discretionary eating budgets for the first time since the onset of the financial crisis. Though it couldn't have been the intention, I think the popularity of the sketch, the lampooning of ethical dining, had a chilling effect, made it an embarrassment to ask these kinds of questions in a restaurant. I heard people reference it, not wanting to be seen that way.

No one wants to be a boor and a buzzkill when eating with friends. But we can't afford to have our regular food-away-from-home spending governed by the moving goalpost of vacation behavior. From a financial, nutritional, and ethical standpoint, we can't dine out or order takeout three times a week and behave the way we do on vacation.

Doing so leaves us broke, unhealthy, and supporting food supply chains that, if we looked at them honestly, would not meet the moral standing we aspire to at home.

I still adore restaurants. They are magical to me. Restaurants are my first love, after superheroes. I want to find a better way, a system, for eating out without supporting horrific business practices. That seems like something other people want too.

※

AS A DINING critic, I sat alone in grand rooms during the Great Recession. I saw the circumstances reshape part of the industry, as a wave of talented chefs dropped out of high-end dining and opened their own thirty-seat restaurants, serving what they wanted while playing their favorite albums as loud as the speakers could go. We did away with tablecloths and reservations. We stopped charging for water and started charging for bread. That postrecession era gave us some great nose-to-tail dining years. Like every phase, it ran its course: people will eat gizzards and tripe for only so long. Butchers wised up, and offcuts of meat, once great bargains, became trendy and therefore more expensive. By the early 2010s, once people had money again, they wanted luxury. As the economy recovered, that golden age of restaurants ended. The trappings of dining—linens, labor-intensive presentation, and ostentatious rooms—all returned.

A similar arc is likely this time. COVID-19 has been a scourge to the dining industry. It's too early to say how our economy or the hospitality industry is going to react long term. What we do know is that people will have money again. And they will eat out. If I had to guess, I'd say that many of the restaurateurs who have pivoted to leaner takeout operations will continue that way, at least for a couple years, and that when pockets are flush again, we'll see the pendulum swing back to a lot of the excess we saw before. It won't look the same; while the Great Recession was a disruption, this is an extinction-level event. The pandemic will leave us with fewer restaurants overall. Many will be smaller and employ fewer people. A sector that already had bad odds (in a "normal" year, about sixty thousand restaurants open in the United States and fifty thousand close) has become an even bigger gamble. Not many entrepreneurs will be eager to risk their savings on a venture that has proved not just risky but uninsurable (in a legal conflict that may not be resolved for years, most insurance companies have so far not recognized "disruption insurance" as covering a disruption due to pandemic).[6]

"I'm personally bullish on restaurants," Zuccarini tells me, nearly a year after our initial call. Like many of the more agile operators, she has spent the interim using every device possible—groceries, meal kits, picnic baskets, government assistance, renegotiating with banks and landlords—to remain solvent. She didn't have to close any restaurants permanently. While she lost a deposit on one of her planned locations, Zuccarini believes that in a post-COVID real-estate landscape she'll be able to get a better deal on a better location. "If you can get over this year of the pandemic, if you can survive and get to the other side of it, I think that restaurants will do very well. People are going to run to go to restaurants. I'm bullish with the restaurant industry in general." I suspect she's right. I just hope we don't lose that feeling of appreciation, the awareness that eating and being served in a restaurant is a luxury, not a right.

After the first lockdown ended dine-in service across the continent, fast food and immigrant restaurants, which have long focused on efficient takeout and delivery, were the quickest to adapt, immediately pivoting to exclusively off-premises sales. Full-service independents, though told to expect this shift in the next five years due to the rise of third-party delivery apps (3PD), were unprepared to execute the change at the lightning speed required as of March 2020. In some cases, they were unwilling, the owners confessing that they didn't get into the hospitality business to package takeout orders (one restaurant manager told me she is essentially operating a very small Amazon fulfillment center). Others, who would have closed, kept the kitchen running in order to maintain employment for undocumented workers who would be unable to access social assistance. Thanks to their financial resources, chains have survived more or less intact; independents have been slaughtered. Most don't have the savings to carry them through the hard times. The ones that are surviving are doing so by flexing the creativity and agility they've always had, buoyed by a level of community support that chains don't possess. While no one is going to rally to save their neighborhood Applebee's, companies that size have money and access to investor capital, plus lawyers and executives dedicated to finding efficiencies. Across the spectrum, the story of restaurants is being rewritten.

Crystal ball or no, here's one thing of which I am certain. What is happening right now is a tragedy. A bigger tragedy would be to learn nothing from it while blindly reproducing the same broken, cruel system. In the wake of COVID-19's dismantling of the restaurant industry, it's time to ask, how can we rebuild a better dining culture and supply chain rather than replicating the inequities of the previous one?

In order to understand some unpleasant truths about restaurants, and how we can make better choices, these eight chapters will break the industry down to a collection of genres. The realities of the chef-driven restaurant are completely different from the immigrant-family restaurant or the franchisee-owned, publicly traded chain restaurant. In each chapter, we will explore one of these models, some of the systemic problems in its orbit, and possible solutions, including choices we can make as diners.

⚜

IF THERE IS a single guiding principle that applies to everything I've learned in the past year, and everything I hope to set down in these pages, it is this: The most important action we can take to contribute to a more equitable restaurant industry is to let go of the idea that the customer is always right. That attitude, philosophy, and prevailing power dynamic is one thing about hospitality that we not only must change, it is shockingly within our power as diners to do so. Asking and expecting working people, who are doing so much, to do one more thing is not a right to which we are entitled.

At every level of the restaurant industry, "the customer is always right" leads to bad outcomes. This takes many forms. It's the cook who runs out the back door to buy a piece of fish in order to satisfy a customer who's ordered a dish not on the menu. It's the server put in the precarious position of deciding when a customer has physically or verbally crossed the line in their sexualized behavior. It's the Dairy Queen employee asked to layer the dispersal of pecan clusters in a Blizzard while a queue of customers grows longer. It's every restaurant staffer, everywhere, placed in jeopardy by customers refusing to wear masks. From the seemingly innocuous to the horrific, "the customer is always right" is a business axiom at odds and out of date with today's dangers and our broader understanding of consent, fairness, and equity.

The mantra has been invoked by restaurants, traditionally as an opportunity for hospitality professionals to display virtuosity at accommodation. It's always an impressive feat, in a way, like those weight lifters who pull a car by their teeth, to see how graceful or charming a professional can be while being treated like trash by an entitled diner. The idea that a person, by taking a job, consents to the whims of anyone who walks through the door, or that our money gives us the right to services and products beyond those that a restaurant explicitly offers, has always been questionable; the pandemic has blown the doors off of our willful collective ignorance about the consequences. Restaurant line cooks, according to a California-based study, led the COVID-19 mortality rate among groups of essential workers that also included warehouse workers, agricultural workers, bakers, and construction workers—all jobs that tend to be held by immigrants in that state.[7] In restaurants, an additional risk factor is that workers are exposed to the unscreened public, which by definition includes those of us who don't respect science or other people's health and safety. Once vaccinations started being distributed, I spoke with restaurant staff, who were eager to get back to work. Their main anxiety was still customers. They remembered how some diners behaved during patio service in the summer of 2020, refusing to put on masks on their way to the bathroom or leaving used masks on the table. Being placed in the position of communicating and enforcing ever-changing public health policy, their tip-based earnings held in the balance during every potential conflict with a customer, left them shaken.

In retail, it may be too late to change this behavior. Amazon, the ultimate expression of "the customer is always right," has reshaped our expectations to the point where getting everything we want, as soon as possible, seems reasonable. Amazon's priority is focusing on customer satisfaction, it appears at the expense of the safety and well-being of its workers. This is achieved in fulfillment centers, where the need to package four orders a minute keeps workers running all day, afraid to pause for fear it will impact their performance evaluations. Injury rates have been increasing every year since 2016. In 2019, the rate of serious injury in Amazon warehouses was 7.7 per 100 employees, twice the most recent industry standard (Amazon disputes the characterization of "serious injuries," though not the rise in injury rates).[8] This too is the consequence of the customer always being right.

The dominance of Amazon in the retail sphere gives it outsize influence on consumer behavior: it is hard to avoid perpetuating this problem by buying from them and, in the process, supporting the company's attitudes and practices. That kind of hegemony doesn't exist in the restaurant sphere: we do all have readily available choices here. There is no simpler action we can take than to recalibrate our perception that the customer is always right—that we are always right. It's not that we're wrong. Or that we're the villain. Only that our ability to pay the price of admission does not put our desires above those of workers. Or, for that matter, above those of other diners.

The customer who believes they're always right doesn't understand what they are asking of staff when they request seemingly simple modifications like splitting a dish, more complex amendments such as noodles prepared without the garlic that is already in the sauce, or the even more impossible demand of snagging a table in a packed restaurant without a reservation. Restaurants, through embracing this philosophy, have trained us to believe that our immediate gratification is achievable and justifiable. It's not either. It's rude. It treats humans, and the hard work they do, as beneath our concern. It asks people tasked to the limit to add one more element to their physical and emotional labor. Worse, when we uphold (or, as the most odious diners do, flaunt) our ability to punish or reward restaurants and their staff, not merely through our choice to dine there but through tipping and Yelp reviews, it's an abuse of power. The threat of bad online reviews or withholding of tips is a shakedown. When our friends and dining companions exhibit these behaviors, it's our obligation to correct them.

From the virtual restaurant to the virtuous restaurant, we'll go into more detail about the problems and solutions within different restaurant types. But if you take one thing from this book, or put it down after reading this Introduction, I hope it is that the customer is not always right.

So what is right? Speaking with experts and innovators in the field, it's my hope to answer this question for myself, and to help you answer it, too: How do we establish a set of principles for choosing where to eat? To suss out not which chefs are good and which are bad, but what ideas and what kinds of workplaces are worth supporting. My quest is nothing less than figuring out how to eat restaurant food without having to look the other way.

·1·

The Virtual Restaurant

> **Manager:** I've got good news and bad news.
> **Boss:** Gimme the bad first.
> **Manager:** The bad news is that we're losing money on every unit.
> **Boss:** And the good news?
> **Manager:** The good news is that sales are up.

SUNDAY, JULY 19, 2020

Because we're moving halfway across the country in a week and we're stressed, we order from Hong Shing. It's been a trying twenty-four hours. We'd rented a car to visit family in the suburbs, to see them one last time before leaving town. Smack in the middle of a pandemic, it's a hard farewell. I can't hug my brother goodbye. My mother can't hold her granddaughter.

Back at home, I pull the rental up on the curb—parking is limited in the city—so my wife, Victoria, can delicately escort our daughter, Scarlett, who's fallen asleep in the backseat, to her crib. Once they're inside, I turn the key, but the ignition won't start. What I don't know is that Zipcar, the car-sharing company with a $500 million market cap, mistakenly believing that the car is late, has deactivated the vehicle. They don't inform me of this. So I spend twenty minutes trying to figure out what's wrong with the engine, asking my neighbor to look under the hood. After thirty minutes on hold, a customer service agent tells me to try starting the engine again. It doesn't work. He asks me to wait again. Sitting in the car during a heat wave, being put on and off hold interminably, only to be asked to try the ignition again, my blood boils. After the company tries and fails, several times, to reactivate the car, we abandon it on the sidewalk. Zipcar promises to pick it up. It's still there in the morning when another vehicle crashes into it.

That's when we get a case of the fuck-its and decide to get delivery instead of cooking dinner. The ordering process for Hong Shing is much like any app, except it's done through the browser. We pick our dishes, the system totals them, adds tax, and offers a variety of tip options. An hour later, someone's knocking on my door with food.

The heat and tension of the day melt away in a nostalgic trip through the Chinese food of my childhood—kung pao chicken with more baby corn than spice, beef dredged in honey and deep-fried into a leathery consistency, chicken wings encrusted with a coating of Szechuan peppercorns and cumin. Long before I learned about doubanjiang paste or the massive regional varieties of mainland China, this was the Chinese food I knew. It's as sweet and comforting as a VHS tape of *The Goonies* recorded off broadcast television (commercials included).

The difference between Hong Shing and the dozens of options I could get via apps such as Grubhub, Uber Eats, Foodora, and others is that Hong Shing does its own delivery. Most third-party delivery app companies take 30 percent commissions from small businesses that operate at 4 to 12 percent profit margins. This had been destroying the profitability of restaurants for the past five years. Within the industry, this has been a source of worry and debate. For diners, the threat these tech companies pose to restaurants had gone largely unnoticed until the pandemic dropped dine-in sales to zero, placing restaurateurs at the mercy of delivery platforms. After a couple of months diners, many believing that delivery was saving restaurants, began to hear how this wasn't the case.

These delivery apps have been training us to value convenience over price, quality, and fair wages. As someone who takes food and the livelihood of restaurants seriously, this is not a trade-off I can accept. Despite the many problems I have with how restaurants are run, I want them to make money. I want them to succeed. So I'd rather order from a restaurant like Hong Shing that, thanks to some ingenuity on their end, is circumventing the stranglehold that tech companies have over online ordering and delivery. The restaurant not only avoids profit-busting commissions, but also maintains control of its consumer data; they are actually making money on our order and strengthening their business for the long-term.

They're not alone. Self-delivery, a challenge taken on by a small number of clever operators, is one of the tools used by the restaurateurs that are not merely surviving the COVID-19 crisis, but are best placed to revive after it.

In San Francisco, Laurence and Holly Jossel cruise through Diamond Heights, about ten minutes south of their restaurant. They're bringing three replacement bags of pasta to a customer who wasn't satisfied with last week's handmade rigatoni delivered with pork shoulder Bolognese and a brick of Parmesan. Maybe the kitchen's water/flour/egg ratio was off. Maybe the pasta dried too long or not long enough. It doesn't matter. What matters to the Jossels is pleasing delivery customers, a part of the restaurant's business that didn't exist until recently. "Go down Clipper, make a right on Diamond . . . ," Holly instructs her husband from the passenger seat of their car.

Laurence is the chef and co-owner of Nopa, a 136-seat Michelin-starred restaurant where, in the Before Times, sunlight poured in through tall two-story windows, bathing dishes that showcased the best of California's organic produce in the warm embrace of natural light. Holly used to work in e-commerce for Levi Strauss. Along with Antonio, a former busser in the restaurant, she is half of Nopa's delivery team.

In the middle of March 2020, along with most of California's restaurants, Nopa closed. After a brief spell the kitchen reopened, cooking a slimmed-down version of the menu for takeout—burgers, kale Caesar, meatloaf, chips, and so on. Soon they were selling groceries based on the inventory of their walk-in fridge. Once the city approved liquor sales for takeout and delivery, they began producing batched cocktails to go.

Quickly they had a new problem: customers clustering outside the entrance. They weren't the only ones. There's a photo from that period that went viral, taken by food journalist Gary He: in it a couple of dozen delivery-app couriers crowd around the door of New York City's Carbone restaurant. Taken just a few days into lockdown, it shocked people just getting used to the idea of staying home, always, and avoiding crowds no matter what, illustrating how hard it is in dense cities, where even outside, wearing masks, there isn't enough space on city sidewalks to do this safely.[1]

So Nopa shut down again, this time for just long enough, three days, to develop ordering software for people to pay online and choose a fifteen-minute slot for pickup, so there is no need to create a bottleneck at the door (here Jossel pauses in recounting the story to acknowledge how advantaged they were to be able to do this: he has regulars who work for Apple or Google, people who know and love his establishment and who can whip up this kind of software like so much fried rice). Before long, Nopa had also found financial support to supplement the cost of meals donated to hospital workers.

"This is what food's supposed to be about," says Jossel, who has spent the majority of his fifty years in a kitchen. His initial reaction to the pandemic was stress, before he began to see the path forward, a role for his restaurant and himself, one more vital to the community than service-heavy fine dining. "And then I was like, this is why we're here. To feed people. To be scrappy. To gather staff and hope. I'm very inspired by all this. I have never had a better time cooking."

SOME 950 MILES north, Iori Kataoka and her daughter drive around Vancouver, the San Francisco of Canada (equally hilly, coastal, and left-leaning, with real-estate values far in excess of the national average), delivering meals from their Japanese restaurant. After also closing for a brief spell early in the pandemic, Yuwa Japanese Cuisine shifted to producing food for takeout. It's a compromise. Items like Yuwa's griddle-cooked wagyu loin steak, the luxuriously fatty beef served on a sizzling platter with sauce made from sake lees (a yeast by-product of the fermentation process), cannot be stuffed into a takeout container. "And you may think sushi is fine," says Kataoka. "Not really." The raw fish is perfectly safe, particularly with an ice pack. As far as the quality, short-grain sushi rice should be human-skin temperature. It hardens as it cools. And unless fish is cut fresh, it leaks moisture.

But early on, Kataoka found that most of her staff, who are from Japan, already owned a couple packages of masks at home. So she pivoted quickly and adapted her menu, with just a few employees in the kitchen, plus Kataoka doing deliveries herself. At first she averaged about 30 percent of her previous revenue, inching up to 65 percent by July. It's not ideal, though Kataoka believes it will serve her in the long run: even though she's only breaking even, it maintains the valuable connection to her diners. As many restaurateurs tell me, if they had closed for the duration of the pandemic, would their customers remember them once it's safe to open up again?

"There is a Japanese saying," says Kataoka. "'Act as if you are grasping the straw to climb up the mountain.' That's what I'm feeling. You don't have anything to hold. It may break anytime. But you have no choice. You have to climb up."

※

ON TUESDAYS SMOKEY John's BBQ delivers food to Irvine, Arlington, and Grand Prairie. On Wednesdays they drive to North Dallas, Carrollton, and Farmers Branch, bringing East Texas–style brisket (more spice than the salt-and-pepper puritanism of central Texas) and ribs (saucy, owing to the proximity of the Carolinas and Memphis). The new hot-ticket queso, a blend of tomatoes, peppers, onions, cheese (cheddar, Velveeta), and milk, simmered with brisket trimmings, the smoky fat of the meat emulsifying into the gooey sauce, is sold by the pint or quart (with chips for dipping). It's available only on Thursdays and Saturdays. So unless you live in Delivery Group C (Oak Cliff, Cedar Hill, Desoto, and Duncanville) or E (East Dallas, Garland, and Mesquite), you've got to come into the shop to get it.

"When the shutdown happened in Dallas, people were not getting out of their houses," recalls co-owner Brent Reaves. Smokey John's was still getting pickup orders. Within two weeks, business dropped 55 percent. With twenty-two employees, things were getting tight quickly. Then Brent had an epiphany. "One morning I said, 'We know where our customers are. They're at home.'" Along with the restaurant, Brent and his brother Juan had catering trucks just idling. Adding up their clientele, product, and wheels, the Reaves brothers formulated a plan.

On March 20, Brent and Juan went on Facebook Live to update their customers on the new delivery schedule, letting them know which areas of Dallas they'd cover on which days. That first week, the brothers promised that if they got twenty orders, they'd sing a karaoke battle. Sixty orders came in. Juan sang Journey and Prince. Brent wrote a parody of Jodeci's "Feenin" called "Feenin' for BBQ." "Spend my last dime, on brisket queso every time," crooned Brent, shielded by aviator sunglasses. "Smokey John's without a doubt, its barbecue sauce got me strung out!"

They've done a live broadcast every night since, maintaining the connection with customers that has long been a core part of the family business (originally named Big John's by their father, John Reaves, until a fire in the late 1970s caused a customer to declare, "Y'all should call this place Smokey John's instead of Big John's!"). A year before the pandemic, Smokey John's had been offering delivery through the app Eat24, at a loss, just to expand the company's reputation and get diners used to ordering online. Now customers in the five delivery zones around Dallas were regularly placing orders by five o'clock the day before, by phone, email, or fax. By the summer, revenue was up 15 percent from the previous year, without a penny of it going to a tech company.

⚑

NOPA, YUWA, SMOKEY John's, and Hong Shing are the exceptions to the rule. These are the winners, the survivors if you will, of March 2020. In the zombie movie, these are the people who first figure out how to attach a crossbow to a chain saw—because they've conceived and executed a version of self-delivery.

Prepandemic, restaurants were being flanked by app companies and left with two choices: they could refuse to participate and lose customers, or they could partner with the app companies and lose money on the ruinous commissions. Once COVID-19 forced an end to dine-in service in most places, restaurants were at the mercy of 3PD, with little choice but to pay an average commission rate higher than the average restaurant profit margin.

Subsidized by the war chest of venture capital, these companies have in the past decade successfully gotten between restaurants and their hard-earned customers, aided by slick marketing that convinces us eaters that they are a convenience we're too busy to live without and promising businesses they'll grow sales while adapting to today's uniquely fast-paced customer. And that's bullshit.

We think we invented being busy. It's advertised at us all the time, in self-mythologizing Instagram posts boasting of our achievements and on magazine covers telling us how to have it all through fifteen-minute recipes that cheat by leaving out steps or ingredients, because who has time to chop vegetables from scratch?

Economists and technologists usually argue that innovations free our time for other, better, tasks.[2] That makes sense on the page. Is it true? Who do you know who has more time for friends and family than even a decade ago? Yes, we have more leisure time than we did in the nineteenth century, when we had to go to a well to gather water, and light a fire to boil it, and when there were no laws governing the length of a workday, paid sick leave, maternity leave, weekends, or overtime. These days we have less private time than fifty years ago, when our employers couldn't reach us twenty-four hours a day by phone, text, or Slack, when a viable middle class saw a pathway to financial stability through education. According to "Leisure Time and Technology," a 2006 paper by German researcher Dr. Stefan Poser, the more free time we have, the more we have filled it with buying stuff we don't need. "If leisure time in the 1950s was characterized by a desire for rest and recreation due to the long periods of work," writes Poser, "its devotion to the purpose of consumption would become the norm in the following decades. Cars, televisions and clothing developed into status symbols. The rise of the consumer society coincided with the development of shopping as a pastime for all classes."[3]

We don't shop online today so we can spend more time with our families. We do it so we can spend more time working. That's because our jobs are unstable, our family lives are overscheduled, our housing costs require a greater percentage of our income, and our futures are uncertain.[4]

We are, without a doubt, too busy for our own good. We spend too much of our days working or, before a pandemic transformed most office jobs into remote positions, commuting in cars or subways. There are many good reasons why getting carryout or delivery for dinner is a necessary expediency. The idea that we have uniquely cultivated an existence that demands convenience to serve our mightily efficient lifestyles, however, is more spin. Some of us get takeout because we are too tired at the end of our second or third jobs to do anything else. Some of us order an Uber to bring us a bubble tea and quinoa salad for lunch every day because the luxury seems reasonable.

Like us, the ancient Romans were busy. They had to make offerings to the gods and view chariot races and public executions with the rushed pace of our breakfast meetings, Pilates classes, and clarinet lessons. Their *90 Day Fiancé* was watching two guys fight a bear. That's why they invented fast food and takeout.

Thermopolia were businesses that sold food on the go, using long counters to store earthenware jars, called dolia, that kept food warm and enabled quick service. Think of the hot table at Chipotle—the one where cooked meats, rice, and beans sit in metal inserts, warmed by steam from below—minus the sneeze guard. Back then, not everyone had a kitchen in their home. At thermopolia Romans could grab a quick bite of meat and cheese, spiced wine, lentils, fish, or nuts with a dash of garum, the liquid extract of fermented fish, similar to the fish sauce essential to Southeast Asian cooking, a condiment as ubiquitous to the ancient Roman diet as ketchup is to the modern American. These takeout spots weren't rare. In the ruins of Pompeii, buried by the eruption of Mount Vesuvius in AD 79, more than eighty thermopolium counters have been discovered.[5] Though the ancient Romans may not have had to pick up the ancient kids from ancient soccer practice, they were busy enough to have created fast food and takeout. So that sensation of feeling "on the go," the need to adopt convenience meals for our fast-paced lifestyles, is nothing new.

The much later invention of delivery is often credited to Italy. In 1889, according to legend, King Umberto and Queen Margherita asked chef Raffaele Esposito to bring a pizza to their palace in Naples. The element of royalty makes for a good fable about the protodelivery. While the history of the thermopolium (along with tamales sold in open-air markets by the Aztecs of Central America) is backed up by archaeological discoveries, this origin story is suspect at best and, like many versions of history in which white people invent everything, probably apocryphal. True or not, it was at the same time that Mahadeo Havaji Bachche launched a Mumbai business shepherding hot meals between offices, homes, and restaurants. Bachche's more formalized Dabbawala system is the clear progenitor of modern delivery. The tiffins, which are nested, cylindrical stainless-steel lunchboxes, are carried about India by train and bicycle with such dazzling efficiency and accuracy that the industry is admired and studied by business academics all over the world.

In America some colonial-era restaurants offered carryout food to be picked up by servants. After the Civil War, an informal economy sprang up around train stops of Black women selling prepared food—one of the only entrepreneurial opportunities available, before or after emancipation. "For African American consumers, take-out was often less of a convenience than a necessity," writes food historian Emelyn Rude, author of *Tastes Like Chicken*. "Blacks on a long journey or simply looking for a bite to eat away from home anywhere in the Jim Crow South were often forced to order their food as take-away in segregated restaurants if they wanted to eat at all."[6]

Until the middle of the twentieth century, carryout was mostly the domain of transit, of train stations and roadhouses. It wasn't until after World War II, when new car sales quadrupled in America, that take-out and delivery exploded.[7] With both the economy and the birthrate booming, Americans migrated from urban centers to newly developed suburbs. The GI Bill subsidized a massive expansion of postsecondary education and home ownership (often with zero down payment and low-interest loans), sometimes with preferred terms for new developments. The move to the suburbs and growth of car culture spurred the proliferation of carryout service, the specific popularity of pizza largely attributed to American GIs, having served in Italy during the war, coming home with a taste for Italian food. McDonald's, created in 1943 and massively expanded in the postwar era, didn't even add dine-in seating until 1963. For the first twenty years, it was all takeout.

The science and mechanics of takeout didn't change much throughout this era. Made by the Bloomer Brothers (now Fold-Pak), the ubiquitous "Chinese takeout" container started life as packaging for oysters and scallops, popular for takeout in early-twentieth-century New York. In subsequent decades, various manufacturing developments allowed for the creation of paper, plastic, and Styrofoam containers that did better jobs of keeping food warm or cold, until the zenith of 1985's McDLT, which came in packaging that kept the hot side hot and the cool side cool. For about forty years, not much else changed. After a half century of mass-market takeout food, we still don't trust a plastic lid to stay on a container of hot soup—the business has never been terrifically tech savvy.

These were the ways that, for a generation, we got restaurant food at home. Local restaurants printed takeout menus and slipped them under the doors of prospective customers. Most of us devoted a drawer in our kitchen to these menus, pulling one out for a break at the end of a particularly stressful week, or grabbed a familiar favorite from a drive-thru on the way home. That was the extent of it.

It wasn't until the 1990s that technology began to fundamentally change this part of restaurants.

❧

RECESSION PROOF AND perennially popular, pizza is inarguably the champion of American food. It is not just widely adored but endlessly adaptable, made dogmatically according to Neapolitan standards, or also adorned with butter chicken or pierogi, its crusts stuffed or composed of cauliflower, enjoyed in beautiful restaurants but also sold in the supermarket freezer aisle. Unlike one of its main competitors for our affection, the hamburger, it holds up perfectly when delivered. Made and sold high and low, it is a complete meal or a snack. Fittingly pizza was the first physical product sold online. That inaugural digital sale, the Yuri Gagarin of e-commerce, was a large pepperoni with mushrooms and extra cheese from Pizza Hut, which launched PizzaNet in 1994.[8] Though money changed hands only at the point of delivery, this was the antecedent of our contemporary one-click shopping experience.

In 2001 Papa John's showed early tech savviness with its online ordering system, followed by Domino's in 2010, which became a trendsetter with its "pizza tracker" app, enabling the consumer to see at which stage of production or delivery their pizza is.[9] In 2014 Domino's introduced "Dom," a voice-operated ordering feature that let you order by speaking, oddly replicating the telephone experience that technology was replacing. "I don't even think that Domino's is a food company anymore," influential restaurateur David Chang told a Domino's store manager on his television show *Ugly Delicious*. "I think of you as a tech company." He intended it as a compliment.

Big chains like Red Robin, Famous Dave's, and Panera Bread, with their economy of scale, resources to devote to digital development, and perceptive leadership that anticipated the growth in e-commerce sales, were able to place themselves ahead of the herd by developing self-delivery before the app-based tech revolution, when the wolves came hunting.

❧

AT THE TURN of this century, online dating was just starting to become a thing. People did it, still with some embarrassment. If they married someone they met on eharmony or Jdate, couples would fictionalize an account of their first date. We still shopped for pants, diapers, and DVDs in stores.

So around that time, accustomed as we were to banging two rocks together to make fire, when Seamless was launched, mostly as a tool for offices to place large orders from restaurants and caterers, it didn't register as a threat. Nor did Just Eat in Denmark (2001) or Grubhub (2004) or a host of others, which all began swallowing one another in a series of mergers and acquisitions that read like a tech version of biblical birth announcements: "And Just Eat acquired hungryhouse from Delivery Hero, and Seamless merged with Grubhub, and Greylock Partners and Redpoint Ventures did invest in Just Eat, which begat SkipTheDishes."

As with humans, the family of companies grew wider and more diverse. Here is a partial list of major competitors and also-ran companies in this sphere: Talabat, Snapfinger, hungryhouse, Menulog, Eat24Hours, Ele.me, EatStreet, EAT Club, Munchery, Postmates, OrderAhead, DoorDash, ChowNow, Caviar, Foodpanda, Menu

Group, SkipTheDishes, SpoonRocket, Deliveroo, gopuff, Hello Curry, Foodora, Dunzo, Swiggy, Uber Eats, Wolt, TinyOwl, InnerChef, Maple, Tapingo, Rappi, Spring, Chowbus, and Glovo. As they proliferated and merged, these companies collected more detailed, more accurate customer data, the information aggregating into a tool that could anticipate and meet customer demands far more efficiently than even the most veteran restaurateur.

The success of Genghis Khan, who conquered half of the known world in the early thirteenth century, was based partly on tactical brilliance and ruthlessness. Another factor was his soldiers' skill at horseback archery. No army in the world could contend with an enemy that moved so swiftly while firing accurately with long-range weapons. To the defending nations of the era, it was the equivalent of aliens landing on earth today and vaporizing whole cities at once.

The arrival of the iPhone in 2007, followed by the 2008 recession and a whole generation of young engineers mobilized to create apps in a get-rich-quick land rush to be the next Facebook, was just such an indefensible assault on restaurants. A host with a reservation book and a landline was underequipped to compete with order-placing technology that was suddenly in every diner's pocket, feeding data into Silicon Valley app companies. Within a few years, these companies knew more about a restaurant's customers—what we wanted, when we wanted it, how much we were willing to pay—than a small business ever could.

In 2016 a number of these companies made news by stopping their so far unobstructed growth. Before shutting down, Bento conceded that there was more money to be made in catering than on-demand delivery, SpoonRocket sold its technology to Brazilian food chain iFood, and Square tried to sell Caviar to Uber or Grubhub.[10]

As word got out that third-party delivery was unprofitable, despite much-heralded sales, the conversation shifted. The problem wasn't that the emperor had no clothes, that these companies—valued in the billions, with more investment cash pouring in every day—had hustled restaurants and investors. It was that of course delivering food wasn't profitable. Not with human labor. When restaurant meals could arrive at our door via drones, robots, and self-driving cars, however, that's when the sector would go from red to black. "If we don't get the [autonomous car] software thing nailed, we're not going to be around much longer," Uber chief executive officer (CEO) Travis Kalanick told *USA Today* in 2016.

In early 2020, California passed a law, AB5, enshrining employee rights for gig workers. Rather than a beacon of change, companies like Uber, Lyft, Instacart, and DoorDash saw it as a challenge. They advanced their own bill, Prop 22, which effectively granted them an exemption to these new labor laws. Able to campaign directly to customers/voters through their apps, they spent more than $200 million on the election and threatened to leave the state if they lost. Prop 22 passed, and Uber's CEO immediately promised to take the fight well beyond California. One month later, Uber sold off its stake in Advanced Technology Group and Elevate, divisions developing driverless cars and flying vehicles, leaving the exploitation of human labor as the only path to profitability.[11]

To me, this was one hell of a bait and switch. Part of the original sales pitch for these apps, in addition to convenience for consumers and sales growth for merchants, was the glory of the gig economy. It seems so long ago now, who could remember? But for about five years following the Great Recession, you couldn't escape the terms *gig economy* and *sharing economy*. Platforms like Uber, Airbnb, and Grubhub promised flexibility and opportunity. They used terms like *shared marketplace*, *collaborative platform*, and *peer-to-peer application* to explain how uploading our cars, homes, and bodies to their digital marketplace would allow our most personal, irreplaceable assets (and rights) to be commodified and sold for as little as possible. And somehow that was good for us. Or at least, at a time when unemployment rose to 10 percent, workers had little choice. Even by 2016, with the economy back to a roar, a McKinsey study found that 30 percent of gig workers were working this way only because their other income was insufficient.[12]

Uber and Lyft torpedoed the taxi industry, and municipalities did nothing because public sentiment was already aligned against cab companies. Airbnb evaporated long-term rental stock, and cities dragged their feet on legislative defenses, because home owners, seen as a property tax–aligned voting bloc, are valued above renters. The delivery apps hustled restaurants like the mark at a poker table because independent restaurants, before the pandemic pushed them to consolidate lobbying efforts into groups like the Independent Restaurant Coalition, had little collective voice.

The tech-company barkers coaxed us into their tents with their talk of collaborations and no-fee delivery, and we bought into it as if P. T. Barnum never existed. Part of the danger they pose is that we too often look at technology as a snapshot of what's possible at a particular moment rather than a trajectory that will unfold over time. We focus on the present tense, rather than down the road, which is necessary for an industry that evolves as quickly as this one. The frequent pattern is to use an innovation and early consumer adoption to attract venture-capital funding, and then use that capital to create a business opportunity that's ostensibly a good deal for everyone. Until the company in question gains a foothold in the market. Then the deal starts to change, incrementally, always toward one that's less equitable and favors the company at the expense of its customers and users.

These enterprises prefer to be known as tech companies, as opposed to taxi, hotel, and restaurant businesses. That's true. They don't deliver food. Many of them farm out the physical schlepping to other agencies, like Relay, Homer Logistics (acquired by Waitr), and Habitat Logistics. Bike and car couriers are never employees but "independent contractors," granting the company the maximum exemptions from labor and employment laws regarding scheduling, overtime, sick pay, and wages.

Committed to the legal fiction that their product is something other than delivery, and that couriers are not employees, these companies skirt around the particulars of what service they actually provide, reminding you that you get food brought to you *because of* them, in some hard-to-quantify way. "Grubhub helps you find and order food from wherever you are." "Uber Eats is the easy way to get the food you love delivered." "Whatever you want, we get it. Order delivery for yourself or with friends and watch in real-time as your Postmate brings you all the things you love." It's an impressive feat of copywriting, implying that they deliver food without stating it and therefore avoiding the liability of identifying themselves as delivery companies.

I would describe them a different way. In my opinion they are a predatory enterprise that has figured out how to use technology to get between restaurants and their customers and then sell the customers back for a cut of the action. From my perspective, that's a scam. It isn't just that some of these companies served the exact same product to roughly the same customers while taking the first thirty cents of every dollar. The media hailed them as heroes for doing it, too.

It's shameful to admit now. But I was one of those useful idiots, a member of the media proselytizing a deal that was too good to be true. In 2015, when Uber Eats launched in Toronto, following a trial in Santa Monica, it was a good deal for everyone. It was a very different system. Back then, Uber Eats had only a handful of options every day. Carefully selected restaurant partners would prep hundreds of orders of one or two items and load them into Uber vehicles, which roamed the densely populated urban core over the lunch period, enabling drop-off of still-hot food within minutes. Consumers got meals out of orbiting cars at whiplash speed, while restaurants were able to minimize food waste and labor cost by pretty much guaranteeing large-volume sales on a dish of their choice.

At the time, I spent a morning in Uber's regional office, observing how the staff tasted and voted on potential dishes from a local Thai restaurant. It seems comically quaint now, the idea of a tech company fastidiously calibrating a delivery menu, like Ettore Boiardi (yes, Boiardi, founder of Chef Boyardee, was a real person) hand rolling and stuffing pasta, before determining that it didn't meet his standards to be extruded into a can. The joke was on me, for believing and promoting the idea that the company cared this much about product quality and equitable partnerships.

Within a year Uber Eats had transformed into a service like its competitors, picking up food from a restaurant's existing menu. No special packaging, no hand-selecting just the right dishes. At the same time, they drastically reduced payment rates for their drivers. The investment of time, the development of personal relationships with restaurateurs, converted customers to ordering through an app that had until then been for taxis. It also bought the tech company oodles of their most valuable asset—data. Soon they were one of the many offering a different version of the same lousy deal: customers in exchange for a commission larger than a restaurant's profit margin. I felt like a real chump.

The apps don't make the process of making food cheaper. They don't make the process of delivering food cheaper, either. They just enable an ease of sales. The tech companies extract value by charging the restaurant a commission, which can range from 10 to 40 percent, usually hovering around 25 to 30 percent. How can you take 30 percent off the top from a business with such thin margins? You can't. "You're not making a profit at that type of a haircut," as one restaurateur put it to me. That's a huge problem at a time when online order and delivery platforms, which barely existed until recently, constitute 10.89 percent of the $863 billion restaurant market.[13]

Some restaurateurs charge higher prices for delivery orders to absorb the commission cost. Some 3PD companies won't allow this. In early 2020, a group of New Yorkers sued Grubhub, DoorDash, Uber Eats, and Postmates, alleging a monopolistic practice that prevents competition, limits consumer choice, and forces restaurants into illegal contracts that effectively fix prices.[14] The companies named in the class action declined to comment or did not respond to requests.

In the early days, a lot of restaurateurs looked at the commissions and turned their backs on the delivery apps, refusing to play ball. They found sales were dropping as these companies syphoned off customers.

So they began to use the apps, many figuring that if their peers were doing it, there must be a way to make money.

The business aphorism "Don't confuse revenue with profit" knows no political loyalty. A hospitality professor put this situation to me as an old management-school joke. "A manager tells the boss there's good news and bad. The bad news is we're losing money on every unit. The good news is that sales are up." This joke doesn't just describe the restaurants. It describes the delivery apps, too.

Remember Uber, and other companies like them, with their big push toward driverless cars and, barring that, diluted labor and wage standards as high-stakes efforts to make third-party delivery profitable? Though these are companies with multibillion-dollar valuations, they're still operating at a loss. In 2018 Uber lost $1.8 billion. Before their initial public offering (IPO) in 2019, the company was rumored to be seeking a valuation in excess of $100 billion. With analysts decrying that as grossly overpriced, they lowered it to $82 billion and still wildly underperformed. DoorDash grossed nearly $1 billion in 2019 and still posted losses of $450 million. Despite that, they pulled in another $400 million from investors. They closed 2020 by tripling revenue and doubling losses.[15]

Big restaurant brands are able to profit from sales made through these apps because the demand for their product enables them to negotiate better rates. Grubhub's (which also lost $155 million in 2020 despite increasing sales 29 percent to $1.8 billion) first-quarter 2020 results show that the average profit from orders placed with independent restaurants was $4. For orders placed with "a partnered national enterprise brand," it was $0.[16] The apps need major brands but don't make any money from them. So it's the independents that pay the cost, your local ramen shop subsidizing a delivery service for McDonald's.

Until there are only a couple players left in the field, making it possible for two competitors to increase fees, the business model of the tech-delivery industry makes no sense. For now at least—that doesn't really matter to customers who depend on the convenience of delivery and are willing to pay for it.[17]

ADDICTED TO DELIVERY

Nowhere is this addiction to convenience stronger than in America's largest city, perhaps the best place in the country for business, lunch, and business lunch. "New Yorkers would rather die than have to make their own lunch," says Joel Teitelman, owner of Mile End Delicatessen. Launched in 2010, as a recession-era America was embracing comfort food in all its forms, Teitelman's deli serves matzo ball soup, Montreal-style smoked meat, salami and eggs, and other Jewish comfort dishes to residents of Boerum Hill, Brooklyn. Teitelman is only partially joking. Because he knows his customers.

Certainly, there are plenty of New York residents who cook. I don't want to reduce a city of eight million people to a stereotype. It's just that nowhere else have I so repeatedly met people who boast that they don't cook. It's understandable. The cost of real estate in New York means small homes and small kitchens. Small kitchens sometimes mean small fridges and ovens or, in a trend that began to surface in recent years, no stove at all.[18] Many New York ovens, Teitelman suggests, are filled with shoes. New Yorkers spend a lot of time in transit, forty-five-minute treks from borough to borough to get to work, visit a friend, or catch a show; turn sideways to pass each other in narrow grocery aisles; and then carry food home in their arms instead of the trunk of a car. As they will also not be shy to tell you, they are surrounded by the greatest collection of food options in the world.

New York is the nexus of delivery in America, where having food brought to your door has been a major part of dining culture for a long time. This used to be done by restaurants. These days, as off-premise orders constitute a growing percentage of our dining spending, it's done by a third party. So who is profiting from this?

Talk to any restaurateur about third-party delivery apps, whether they've found a way to work with them or not, and you'll hear the phrase *necessary evil.*

Prior to 2016, when he became the owner of Il Mattone, a pizza shop in Tribeca, Manhattan, Michael Lombardo worked in finance on

Wall Street, specializing in retail and hospitality. "Before I left Wall Street there was this big movement of e-commerce. The catchphrase was *omnichannel*." The exciting word refers to syncing advertising and sales at every physical and digital level. "All these retailers had to adopt their business model to people ordering things online. I can't help but parallel that to what I'm seeing now in the restaurant space. But restaurants have been strong-armed into using these middlemen that take unrealistic take-rates on each order."

Il Mattone uses a dozen different services for online orders. Lombardo estimates that maybe three are profitable for him, based on the agreements and the constant promotions used to drive customers. "They push that they're driving incremental sales to the restaurant. I would strongly argue that, if you look at overall spending, and what people are ordering, it's just shifted the dollars from one pocket to the other. The orders move from one service to another, depending on where the promotions are. It's really just a giant shell game."

⌗

JUST BEFORE THE pandemic, on the other side of the country, Reem Assil caved and started using the Caviar app for her restaurant. Reem's sits in the shadow of the Fruitvale station, where Bay Area transit police killed Oscar Grant on New Year's Day, 2009. It gets less foot traffic than you'd expect. Even delivery drivers had trouble finding it. Still, the added sales justified the commission, and the app's reach helped extend the restaurant's fan base. "In the end, the increase and the ease with which our customers could get delivery outweighed the cut they were taking. We needed that cash flow and that revenue." Assil was unhappy with how the focus on off-premise sales created a bottleneck of orders when the restaurant looked almost empty, impacting the experience of diners. If you come in to eat when there are only a few customers, you might think, why are they so slow, not knowing that the kitchen is jammed with "off-prem" orders.

Beyond the unsustainable commissions, the lack of control over food and packaging is an issue that drives restaurateurs wild. They don't know if their milkshake is going to get squeezed in a bag with another restaurant's shrimp po'boy. It sucks to hand over control of your food, to watch a stranger, who is not your employee, handle and represent your product. Not to mention peak delivery hours that drain focus from the kitchen staff and couriers who are not properly screened or trained. One restaurateur told me the final straw was a delivery driver who tried to put her meals into a duffel bag.

But while the deal still ate into the restaurant's bottom line, Reem's didn't lose money. This was thanks to negotiating the commission rate down to 10 percent for pickup orders and 10 percent for orders that came directly through the website's traffic (as opposed to the app), and most important, raising prices on delivery orders. "Even though Caviar doesn't like that, and they say not to, we would upcharge on the pricing to account for that percentage of the cut," says Assil. "The way we reasoned it was, the tech professionals that are, without sounding too crude, too lazy to come out of their home, they're subsidizing us to be able to keep feeding our own community."

When COVID-19 hit, there was an opportunity to recalibrate. Reem's had been using Toast, a point-of-sales system, which, like other POS companies, pivoted to handle online sales. There are other e-commerce solutions to handle the ordering component of off-premise sales, developed by restaurateurs, such as Tock by Chicago's Nick Kokonas (Alinea, The Aviary), with a 3 percent commission, or Ambassador from Toronto's Nav Sangha (SoSo Food Club, Otto's Bierhalle), which charges only a flat monthly fee. Happy with Toast but seeking a new partner to handle the actual delivery, Assil found Candlestick, a co-op owned by cyclist couriers. Though the delivery zone was smaller, it fitted better with Assil's values. Toast charges a flat fee. Candlestick takes just 6 percent, plus an even split of tips. Because Candlestick is worker owned, Assil doesn't have to worry about where that money is going.

Like Assil, a lot of restaurateurs got into the game reluctantly, signed up with these services only after they saw sales dropping, or growth stagnating, in tandem with the rise of the apps. The problem was that the deal was getting worse all the time. The same went for couriers, who, enticed by the promise of autonomy and an income directly related to how hard they worked, were happy at first. "The harder you hustled, you'd be able to do more deliveries and make more money," recalls Alex Curth, a former courier for Foodora. "I liked that immediacy. It was constantly stimulating. Almost like a fun video game."

But gradually the work changed. Guaranteed shifts disappeared. When the system changed how it prompts customers to tip, those tips dried up. Curth went from about two-thirds of customers tipping to one-third. The algorithm, which controls the dispatch, didn't seem to factor in the distance to pickups, for which couriers don't get paid.

The "independent contractors" who work for third-party delivery companies are not entitled to minimum wage, overtime, holiday and vacation pay, or the required additional insurance for a vehicle they use to deliver food.[19] DoorDash, for example, provides "excess insurance," which applies only after drivers have gone through their own insurance first and only when drivers are "in possession of goods to be delivered." Meaning that when they're on their way to a restaurant, which they are for about half of every shift, they're not covered.

According to Curth, "All those started becoming bigger and bigger factors in whether or not you were making decent money. It wasn't how hard you were working or fast you were going. You couldn't just make up for it by going harder. It was beyond your control. You were at the mercy of the algorithm. Anytime that things changed for the worse, it would always be a little bit at a time. And we'd say, 'They can't do this.' And actually, they can. We have no power in this relationship."

THE TYRANNY OF CONVENIENCE

Beyond the complaints from restaurateurs and couriers, the other mark at the table is us, the eaters. We're not getting any real value out of this deal either.

Toronto is a densely populated city where I can walk out my door and find pretty much any food I want. It's an extra convenience for someone to bring it to my door, but the premium is steep. Between delivery fees and tip (yes, we have to tip people being paid this poorly), a ten-dollar burger quickly becomes a fifteen-dollar burger. When it's crunch time and I'm up against a deadline, saving the time it takes to go pick up food feels worth it. But eating like that all the time is expensive.

A couple of years ago, while working on a podcast, I was struck by how often the producer, who was always telling me how broke she was, ordered lunch and dinner delivery. "What am I saving for?" she asked, pointing out that home ownership was forever beyond the reach of her generation. So why not spend it on nice meals? I was stunned by the pessimism.

According to Eve Turow-Paul, author of *Hungry: Avocado Toast, Instagram Influencers, and Our Search for Connection and Meaning*, that attitude has been a core element in the rise of food culture. "In terms of control and foodie behavior, the fatalism is absolutely one driver," Turow-Paul tells me. A previous generation might have worked longer hours to afford extras. The current generation works more to stay afloat. Food delivery is both an extravagance and an act of control within our reach.

In Korea it's called *shibal biyong*, loosely translated as a "frustration expense" or "fuck-it expense." It's the same emotion that drove us to order from Hong Shing after our Zipcar episode. Seoul National University political science scholar Jeongmin Kim describes the term as "an expense that might seem unnecessary but that helps you get through a bad day. It's the $20 you splurge for a cab home instead of taking the subway after you've been denied a promotion or the comforting but expensive sushi you buy after you've been berated by your boss. The term implies that you might as well make yourself happy right now because your prospects in the long term seem bleak. Buy that nice coat, because you'll never get on the housing ladder. Eat that steak, because you'll never save up enough to retire."[20]

The contemporary obsession with restaurants, the willingness to devote so much of our income to them, originates in some good places.

Like caring about where your food is coming from and a democrati-zation of better restaurants that rippled from the Great Recession. Turow-Paul's interviews led her to the bleaker conclusion that food had become the new aspirational lifestyle choice for a generation that has been robbed of the opportunities their parents took for granted: job security, home ownership, family. "If you're feeling extraordinarily anxious, you're gonna want to use food to feel better," says Turow-Paul. "Foodieism was born out of the 2008 recession. It wasn't rational. It was escapist."

The idea that generational economic instability is a choice, a "hus-tle," is spin. In fact, the entire notion of eating on the go while hustling to get ahead is itself aspirational. Despite the image that we're all order-ing salads so we can keep burning the midnight oil in our lofty creative fields, the highest users of meal delivery are the lowest income earners. According to data from Zion and Zion, in a study of 2,928 US con-sumers the largest group of respondents that ordered through delivery apps within a ninety-day period earns less than $10,000 a year.

And we don't order salads. We order burritos, ramen, burgers, cake, tacos, noodles, fried chicken, pizza, and more tacos.[21] These are our re-wards for getting through hard days. I've been known to self-medicate with spicy noodles. No matter the price point, we pay for this conve-nience with our health, because delivery increases the availability of, with all due love and respect to the foods listed above, what my bubbie would call *chazzerai*—junk.

SOME LOVE FOR 3PD

Not all restaurants are against these apps. Some have found a way to make them work, either as a loss leader for marketing purposes, a prof-itable sales method for high-margin items, or because the restaurant is popular enough to negotiate better commission rates (any restaurateur in this position asked me not to disclose their preferential deal).

Pittsburgh-based Primanti Bros., a sandwich chain (known for putting french fries in the sandwiches) with forty-two locations in six states, works with a variety of different apps in different cities. "Third-party delivery is the necessary evil in the restaurant business at this moment," chief marketing officer Adam Golomb says, invoking the mantra. "Fact of the matter is, you're giving a percentage of your sales to them. But they are driving business, and we're paying them to drive business."

Heng Shi believes the apps are worth losing money on for their potential as a marketing tool. Moving from Beijing to Kent State University to study hotel management, Shi then headed to Chicago, for no more reason than he loved basketball, the Bulls, and Michael Jordan. Though the legendary Jordan hasn't played a game in more than twenty years, Shi is happy in his adoptive city. In 2019 he bought into A Place by Damao, a Chicago restaurant serving Chengdu street food.

Shi increased efficiency in the kitchen and cut out the existing marketing streams—Google, OpenTable, social media—that weren't generating customers and then focused on the Chowbus platform, which has doubled revenue, but not profits. "To be honest, I'm not making money," admits Shi. Chowbus, which usually charges 30 percent, has been capped at 20 percent thanks to pandemic-related limits put into temporary place by Chicago's city council.

Even with the limits in place, using the ordering system means sales through Chowbus are unprofitable for Damao. Instead, Shi considers the commissions his marketing fee for using the platform to reach customers and build a reputation for the restaurant. "I'm looking at the big picture. I want, after two to three years, all my commissions to add up to a brand." It's not a ringing endorsement of this model that its restaurant proponents are businesses that can afford to lose money for years or are special enough to get sweet deals.

A GHOST STORY

Using apps to massively expand delivery isn't the only way restaurants are going virtual. Over the past few years, another trend has emerged: restaurants that only deliver. They have a name and a brand and you can order their food—if you saw them on Uber Eats you'd have no idea there was anything different about them. These are establishments that, in the conventional sense, do not exist. When in-person dining is a thing again, you won't be able to go sit and eat in them. These enterprises were first called dark kitchens, then evolved into the slightly friendlier ghost kitchen—think Casper rather than Freddy Kreuger or Hamlet's dad. They are enabled by 3PD. It would be impossible to run one successfully without these platforms, and they take the idea of a virtual restaurant encounter in a whole new direction.

The premise is that a ghost-kitchen company invests in the physical infrastructure, buying or leasing real estate and developing a commercial kitchen facility that can service multiple businesses, as well as the digital marketing and sales platform. Within a building that houses five or ten kitchens, the restaurant-business tenants make the actual food. Some of these restaurants are new businesses with no physical store presence you can visit. Most are expansions of existing restaurants.

For a few years now, industry watchers have been predicting a shift to delivery first for full-service restaurants. Within five years, they kept saying, restaurants needed to reconfigure for the majority of their revenue coming through off-premise dining (takeout and delivery, sometimes abbreviated as "off-prem"). When COVID-19 ended dine-in service for any foreseeable future, that rate of change was accelerated from a matter of years to weeks.

Before March 2020, Kim Alter's San Francisco restaurant, Nightbird, served a ten-course tasting menu. Between crime and pollution, she says, her location didn't allow her to offer outdoor dining as a pandemic-coping strategy. Very quickly, she switched to providing meals for churches and hospitals, which at least kept her workers employed and put to helpful use.

Alter had always kept food cost at 19.6 percent, which is low. But her fixed costs (rent, water, electric, insurance, workers' comp, and so forth) made it impossible for her to so much as break even after all these adjustments.

Instead of trying to sell Nightbird's food for delivery, she created a virtual brand extension, Nightburger, using Tock for sales and Door-Dash for delivery.

When the pandemic devalued the dining rooms that account for so much of a restaurant's fixed cost, the ghost kitchen became an appealing business model. If we can't eat inside restaurants, why do restaurateurs need to be paying for dining rooms in the most expensive locations?

Small moves from big companies like Uber or Amazon demand industry watchers' attention. In March 2019, *Bloomberg News* reported that Uber Eats was testing a program in Paris leasing commercial kitchens and renting the spaces for delivery-only restaurants. There were few details, and Uber declined to comment on their plans. Leasing kitchen space would put Uber in competition with similar ghost-kitchen enterprises, such as CloudKitchens (run by former Uber CEO Travis Kalanick) and Kitchen United, which both offer turnkey commercial kitchens optimized for delivery service.[22]

As president of the Cornerstone Restaurant Group, Josh Zadikoff oversees thirteen restaurants, from Michael Jordan's Steak House in Chicago to ENO, a wine bar in San Francisco. A few years ago, after testing out third-party delivery apps with the steakhouses, he found that value, quality, and experience were too difficult to maintain. There isn't a huge market for a $123 Japanese wagyu ribeye that was cooked a half hour ago. For another of their brands, urbanbelly, a fast-casual counter-service concept by chef Bill Kim, serving noodles, dumplings, and rice, the system worked perfectly.

In 2019 Cornerstone opened two new urbanbelly locations. One was a ghost kitchen in the River North neighborhood of Chicago, a Kitchen United space, with the food delivered through Caviar. "For us to expand, we need to find locations that we can service," said Zadikoff in 2019. At the time, he was happy with the ghost-kitchen model as a way to expand while lowering the cost of entry into an upscale neighborhood where it would be extremely expensive to open a brick and mortar.

However, it took years of partnering with different 3PD apps for Caviar to become a viable, long-term, profitable revenue stream for

Cornerstone. By 2020, they had pulled the plug on the ghost-kitchen operation. That's another advantage that bigger companies have: the time, capital, and resources to experiment while operating in the red.

There's a lot of potential upside to these ghost kitchens for the right kind of business. The cost of build-out for a full-service restaurant (the construction of a kitchen with an HVAC system, plumbing, wiring, a glitzy dining room) is a fraction for a ghost operation. Though it's way too hard to build a reputation and customer base on digital sales alone. So it's a highly risky prospect for a first-time restaurateur. For established, successful brands, it's a way to increase overall sales by producing food out of an off-site kitchen where delivery orders don't interfere with their busy lunch or dinner service. Location matters too. Ghost kitchens make the most sense in high-density urban areas where the cost of commercial real estate is prohibitive and consumer demand is at its peak.

The concept also enables experienced restaurateurs to pivot (yes, everyone in the restaurant industry is as tired of this word as you are) quickly. After the pandemic forced Aki and Koji Kanematsu to close down most of their Onigilly restaurant operations in San Francisco, they struck a preferred deal with CloudKitchens: a six-month lease for three spaces at once. Due to the newness and volatility of the sector, ghost leases are typically for one year, as opposed to a traditional five-, ten-, or fifteen-year lease for a brick and mortar, where both parties want to lock in a long-term commitment. Onigilly's core product is the Japanese snack onigiri, a triangle of short grain rice, wrapped in nori, stuffed with things like pickled mustard greens or spicy miso beef. They made their signature Onigilly dish in the ghost kitchen, but the Kanematsus also immediately started developing two additional concepts to produce out of the same kitchens. "If we have a sub-brand online," says Aki Kanematsu, "Tokyo Poke House or Curry Ninja, we can operate with the same staff. Because they are simple operations. Same ingredients. Same labor." These alternative brands sell different foods than Onigilly, ones that their cooks know how to make but don't necessarily make sense at their original restaurant.

This kind of brand extension, sometimes called a virtual restaurant, is happening on a much broader scale. Virtual restaurant Wing Squad, for example, operates out of Planet Hollywood and Buca di Beppo kitchens. Pasqually's Pizza & Wings is really Chuck E. Cheese.[23] Even more fascinating is the concept of virtual franchising. Tyga Bites is a collaboration between rapper Tyga and restaurant mogul Robert Earl (founder of Planet Hollywood) that sells the concept and branding of an oven-baked chicken-nugget menu, with a heavy focus on dipping sauces, to existing businesses that want to run virtual restaurants out of the same kitchen. "It's kind of safe," explained Tyga in a promotional video. "I don't have to deal with the headache of opening a restaurant, hiring staff, doing all that extra stuff. People that already have that in place can just franchise it and do it themselves." Restaurants don't need Tyga to teach them to make chicken nuggets or tamarind chipotle dipping sauce. The value is in the celebrity's marketing power. Without a gimmick, it's hard for a neighborhood restaurant to transition to a ghost model and stand out in the 3PD sales stream.

It's not just the cost of rent and build-out that makes a ghost kitchen more attractive but the way traditional restaurant locations are laid out. Even if traditional restaurants can find a way to make a delivery-first model work financially, they're up against a physical obstacle—their kitchens are too small. The traditional allocation of floor space in full-service restaurants, with the aim of maximizing the dining area (where seating equals potential revenue), makes it hard to pump out to-go meals. It's a software update that doesn't truly function without a hardware upgrade.

Restaurant kitchens have always been too small. So many are designed and constructed less for functionality than to fit into the existing architecture, like in New Orleans, where you sometimes have to walk through the kitchen to get to the bathroom. In the battle for space, trying to make a workable restaurant inside a century-old building, the kitchen traditionally loses to the front of house. The thinking is usually that it's better for the cooking staff to be a bit uncomfortable than the customers. Now we are entering an era where the lack of cooking, prep, and storage space is an impediment to production capacity and, therefore, financial viability.

By the time this sees print, most Americans will be vaccinated. But in the postquarantine, prevaccine Between era, when Uber Eats reported that its roster of restaurants grew by 75 percent, the value of the dining area immediately dropped even further, and the ghost restaurant presented an even more unique opportunity for a successful business model.[24]

"The infrastructure was never built to support off-premises dining." That's Corey Manicone, who goes on to describe the sea of couriers you'd have to wade through, pre-COVID, to get to the cash register in a New York City restaurant.

Manicone grew up mopping the floors in his parents' International House of Pancakes franchise. After finding success, they overextended themselves by opening a second restaurant that bled cash and forced them to sell the IHOP to cover the losses. His father went from being named Midwest Franchisee of the Year to losing it all. "I told myself I'd never be in the industry," says Manicone, who very much ended up in the industry and has found a way to deal himself a better hand.

In 2015 Manicone was the first employee at Relay, a company that bridges the gap between 3PD platforms and last-mile logistics—or, to put it into English, the people who actually do the delivering. On Manicone's first day, Relay did fifty deliveries. On his last day, three years later, they did close to twenty thousand. So he got to know quite a few operators in New York City and saw just how big the shift toward off-premise dining was. He saw an opportunity to design an infrastructure to support that next phase of dining. "I helped build the optimal delivery playbook. The best products to deliver. How to optimize for your zone, for speed. I was starting to see the majority, 40 or 60 percent, of revenue going out the door with the courier. I remembered all the historical challenges that my parents faced. From HR [human resources] and accounting to cooking the product and creating an experience for the consumers. The reason why it's such a risky business is because there's so much that goes into it. And there's this new one, which is logistics." Manicone, knowing he's got a good line, pauses for effect. "No one gets into the restaurant industry because they're good at logistics."

Except he is good at logistics. And despite his protestations, when he talks about bringing multiple restaurant brands under one roof, benefiting from the economies of scale, aggregating the sum of labor and operational support, or strategizing for getting food out the door and into the customer's hands as quickly as possible, that sounds a lot like the restaurant business. "We allow the brands to do what they do best," he distinguishes. "Which is cook." Manicone sees the broken model of restaurants, a razor-thin margin made worse by the techno-disruption, as an opportunity.

So, in the summer of 2019, he launched Zuul (named after the minion of Gozer the Gozerian, the antagonist from *Ghostbusters*), a ghost kitchen with six tenants in its Lower Manhattan kitchen: Sarge's Deli, Naya, Sweetgreen, Positive, junzi, and Stone Bridge.

That summer, when Manicone approached restaurateur Hady Kfoury about opening a ghost kitchen, Kfoury didn't know what a ghost kitchen was. Starting in 2008, he had successfully grown his Lebanese restaurant, Naya, from one location in midtown Manhattan to seven. Zuul presented the opportunity for Kfoury to expand into Soho, a section of the New York market beyond Naya's delivery reach, at a fraction of the start-up cost for a new restaurant. "Going to Zuul on Zandam Street, which is in Soho, was a completely new territory for us. That was a whole area we were not serving. That was the motivation," says Kfoury, happy to have the landlord, Zuul, take responsibility for leaks, breaks, even dishwashing labor. "Rent made sense for us. It's a plug-and-play setup. Worst-case scenario you pull out after a year. It's a one-year contract. The start-up cost is way lower than any brick and mortar. The risk is so minimal."

By the end of the year, Kfoury launched Naya's ghost kitchen. For about $50,000 (rather than the $1 million another full restaurant would have cost), he ended up paying a third as much as his highest rent ($33,000 for Madison and Fifty-Second).

A few months later, COVID-19 not only wiped out dine-in service but also emptied office spaces and the lunch sales that go with them (diners who, with our shift to remote work, are not returning in the same numbers). Naya's sales dropped to 30 percent of the previous year. But the ghost-kitchen experiment was a success, enabling Kfoury to prove the growth potential of his business and finalize the sale of his majority stake in the company.

At Zuul, all deliveries are done by bike within a radius of a mile and a quarter, which equals about twenty blocks north or south. Keeping the delivery zone tight, the businesses within Zuul are able to guarantee a fifteen-minute delivery. That's start to finish, order to doorstop.

Those tenants are, in the best tradition of *The Dirty Dozen* or *Ocean's 11*, a ragtag mix of legacy businesses, like Sarge's Deli, and modern chains such as junzi, run by an aggressively forward-thinking group of entrepreneurs who studied forestry before turning to hospitality. What they all have in common is a refusal to be tethered to the restaurant rules of the past. "The model of the ghost kitchen is the future," says Yong Zhao, one of junzi's cofounders. "We saw the future back in China."

Junzi was thinking so far in advance of this pandemic that in December 2019, Zhao had ordered masks, sent them to China to help friends there, and then had them sent back to New York in time to still be ahead of the game for mask wearing in America.

Zhao sees huge potential in the ghost-restaurant model but knows it's very hard for traditional restaurateurs. "They have to change their whole mentality. In the future, delivery is not going to be incremental. It's going to be the core of sales. The P&L [profit and loss] for a restaurant like that is quite different."

When delivery is still the minority of your sales, you can consider the app commissions as an affordable marketing tool, as Damao is doing. When it is the majority, you have to play a different game or get out. Zhao believes that Chinese restaurants are uniquely positioned to make this shift. "Chinese was the original ghost kitchen," says Zhao.

"More than half of the Chinese restaurants in America are takeout, with less than ten seats. They're like ghost kitchens. They depend on delivery rather than foot traffic. [At first] the demand for Chinese food declined. Because of discrimination and the association with the coronavirus. But when the coronavirus happened in America, and the whole restaurant industry got hit, the delivery of Chinese food increased. Because Chinese food is fundamentally delivery food, ghost-kitchen food."

While certain cuisines may adapt better to delivery, the structure of the ghost kitchen offers opportunity at multiple strata. Crave, a vertically integrated ghost-kitchen and delivery business, partners with higher-end restaurants that don't want their fancy food carelessly stuffed in bags. The company, which launched in Boise and is building facilities in Dallas, Phoenix, and Salt Lake City, actually employs their couriers. They're not gig workers. Their restaurants create dishes specifically for delivery rather than try to replicate their dine-in cuisine. "When you know something is going to sit during delivery, you do something different," says director of strategy Shannon Bloemker. "We separate hot and cold things. Such a basic thing to do. But it doesn't get done. Delivery is not going to go away. But let's do it with intention."

Thoughtful variations are exciting, if limited to a smaller audience. From what I've seen so far, the ghost model offers real potential value to all parties. The basic 3PD structure, the one that's dominated our restaurant landscape and, since the onset of the pandemic, shifted ordering behavior for so many of us, is still a lose-lose proposition. "There's nothing in this model that I can see where there's a path to profitability for everybody," says Lombardo, the pizza slinger. "It works overseas in parts of Asia because the labor cost is so ridiculously low on a comparative basis. And you're not even close here in a city like New York where it's difficult enough to keep a talented cook."

For several years, industry watchers, both those with and those without skin in the game, didn't believe there was long-term profitability in the delivery-app game. What would make it profitable is vertical integration, which basically means that you own the businesses you're supplying, like a car manufacturer owning an oil refinery. While I'm excited about the potential of ghost kitchens, it worries me that they could be used to leverage even more control away from restaurant operators.

What happens if these large companies, ones that rent kitchens and others that deliver food, continue to merge as they've done for the past decade? A combined entity would have the ability to throttle or promote certain restaurant partners based on preferable sales commissions. "There is huge potential for conflict there, and I'd be very wary and probably likely not go near something like that," says Zadikoff, who for the moment is not worried. "It's not what their core business is."

The tech industry changes strategies quickly. Most of these companies are still unprofitable. Yet, thanks to a steady supply of low-interest investment cash and arguably predatory pricing (a common strategy in which companies eat the loss on a sale by subsidizing the cost of the product, hoping their war chest can help them eliminate the competition while operating at a loss), these paper tigers keep walking tall, talking tough, and trying to go public with ludicrous overvaluations.

As fierce competitors buy each other out, consolidation in these still-new sectors is already under way, with no regulation to slow it down. Amazon, now a leader in food retail thanks to its purchase of Whole Foods in 2017, invested a half-billion dollars in Deliveroo, one of Uber Eats' main competitors in the United Kingdom. Kitchen United is funded by Google. So it seems naive to look at ghost or virtual restaurants as an isolated venture. What will happen if and when one of these tech giants ends up being both landlord and distributor for our restaurant industry?

That fear of vertical integration might have seemed paranoid fifteen years ago, when Amazon was still thought of as an online bookseller. As that company has grown into one determined to sell us everything, it has also evolved to produce in-house versions of popular products. Its founder is the richest man on earth, and employees at his fulfillment centers suffer injuries at twice the industry average.[25]

By now the public has learned from Facebook's many privacy scandals that consumer data is the most valuable asset these companies possess. As for what virtual kitchen companies will do with it, the most likely suggestion I've heard is cannibalization. Tech leaders are probably not interested in being real-estate magnates. If they were, they'd be investing in commercial properties less volatile than restaurant locations. What they're doing with virtual kitchens feels similar to what they did with delivery—getting their toehold in the market to leverage it into something bigger.

Traditionally, in their first few years in a new sector, tech companies have been less concerned with profitability than obtaining consumer data and cornering whatever market they're entering. In the case of the food-service industry, I don't think they are interested in collecting rent from restaurants as much as building out a monopoly over the whole ecosystem of online food sales. The end goal, if I had to guess, would be pushing restaurants—whether these operate out of traditional storefronts or take up tenancy in a ghost kitchen—out of the sector entirely.

That's why it's a mistake to examine these companies only in the present tense. Past behavior is a better predictor of future behavior.

With their roster of virtual restaurants grown into virtual food courts, Kitchen United and CloudKitchens can battle each other over exclusivity with the most popular local brands (who's got a Shake Shack, a Momofuku, and so forth, for any particular delivery zone), before ultimately cutting out the restaurants and producing virtually identical food in-house at lower cost to them and the consumer. Again, this is what Amazon did: collecting consumer data on what sold, at what time of day, and at what price, before cutting out the supplier and manufacturing their own products.

Joel Tietelman, the owner of Mile End Delicatessen in New York, isn't worried about copycat matzo ball soup. "I'm in New York City, where the customers are extremely discerning. If they can't go to visit the restaurant, it is very doubtful that they're going to patronize it."

I want to believe he's right, that diners value his product too much to be swayed by digital trickery. Imagining for a moment that I am a tech mogul looking to expand into the food-service space, let's say I lease a five-thousand-square-foot building and construct ten kitchens inside, each with their own ovens, hoods, storage, and so on. Then I get ten tenants who make a variety of staple takeout foods—tacos, burgers, fried chicken, and more—and sign them up for my full-service support package as well, taking care of everything from online ordering to credit-card sales to delivery. Now comes the fun part. Maybe a business called Taco Deliciosos already has a steady lunch and dinner following. Great. My company's data inform us that there's a demand within the delivery zone for breakfast items or healthy lunches. We can easily reconfigure the food inventory to make breakfast burritos or healthy-sounding "bowl" food, some permutation of beans and avocado, maybe served with brown rice and whatever fruit is currently purported to have medicinal qualities. We can experiment with the name, A/B testing different identities for the restaurant, to see which best captures the ethnicity, age, gender, or income of the audience we're targeting. Once I know all that, won't my customers be just as happy with Corey's Tacos as they were with Tacos Deliciosos?

If this sounds like I'm making it up, there's a CloudKitchen at 1842 West Washington Boulevard in Los Angeles that lists food on Postmates from Thai Market, Send Noods, Thai Thai Thai, Salathai, and Crazy Rich Asian Foods. They have nearly identical menus because they're the same kitchen. According to the Postmates menu, Thai Market's "phuket wings" are "Thai style Buffalo wings cooked with one of a kind Southern curry sauce. To die for." They seem to me the same dish as Crazy Rich Asian Foods' "bougie phuket wings," described in the exact same words: "Thai style Buffalo wings cooked with one of a kind Southern curry sauce. To die for." Ditto for the "new money pad thai," which evidently "won several awards" according to the Crazy Rich Asian Foods menu on Postmates. Not coincidentally, Thai Market's pad thai also seems to have won the same awards. The Crazy Rich Asian Foods brand simply adds the words *wealthy, VIP, baller, chic, loaded, new money, bling, fancy,* or *bougie* in front of the same menu items.

So if you're a ghost tenant and you believe your customers will never abandon you for a copycat because it's a dollar cheaper, or delivers one mile farther, know that your landlord is investing a great deal of money to gather the data to prove you wrong.

Brad Slingerland, cofounder of investment firm NZS Capital, doesn't see any value being added in the delivery-app racket. He does see potential in the tech companies' ability to vertically integrate the food brands they distribute. And he is not so devout as Teitelman about consumer brand loyalty. "Do I want a Shake Shack burger, or do I just want a good burger? If all I want is just a good burger, delivered in a way that's fresh, then I don't care if it's Shake Shack or Shake Shimmy by Uber."

Cannibalizing their restaurant partners may sound like a conspiracy theory. But the value has to come from somewhere.

As long as they still have to use humans, these tech companies use every trick in their vast legal arsenal to prevent classifying their workers as employees and being liable for employee benefits or vehicle insurance. For example, when couriers signed up to deliver food for Uber Eats in Canada, they agreed that disputes had to be pursued through an arbitration court in the Netherlands, incurring upfront administrative and filing fees of $14,500 USD (eventually invalidated by the Supreme Court of Ontario on grounds of unconscionability).[26] "We always knew the independent-contractor classification was a scam," says Curth, the former courier for Foodora, "and in no way indicative of our actual relationship with the company, which is very much an employer-employee one. But we were happy to put up with it because we were happy in our jobs and getting paid well."

In late 2019, Curth and fellow Ontario Foodora couriers organized in an effort to change that classification. Early in 2020, the Ontario Labour Relations Board ruled that Foodora's couriers were "dependent contractors and must be treated as such under the [Employment Standards] Act. As the evidence bears out, couriers more closely resemble employees than independent contractors." This victory paved the way for the roughly nine hundred workers to unionize.[27]

Two months later, Foodora ceased operations in Canada. So it seems they'd rather quit than pay workers a fair wage. Fully automated vehicles are still not here; they can't eliminate workers yet. Meanwhile, the cost of labor keeps pushing delivery profitability further away. That means they need another path. If I'm a tech company, helping you sell your tacos, once I've learned everything I need to know about your product and customers, why do I still need you?

SELF-DELIVERY

This is a lot of information to consider before ordering dinner. Too much. It does help to highlight the two types of survivors in the altered restaurant landscape: those who are able to adapt to massive disruption and the ones who were already planning for it.

Without intending to, Colin Li had spent two years preparing for a pandemic. In the late 1980s, Li's parents came to Canada from Guangzhou. They had been restaurateurs back in China and spent years saving until they could afford their own spot, Hong Shing, in 1997. In 2016, after graduating with a human resources degree, Li began working in the family business full-time, transitioning to eventually take over so his parents could retire.

It was difficult at first, working from 11:00 a.m. to 4:00 a.m., his mother and father insisting that he replicate their methods. They wanted their son to succeed, but they were reluctant to see the business change.

There is no official rule for how many items a full-service restaurant should have. The popular, high-volume Momofuku Noodle Bar has 24. Applebee's, a chain known for a big menu that offers a bit of everything, has 55. The Cheesecake Factory has 197. Old-school Chinese restaurants tend to have long menus. House of Gourmet, not far from Hong Shing, offers more than 500 dishes.

When Li started working in his parents' restaurant, they had 200 menu items. They resented the idea of shortening it at all. Li argued for efficiency. Why have a staff member spend all day making six types of spring rolls when they could focus on the most frequently ordered one?

Gradually, Li managed to court a new audience with an updated menu and modern social media strategy, while maintaining existing clientele by holding on to key dishes and cooking methods. Two years ago, Li began developing an online ordering system. The problem with the delivery-app companies wasn't just their commissions, thought Li, but their control of customer data, which is necessary to know where to allocate your labor and marketing.

Like the Jossels, Kataokas, and Reaves brothers, Li had never offered delivery before March 2020. Now he spends his dinner hours packaging orders, managing drivers, taking phone calls from customers, and occasionally stepping behind the wok to get meals out the door faster.

Whenever there's a free moment, he'll pull his phone out to reply to Instagram comments or crack open his laptop to peek behind the curtain of his ordering software, which enables him to see how much time customers spend on his website, where web traffic is coming from digitally (Google, Instagram, or wherever) and geographically (enabling him to open up delivery zones based on demand), even where on the page they are resting and for how long. For example, he's able to tell me that I spent most of my visit looking at the beef section. It can automatically send enticement offers to individual customers. So, if you're specifically looking at vegetarian dishes on the site, it can instantly send you an email for a promotional discount on vegetarian dishes or an offer of a free half serving. Li is very confident that once diners are within his system, he will bring them back to become repeat customers.

Thanks to this fortuitous planning—the development of his own online ordering system—Li was in a rare position to benefit from the early pandemic chaos of the restaurant industry. Within a couple months he hired back 90 percent of the front-of-house staff he'd initially had to lay off, putting them to work as couriers. In a stroke of good fortune, Li launched his ordering platform at the beginning of March 2020, two weeks before everything went haywire. By mid-March, he was already up and running. "When COVID happened, the first thing I thought of was, Chinese restaurants are always built for takeout and delivery first. So there wasn't too much to change. Biggest thing we did was open up areas for delivery at the click of a button."

Seeing Chinese restaurants closed all over the suburbs, Li launched a social media campaign, asking people to tag their friends, promising he would deliver wherever there were the most tags. Once he knew where his food was wanted, he began what he called delivery pop-ups, announcing that Hong Shing would be available on certain days, in certain areas, just like the Reaves brothers in Dallas, except that he had all the back-end data as well. So he knew where demand was coming from.

Most customers have become used to making food choices at the last minute—what we want, when we want. That's part of what these apps prey on. The convenience they sell is not just choice but also free-dom from commitment. We don't have to plan, shop, or even think about dinner during the day because we can use our phones to make all of that happen at seven o'clock. That's a huge luxury, which many of us have grown to depend on. Changing consumer behavior is hard. We've learned that it's possible. Quarantine isolation and public health guidelines changed so much of our daily routines overnight, enabling clever restaurateurs to redefine that relationship to the point where people will order dinner in advance, because it's the food they crave or because they want to support that restaurant.

Within a few weeks, Li's database of repeat customers jumped from 80 to 150 to 4,000. The operating hours changed radically. In-stead of heavy lunch crowds from the nearby law offices and late-night service filled with the after-party crowd, including occasional appear-ances from Toronto Raptors players, it's all dinner-hour delivery now. Revenue quickly returned to pre-COVID levels.

In 2020, when more than half of the restaurants in North America may have closed for good, and those that survived were struggling to turn a profit amid harsh conditions, Li was not just surviving but grow-ing. "When things change, we're thinking of expanding," says Li, still in his twenties, looking forward to a postpandemic restaurant landscape. "We're looking to open up a five-hundred- to two-thousand-square-feet place devoted to takeout and catering. If I open two in a few years, I can open a central kitchen and do quality control."

The physical element isn't the biggest obstacle to restaurants offering self-delivery. It's migrating customers, back from the grazing ground of the apps, to direct ordering. Restaurants are capable of doing this on their own, Robert Guarino tells me, if they're prepared for the challenge. At the start of the pandemic, the CEO of the mini chain 5 Napkin Burger, with twelve locations in Manhattan, was able to hold on to all his units and about 200 out of 350 employees by implementing a combination of solutions. Five years ago, the company did no delivery. By 2019 it was 20 percent of sales, jumping to 65 percent in March 2020. Using Bbot, an online ordering platform (with a flat fee), and Relay for delivery (paying about five dollars a hit and charging the customer three), the company has been able to stream about 30 percent of ordering traffic directly. This is all done through talking up customers, offering first-order discounts, and running social media ads in targeted neighborhoods. Some restaurants pursuing a similar strategy put self-delivery flyers in the delivery bags for Grubhub. Guarino doesn't. But given Grubhub's alleged scam of creating phony websites to trick diners into ordering direct from them, slipping flyers into a paper bag seems almost quaint.

In the early days of our COVID quarantine, there was a general call to support our most cherished local restaurants. With their doors closed, some advocated that those who could afford it should buy merch or gift cards. Restaurants weren't going to stave off bankruptcy by selling T-shirts. If they never reopened, of what use were gift cards? As restaurants started operating takeout and delivery, and the public felt that this was a way of supporting these businesses, I hesitated to start haranguing people yet again that the apps are a money loser for most full-service restaurants, even when I started hearing the ad copy in podcasts: "Continue supporting restaurants in your community safely. You've counted on restaurants. Now they're counting on you."

But almost as quickly, the situation seemed to hit a trip wire. Suddenly the conversation about the predatory nature of these companies was mainstream, with every news outlet publishing stories about how ordering through apps wouldn't save local restaurants. As public perception about the business practices of these companies grew, cities like New York, Denver, Seattle, Los Angeles, San Francisco, and Seattle were able to pass temporary legislation imposing commission caps on delivery services. In Toronto Mayor John Tory politely asked the 3PD companies to do it voluntarily. "You've got to hope that corporations have the good sense to do something on their own without being forced to do it," said Tory, feigning a political innocence not seen since before Mr. Smith went to Washington.

DELETE YOUR APPS

Those temporary measures are hopefully the legislative foot in the door that enables local governments to enact more meaningful policies to protect small businesses from predatory business practices. In New York, for example, Councilor Mark Gnojaj (who worked in a pizzeria and ran a restaurant with his brother) has been pushing legislation to hold these companies accountable. Or at least it might be possible to renew these laws indefinitely, like a certain Patriot Act I could name but won't. Certainly, many cities and states, in order to support small businesses, were willing to sacrifice lives by refusing to impose lockdowns or require mask wearing. Until our town puts some legislative teeth in the fight against these tech companies, we can do something ourselves.

The only thing certain about third-party delivery is that we cannot predict the next steps from these companies. Not five years from now or even one. A decade ago they didn't exist. Now they are more than 10.89 percent of the restaurant market and growing.

But it's a corner of the restaurant industry where we can take simple, direct action through our choices. We can stop using these apps. Delete them from our phones. I just did it. Before we could use apps to order food, did we all starve to death? True, it means that I can no longer choose dinner from two hundred different restaurants. I don't think I ever did. Most of us order from the same half dozen places on repeat. If I really want food from a particular restaurant, I'll call it in and pick it up.

If I find a restaurant near me that's doing self-delivery, whether as a disaster adaptation like Nopa and Smokey John's or because they're a pizza or Chinese restaurant that has always provided their own delivery, I'm gonna support the hell out of them. When it's my cheat night and I'm going to indulge by eating something rich and delicious without cooking, I want the restaurant I'm ordering from to be making money.

But let's say we're at a friend's home (still an impossibility as I type this) and they're ordering dinner through some app. We don't want to be a grinch by telling them not to. In the postvaccine world, when we finally get to hang out casually with our friends again, we don't want to start by chastising them for using Grubhub. If we're in this situation, there's a compromise solution—tip cash. We don't want to Google the company later to find it's one of the many that uses tips to drivers as a deduction from the promised hourly wage (like DoorDash, which stopped the practice in 2019 following public criticism).[28] So at the very least, let's make sure the courier gets a solid tip and that we get it directly into their hands.

I always have cash on me. (I probably shouldn't be admitting this to the many professional thieves who identify big-money targets by reading nonfiction food books.) We still haven't arrived at a cashless future society. Until then, you never know when you're going to encounter a tow-truck driver, kidnapper, or meal courier for whom cash is still king.

Deleting these apps may be difficult for some of us, hooked as we are on the convenience or routine. But the action and the way it helps restaurants is one of the simplest, most black-and-white of those in the dining sphere. Once we start looking inside the restaurant, at how workers are treated, it gets much more complicated.

· 2 ·

The Chef-Driven Restaurant

My right hand hasn't seen my left hand in thirty years.

—J. J. HUNSECKER

JULY 2020

A year ago, Amanda Cohen's restaurant offered only a tasting menu. From Tuesday to Saturday, the fifty-seat Manhattan room served about eighty-five people for dinner, ensuring that diners had a table for three hours to leisurely enjoy ten courses of elegantly plated seaweed caviar with crème fraîche, towers of foraged greens, tomato tarts and tomato lollipops, mushroom mousse, fennel tajine, carrot burgers, corn pasta, beet yakitori, and other exquisite creations made without animal products.

By the pandemic summer of 2020, Dirt Candy is open from noon to 9:00 p.m., serving sandwiches and salads at lunch, with a prix fixe at dinner. The plates are only slightly less composed—smoked and grilled broccoli, Thai basil pesto with spinach ramen, oyster mushrooms al pastor. But most of it is prepared to go or to be eaten on the twenty-seat ad hoc patio.

Like so much of New York City this summer, the sidewalk and former parking spots outside Dirt Candy on Allen Street have been transformed into a grubby piazza, with smaller crowds and more noise and diesel fumes from delivery trucks than your typical Italian town square. It's like a summertime Halloween, with America dressed as Europe, the city's seasonal zoning solution to a dark spring that saw the dining rooms of the nation's eating capital shuttered by a plague for which few were prepared.

While Cohen is happy with her choice of a wide restaurant space (most New York restaurant real estate runs deep), enabling her more sidewalk seating room during a time when food can't be served inside, the location is close to both the Williamsburg and the Manhattan Bridges. It's a busy commercial drive, a preferred route of ambulances and fire trucks, on which no one ever fantasized about dining al fresco. Worse, this far north, patio season lasts only half the year, at best.

With all this effort to make the best of difficult conditions, between a lower-priced à la carte menu and a lack of large parties, Dirt Candy's average check size has shrunk to a small fraction, with revenue hovering around 35 percent of where it was a year ago. "If I didn't have government money, I would be hemorrhaging," says Cohen, who has been able to rehire six of the thirty-five staff members she had to lay off when she closed in March. "I'm able to pay rent because of the PPP [Paycheck Protection Program]. In October, when my PPP runs out, I'll have to be renegotiating with my landlord. There's no way I can pay that. I'm clearly not doing the amount of business I was. But my insurance hasn't gone down. The cost of food hasn't gone down."

She's also got new costs, like takeout containers and building a patio. Her only solace is regular group chats with other chefs and restaurateurs, all in the same situation, all trying to figure how their businesses can make it to a postvaccine world, attempting every conceivable idea just to bring in a quarter of their usual sales.

Yes, there are a handful of stories that sound like successes only because a cataclysm makes survival the new standard of victory. The

$38 bento boxes from n/naka in LA, lined with wagyu-stuffed shishito peppers and tuna karaage with burnt tomato puree, sold out instantly.[1] But they need to be selling out. A prepandemic meal at the restaurant cost $275.

Mostly, COVID-19 has been a throat punch to the genre of chef-driven restaurants. Since the pandemic began in March, fast-thinking restaurateurs and chefs have thrown everything at the wall to see what sticks—patio service, meal kits, delivery, and online classes. None of it is enough to meet Cohen's revenue needs. "It's a huge disaster, and I don't think we understand what is going to happen. I am not sure we can understand what is about to happen. Most of my colleagues are on the brink of closure."

Cohen, because she has always been willing to challenge industry norms and redefine what her restaurant is, what it means to both workers and diners, just may survive this crisis. "If as a restaurant you are willing to completely reconsider what it is that you think a restaurant is going to provide, then there is a chance," says Vaughn Tan, author of *The Uncertainty Mindset*, a view of innovation formed by observational ethnographies of high-end culinary research-and-development (R&D) teams at world-celebrated kitchens like England's The Fat Duck, American food-innovation labs like Modernist Cuisine, and José Andrés's ThinkFoodLab, and an unnamed restaurant that sounds a lot like Denmark's Noma. "I'm not sure if the world in this book is coming back."

It's not. Noma, the world's most vaunted restaurant, is now making burgers. Not that there's anything wrong with that. "This is what's been problematic about our dining culture," says Tan. "We've managed to conflate why food is important with the trappings that surround food."

The practicality of chef-driven restaurants built around the persona of the chefs, the subgenre to which Dirt Candy belongs, has long been on the edge. Pandemic conditions are just finally pushing it off the cliff. "We have an opportunity," says Tan, "to make a new normal that is a better normal."

That's something I've heard a lot this year. I'd go further. We have an obligation to make a better normal. Following the forest fire of

COVID-19, we have a once-in-a-lifetime opportunity to regrow our food culture from its roots. How do we want that to look?

For me, as a diner, good food is a given. I suppose there are foodsters who will eat a lousy meal just to say they've been somewhere hot, but I wouldn't knowingly pay for bad food, no matter how noble the cause. The issues that bother me are systemic and hard to change: wage theft (withholding of legally deserved pay, through a variety of schemes) and abuse of all kinds (physical, emotional, verbal, sexual, racial). They are exacerbated by the structure of chef-driven restaurants, the dominance of chefs both within the hierarchy that rules a particular type of restaurant and externally, through the food media that perpetuates it.

I never again want to hear about how great a chef is unless it's about how great an employer they are. We have been celebrating a clichéd, larger-than-life concept of a chef—brilliant, abusive, insulting, demanding, loudly cruel—for the past twenty years. We have promoted the idea that this is what a winner looks like in the world of restaurants, filtered through the TV trope of the screaming mentor who will change your life and the ubiquitous print profile of the "difficult genius." It wasn't even that we held these people up as leaders, despite their cruelty. We exalted them as leaders because of their cruelty and allowed their corrosive personalities to define workplace culture, because that was somehow a mark of their dedicated pursuit of perfection.

They'll change only when we change how restaurants are run.

It may seem counterintuitive, but an unfair reality of the industry as it currently functions is that the better the restaurant, the less the cooks are paid. Because eager young cooks will put up with anything to learn from their idols, within any city's top-ten dining destinations, wage theft is rampant, income disparity divides workplaces, and abuse and addiction are common, all of it enabled by the cultlike toxicity of a certain brand of kitchen culture, the deification of chefs, and the brutal economics of tipping.

After a fire that destroyed California's Restaurant at Meadowood, I read a generous elegy in which people remembered fondly what it was like, including how horrible it could be to work there. The chef (who declined to comment on specific allegations) was accused of yelling, throwing dishes, and throwing fish in a worker's face. Several former cooks commented that the environment was "standard behavior for a Michelin-starred kitchen and it didn't bother them."[2] I've encountered this narrative repeatedly, in both my cooking and my writing careers. You'll find people in these kitchens who will say that they were treated and paid horribly, illegally even. There are just as many who will say that the harsh conditions turned them into who they are today, for which they are grateful. I could say the same. Their accounts of what work is like—minimum wage or less for twelve-hour days, screams and ridicule in front of peers for anything less than perfection—rarely differ.

It's not all restaurants, of course. That's the good news. There are owners using different structural models for running a business or compensating staff and chefs who make great food without treating people terribly. What are they doing different? What's the system that they are agitating against?

Let me take a step back for one moment. When I say "chef-driven restaurant" to someone in the industry, they nod. For people outside the industry, the term probably seems vague or redundant. Don't all restaurants have a chef at the helm? Often, but they are not always the center of attention.

Chef-driven restaurants are ones that operate and orbit around the persona of the chef. Sometimes their culinary imagination is the center of attention. Or it's just their personality. They stand in contrast to other categories: Quick Service Restaurants (a.k.a. fast food or fast casual), full-service chains, immigrant restaurants, and so on. Unlike these other forms of the business, chef-driven restaurants are the ones that ate up the largest percentage of media coverage for the past twenty years, when we started putting chefs on the same pedestal that film directors were on in the 1970s—auteurs credited with responsibility for all elements of what is clearly a huge collective effort. In this genre, the personality and vision of the chef define the restaurant, from investment to management to marketing.

This started with the regrettable aphorism that chefs are the new rock stars. I remember the era when this started because I was there. I was part of pushing that unfortunate trend. For work, I was eating a tasting meal in a fancy restaurant, a new life to which I'd quickly become accustomed after years of frugal living and eating. The diner next to me whispered, "You know, chefs are the new rock stars."

Following years spent as a kitchen minion, I looked up to chefs. They taught me everything I knew until that point—how to transform flour and eggs into noodles or how to tell when a steak is medium rare just by touching it. So I was primed to be a spokesperson for the celebration of chefs. When I interviewed for the job of restaurant critic, not too long before this dinner, I was asked what percentage of the review should be about the food versus everything else. "Seventy-five percent," I said. "No wait," I retracted. "Eighty." It seems so stupid now. As much as we love our rock stars, no one talks about what a great employer Nikki Sixx was (my apologies to the Mötley Crüe bass player, who, for all I know, is a kindly boss, making sure everyone gets dental coverage and takes scheduled meal breaks).

If somebody asked me that question today, I'd place it at exactly 49 percent. If those were shares in a company, they'd be important enough to get a vote, but not enough to be in charge.

In just two years as a critic, eating in the best (and worst) restaurants, I put on twenty pounds. Eventually, I learned two things: I had to start exercising. And while the best chefs are leaders and teachers who care deeply about their workers, too many are merely great at cooking and have more regard for an animal they put on a plate than the humans they need to help prepare and serve it.

When cooks complain of the monotony of their tasks, chefs remind them that while they aspire to artistry, they are, for now, skilled tradespeople who should take pride in perfection and pleasure in repetition. Then, when they complain about low wages, that they are not paid like electricians, plumbers, or any other skilled tradespeople, a chef will reverse course to remind them that they are artists and must suffer for their creative pursuits.

I've worked on the inside of that paradox (though I was fortunate to never have a chef who regularly yelled at us). I've thrown out my back while working sixty hours a week for less than minimum wage, only to have the restaurant pretend to file an insurance claim and, at tax time, for their accountant to hand me a form that falsely stated I worked forty hours a week. So when I hear about how mind-blowing the food is at some celebrated chef's new restaurant, it's hard to divorce that from how the employees are likely treated. I'm glad to see that we are starting to move away from exclusively glorifying the guru chef.

The James Beard Awards, in its most mainstream, visible activity, could be referred to as the Oscars for restaurants. The nonprofit also supports the industry through scholarships and a suite of educational programs designed to spread diversity and sustainability strategies via chefs and owners, such as the Women's Leadership Programs or the Chefs Bootcamp for Policy and Change.

In 2018 the foundation started the Good Food 100 list, a survey and guide of restaurants committed to sustainable sourcing practices throughout the supply chain (with ratings, for some mystifying reason, on a scale of 2 to 6). Lists like this are everywhere. This one, I was thrilled to find, incorporates treatment of employees—though it does not yet make it mandatory for restaurants to submit their wage data to be considered. "My hope is that over time it will be a requirement and that people will be more socialized to share it," says the organization's vice president of impact, Katherine Miller. By the year's end, Miller had left the organization to write a book about chef activism.

It's hard, she tells me at the time, getting owners who are subject to such a fragile business structure to share financial data. "The model is complicated and limiting. It's not as glamorous as everybody thinks it is. Most restaurants are operating at somewhere like a 6 percent profit margin. These folks aren't pocketing away millions of dollars unless you're up in the food-television celebrity where you probably don't own a restaurant anymore. That's why I think a lot of chefs are turning to fast casual. Your profit margins are higher at counter service, where you have limited workers on the floor, where you are buying high-quality ingredients at a larger scale."

A DAY IN THE LIFE OF A FANCY COOK

There's a lot going on beneath the phrase *workers on the floor*. The celebration of chefs obscures the labor and lives of cooks, and if you haven't worked in one of these kitchens, the number of bodies needed is abstracted. So let's take a look inside one of the top restaurants in the United States.

Without naming it, you know this restaurant. If you're a dining fanatic, you've either eaten there or watched a slide show of the tasting menu. Google "ten best restaurants in America." No matter which publication you're looking at, it's on the list. For the purpose of this story, let's just call it the Restaurant.

Before March 2020, the kitchen had about sixty employees. For a while, Tina (whose name is changed here) was proud to be one of them. After graduating from the Culinary Institute of America, where tuition is $32,000, she worked for a few years for a well-respected New York caterer. But she wanted more. Contacting the Restaurant, she was invited for a trial shift, sometimes known as a stage (rhymes with *garage* or, unless you are William Shatner, *sabotage*), an unpaid learning period in a restaurant that can run anywhere from a day to six months.

Asked to arrive at 2:00 p.m. in black pants and a white T-shirt (she heard they turned people away if they were wearing the wrong color pants), Tina showed up at 1:30. She snipped green beans, then helped with the staff meal, and then moved among various kitchen stations for a couple hours each. Finally, the chef de cuisine gave her a piece of halibut and told her she had ninety minutes to create a dish.

I've done a trial shift like this a few times. You never know where anything is and have to ask constantly for tools or ingredients. For Tina, this was during service in one of the world's top kitchens, where she had to whisper her questions while sharing flattop space. Because it's a silent service, she couldn't use heavy machinery and had to take the blender upstairs if she wanted to puree something. In the kitchen of the Restaurant, you can't place metal on metal. If you want to put a baking tray on a table, you have to place parchment down first. This silence is observed by thirty cooks. On weekends, during a two-hour overlap as the lunch shift breaks down, sixty people share the same space.

In a restaurant like the Restaurant, dishes must arrive at the table simultaneously. Diners paying this much for a tasting menu are not going to stare at their scallop course while the server goes back to the kitchen to fetch their friend's plate. In the kitchen, cooks coordinate by asking each other precisely how many minutes or seconds are left on their particular elements of each course. An expeditor, usually the CDC (chef de cuisine) or sous, acts like a field general, initiating courses with a call of "fire table 3 mains," checking the progress of each station, ensuring that the garde mangers (the cooks in charge of plating dishes and assembling cold items) are handed hot pieces of meat and bubbling pots of sauce, and are assembling the dishes neatly and precisely with the array of garnishes they've spent the day preparing. Meanwhile, a queue of servers awaits the command to begin carrying food to the dining room. When a call goes out, everyone in the kitchen says "oui."

If this sounds like a French remake of a Shaw Brothers *Shaolin Temple* movie, remember that these are not monks, seeking spiritual enlightenment through repetitive tasks and physical conditioning. They are cooking dinner for customers paying more than $300 per person.

After presenting her trial dish to the CDC for a critique, Tina went back to the kitchen to help clean, a process of breaking down stations, transferring the contents of every metal insert to a clean one, sweeping the walk-ins, and consolidating and scrubbing until one in the morning, the last half hour spent buffing and shining those sacred metal surfaces. At the end of the nearly twelve-hour day, she was offered a job.

A week later, as soon as she started, Tina noticed how often her coworkers quit. "The turnover is insane there," Tina recalls. "It's hard to find people who want to stay."

Tina was paid minimum wage, like everyone in the kitchen except for sous chefs, who were on salary. Below sous chefs, there were line cooks and, below them, the commis cooks. Commis cooks promoted to line cooks were frequently demoted back down to commis, the lowest rung on the ladder.

During her tenure, Tina got promoted, which meant longer hours but no more money. Because they were constantly hemorrhaging employees, she wondered if the promotion was based on her performance or because they needed someone to fill that space.

There was no time for self-doubt. Not with what was expected from her in a day. "There's so much to get done in so little time. You're constantly in the shit. Every day, everybody is in the shit all the time. You're never not in the shit. This goes for every single station and all the sous chefs, 100 percent of the time. There's so much anxiety to work there." She permits herself a giggle at the ridiculousness of it. "I'm laughing because we don't have to do it anymore."

Her promotion coincided with a seasonal menu change, when every dish was replaced simultaneously. For three days, no one knew what was happening, and everyone was yelled at for not knowing. It was up to each line cook to reconfigure their station, with more yelling when anyone failed to read minds or do it perfectly with no instruction.

Tina still respects the Restaurant for the culinary heights they achieved. She does question the necessity of the management style. "The way they ran their kitchen was very fear based. Nobody wants to get yelled at. Especially in front of all their friends. You feel really shitty about yourself when that happens. The motivator in that kitchen was fear. Not to be a better cook, but because you didn't want to get yelled at."

One of Tina's many new tasks was spending two hours a day sculpting root vegetables before vacuum sealing them in bags with brown butter to cook, one of many elements in a dish that was ultimately covered by foie gras and other garnishes. Tina laughs as she recounts the methodology of what now almost seems like a prank on her. Concealed by a garnish and rendered largely invisible, the effort expended to shape them was pointless. "I wish I could tell you why. That's how they wanted it done. You're constantly asking yourself, 'Why are we doing this?'" recalls Tina. "I said, 'This is what I signed up for. And if I don't do it, and do it right, I'm going to get reamed out by my sous chef.' Even if you are perfect, no one's going to give you any praise. It's an expectation that you do stuff perfectly, and all the time."

Most of the cooks were in their late teens or twenties. During ten-minute breaks (technically they had thirty minutes, but no one could afford to take that long), they'd discuss their anxieties about working at the Restaurant and question why they earned less than employees at fast-food chains. "Why don't we just work at McDonald's?" Tina would ask rhetorically. "We'd always talk about why. Nobody had an answer."

When coworkers heard about her quitting, the ones on J-1 visas (nonimmigrant visa for work and study-based exchange visitor programs) told her they were jealous because they wished they could too but were under contract and would have to leave the country if they did. "That solidified my feelings on this decision. A lot of people left while I was there. And the people that were there wanted to leave all the time."

There are good kitchens and bad. The methods at the Restaurant are not universal. This volume of labor and militaristic hierarchy, however, is how we make the kind of food that wins awards.

Tina was lucky. She may have earned only minimum wage for working in one of America's top restaurants, but at least she was paid for all her hours, in a segment of the industry that frequently indulges in wage theft: day rates that add up to less than minimum wage, or hourly pay with the expectation that everyone shows up to work a couple extra hours before clocking in for every shift. Two extra hours a day adds up to ten hours a week. That's forty hours, a full week, 25 percent of wages, unpaid, per month. So for every $100 earned, workers are paid $75.

This doesn't happen everywhere. But I've spoken to cooks and owners, from San Francisco to Toronto, Boston to Buffalo, New Orleans to New York, who confirm that this bullshit is still in full effect, or was, until March 2020.

It's worse in Europe, with the stagiaire system—where a cook's unpaid trial at a restaurant can last for months rather than a single shift or a few days. In America, labor enforcement cracked down on the practice. In many of Europe's "best" restaurants, stages can still run for six months. At the time that El Bulli was ranked as the world's "best" restaurant, I interviewed chef and owner Ferran Adrià, who told me that twenty-five of his cooks were unpaid stagiaires. "It's not a business. And it's not a restaurant," Adrià told me. "It's a way of understanding life."

The reason I put *best* in quotations is not to digress into questioning the ranking of subjective experiences, but because none of the restaurant-ranking lists place any value on how employees are treated or paid. Without detracting from the talent, dedication, and creativity of these restaurants, they could not perform at that level without the legion of unpaid help.

When we anoint status on restaurants as the best in the world, what are we saying when we celebrate their level of performance while ignoring how they achieved it? According to *Hospitality Magazine*, Italy's Osteria Francescana receives nineteen hundred stage applications a year. "Noma, which employs 25 full-time chefs, usually has up to 30 interns in the kitchen at any one time," reported the *Guardian* in 2015, when Noma was ranked at number three in the world, in a piece about how great the experience can be. A memoir from a former Noma stagiaire, published in *Los Angeles Magazine*, alleges seventeen-hour days.[3]

I've heard all of the justifications for the unpaid staff. I've even had chefs suggest that, for the education they're getting, stagiaires should be paying the restaurant. This isn't a new idea. In the Middle Ages, children as young as seven were sent to work as apprentices, sometimes paying to learn under a master craftsman of the highly controlled craft guilds, such as printmaking or goldsmithing. These labor standards are literally medieval.

In the restaurant world, the basic case for staging is that it's like going to school for free. That's a reasonable enough proposition that I won't argue against it. Every truly great chef I've known is also a great teacher. I went to cooking school and spent most of my twenties in restaurants. As I made the transition from cooking to writing, I did a couple stages. One was in a Japanese restaurant, the other French. Though brief, they were rewarding experiences that expanded my understanding of those cuisines and built lasting relationships. If I could afford to work for free, I wouldn't mind staging at this very moment.

But this system perpetuates a culinary class divide between those who can afford to stage and those who cannot. These positions, while educational, also help carve out a pathway to success. So while I encourage those who can afford it to go stage, who can afford it? For young people already living in expensive cities, earning minimum wage or less, how are they expected to save for six months in Spain? While many do somehow manage to put money aside for these trips, it's one more hurdle for low-income people, which means one more leg up for children of privilege. That advantage doesn't just mean some cooks are able to get much better training than others. It contributes to a dominance of white cooks in leadership roles, who disproportionately benefit from the experience.

In England, always looking for a way to not quite be part of Europe, chef/restaurateurs have found other ways to get out of paying their cooks. In 2016 chef Michel Roux Jr. was busted for paying cooks less than minimum wage at his London restaurant, Le Gavroche. Though a spokesperson, who admitted to the subminimum wages, told the *Guardian* that a 13 percent service fee was split between employees, Roux later confessed that the business kept the money and counted it as revenue.[4] Le Gavroche is not a struggling local trying to feed the neighborhood. It's a Michelin-starred restaurant that serves champagne butter sauce over lobster mousse with caviar. It didn't lose any stars over this.

In 2018, reporting by the *Sydney Morning Herald* revealed that cooks at one of the restaurants fronted by Heston Blumenthal (The Fat Duck, Dinner by Heston Blumenthal) regularly worked twenty-five hours of unpaid overtime a week, while ownership of the companies was set up through the tax-haven island of Nevis (see Steven Soderbergh's *The Laundromat* if you'd like to quickly learn more about the Caribbean tax haven while enjoying a Meryl Streep victory lap). A spokesperson for the company denied knowledge of staff underpayment, stating, "The group operates internationally within an existing trading structure, in a way that allows the business to work efficiently in its chosen markets," but did not directly answer the *Sydney Morning Herald*'s questions about the use of tax havens.[5]

All of this seeming worker exploitation happens for two reasons: weak labor-law enforcement and a kitchen culture best summarized by the phrase "Yes, chef!" Imagine if everyone in your office, every time the regional manager sent a memo, had to chant "Yes, boss!" That would be insane, right?

But I've been in the shoes of these cooks. Just like Tina, I know the mania of exhaustion in pursuit of excellence, your best never being good enough and constant wondering why you're putting yourself through it, the identity crisis of preparing food for the wealthiest people while you can barely afford the Grand Slam breakfast at Denny's.

It helps to start as an empty vessel, to arrive in these kitchens without allegiance to any other ideologies. When I started writing about food, most of my view of the world came from years of cooking in professional kitchens. So my values were accrued from the people around me in the back of the house, a work environment that fosters belief in meritocracy, as if privilege, gender, and racial bias don't exist. Maybe it's the military hierarchal structure (the kitchen brigade's org chart is borrowed from the army, another workplace where it's normal to affirm your boss's rank in response to every command) that causes most cooks I've known to espouse the belief that greatness and success, both personal and artistic, are attainable through hard work. In other words, the American dream. Yes, hard work is essential for success. Let's be real, though. It isn't enough without talent and luck, which includes privileges of birth, health, and the absence of bad luck.

WHY ARE YOU HITTING YOURSELF?

I'm also one of those people who would say that I am who I am today, as a husband and a father, thanks to this kind of cooking training. It drilled into me the expectation of doing my best at every opportunity, of seeing joy in repetition, rather than drudgery. It's why making my wife her morning coffee is one of my favorite parts of the day. It's why I put the same energy into every reading of *The Paperbag Princess* or *Goodnight Moon*, as if my little girl were a paying Broadway audience who would rightfully feel disappointed if I phoned it in.

My kitchen mentors taught me to love food, that there was nirvana found in the ideal ratio of moisture and chew within a grain of arborio rice infused with porcini and chicken stock. They taught me to care about the quality of every ingredient. They trained me to inspect every delivery that came through the alley door. If a case of white asparagus arrived looking blotchy, or dried, I'd send it back. If our ingredients were imperfect, we could not achieve perfection with them. A bruised basil leaf was not fit to be served to customers. Discipline continued in the care of these ingredients, storing them properly, rotating the old stock to the front of the shelves in the walk-in fridge we cleaned every day. At night, after service, I would dampen a paper towel and lay it over a metal tray of micro greens with the protectiveness I now reserve for placing my sleepy baby in her crib.

We'd watch the servers return from the dining room with plates, aghast if more than a crumb was still present. Did the customer not like it? Was it not what they were expecting? Our personal investment in the food we cooked muted awareness that other people have identities, tastes, lives, and circumstances that have nothing to do with, and are in no way a judgment on, our cooking. It wouldn't occur to us that maybe the diners had spoiled their appetite with an afternoon snack or that a romantic meal had soured into an argument. It was all about the food.

Other than the few people who periodically updated each other about sports, we spoke only about food—what was good, what was bad, and how we could make ours better. At the high, competitive edge of medicine, technology, filmmaking, or stock trading, you'll find people singularly obsessed with their craft, often working in similarly high-stress, cultlike situations, which creates opportunities for exploitation.

For many years, I'd noticed that young cooks, who have only ever studied or worked with food, don't question this system. It's the people who have experience in other industries, or have spent some time in postsecondary education, who are the ones to occasionally give voice to the unfairness of their unpaid work. For the most part, for a very long time—and even more so over the past fifteen years—there were simply far more novices eager to get into the kitchen than chefs had room for. Anyone who complained too loudly could always be replaced.

The rise of food television programming, in particular, helped inspire a generation of young people to pursue a career in cooking. This swelled the enrollment of cooking schools—and, because of that, as the economy recovered after the 2008 crash, postrecession dining quickly grew from small nose-to-tail hangouts serving good food with a minimum of fuss to luxury palaces serving prime cuts with eighteen other elements on a plate. Restaurants began making their own bread, curing their own meats, brining their own pickles—all products they used to buy. You just can't create that kind of food while compensating people fairly for all their work. Not without charging $500 a plate.

Then, a few years ago, I began to notice something new. Chefs started complaining of a labor shortage.

One day I was in a fancy kitchen. The chef/owner, who was having trouble finding cadets, inquired if I knew anyone. I asked what he paid. He happily quoted me a day rate that, divided by twelve (everyone there worked noon to midnight, eating the staff meal on their feet as they continued prepping for service), was less than minimum wage. Soon I was hearing the same complaint from chefs all over. None was willing to connect the low wages and hard work with the lack of willing candidates. The system had worked for so long. Why would it change?

Just as with the Great Recession itself, this boom-time restaurant bubble burst, a victim of empty sales pitches and inflated expectations. This generation didn't want to be cooks. They wanted to be chefs. Which is like enlisting in the army and expecting to be a general by the end of basic training. One cooking school told me their enrollment had doubled in the past decade. At another, an administrator said that only a third of their graduates even stay in the business.

"A lot of kids that I see that have come from school don't know their ass from their elbow," Ang McCluskey told me, while filling popsicle trays to make pineapple and guajillo paletas in the back of a taqueria.

McCluskey is a three-decade veteran of the industry. Instead of working full-time, at a single restaurant, she'll rotate between two or three, usually leading a day shift on prep in order to train and mentor the new hires. "Cooking school is a business. When they come to me, or come to any restaurant, they're on their way to being a 'chef.' And you're not a chef for many years. A lot of people are never a chef." The problem, says McCluskey, is that many of them call themselves chef. "They're twenty. And it's very difficult to somebody who has paid their money [for schooling]. They want validation for that. I feel strongly, me as an individual but also the responsibility of the industry, to teach somebody how to be a good cook and how to be a good chef and a good manager. But not every kid wants to be taught. Because they feel that they've already learned."

Was it a coincidence that I was seeing more and more young people aware of, and standing up for, their rights, at the same time that chefs were complaining they couldn't find cooks?

The drudgery and low pay created an attrition problem with the wave of cooks lured by the unintentional recruitment ads of food television. They were coming in high numbers, but leaving in higher numbers. By 2015, it had become nearly impossible to staff kitchens in all but the most celebrated restaurants, where international fame was still a siren call to young acolytes. "Even though people are constantly leaving, they're never gonna stop getting people that want to work there," Tina says of her experience at the Restaurant. "Because of its prestige and its name. So they're never going to stop getting new people."

Below this top tier, chefs were having problems. If they scheduled twenty interviews for a position, only a handful of applicants actually showed up. Once hired, half of their new recruits quit after one or two shifts, often just ghosting rather than informing their employer that they were leaving. These chefs never struck any deal with television to act as an enlistment tool for cooking schools. They just benefited from it, for a good long while, in the form of bodies needed to feed the machine of their restaurants. Which is different from diners benefiting from it in the form of getting a well-prepared meal at a genuinely fair price.

"It's getting too complicated," Fred Morin, co-owner of Montreal's Joe Beef, told me prepandemic. "Part of it is the chef's ego. How many people work for nothing just so a guy can see himself in the pages of the *New York Times*? There's a lot of vanity in that."

Morin takes aim at ambitious chefs, and the demands that their long, complicated menus put on cooks, as partially responsible for creating their own labor problems. "The future is cooks making more, customers paying more," says Morin, "and the food itself, the menus in the restaurant, the whole industry, and the media around it promoting a more simple type of restaurant experience."

Some chefs justify producing everything from scratch on the basis that they really do make things better than anyone else. In truth, how many can be the best, rewarded with placement on top-ten lists? Why should everyone else in the midrange of the dining sector have to live up to that standard?

This demand for perfection, for everything to be made by hand, coupled with the public's expectation for artisanal everything, has kept the restaurant industry from making progress with its labor problems. "That simple menu, you're going to save money on time and losses from ingredients," says Morin. "That money is right there to be used to pay people."

A common managerial strategy in kitchens is to always give a cook a longer prep list than they can achieve during their shift. The pressure will keep them striving to get faster and better, and the social order of the kitchen will make them feel weak if they can't or won't achieve the expected output.

Even those cooks who survive the gauntlet of burns, cuts, and exhaustion, who become ultraefficient machines, in the end still come up against the obstacles of how they're paid, how they're treated, and how much they work. In their early twenties, most aren't thinking of health care, starting a family, or even comfortable living spaces. Leaving, to do anything else, is often talked about as treasonous. Quitting an ambitious kitchen is a mark of shame. Then, as they near thirty, settling into long-term relationships with partners who may be considering parenthood, beginning to feel more than occasional pain in their lower back, with little or no savings, talk of getting out seems less and less like sedition and more a matter of survival.

I know a chef who owns multiple restaurants. He's popular enough to have young cooks lined up to work for him, even for free. One day he called me. He could sense the change brewing in restaurants and wanted to be ahead of it. He wanted to let me know that cooks in his kitchen would no longer work for free, that he was in the process of revising his company, to make sure things like national holidays and vacation pay were accounted for. He was looking to learn what more he could do to be at the vanguard of the cultural shift he saw happening.

I made a suggestion that would cost him nothing. What if you didn't badmouth people for leaving? The industry at large fostered the attitude that working in fancy, ambitious restaurants should be the only aspiration for young cooks, which in turn contributed to the abusive and exploitative environment of these kitchens. When cooks take a lateral move in their careers, I suggested, how about congratulating them and citing it as an example of all the opportunities that their hard work and experience on the line might open up, rather than trash-talking them as traitors?

The chef listened patiently before asking, in all sincerity, "Why would I congratulate quitters?" Not only would he not consider the suggestion, he was insulted by it.

"For a lot of people in the industry, there is this feeling that you can't ever leave," says former chef Alex Dettwyler. "That your skills aren't transferrable and no one's gonna want to hire you. I experienced a lot of that." Dettwyler has just finished the final exams for his first year of law school. A year earlier, he'd been standing over a flattop, searing pork bellies and calling out tickets.

Dettwyler had done everything fast. By his twenty-fifth birthday, he was married, with a BA in anthropology from the University of Pennsylvania, and his first chef de cuisine position, for which he now acknowledges he was too young. Stepping back into a line cook's role (and eventually CDC) at Pittsburgh's Cure, where the hours were more reasonable, he realized that after years of twelve-hour shifts, six days a week, he was missing out on his life. "Cure was as good as a restaurant could possibly get for me." Under chef Danielle Felix, cooks worked ten-hour shifts, four days a week. "The food was amazing. The team was amazing. And then I got promoted and realized that this is as good as it gets, and it's still not making me as happy as I think a job should. If this isn't doing it for me, the French Laundry is never going to do it for me. Alinea is never going to do it for me. Nothing's going to do it for me. And maybe this is the wrong thing for me to be doing with my life. One day I walked out the side door and called my wife and said, 'I don't think I want to be a cook anymore.'"

Not everyone who aspires to chefdom wants to be the boss. Dettwyler, like many others, just wanted to cook. He loved running a kitchen, putting food on plates, leading a team, teaching people, and giving guests a wonderful experience. There's no future in that without continuing to work for a beginner's wage. "I didn't see any way forward for me," recalls Dettwyler. "This is fun now, but where does it end? Where do the sixty-hour weeks stop? Where does making $32,000 a year stop? When am I ever going to be able to have a family?" His problem with cooking wasn't the work or the money. It was knowing that there'd never be less work or more money. "It was never going to get fixed. There's no way that the economics of it were going to work themselves out in time to save my career."

While Cure was a rare healthy work environment, in other parts of his career Dettwyler was both witness to and complicit in the industry's various forms of wage theft. "There were places I worked where it was normal to come into work two and a half hours early and not clock in until your scheduled start time. And if you were running up against overtime in the middle of a Saturday-night service, the chef would tell you to walk off the line, clock out, and walk right back onto the line and keep working the next four or five hours of your shift until two in the morning."

Worse, he found himself doing the same things when he was running the show. "As a chef, you need that. It wasn't clear how the restaurant is supposed to function without the amount of labor you needed. At the same time, you could not afford to pay everybody the amount that would be required if you did pay everyone the overtime they would be getting every paycheck. At least not without raising the cost of the food 20 or 40 percent. So a young line cook is the weakest link in the chain and the easiest person to exploit. You tell them this is what it takes if you want to become the best. In fine dining, it was framed as a self-sacrifice that was necessary to learn the skills you needed to learn and get the opportunities you wanted to have."

I've been there too, drawn in by the perspective that serving someone else, the chef, was a pursuit of my own physical and mental enlightenment, which would result in a professional elevation. At best, that's true for maybe a tenth of the kitchen. The rest are cannon fodder. And as soon as you prove yourself and get promoted, you're switched from hourly pay to salary. And now it's your responsibility to get staff to work longer, harder, and faster or put in more hours yourself to make up for their shortcomings, all of which grinds you down further. "It doesn't really pay off," says Dettwyler. "Because you never really end up working much less or making any more money. And a lot of people are doing those things with no chance of ever getting any return on it. There were many cooks I worked with who worked just as hard and did just as much 'self-sacrifice' and never got those rewards."

Part of what helps people buy into this system is the pervasive attitude in chef-driven kitchens that there is honor in suffering. The symptom of toxic masculinity is a character-defining element of the laconic hero myth—Yojimbo, Wolverine, the Road Warrior, and the like—the male fantasy that enduring pain is a virtue unto itself. Dettwyler calls the kitchen version a "fetishization of not getting paid enough and working too hard." The chef-driven kitchen, with its time- and labor-intensive cuisine, food that needs humans to apply garnishes with a surgeon's tools, demands this level of endurance. The self-mythologizing is just a way to justify or romanticize these outdated attitudes in a contemporary workspace. "We do it to ourselves. I did it to myself for years. And I did it to other people as a chef. I expected people to work for free. I did my share of screaming at people and throwing plates and being a total asshole."

In the end, Dettwyler couldn't see a way to make the scenario work for himself. I also spent the last couple years of my cooking career certain that I was in the wrong field. But as a high school dropout, I couldn't see any other opportunities for myself. When Dettwyler reached that stage, his wife was working full-time in her field as a genetic counselor, with health insurance that covered both of them. Plus he had a degree. "Because I finished college, I could fuck off anytime I wanted and go to law school. I feel bad about all the people I left behind." The former chef knows that being able to build on his undergraduate degree was a privilege his coworkers didn't share. That's part of a contradiction at the heart of these restaurants. Is advancement (or the ability to move on to a more lucrative profession) primed for people from well-off families, young cooks who can afford to stage and work for free? Are they opportunity centers for underprivileged people who have fewer career options? The truth is that they are both, somehow both classes of worker overlapping, with leadership needing to maintain the illusion of a meritocracy where everyone has the same chances.

"People in the industry like to talk about how the restaurant kitchen is like the last great meritocracy that's left," says Dettwyler. "And it's a complete crock of shit. The only people that can really afford to do these things, to live in San Francisco, are people that have some other source of support. They have a spouse, or family money. The number of people that I've known that worked in fine dining in expensive places, there's always something like that going on. There are people out there doing it 100 percent themselves and living in a shoe box in Queens. But calling it a meritocracy is really disingenuous."

For a few years, Umi Kong was one of those people earning minimum wage while pursuing her pastry career in a high-end Manhattan bakery. "There is no way that I would be able to afford where I was living on that salary." Her partner at the time was a software developer. She paid a quarter of the rent, and he paid the rest.

Everyone in Kong's kitchen had a different story for how they afforded New York. One coworker lived in the subway for a week. Another had a partner who earned tips. One came in from an hour away for her 2:00 a.m. shifts. There was an undocumented guy who worked another job before starting his eight- or ten-hour days at the bakery. There was a single mother who lived in Queens or the Bronx, plus younger people who were more content to share a very small apartment. No one below the chef could afford anything resembling comfort.

Growing up in Australia (where cooks are paid better and food prices are higher), Kong followed her parents' wishes and studied economics. Not wanting to make corporate taxes her life, she switched over to law. Moving to the States with a boyfriend, she applied for two jobs. One was in pastry. The other was at an international organization. She got the pastry job. After working in New York, she settled in Canada, where she teaches pastry at George Brown College, a cooking school in Toronto.

Maybe because of Kong's background in economics, what I call exploitation of kitchen labor, she delineates as the basic realities of market forces. "Fridges, ovens, machinery are very expensive," says Kong. "So when you do have an efficient person who's willing to work for twelve hours, the market doesn't allow for that anomaly." A $60,000 oven doesn't have much wiggle room on price. Humans, on the other hand, are more likely to undervalue their cost. The supply and demand of restaurant cooks, suggests Kong, dictates that the more people you have willing to work at minimum wage or less, the less incentive there is to change the system.

Other than the occasional journalistic exposé or class-action lawsuit, this structure continued unabated, with no rift in the status quo, until the pandemic shuttered everything in March 2020. When the meteor of COVID-19 hit our dining industry, predictions for permanent closures quickly rose from 10 percent to 25 percent within a couple weeks. By mid-April analysts were saying 50 percent at least. The Independent Restaurant Coalition, which defined 70 percent of America's restaurants as independent, estimated that 85 percent of those would go out of business.[6] This was based on a survey conducted at the earliest, most uncertain point in the pandemic. A year later, while the numbers may be a bit out of date, the projection is still grim.

As of 2019, there were 657,000 food and drinking establishments in the United States, employing twelve million people. There is no contingency plan for that many people out of work or that many businesses shuttered. Not to mention the cascading impact of those closures: dropping values of both commercial and residential real estate (how much is that house worth now that it's no longer near so many great places to eat and drink?), which precipitates a decline in the property-tax base and the municipal services those taxes fund, and so on. Canada may have reacted quicker to close down nonessential services and offer better supports for workers, employers, and landlords. Neither country had an industry-specific plan. That's partly because the economists who advise governments are sweet on energy extraction and trade, leaving a huge blind spot for the hospitality industry.

This is a tragedy. What would be an even bigger tragedy is if we rebuilt our dining culture as it existed before, baking in the same inequities.

There are, I'm happy to discover, restaurateurs out there practicing other structural styles, making good food, and treating staff well, using methods other than the rigid hierarchy. But how can we imagine the type of chef-driven restaurant worth supporting without talking about the elephant taking up 20 percent of the room?

YES, WE HAVE TO TALK ABOUT TIPPING

High on the list of factors contributing to the inequities of life in chef-driven restaurants, on top of wage theft and unreasonable hours and a workplace culture that's not too far from *Fight Club*, is tipping. The general public seems to have no idea how tipping works. People don't necessarily know who gets the money they leave at the table and certainly do not understand the byzantine system of gratuities, which allows employers to pay tipped workers less than minimum wage and hurts cooks as much or more than waitstaff.

But it's not the norm everywhere. If you're from a country that does not tip in restaurants—Japan, China, South Korea, Georgia, Iceland, Peru, Spain, Thailand, Australia, Finland, Norway, Denmark, Belgium, the Netherlands, Switzerland, Croatia, Iran, or Brazil—let me try to explain tipping.

Most jobs involve an employee performing a function for their employer, who provides compensation for this labor. In certain jobs, like restaurant server, employers do not have to pay a full wage, because that's the customer's job.

Hang on, that can't be right. Customers are not supposed to manage payroll at the places they patronize. Let's try this again.

There are certain kinds of work, like restaurant server, where customers have the right to decide the value of a worker's earning.

Is that better? It doesn't seem better. Let's take another crack at this.

If restaurants had to pay their staff in full wages instead of relying on tips, they'd have to charge customers what it actually costs to prepare and serve their meal. Customers would revolt. So prices are kept down through the unwritten expectation that customers will pay the remainder voluntarily.

But wait a minute—how does the restaurant save money if the customer is paying the same amount either way? This formulation seems suspicious.

Let's give it one more shot. I know that I can find an explanation of tipping that makes sense of it. How about this?

In the nineteenth century, the custom of tipping migrated from Europe to the United States. It did not gain popularity until after the Civil War. Formerly enslaved people had few employment opportunities. Restaurant (and railroad porter) work came with the caveat that many employers would not pay workers, who were instead compensated through voluntary monetary gifts from customers, which was expressed as an act of generosity rather than an obligation from employers. Over time this evolved into the codified expectation of tipping 15 to 20 percent, with laws (the 1938 Fair Labor Standards Act [FLSA] and the tip credit, introduced in a 1996 amendment) enacted to suppress wages in order to perpetuate this legacy of slavery.[7]

This last one is the most accurate of the bunch. So that's something.

It's a far cry from the often believed and repeated idea that tipping is how we ensure good service when we eat out. If that's true, how much do you tip your dentist? Or do you expect professionalism from them and pay what they ask for their work?

One night, when I was nearing the end of a cooking shift, I watched a server in the kitchen, counting cash. One of his peers admonished him, "We *never* count money in the kitchen." I asked him why, and he explained that it was etiquette among professional servers of their caliber, given the pay disparity between the front and the back of the house, to avoid rubbing it in by displaying their earnings in front of us.

In nice restaurants, servers make double what cooks make. All the talk about teamwork and how we're all in this together is nonsense if one half of the team walks away with double the loot. And, if we can forget the money for a moment, what does it say about the unity of the team when it's believed that one group of employees will not perform their duties well without the system of bonuses, while the other will come in early to earn less than minimum wage?

Talk to ten restaurant workers, and you'll hear ten different explanations for how tips are divided. There are nearly infinite permutations for who (servers, bussers, hosts, bartenders, cooks, dishwashers) gets a cut and how much. Sometimes tips are pooled. Sometimes shares are based on a percentage of gross sales. There are no rules (other than a 2018 amendment to the FLSA prohibiting employers, managers, and supervisors from taking a portion of tips), in law or common practice, for a standardized way of dividing tips. As we see from cases where employees have sued high-profile restaurants such as Per Se (settled for $500,000) and Babbo (settled for $5.5 million), laws are frequently circumvented.[8]

So when you leave money on the table, unless you have a relationship with that particular restaurant and know how it's run, there's no infallible way to know who gets a share of it. "For the most part, customers in America have very little understanding of anything with regards to tips," observes Saru Jayaraman, cofounder of Restaurant Opportunities Centers United, a hospitality labor organization. "Some people think it's for exclusively their server. Some people think it's shared with everybody. Almost no one knows, unless they've worked in the industry, that it is a replacement for the wage, not on top of the wage in America."

But the issue with tipping is not just transparency or pay disparity. The system also increases the impact of customer biases, based on things like race, gender, and age, as well as the harassment and abuse of service staff. The ability of managers to schedule the most lucrative shifts, and the power of customers to withhold or reward with tips, exacerbates much of the horrific sexual misconduct that has always been part of the industry but has only recently become so public, via the now familiar downfalls of characters such as John Besh, Mario Batali, Mike Isabella, and others (Besh has denied allegations of sexual misconduct, as has Batali, who has also pleaded not guilty to criminal charges of indecent assault and battery, while Isabella settled for an undisclosed sum).[9]

While Katherine Stokes has worked all over, the most consistent sexual harassment of her career was in Louisiana, a state known for its hospitality. At one job, a manager got drunk and sent dick pics to staff. A different manager threatened to take off Stokes's pants. After she reported him, her shifts were cut down. One night, four men came into the New Orleans restaurant where she worked and requested her. "It was a bunch of doctors," remembers Stokes. "And they asked how high would the tip percentage be for me to sit down and talk about masturbation with them. What am I supposed to do? Complain and then have my hours cut because I don't want to deal with a bunch of horny old men?"

At the time, she worked under a manager and chef who would get drunk during shifts. She caught the manager in the stairwell making out with a guest. Soon after he tried to fire her via text at two in the morning. Another night, the chef jumped in her Uber, grabbed her phone, and changed the location to meet his coke dealer.

In short, she is one of millions of servers who is at the mercy of abusive bosses and customers, because customers control tips and managers control who gets the shifts with the best tips. "I don't feel like it should be my customer's responsibility to reward or punish me without a tip. It's the restaurant's job to make sure that I'm being paid a fair wage. But I think people want to have that control."

For all the problems with tipping, getting rid of it is famously difficult. There's a public discussion about it that rears its head every few years. But like any good monster—Dracula, Freddy, Jason, Candyman, Tom Hanks in *You've Got Mail*—it seems like tipping cannot be killed.

In 2015 the Union Square Hospitality Group (USHG) announced that it was eliminating tipping in all its restaurants. As an industry leader with eighteen hundred employees, this was a big deal. The announcement generated a lot of attention and reignited the public's perennial conversation on the matter. A wave of restaurateurs followed the USHG's example. Behind the scenes, many owners told me they'd like to do it. They were reluctant, fearing customer sticker shock over the necessary higher prices and losing their best servers to restaurants where more money could be made in tips. Which is exactly what happened. By 2018 tipping was back at New York's Roman's, Diner, Fedora, Agern, and Momofuku Nishi.[10]

"For a couple of years, every journalist I talked to was certain that this was a movement," says Thad Vogler, who tried getting rid of tipping at his San Francisco restaurants, Trou Normand and Bar Agricole. "And it didn't happen." Earlier in 2015, with minimum wage in San Francisco set to hit sixteen dollars, tired of the quasi-legal nature of the business, Vogler went tip free. "You just want to be a grown-up with a real business, charge what it costs, pay your people, figure out a bottom line, and move on," says Vogler. "It requires so much work to keep it this gray-market cash thing. Or a nonrevenue thing. Having lived and worked in Japan and the UK, it always felt kind of civilized to just have a bill and pay it."

After nine months of trying to dispense with them, despite his feelings, Vogler reverted back to accepting tips in his restaurants. Not because of his diners, who he felt were generally ready for the change. "Why we ultimately stopped is there's a population of workers who prefer it a certain way. And they see themselves losing agency over their income. That was the main reason. We couldn't keep a certain quality of staff. It's been popular or easy to be resentful of the server mentality. But you need them."

As there are all types of restaurants, there are all types of restaurant servers. Across America, where the federal subminimum wage for tipped workers is $2.13 (unchanged since 1991), workers subject to this system are twice as likely to live in poverty than the national average.[11] But in a big city, at a hot chef-driven restaurant, some servers do very well. "There is a type of server that makes a ton of money. And is empowered and in great demand. And goes where the money's best," says Vogler. "They want to make around $100,000 working four days a week. That's a real category of professional person. And there's a certain personal freedom that attends that. They might not be as ideologically driven as an owner. But they're going to do their job—learn the food, the beverage, the culture—and manifest it as well as they can. That doesn't mean they're a Japanese assistant-assistant-assistant sushi chef working for ten bucks an hour and treating this as if it's his life's work. But it does mean that they're good and they get the job done. And that's generally the type of server I've been competing to keep."

Vogler estimates that while a hundred grand is at the high end, it's not uncommon in places like New York, LA, and San Francisco. "Being a server is a hard job. It takes its toll on people psychologically. The ones that are able to do it, it's a real quality-of-life thing. They serve. They're in school. They have kids. None of them ever want to be managers. Ever. They never want to move vertically. It's maddening."

One of Vogler's best servers is forty, has two young children, has been with the company ten years, and won't work more than three days a week. "He just will not take any more responsibility. Not that he's lazy or irresponsible. He's tremendous at what he does. He makes probably about sixty grand a year, working three days. He and his wife are frugal. They have amazing relationships with their kids. They volunteer at their preschools."

The problem is that when the front of the house gets such a large slice of the pie, enough that some people can afford to work three days a week, the back of the house has to settle for smaller slices. Vogler has long offered any kitchen employee to train for a front-of-house position, so they can make more money. He'd be out of kitchen staff if they all took him up on the option. Only a handful ever have. "You can't underestimate the value of pride. A cook has to keep his or her pride and dignity on some level. And a server has to spend that."

Amanda Cohen, having swallowed her pride to toss out her tasting menu and make salads for takeout, still believes that great service and fair compensation are not mutually exclusive. In 2015 Cohen was moving her restaurant, Dirt Candy, to a new location and leveraged the shake-up to eliminate tipping.

The fresh start in a new space was key to minimizing the blowback from customers (Cohen's thick skin helped, too), which has almost entirely subsided in the years since. Cohen believes that a silver lining to the current catastrophic disruption of service is that it's the perfect chapter break to restart this conversation. "Everybody is starting to rethink how to run their business. A come-to-Jesus moment. The way we run our restaurants has left everybody vulnerable. Because we don't charge enough for food and we don't pay our employees enough. And I hear people saying they don't want to participate in this system anymore. We have to provide better for our workplace. And customers will have to pay the cost."

During the liminal period between pandemic outbreak and vaccine immunization, with stop and start closures, without seating capacity, plus the expected recession to follow, says Cohen, servers don't have the same opportunities to earn the majority of their income from tips. "I think restaurateurs are wary of bringing back tipped employees. You're not going to make $500 a night in tips. And definitely not in cash. The only way to properly compensate employees is to have them not work on the tip system."

Amanda Peticca-Harris, a former restaurant manager and now associate professor of people, organizations, and society at the Grenoble School of Management in France, is circumspect about this possibility. The business professor in Peticca-Harris says, yes, there's an opportunity for a no-tipping movement. Her firsthand knowledge of the industry does not make her think that owners will shift in this direction. "COVID-19 isn't going to be the time that they go, 'I've just had this epiphany. Let me innovate with no tipping.' They're going to draw those purse strings even closer. Because they're going to be scared."

Peticca-Harris predicts that the period of economic uncertainty—mass closures, workers worried about having jobs, employers worried about losing their businesses—is more likely to prompt a cycle of exploitation. "That's a bad climate for employees and employee rights. 'I'm grateful to have this job' as a mantra can be a bit of a dangerous terrain. If you shake people to their core, how motivated are they to voice their rights?"

That's something we saw quickly—furloughed workers with employment benefits running out, financially pushed back into restaurant work before it's safe, and too insecure in their job prospects to object to conditions. Or worse, states where employers were required to report employees who declined to return. During a year of closings, reopenings, and reclosings, restaurant workers were cornered—pressured to do their jobs while navigating hazardous situations with customers, with every life-threatening interaction tied to their compensation through tips.

Yes, this could be the time to get rid of tipping. Though it's seemed so before. One of the crazy things about our tipping culture is that the movement to get rid of the system is cyclical, instigated every few years when a prominent restaurant announces that they're doing it. Will it ever change?

When he's not flintknapping (making knives and tools out of stone), Cornell University professor Michael Lynn has spent the past three decades researching tipping. He didn't intend to.

To pay his way while at the University of Texas in Austin, Lynn waited tables. "I loved it," remembers Lynn. "It paid more than any job that I was qualified for." Lynn didn't know what the cooks made, but he could sense the clear tension between them and the servers. It struck him as odd that he earned more than his manager.

When he began grad school in Ohio, there was a gap when he wouldn't get paid as a research assistant for seven weeks. Lynn asked his adviser if he could work as a bartender and was told sure, so long as he turned it into a research opportunity. That necessity, to turn a paycheck into an academic exercise, set Lynn on the path of his life's work.

Starting as an economics major, he got better grades in psychology. As tipping is at the confluence of these two disciplines, the subject was a natural for his master's thesis.

Those bits of trivia you may have heard about tipping, how tips can be increased when servers introduce themselves or touch the customer on the shoulder or elbow? Those are from Lynn's more than seventy papers on the subject. Over the past thirty years, Lynn has published on aspects such as motivations for tipping (desires to help servers, reward service, buy future service, buy social status or esteem, avoid social sanctions, and fulfill internalized social obligations), racial and ethnic differences in tipping (in US restaurants, racial and ethnic minorities often tip less, and these differences create numerous problems ranging from discriminatory service to restaurant executives' reluctance to open new restaurants in minority communities), Black-white wage gap among restaurant servers (both white and Black restaurant customers discriminate against Black servers by tipping them less than their white coworkers), and, obviously, the efficacy of eliminating tipping.[12]

But over time, he hasn't seen the dialogue around this change. "Danny Meyer and others get a lot of press attention," says Lynn. Meyer is the CEO of the Union Square Hospitality Group, which in addition to high-end eateries also created Shake Shack. In 2015, shortly after taking Shake Shack public, armed with the money generated by the burger chain's IPO, the entire USHG shifted to eliminate tipping. As an industry leader, the USHG's move reignited the "Will they? Won't they?" conversation over tipping. "But back in the late '70s, early '80s, there was a similar movement. And it tended to die out. And this one's gonna die out."

Prior to the 1970s, if the Internal Revenue Service (IRS) wanted to audit a server, they had to be able to identify who was underreporting. Then it became legal to conduct class audits. Because the restaurants were responsible for paying FICA taxes, they were liable for underreported tips. That made it easier for the IRS to do these audits. The threat of audit reduced the benefits for tipping. So a couple restaurateurs eliminated it and got some recognition. The momentum didn't last. "There are cycles to it. Some try it. But it never ends up going anywhere."

Lynn says he is neither for nor against tipping. He simply believes in following the data, examining who benefits and who doesn't. The winners, he says, are servers. "I do believe tipping overpays servers," says Lynn, excluding situations where servers don't make a lot in tips. There's a clear division between servers in an upscale Manhattan restaurant and their counterparts in states with a lower tipped minimum wage, who have higher poverty rates.[13] "I don't see any justification for making two times what cooks make."

Which is what Lynn found in a survey he conducted for the New York Hospitality Alliance. The government, he says, does not benefit. Subminimum wages appear to benefit diners, through lower menu prices. But then those diners subsidize the lower wages and prices through tips, which mostly don't get taxed. "So the government is a clear loser."

On an emotional level, customers are beneficiaries because they get the freedom of choice. "They get some psychic enjoyment. They can show off. Overall customers are happier."

Consumer psychology, Lynn believes, is at the root of this problem. Tipping constrains a restaurant's ability to control menu prices. If tips could be redistributed in the form of higher menu prices, that would be a better system in Lynn's view. A huge obstruction, as any tipping-abolitionist restaurateur I've spoken with tells me, is that customers perceive the menu as more expensive, a view borne out by Lynn's research.

I have a hard time accepting that. So I ask Lynn. I barely squeaked by in grade 10 math. If I can grasp that ten dollars plus tip equals twelve dollars without a tip, why are we so unable or unwilling to make that calculation? "We're lazy," says Lynn. "We can do the math. We just don't. People are lazy, and they particularly hate math."

Charlie Redd, the owner of Dragon Pizza in Boston, has a different take. "You can tell your professor at Cornell, until he runs a restaurant for ten years, he has no fucking idea. You can analyze it top and down. But until his life depends on it, he can't really fathom."

The obstacle, says Redd, is not a dislike of math. It is an assumption of expertise. "The general public has opinions on how government is run, with no experience. I think business is the same way. The American personality has strong opinions about things. And everybody goes to restaurants. So there's a strong opinion about what a restaurant is and how it works. There's a sense of ownership."

That mentality, with an assumption and opinion on how restaurants are run, is manifested in the diner who feels it's their right to decide what a server earns.

When Redd graduated culinary school in the 1990s, he cooked in restaurants in North Carolina and Oregon. He had the opportunity to work at more prestigious restaurants in New York, but the workload and compensation (about half of minimum wage) were too far apart for the amount of student debt he was carrying. "The one thing that was frustrating at that time is that all those great restaurants, which had huge staffs, were all functioning in illegal labor practices. And I was unable to balance my budget to work in those places. I wanted to. I wanted that experience, and the cachet, on my résumé. I really just wanted to cook food on that level. But I could not afford to live in the places where they were. So I made some different decisions."

Over the course of his career, Redd has veered away from the finicky chef-driven-restaurant concept, paring away those trappings of presentation, service, and management, to settle on a format more equitable for all involved. After a change in liquor licensing effectively devalued his original location and its license, forcing Redd to close his previous restaurant and relocate to a different Boston neighborhood, he restructured his model for Dragon Pizza, incorporating his previous kitchen staff as partners. Along with the smaller footprint of the new restaurant, Redd shrank the number of employees, eliminating front of house, which enabled him to retain long-term, loyal workers and incentivize them through equity in the business. "We wanted consistency in our work team. We wanted a diversified skill set and a devotion to this business, which the kitchen staff brings but we weren't getting in the front of the house. And we looked to boost their income." Using the simplified model, counter service, cross-training everyone, and sharing tips with the whole team, Dragon Pizza is able to do that.

What intrigues me about Redd's approach is the insistence on ownership as a necessary component of changing the often mercenary dynamic of front-of-house employees. Profits at Dragon are distributed based on percentage of ownership. Tips are split based on hours worked. Not only do staff perform better when they're invested, they also stick around, which solves the cook-shortage side of the equation.

What really helps his model, and others I've seen that have taken a similar route, is going from full service to limited counter service, which cuts out a lot of labor, specifically those who demand the lion's share of money coming in. We were already seeing service going in this direction prepandemic in cities like San Francisco, where savings had to be found in the runaway cost of operating a restaurant. They can call it fast casual if they want, but from Chicago to DC to Denver, chefs have been keeping the value in their food by ditching table service.[14]

But what if a restaurant wants to maintain a style of dining achievable only with full table service? "When you refer to chef restaurants, these are mostly independent restaurants with a specific vision tied to a person," says Joshua Lewin, co-owner of Juliet and Peregrine, in Somerville, Massachusetts, just northwest of Boston. "The trend in these kind of independent restaurants was this worship of the kitchen as being the voice that mattered—a result of the media and the public caring about the stories of these chefs. And TV had a lot to do with that. The chef kind of became the everything."

Lewin doesn't quibble with the various potential problems of restaurant work: fair pay, wages, diversity, safety, and security in the workplace. But for him and partner Katrina Jazayeri, they all fall under the umbrella of a power structure that mostly rewards white males. Meanwhile, another segment of employees, largely Latin Americans, often in support positions—food runners, prep cooks, dishwashers—don't get the same promotions and opportunities for career development.

So as Lewin grew from cook to chef, toward the path of ownership, he and Jazayeri took time to consider how they wanted to approach that phase of their careers. They wanted a reason, beyond their own professional ambitions, for their restaurant to exist.

Career development became their reason. Because the pay is so low in high-end restaurants, people who are empowered to seek information and training beyond their daily responsibilities, in order to rise in their careers, tend to be those with assistance of some kind. The stages and trial shifts, which are hugely educational, are not accessible to people who need to support a family or even just themselves with a steady income.

The partners' mission became creating a safe working environment, one that does not tolerate the types of dangers that are common in the industry, that pays people well for a job well done, and that values people long term with money and access to training. In 2016 Lewin and Jazayeri launched Juliet, and later Peregrine, where tipping is optional, though not expected. Four years in, tips are rarely left.

At the time, the subminimum wage in Massachusetts was $3.15 and the full minimum was $11. Opening without tips meant mitigating financial risk by finding a smaller space and doing most of the work themselves. That limited the size and scope of what they wanted to do. In the end they went with something that was less than a thousand square feet that didn't require more money than they had access to and required less staff to operate.

At the same time, Lewin and Jazayeri took on the majority of labor hours, serving breakfast, lunch, and dinner seven days a week. "I don't think that we would have been successful had we tried to do something larger."

Within the first year, Juliet added to wages by introducing profit sharing for staff and clear internal benchmarks, empowering employees to make more money. With the additional income, staff earned about $14.50. Since then, they've set a company minimum of $15.

The next aspect was career training by way of total transparency, the kind of open-book management that is extremely rare. "In all my years being a manager and chef for other people, if financial information was shared with me about how the business was doing or what the goals of the business were, it was very compartmentalized to my specific department. So I never knew the overall health of a business."

A lot of restaurants organize staff education around wine, because it's essential for sales. At Juliet they scheduled regular meetings to teach basic literacy of finances and other skills that are transferable outside of the restaurant. The goal was twofold: professionally educate staff so they are able to move beyond the limitations of hourly work and invest in people to keep them longer than a one-year tenure.

Juliet turned a profit in its first year and for every year until 2020, with almost zero employee turnover. Their staff has grown to fifty. That was why they opened a second restaurant: because so many people had stayed with them, and they needed new horizons. "We shifted our thinking from 'If people work for us, they should be paid more' into thinking about it as an investment in the future of the business. To train them to be worth that much more. What's made it successful has been a theory about how it would pay for itself."

Because the benefit of a well-paid staff is realized only once they've reached a level of training and experience to help run that business, all that time until they get there is a sunk cost. "Had they all left at six months in, we wouldn't have been able to cash in on that investment. That was the crux of the experiment. We didn't know if it would work."

The structures at Juliet, Dragon Pizza, and Dirt Candy are not the same. For example, Cohen's plans for reopening dine-in service at Dirt Candy include significantly raising prices to finally pay staff what they are worth. As for the tipping battle, she's ready to charge the true cost to the diner and find out if they share the value of respecting workers. Still, these businesses have far more in common with each other than with the legacy hierarchy of the average chef-driven restaurant. And their ideas are possible within other genres.

SERVICE WAS ALWAYS A LUXURY

As a pandemic pivot, all restaurants needed to shift to takeout and delivery (sometimes at a loss, through the app companies). Chef-driven restaurants tried to augment revenue through meal kits, online cooking classes, groceries, and more. Mary Attea, owner of Musket Room in New York, told me that she was considering turning her dining room into a temporary child-care space. As they struggled to survive with limited seating, and the prospect of a likely recession, owners have had to reconsider everything about their businesses.

At the start of the pandemic, many restaurateurs thought that closures would last a few weeks. As the situation worsened, and people came to understand the science of vaccination trials, an expectation grew that this could last a couple years. Before the end of 2020, when the rapid pace of vaccine research produced results, a lot of thought was given to changing what restaurants needed to be if dine-in sales, office business lunches, and tourism traffic were not returning for a long time.

At the very high end, at places like the French Laundry or Noma, the value of exclusivity is so prized that they can incorporate the cost of reduced capacity into an increased price, to a degree. Most chef-driven restaurants in the midrange cannot scale up that high. They could reconfigure as quick-service takeout spots, selling fried chicken, burgers, and grain bowls (as many chefs were already transitioning to pre-2020). They might attempt dynamic pricing, the method used by airlines and hotels, adjusting prices up and down based on periods of peak demand (an even more electrified third rail for restaurants than no tipping). Or they could radically depart from the traditional inequities of how their businesses are run.

What I see as essential to what restaurants like Peregrine and Dragon Pizza have done, beyond reconsidering the diner's experience or how a restaurant works for employees, is diminishing the status of the chef's persona. "If there is a way for the restaurant that's supposed to be about the chef to survive an investment in labor of the type that we made," says Lewin, "it can't be about the chef."

People dine out for a lot of reasons. One is to say you've eaten at chef so-and-so's. Another is to feel like you are a part of something, the unique intoxication of a room full of strangers eating, drinking, laughing, and flirting. Many restaurateurs do what they do for that same reason, the wonderful feeling of a spellbinding room, lit to complement, from every angle, comfortable banquettes packed with happy diners clinking glasses and sharing memories. Too often, though, that magic is achieved by working conditions that make people unwell—constant demand for perfection compounded by late nights and the availability of alcohol.

Drinking on the job is another area where every restaurant is different. In some places, it's strictly forbidden. In others, it's part of the workplace culture. Certainly, it's easier to get away with in the realm of independent chef-driven restaurants than in larger chains with more exposure for liability and more eyes on inventory. In addition to the financial inequality, intoxicants fuel conflict between coworkers.

In no office today would it be acceptable for staff to drink a glass of wine at their desk at noon. But in a restaurant, halfway through your shift, it's already eight o'clock. A sip here and there, sharing a drink with a customer, sneaking booze, and so on. It takes on many forms. Hospitality beats out mining for the highest rate of addiction of any professional field.[15]

There are a lot of clichés about substance abuse in the industry, many fueled by Anthony Bourdain's influential memoir about cooking and addiction, *Kitchen Confidential*. Personally, I never saw anyone doing coke in the walk-in, never worked with anyone who seemed high or drunk. Yet even in the relatively sober kitchens where I've cooked, it was standard to hand out beers at the end of every shift. Not just on Fridays. Every night. "It's supertoxic to reward people with a substance," says Hassel Aviles. "I think that sends a really bad message."

After cofounding the popular taqueria brand La Carnita and the food festival Toronto Underground Market, Aviles has been focusing her energies on creating conversations and solutions for the mental health crisis she sees in her industry in recent years. Through her nonprofit, Not 9 to 5, Aviles has been organizing workshops and spreading support resources for hospitality workers dealing with anxiety, depression, and addiction.

A lot of these problems are fueled by consistent access to intoxicants, the everyday after-work beers and the snowballing they can precede, which prevents staff from confronting the emotional toll of their work while creating conditions for inappropriate sexual behavior. "Normalizing all of that substance and alcohol abuse, and encouraging your staff to partake, leads to sexual harassment. That still happens all the time. Because people are coked up. Postwork, doors closed. And it goes and goes, and terrible things happen."

Adding kindling to the fire is the lack of anything resembling human resources in restaurants, even within larger restaurant groups, with anything less than a thousand employees. "The little places, the small to medium-sized restaurants, get away with murder," says Aviles.

If anything, HR in chef-driven restaurants usually consists of consultants who come in to get the books in order. "We think we're pirates," Aviles says, citing the oft-repeated mentality of restaurant people that the hours spent in literal and figurative shadows, the prevalence of cash and alcohol, and the rejection of workplace rules, hours, and customs by which the square world operates makes them outlaws.

If you've worked in restaurants for three years, Aviles argues, there's a high chance that you have some form of undiagnosed PTSD. "Because the things that happen in our industry that are so normalized and socially accepted, and the way that you're treated, leaves you with some level of trauma. And you just don't deal with it. And the whole thing that keeps it going is the silence around it. Instead of causing a problem in the place you work at, you end up going to another place, because you heard it was better there. And then you go to another place because that wasn't the case."

For a long time, living in that cycle of trauma, Patrick Mulvaney didn't know what to do about it. "For anyone in crisis, we had four answers," says the chef and owner of Sacramento restaurant Mulvaney's B&L. "Go home, get back on the line, stop drinking, do a shot. And we knew none of those were good." By the end of 2018, four colleagues had died by suicide, prompting Mulvaney to seek some way of lowering the stigma of discussing mental health, thereby raising the likelihood of people getting help before it's too late.

One of the actions he took was deceptively simple. When staff clocks in at B&L, they select one of four cards for happy, neutral, sad, or angry/in the weeds. There are no words on them. Just colors. During the staff meal, someone pulls the cards out of their box to take the temperature of the restaurant and discuss how they're going to change it. "If there are two people who are blue, or in the weeds, what are we going to do to make sure that we have a successful night? If you are one of the blue people who walk in, what can we do for you? And what are you going to take from tonight, so that next week, when you're not blue, when you're happy or neutral, how are you going to take tonight's experience to help someone else who's having trouble next time? And that's it."

The system is anonymous. There's no requirement to identify the exact problems people are facing that day. What it does is alert every-one that there is pain in the air. Later, when people are picking herbs, making stock, buffing glasses, or any of the repetitive tasks that tend to instigate dialogue, people start talking about what's troubling them. "Just having that check-in opens the conversation," says Mulvaney, "and allows the conversation, without dictating it. So it's not forced. And if you're ready, and you're with someone who can talk, then you talk about it."

Mulvaney thinks staff found the system a little unmacho at first. Despite this, they were respectful, and the mood in the community was dire, with people looking for hope or direction. "Everyone in the Sacramento food world was upset. All of us have seen untold num-bers of people who have quit or fallen out of the industry because of alcoholism or drug use or anxiety. And we didn't know what to do. So there was a willingness for people to engage. But I think the most im-portant piece is that that box gave people permission to talk about it. It reduces the stigma and increases conversation. That vulnerability that you show at the end of the day, it turns out it gives you more strength." As the actions, including a staff member trained in peer counseling, evolved into the system called I Got Your Back, it was supported by customers and adopted by other restaurants in Sacramento, picking up public attention and political support as it grew.

SHIT IS TOO FANCY

Now, a warning. Though hidden from diners, the various mechanisms for cheating workers out of the money they deserve are not the problem. They are just the symptom. The problem is a dining culture that has grown to expect extravagance without paying luxury prices.

Great food and service allow us the opportunity to buy the experience of being a rich person for an hour or two. It's a glorious illusion. Unfortunately, it's primarily available through the exploitation of workers. It's also unsustainable. Even before 2020, we've been watching the midrange of chef-driven restaurants evaporate in the face of economic pressures: the rising rates of rent, fuel, food, labor, and the bite of third-party delivery. I've seen menu prices rising. I've also seen chefs and restaurateurs in this segment going downstream and opening chicken shacks. They can't make money in a forty-seat high-labor restaurant. "The golden era of restaurants in the US is coming to an end," says Vogler, who by the summer of 2020 has closed three of his four businesses. "Which means that places are going to have to be very expensive or very cheap."

Vogler is comforted to learn that he wasn't alone in failing to have six months' operating capital in the bank. He's honest about his mistake of expanding too far, too fast. While there's a tremendous pain in losing what he's built, there's a relief too of getting out from under the pressure of an untenable business model. "I remember thinking every day," says Vogler, "'How am I going to get out of this?'"

It's possible that the pandemic could usher in a new age of the simple neighborhood restaurant, the type of place that is common in France: twenty seats, ten menu items, two servers, and two cooks. In the early 2000s, before the legitimate small-plates trend, American restaurants tried to make tapas happen. Outside of a society where people go out to eat at ten p.m., or the agglomeration of multiple other businesses serving similarly tiny dishes, enabling customers to hop from one bar to another, you can't just transplant a cultural activity like an orchid. In France people take breaks for lunch. It's uncommon for workers to eat at their desks. So in America, where we pride ourselves on productivity, and shame each other for taking a long lunch, there is little chance of replicating France's meal-ticket system, in which government and employers cosubsidize the cost of meals at local restaurants. We don't need the bureaucracy. The romance and intimacy of a nice restaurant are still possible, if we let go of the fanaticism over handmade everything.

We, as diners, don't get to decide how a restaurant pays its staff. Private enterprise can do what it likes. It's up to entrepreneurs to choose how to structure their companies. But we do get to decide where to eat.

Real-world progress starts with changing the way we think. In pursuit of the equitable restaurant industry we want, this begins with us calling baloney on chef culture. One night, I came into the fancy restaurant where I worked to have dinner. It was my birthday. As a gag, the kitchen sent out a course, plated for four of us, with a thinly sliced cross-section of staff-meal burrito, punctuated by three red dots of sauce I knew to be sriracha. The waiter and I giggled to each other. My friends, to whom the dish looked like a complicated terrine and smelled delicious, needed it explained that my boss had sent out joke food. Was it really? We made good burritos in that kitchen. The gap between high-end and low-end deliciousness can sometimes just be presentation.

As readers, we need to reject the chef-interview profile. You know what's in every chef's fridge? Expensive butter, half of a roti, and whatever props they decided to decorate it with the day of the magazine shoot.

Workers need to question their allegiance to the guru/jedi/priest status of the chef. As long as there are long lines of eager applicants, ready to supplicate and be exploited, these restaurants won't change. The occasional mea culpa from celebrity chefs, the essay about how they used to yell at staff and they'll try not to anymore, taken in good faith, is a sign of a willingness to evolve. But it's just lip service until they start paying staff like professionals.

At the very least, as Hannah Selinger argues in her essay about the abuse she says she endured and witnessed under Momofuku founder David Chang, restaurateurs should end the practice of requiring employees to sign nondisclosure agreements and release former employees from said agreements. Unless restaurants are developing an atomic space displacer or unstable molecules, there is no justification for expecting employee NDAs.[16] It's just the desire for control.

As diners, in a postvaccine landscape, don't be afraid to ask how restaurants are run, how staff is paid, how tips are divided, and if the boss ever yells at them and what for. If it's impolite to ask these questions, consider what that implies about the answers. We need to think of it as a conversation, not an interrogation. I don't think that, as customers, we are in any position to audit the restaurant's practices. Inquiring if the kitchen is tipped, if it's a percentage of tips or of gross sales, at a certain point becomes too much thread to pull. What about the bussers? What's the proper percentage for the host? The answers matter less than that we start talking about these things, that restaurants notice our interest, and that the practice of dividing tips moves from under the table to something for which businesses are publicly accountable. Models that challenge the system won't be as rare if we support them with our money and our voices (Lynn's research indicates that gratuity-included higher menu prices result in lower online-review scores).

On the other side of this crisis, the chefs who terrorized their staffs, collecting accolades for their abusive personalities and credit for the group's cooking efforts, should be afraid to go back to their previous behavior. The insistence on running it the old way should be radioactive. The idea that excellence is achieved only through the abuse and exploitation of workers is a corrupt premise. Its time is done.

· 3 ·

The Insta-Bait Meal

My favorite collection of short stories
narrated by highly unreliable narrators.

—JUDGE JOHN HODGMAN, describing Yelp

ONE DAY, SOON AFTER I STARTED REVIEWING RESTAURANTS
at the *Toronto Star,* someone showed me a pillar in the newsroom
decorated with crackpot reader letters. Even by 2008, only the truly
touched were writing physical letters to newspapers. Occasionally,
you'd get a lovely handwritten note, thanking you for a meatloaf recipe that turned out just right. These were more death threats and calls
for writers to be fired. There was one letter that suggested the paper's restaurant critic (the letter was old even then, addressed to one
of my predecessors) had no business reviewing an Indian restaurant,
because she wasn't Indian. It went on to advise the paper to have a
different critic for every type of cuisine. Of course, a newspaper can't
employ 180 different restaurant critics, or even 10. That was silly. The
letter writer's complaint was not.

What business did I have to judge an Indian, Jamaican, or Thai restaurant, to understand how the food being served fitted into a local or global community or history? No, I shouldn't have been relegated to reviewing only bagels and smoked meat. It was my duty, I believed, to conduct as much culinary research as possible and try my hardest to assess a restaurant, always with the goal of comprehending the business's ambitions and weighing that against its achievements. I did my best. The truth is that I was part of a food-media culture that did not represent the diversity of the community we were serving.

White supremacy is now the term being used. Which doesn't necessarily mean white southerners in hoods burning down Black churches, but the oppression and marginalization of racialized people through the persistent whiteness of political, professional, and cultural gatekeepers. In my own work, I've attempted to unlearn previous behavior, putting in the time to balance reporting with a wider variety of voices, women and people of color, rather than the easy route of populating stories with the white male chefs who already have a public profile and frequently seem more accessible for self-promotion.

The deification of chefs that I discussed in the previous chapter has started to diminish lately, which is a positive development. So is the emergence of new media spaces, such as *Whetstone, For the Culture, The Cleaver Quarterly, Mold,* and *Dill,* that are much more diverse, while the mastheads of legacy publications are targeted for their transgressions. Even since I began writing this book, Adam Rapoport (who denied that a photograph of himself was brownface), Alison Roman (who apologized to women of color she had criticized in an interview), and Peter Meehan (who made a public apology that was also a denial), following alleged racist or abusive behavior, have left their prestigious positions at *Bon Appétit,* the *New York Times,* and the *Los Angeles Times.*[1] No, we didn't solve racism. But five years ago, these people would all have kept their jobs. And in the past few years, in the wake of the Me Too and Black Lives Matter movements, food media is trending in a more equitable direction.

A trend, if you'll excuse a bit of semantic pedantry, is a direction in which things are heading. (Beyond pedantry, this will seem to be a very unexpected change of subject. Bear with me for a page or two. I promise not to drop the thread.) A fad is a short-lived, popular fashion. Fads are frequently (if inaccurately) upgraded to trends for the ubiquitous story format, found both casually throughout the seasons ("Why Are Iced Beet Chips So Hot Right Now!?") and in abundance at the year's end, through annual summaries and predictions. There's a journalistic joke/rule of thumb that it takes three of a thing to make it a trend. Three steakhouses are serving tableside Caesar salads? It's a trend. In November and December, a food writer gets inundated with PR pitches for food trends—celery juice, Burmese cuisine, hidden vegetables—that are rarely accurate and always have at least one of their client's products embedded in the list.

Trend lists are just one facet of food media, as it grew from a section of the Wednesday newspaper to a huge subculture with its own cable channel, leaning toward superficiality. Chasing fads is a symptom of a larger issue—prizing food as entertainment rather than news. It can and should be both. It rarely is. In 2020, though, this partially reversed course due to the pandemic putting the precarious realities of the food industry into stark, unavoidable relief. There were no ambitious tasting menus to rank. The only trends were the unpleasant realities of unemployment and bankruptcy.

Because the pandemic closed so many restaurants, the PR wing of the food industry, and its mission creep over food media, lay dormant for most of 2020. As soon as we've got dine-in service and a functioning economy again, media dinners will be back.

Even if you've never been to one of these, you've read about them, without knowing it. Pretty much any time you've heard about a hot new restaurant, there was a media dinner the night before. A couple dozen guests, who used to be primarily editors and writers, though more and more now are composed of social media influencers, spend an evening under a cascade of cocktails, passed hors d'oeuvres, more cocktails, course after course of food, wine pairings, dessert, gift bags, and more. The crowd eats and drinks without ever putting their hand in their pocket, ostensibly getting a taste of what the restaurant serves, without ever having the option of connecting that experience with actual value to a customer or approximating the experience that a non-VIP diner encounters.

If they've done their job right, the restaurant is suddenly inescapable on your social media feed. You feel left out because you haven't been yet. Not one mention is made of the evening's implicit transaction, which is a free meal in exchange for the expectation of coverage. Not the demand, merely a suggestion.

After studying molecular genetics and working in tech, Nik Sharma pursued a career in food writing and soon found he was invited into, but did not want to be part of, this free-lunch crowd. Sharma, the author of *The Flavor Equation*, and a recipe contributor to the *New York Times*, *San Francisco Chronicle*, and *Serious Eats*, among others, does some influencer work for brands that relate to his area of expertise (cookware, vegan cheese). Always as transparent as possible, he declares "paid partnership" with the name of the sponsor at the top of the post. Sharma has even been approached to do influencer work for car companies, which is not related to what he does, as well as restaurants. "Restaurants offer less money. Not all of them will offer money. A lot of them will ask for a trade. You get to eat a free meal at the restaurant, but you have to post about it." If a food writer had no moral qualms about it, they could eat out for free most nights of the week. If they took home a doggie bag, they could feed a small village.

Once you are on the list of food media with their hand out, the invitations never stop. It's been years since I've written the kind of material these publicists seek—promotional opening previews, chef profiles, best-of lists, travel guides, social media testimonial, and the like—and a decade since I've reviewed a restaurant. And here, despite that, is a list of the media dinner invitations I received in January 2020 alone.

January 8: media preview dinner for kaiseki restaurant, where dinner is $195 or $330

January 14: media preview for Dinner with a View, an event where luxury meals are served inside terrariums big enough for six, "perfect for sharing via social"

January 15: Lobster Burger Bar asks me to join them in "curating your own unique butter, de-shelling lobsters and learning about 2020 plating trends"

January 19: the Enlightened Dining Club—a microdose-infused five-course feast somehow in collaboration with a local artist and "digital experience specialists"

January 22: Pecorino Toscano tasting dinner at an Italian restaurant where a bowl of olives costs $9

January 27: Scotch tasting at an art gallery

January 29: dinner and a cooking class with a chef promoting a packaged sauce

January 29: three-course Greek meal of peaches and meat with Greek trade delegation who are in town to promote Freshcano: Fresh Canned Peaches from Europe, a European Union–funded program

January 29: cocktail party at an upscale department store that's just finished renovating

January 29: media dinner at an upscale Italian restaurant focusing on the regional tastes and wines of Emilia-Romagna, featuring porcinis, cacciocavalo, goose sausage, and the like

Keep in mind that January is the slowest month of the year.

Okay. So there is a well-financed, media-savvy hype machine, geared to promote new restaurants that can afford the cost of publicity. The kind of content this generates is glossy and ubiquitous, with its advertorial nature hidden from its audience. Except for the handful of influencers who adhere to the Federal Trade Commission's requirement that they clearly and conspicuously disclose any material connection to advertisers, hardly anyone informs readers, for whom opinion becomes indistinguishable from shilling. So what? How does this relate to, or matter in comparison with, the business practices and industry conventions that affect the lives of restaurant workers? If people want to see pics of a chef's home fridge, watch a video of a PB&J sandwich machine, take dining, fashion, or travel advice from shills whose endorsement can be had for the price of a meal, who cares?[2]

Guess who has money to launch publicity campaigns? The answer won't shock you. It's predominantly white people, the ones with a hospitality group launching its eighth restaurant. What this whole self-reinforcing foodie hype machine helps maintain is a status quo of abusive restaurateurs and disempowered workers. Also, that complacency from both publications and audiences, looking the other way on the easy PR-generated content, the lack of investment in food as news, has helped pump hot air into a generation of abusive chefs. There's no room (or budget) for reporting on labor practices when the mission is entertainment rather than nourishment.

※

THE RESPONSIBILITY FOR taking food coverage more seriously, as a matter of culture, labor, and climate, and other kinds of reporting beyond puffery, cannot just rest with BIPOC folks. That's a ridiculously heavy load. It's not merely that food media is too white. It's that the sameness is reflected in the sameness of how food is covered. If food media was more diverse, the hype machine wouldn't take hold so effectively in the first place because there would be a wider variety of experiences and perspectives. There would be interest in a broader array of food stories, with more people covering stories that matter. There would also be fewer people in the office agreeing with the boss that "Top Ten Sexiest Chefs" is a good idea.

The impact of this homogeneity in food media isn't limited to what gets covered. Its influence extends to what gets cooked.

It has helped foster a generation of restaurants, more carnival tent than dining experience, that kind of sucked. It gave rise to the It Spot.

At any given time, there's an It Spot restaurant in your town. Depending on the size of the city, maybe two or three or even ten. The status of the It Spot—impossible to get a reservation because everyone wants to eat there right now—never lasts. The crowd always grazes toward another spot, newer and more "it," every six months. The It Spot can be that little chef-driven thirty-seater that's become the late-night hangout of the fashion scene, or a Japanese soufflé pancake shop anointed as the latest fad, or even a chain restaurant.

Sometimes this flavor of the season is "it" because the food, service, style, location, and music are both outstanding and brilliantly of the moment. Too often it's one more place to get a mediocre bowl of pasta with blistered tomatoes or flip through a novella description of Prohibition-era cocktails, a business the owners have elevated to zeitgeist status by buying the public's attention through media dinners and sponsored Instagram posts. Frustratingly, local media will always cover these novelty and It Spots as if they have never heard of supply and demand and that the unfathomable lineup is the story.[3]

Owners who create a queue in front of their restaurants are smart operators who have examined the demographics, location, and price-point data to bait their hooks perfectly. That's a great business narrative about how successful research and marketing pay off. Instead, these stories are told as mysteries, an incredulous reporter asking how good the food must be to justify the lineup—as in "We waited in line two hours to try ghost-pepper bone-broth tea. Was it worth it?"[4]

I get the fun of the spite read. "Look what people are lined up for" or "Look what people spend money on" is not without its charm. All I'm advising is that, when new restaurants start opening again, we'd do well to remember, as diners, that It Spots are a waste of our time and money. We would have infinitely more fun at a restaurant we already know is good. Or we could be seeking out the true undiscovered greats, which are not It Spots. They are in strip malls and parts of town we don't know as well (a journey we'll dive into in the next chapter). True, we would miss out on the potential of something new to surprise us with its excellence. More often, the value of newness is saying, "I've been to so-and-so." The phenomenon of FOMO has made this scavenger-hunt style of dining, the cachet of telling people where you've eaten, more desirable than a pleasurable evening. Cultural status has supplanted personal experience.

Perhaps, in the early twenty-first century, as the dawn of the "chefs are the new rock stars" era, food seemed more honest or essential, maybe less corruptible, than the decadent music industry. Despite food's genuine capacity to bring people together, the ascendency of food's societal relevance instead reduced the whole experience of eating out to a status symbol.

Worse, that obsession with newness is a constant threat to every quality established restaurant, those that have been struggling harder than ever to survive. I used to write for a magazine where the editors asked contributors to convince the readers that every restaurant featured was the best, that they served food so unique or superior, that if it was new it was one of a kind. This is rarely true. A lot of publications, with no budget for restaurant reviews, have replaced critical coverage with the "just-opened" feature—a photo spread of dishes taken at a media dinner. This material is just PR for chefs and restaurants, content SEO-designed to appear at the top of diners' Google searches for new restaurants. While local media, foodsters, and influencers declare, "We've been to the new place!" in an attempt to sway you that you're missing out on something special, truly great restaurants have been working twice as hard to maintain the clientele they have, or had.

For a long time, after I was done as a critic, I kept checking out new restaurants because I thought it was necessary for my professional identity. A few years ago, I stopped. I don't want to spend my money on new restaurants, because they are rarely good. Most don't last. Those that survive, even the rare gems that show the potential for greatness, won't have hit their stride yet. Even worse, the handful that are blessed to be the new It Spot are likely underprepared and overwhelmed by demand.

Unlike precocious species of animals—horses, giraffes, elephants—that are miraculously able to walk the day they are born, restaurants are more like humans, who need about a year before they can stand confidently on their own. The occasional restaurant that arrives ready to gallop, usually operated by an industry veteran rather than a first-timer, is an anomaly. That's not a flaw, but a function of an open design system.

Chefs can and will tinker. That's their nature. It's also how they get better. Unworkable ideas get thrown out. After a year of operation, if a restaurant is still in business, half of the menu and the entire front-of-house team has usually turned over. Restaurants are built to age gradually into their best selves. The moment at which we shower them with attention is precisely when they're not ready for it.

Our obsession with newness is not constrained to restaurants. We fawn over new technology, new musical genres, and new friends, always ready to celebrate as shiny and exciting what may merely be cosmetically refreshed or rebranded. It's understandable. We want to be where things are happening, surrounded by a crowd that reaffirms our choices. We want to feel relevant. After being stuck inside for so long during our pandemic, we want that more than ever.

Back when I reviewed restaurants for a living, the debate still raged over how long to wait once they opened. Two months, I'd say. Two weeks, editors would counter. Zero days, concluded the good people of the Internet. "If they're charging money, they're ready for a review" went the refrain of the public, drunk on the power of social media and without the sobering empathy of having worked to open a restaurant.

While writers and editors were busy with high-minded debates over their duty to readers versus their fairness to business owners (who for the most part are not corporate fat cats with a just-launched product, but private citizens who have poured their life savings into a business), online behavior quickly rendered the argument irrelevant. Social media was not going to hold back opinions for any journalistic-principle nonsense.

Message boards on Chowhound and Yelp began talking up restaurants months in advance, often speculating on what would be revealed behind storefronts under construction. Soon the speed of these forums capitulated to the immediacy of Twitter judgment, and then the visual demand of Instagram, where criticism mattered less than documentation. The conversation firmly shifted from what was good to what was new.

THE MISINFORMATION AGE

Taking advantage of our hunger for the cultural capital of newness, the low-level scamming of free media dinners, influencers, and hidden ads floods our bandwidth. In my opinion, it detracts from food stories of any real value, and it defrauds readers and diners.

That opinion is far from unanimous, even within legacy food media.

"Don't you think that readers are smart enough to figure it out?" asks Susan Edgerley, the former *New York Times* food editor, turning the question back on me. Edgerley was twenty years into her journalism career before she segued into food.

It was primary election day in New York. After twelve years at the *Times*, she was deputy metro editor, coordinating reporters sent all over the city to cover notoriously bad polling machines and conditions. Elections are long days in newsrooms, so at 8:30 that Tuesday morning, when the first plane hit the World Trade Center, she was still heading into Manhattan on the subway.

After the attack she became passionate about food: reading travel memoirs, moving her family to France, growing strawberries in a window box. "I don't think it takes Freud to tell you what that was about. It was great to have an idyllic lifestyle that you could control, through those books about food and travel."

When *NYT* dining editor Pete Wells succeeded Frank Bruni as restaurant critic, Edgerley threw her hat in the ring to step in for Wells and lead the food section. "I approached it as a reporter approaches a news beat," says Edgerley from her home in Ashland, Oregon, where she now grows figs and peaches.

Serving as dining editor for five years, during the postrecession period when our mania for food exploded, she sees audiences as sufficiently savvy to seek good information over bad. "I think that readers are discerning enough," Edgerley contends. "If they don't care, then it doesn't matter. But if they do care, I think they can get to some approximation of the truth. If they really are passionate diners—and the last decade has shown an increased passion in food, in all its permutations—then I think those diners are going to get to it and figure it out. Because they care that much. If it's just someone who wants to eat at whatever place is new, then they can figure that out."

I want to cast off my cynicism and agree with her. However, I don't think it's a matter of intelligence but media literacy, which we've barely begun to teach in school. The ways we get information have changed so much in our lifetimes and continue to change so rapidly. I don't think most of us have the time or energy to dissect the meaning and agenda of every story and detail we hear—to sift through the sea of what is now called "content," sorting it into neat piles of fact, opinion, advertisement, advertorial, and propaganda. At the risk of disagreeing with Edgerley, while also kind of complimenting her, maybe she had smarter readers.

Again, I'm not insulting anyone else. I bought my first DVD player so I could watch *Hudson Hawk*. I'm not a smart man.

Kate Telfeyan, a former publicist, was thirty-seven when she started cooking professionally, quickly rising to head chef at Mission Chinese Food New York, a restaurant where allegations of horrific abuse, including burning an employee with a spoon dipped in hot oil, remain undisputed, though various people in ownership or management have shifted responsibility onto one another.[5] "In my years in PR, it was never explicit. But the ask on the restaurant side was always, bring media. And on the media side, depending on the hotness level of the restaurant you were working with, you almost acted like a VIP concierge," says Telfeyan. "As far as pay-for-play, that happened. There were definitely journalists who said, 'Give me a free dinner and I'll write about it.' They weren't the big fish that you wanted, but it was still coverage. And now with influencers, it's a whole different ball game." At the time she believed, like Edgerley, that people knew the difference between editorial and advertorial. Then friends would tell her about cool restaurants based on coverage she knew was bought and paid for.

Having worked both in PR, arranging "earned media," and then in a restaurant, cooking for influencer events, Telfeyan no longer thinks that diners know or care where their food information comes from. "I think they're not savvy about it because they don't want to be. Nobody wants to think there's something devious going on."

Is that true? Do people just not care about the difference between real and fake? I reach out to Jane Lytvynenko, a *BuzzFeed* reporter who focuses on misinformation, a catchall term for activities that range from phony stories put up on websites meant to look like real newspapers, deceptively edited video clips, online discussions that get sidetracked with inflammatory content, astroturfing (disguising the sponsors of a paid message so it looks like a grassroots movement), and hoaxes. Immediately following any disaster, whether it's a tornado or mass shooting, Lytvynenko has to take to social media to debunk the misinformation in real time—no, Antifa didn't derail an Amtrak train or start the California wildfires and the same man hasn't gone missing in every earthquake, flood, etc., for the past five years. "A lot of false information, a lot of online manipulation campaigns, take advantage of the volume of information that we're faced with day to day, cross their fingers, and hope we don't know that something is off," says Lytvynenko, pointing to the example of Philippines president Rodrigo Duterte. Dubbed by Facebook's public policy director, Katie Harbath, as patient zero in the weaponization of misinformation on digital platforms, the Duterte campaign successfully used all of the misinformation tools, including influencers, to breed distrust of the political opposition, journalists, and activist groups.[6] "For a consumer, who's already bombarded with a lot of information, they're not going to pause to investigate where this information came from. So the volume of information we're faced with plays directly into manipulation techniques."

A Dartmouth study from 2016 found that, duh, absence of labeling makes advertorial material more persuasive.[7] The problem isn't that we're dumb or lazy. It's that we're swimming in bullshit.

But influencer marketing didn't materialize out of nowhere. The host body of food media was already unhealthy before this parasite attached itself.

Ten years ago, these media dinners were smaller, often a single table of writers being courted by the category of restaurants that have enough backing to afford publicists and give food away. Social media changed that. Back then, when Chris Nuttall-Smith was a magazine food editor, he would occasionally go to these affairs to keep tabs on the industry, a practice that stopped when he became a critic. "If someone serves you food, you're going to feel like you owe them. As soon as you take free things, there's an expectation. It's never, ever free."

You do make friends with salad, when the salad is composed of baby gem lettuce from the rooftop garden, topped with grilled white asparagus, peaches, and a slice of prosciutto from acorn-fed pigs that the chef's been curing for eighteen months, paired with a crisp, off-off-dry Riesling.

It's December 2019. Over breakfast this morning, my wife, who has been telling me I should be worried about something called "coronavirus," asked me what Eataly is and why she has to care. The luxury Italian food retailer has just launched their Toronto location through a series of previews, tastings, and parties, adoringly promoted by the city's dining class.

"If you were on Instagram, over the course of forty-eight hours last week, every third image was something from Eataly," says Nuttall-Smith. "Smiling faces, dishes, crowds, people raving about their experience. Every single one of those people went to Eataly without ever taking out their wallet."

Do readers understand that they are effectively looking at ads, that advertisers have figured out how to transform everyone's social circle into a marketing tool? "I think in most cases they just don't care," says Nuttall-Smith. "The people who take free meals in exchange for advertising, who take free trips in exchange for advertising, who take favors in exchange for rave reviews, look at the numbers of followers they have. You'll get hundreds of thousands, if not millions, of people who will willingly sign on so they can be a part of that. And followers equal influence. They're winning."

There are people who want to read credible restaurant reviews and consumer advice without payola. Unfortunately, these are expensive to produce. Whether a restaurant critic is on staff or freelance, the budget to employ them should add up to two full-time salaries. That's a hard pill to swallow for publications already feeling the crunch. "Most media companies, not all, have utterly ceded that terrain," Nuttall-Smith says, noting that newspapers have, to a large degree, refocused their resources on essential services such as finance, business, politics, or investigative work. "And we'll let people get their restaurant advice from Instagram or websites that don't ever pay their bills. They don't ever get bills. The expectation is that they can come in and eat for free, and they'll write a BJ about your restaurant."

Ben Leventhal, who has had a foot in and out of food media for the past fifteen years, isn't so quick to dismiss coverage generated by free meals as fruit of the poisoned tree. "We have a perception in food media that all comped meals are tainted and all paid-in-full meals are legit. I don't think that's right," says the cofounder of the food publication *Eater* and the restaurant booking software company Resy. "I think that there are tons of free meals that result in excellent criticism. And there are tons of paid-for meals that result in extremely biased coverage."

Reviews are inherently biased. That's their purpose, to express a point of view. My approach, as a critic, was always to attempt to be as objective as possible about this reality: never bullshitting myself or the reader that absolute, scientific, triple-blind-study detachment was possible or that that's what I was offering.

"I think the public wants food writers and food writing to be very clean," says Leventhal. "They want food writers to pay for every meal and to be anonymous."

On this issue, there is no debate. People love the idea of the anonymous restaurant critic. I believed it was important too, having read Ruth Reichl's memoir *Garlic and Sapphires*, about practically becoming an undercover spy just to do her job as a critic. The public perception of the restaurant critic, shaped by Reichl's memoir as much as the imperious Anton Ego character in *Ratatouille*, has enjoyed a robust pop-culture presence, bordering on mythological.

Critics don't wield the power they did twenty years ago. And once everyone had a camera in their phone, it wasn't possible for critics to maintain their anonymity. Even a decade ago, when I was reviewing restaurants, the ship of anonymity had sailed.

Like any good legend, we've wanted to keep it going. I respect the power of myth. But we are only recently retiring the legend of anonymity, when it has been over for fifteen years. We're still pushing the folktale of the critic's power. When I started my career, my hometown had five full-time critics. Now, in that city of three million people, with as much culinary diversity as you'll find anywhere on earth, there are none.

It feels late to mourn the loss of the restaurant critic. Their reign has been over for some time, at least the way we thought of them. Over the past ten years, flanked by the twin forces of dwindling ad sales and the rise of social media/user-generated reviews, the role has shrunk from All-Powerful Oz to the man behind the curtain. Most of the critic jobs have evaporated. Those that have remained have given up their anonymity, admitting that they haven't truly been anonymous for some time. Writers like Soleil Ho, who has broadened the restaurant reviewer's role at the *San Francisco Chronicle* to include a cultural, political, holistic view of food, are leaders, though still outliers.

Few cities have papers as robust as that, or the *New York Times* or *LA Times*, with budgets for a food team. So this generation of diners continues to gather restaurant recommendations from the rogues' gallery of sources that have replaced traditional reviews.

Talk to a restaurant owner about Yelp, and they'll tell you how often customers attempt to use the platform to blackmail them, under threat of a one-star review, for free food. For politically outspoken restaurateurs, willing to use their social media platforms to express their views on divisive topics, Yelp is a one-stop shop for vengeful opponents to hurt their business through mean-spirited, fake reviews.

In 2018 the *Times* of London reported that a third of reviews on TripAdvisor are fake. *Eater* followed up with a story that all but accused a New York restaurant of committing fraud in order to position itself as the city's number-one destination.[8] As the restaurant industry regroups postpandemic, so will these problematic design flaws, unless we rewire ourselves as consumers, not just in which restaurants we support, but what kind of food media we consume.

The good news is that this is a lot easier than it sounds. It's mostly a matter of asking where information is coming from, who is seeking to benefit by influencing our dining decisions, and what is motivating us when we feel compelled to eat at a new restaurant.

When we dine out with friends again, let's reverse the "What's new?" question. A better prompt is, "Do we want to check out a new restaurant or a good restaurant?" That's particularly so when we see how hard our favorite places have struggled to stay in business, to keep their suppliers afloat, and to provide jobs for often undocumented workers who have no access to unemployment benefits. That one straightforward act won't cost you a penny and will do a lot to support the kind of businesses you believe in.

Still, the incremental takeover by PR and influencers is just part of the sea change of the past decade, a gradual swing in food media toward style over substance, until the pandemic forced most publications to contend with the uglier realities of our dining system.

Lately, food media has been the subject of a larger conversation about necessary changes in our society. A lot of the criticisms seem fair. Overall, food media is too white and has done too much to build up the persona of celebrity chefs and too little to investigate their misconduct. At the center of these critiques is a key tension that is a clear, literal disagreement between writers and editors that I don't see discussed in public. Is food news or entertainment?

This isn't just a food issue. It's an echo of a larger problem in journalism, a long-term trend away from a time when every paper had a reporter on the labor beat. "Unions were at their peak from the '30s to the '70s, when they represented one in three workers," says Steven

Greenhouse, labor reporter for the *New York Times* until his retirement in 2014. "In the '40s, '50s, and '60s, every paper had labor reporters. It was one of the main beats. Unions were a big f'in deal." Greenhouse actually says "f'in" instead of cursing.

In the 1970s and '80s, as unions started to decline in prominence and membership, their leaders no longer exciting, so did the media focus on the subject. "Many Americans were in the middle class already, so they didn't feel the need to mobilize and be militant about it. Union density fell from one in three to one in ten. There were far fewer strikes. Labor coverage subsided, and eventually a lot of papers stopped having labor reporting. Newspapers went through a huge financial squeeze in the first decade of this century. Many of them got rid of the position of labor reporter. For a while, I was the only full-time labor reporter left in the nation."

Then came the Great Recession. With so many people laid off, suddenly there was much more coverage of workers again. The rise of digital media tilted to a younger audience that, with higher student debt and far less job security than their parents, had more interest in labor issues. No longer focused so specifically on covering unions, labor reporting became more expansive—dress-code discrimination at chain restaurants, protests from rideshare drivers—with a less clear connection between government labor policy and the lives of workers.

Though work has gotten only more precarious, and interest in the politics of labor is renewed, it's still the case that few publications have the budget for multiple food writers, let alone for dedicating reporters to cover workers in the food industry. When I first started as a restaurant critic, I was shown around the newsroom, and half of the people who shook my hand told me, "You don't have to remember my name, kid. I just took a buyout." After losing classified-ad revenue to Craigslist, giving content online for free, and selling digital ads for pennies on the print dollar, newspapers and magazines spent the first decade of this century scrambling. They haven't caught up.

At the same time, social media came along and ate the lunch of legacy-media ad revenue. While traditional publications have spent fifteen years asking how to get readers to pay for their costly product, new media companies, agile and unencumbered, were able to monetize overnight. Within a few years, Facebook went from a place to spy on friends from high school to an election swinger. As of 2019, it collects 20.9 percent of the digital advertising revenue in the world.[9] Instagram, launched in 2010, bought by competitor Facebook two years later for $1 billion, quickly segued from a tool for selling yourself to a tool to selling goods. In 2013 Instagram introduced ads. Within four years, there were a million advertisers on the platform, with the company constantly finding more ways to shorten the number of clicks between viewing and purchasing.

As eyeballs have migrated from print to desktops to phones, from webpages to apps, words have taken a backseat to images. It's no wonder that we've seen a rise in bottom-scraping food ideas, fads rooted 100 percent in images, bearing even less flavor or substance than they do nutrients.

Some of the best legacy publications are able to wear both hats, balancing lighter fare with essential food journalism. That's very expensive. Most media outlets, old and new, have focused their efforts, either on food reporting (*Civil Eats*, *The Counter*, *FoodPrint*, *Edible*) or lists, recipes, product endorsements, and chef profiles (*Bon Appétit*, Food Network, *Food & Wine*).

I'd be a fool to suggest that pictures don't matter. I eat with my eyes first like anyone else. In cooking school, they tried to impart to us the importance of presentation. Food cannot simply taste good, our instructors said. It must look good, too. At the time the trend was to stack elements, a wedge of black cod perched on top of a Jenga tower of braised salsify. Stacking was succeeded by clean lines of sauces—zips of green oils and dots of sticky reduced balsamic squeezed out of tubes—used to frame the still too large hunks of protein on the dish. Then it was Danish asymmetrical minimalism, discs of fermented heirloom carrots and a small cube of sous vide elk belly hiding along one edge of a steering wheel–size plate. Somewhere in there was a moment when every ambitious chef had to create their own plates, either custom-made porcelain or hacked out of a tree stump. These styles came and went, but were never as important as how the food tasted. Until about 2015.

It was about that time that I encountered the floating noodles. I was at a restaurant that served a dish, promoted on Instagram, featuring noodles that seemed to float in the air. We had to have it, right?

When the dish came, a waterfall of noodles hovered a foot above the plate, a pair of chopsticks embedded in the food as if held by an unseen hand. The owner told me of his experimentations with the dish, using a hidden fork and potato wedge to create the illusion. What he didn't talk about was the taste, because it did not matter (short of bacalhau, it was the saltiest thing I've ever put in my mouth).

And what right do I have to complain about the flavor of something I bought purely on the basis of its appearance? That goes for the donut burgers (who ever said, 'This ketchup isn't sweet enough. I need the entire burger bun to be candy too"?), monster milkshakes (you're going to drink a milkshake after eating the half cup of M&Ms, waffles, lollipop, and Twizzlers that were sticking out the top?), and cotton-candy burritos (the wrap component is made from a substance famous for its lack of flavor and the unpleasant residue it leaves on your hands). These image-based foods that have hijacked our attention are designed to be photographed, not eaten.

One day I saw a woman on the sidewalk taking photos of her charcoal ice cream cone. A common sight these days: food arm extended, phone held close to face. After getting her shot, she dumped the ice cream in the trash. A friend of mine who owned a café next to the ice cream place complained that people came in every day asking to use the bathroom to wash charcoal ice cream off their hands.

When style trumps substance, food and money poured out in pursuit of social media engagement, likes and faves harvested like corn and wheat, it changes the face of our food culture. When people open restaurants now, at least some part of the menu or dining room, or both, is conceived purely for photography. "Every restaurant that gets any sort of buzz has at least one dish that is complete Instagram fodder," says San Francisco chef Naomi Elze-Harris making break-fast as we talk. "It might not even taste good. It's just there to photo-graph well, to be the thing that everybody orders so they can put it on their Instagram. And it costs no money for the restaurant." Makes sense, doesn't it, to design a higher-margin item for this purpose? "But they're gonna charge out the butt for it. Because people just want to take the picture."

A smoke alarm interrupts our conversation. Elze-Harris apologizes as she goes to go open a window. Last night the chef hosted a pop-up. She's using leftovers to make hangtown fry, a bacon and herb omelet stuffed with fried oysters. The classic dish, which originated during the gold rush, predates food photography. Though bursting with flavor, it is a mess of brown, gray, and pale yellow. It would never appear in a contemporary restaurant without a makeover of colorful and crispy garnishes to conceal its appearance. Instead, she's currently developing a variation on fairy bread, Wonder Bread with sprinkles on it, for her menu. "I'm essentially gonna recycle some of the bread I make in-house into a bread pudding, slice a piece off of it and brûlée it so it's got a nice crispy crust, put Chantilly cream on top, and dump a bunch of sprinkles on it." While Elze-Harris is committed to making sure the dish actually tastes delicious, she dejectedly admits that it's "a gimmick that photo-graphs well just to put butts in seats. I'm guilty of this too."

The cycle continues through publicists, who write pitches describ-ing the food or decor as "Instagram worthy" and letting you know what lists—best cocktails, best date night for South American cuisine, best restaurants for private events—their client's restaurant would be suited for. A recent press release announcing a restaurant opening devotes five paragraphs to the sommelier, restaurant designer, and detailed descrip-tions of the interior's "original brick and beam," "copper, Italian wool and red oxidized steel accents," "blonde wood and terrazzo," "corru-gated carrera marble bar," and "wall-to-wall glass." The food showcased in this temple of design was summed up in three words: "traditional Italian fare." That was it. A wedding speech about the appearance with a footnote for the food.

The downside for the restaurant is that the people who come "for the 'gram" are not the repeat customers they need for long-term success. Diners who came just to take a picture are not going to order takeout so your business can survive a pandemic. As restaurants cultivate this kind of patron, it changes the nature of the dining experience. It becomes more important to design space for an "Instagram wall" than acoustics that allow diners to hear each other talking. "When your entire advertising depends on 'Will people take pictures of it?' you end up with a clientele that doesn't care about the food," says Elze-Harris. "They don't care about what you're serving. They don't want to talk about the sustainable pork. The people who want the photo are only coming in one time, to take the photo."

Yes, people still value good food. And, yes, traveling carnivals have long tricked rubes into buying gimmicky snacks. Overly styled photos of food are not new. Magazines have been stacking impossibly high sandwiches to fit the rectangular shape of their covers for as long as I can remember.

I'm not immune to the lure of pretty things. But Instagram has turbocharged the hustle of image-based food, extending the reach of the carny's megaphone by transforming consumers into shills who will in turn help the business market its product on their customers' social channels. So dining becomes more of a video-game fetch quest than a communal experience, with diners chasing the social cachet of proving that they've eaten the latest food-shaped bauble.

The joke is on us, because on some level we probably know that we are being duped, that the flatteringly lit industry of aspiration is selling us something unattainable that doesn't taste as good as it looks. We do not care. And as we subscribe, like, and share (often with ironic detachment), we invite these images into our lives, further blurring the distinction of what is an ad, because the attention economy doesn't differentiate between good and bad attention.

The further I go down the "who cares?" rabbit hole, seeking perspective from food writers and editors, the more I doubt that anyone answered this better than comedian Jerry Seinfeld, speaking to an audience of advertisers. "I love advertising because I love lying," said Seinfeld, getting laughs from the crowd while accepting a 2014 Clio Award for advertising. "In advertising, everything is the way you wish it was. I don't care that it won't be like that when I actually get the product being advertised—because in between seeing the commercial and owning the thing, I'm happy. And that's all I want. We know the product is going to stink. But we're happy in that moment between the commercial and the purchase. And I think spending your lives trying to dupe innocent people out of hard-won earnings to buy useless, low-quality, misrepresented items and services is an excellent use of your energy, because a brief moment of happiness is pretty good."

There is however, a glass-half-full side to the rise of social media and the mostly junk content that dominates the medium: the public's ability to amplify their voices, to take part in a conversation too long dominated by gatekeepers, and begin to reshape it.

And as much as I've crapped on Yelp, its design is democratic. There's a straight line between the decline of legacy media and the rising visibility of immigrant restaurants, with user-generated content as a conduit. In the past five years, particularly after the 2016 US election and the anti-immigration, isolationist attitudes that helped win the presidency, we've seen a renewed, focused energy on immigrant-owned restaurants and their stories. The publications with the resources have been spending the money and putting in the work.

I love Canada. But our population is about the same as California's spread over a land mass equal to the entire United States. Except for Quebec, a province that has its own lively and profitable French-language media economy, Canadians get much of our news and entertainment from the States, leaving our newspapers and magazines with an audience, subscription base, and budgets that are too weak to sustain food journalism. The country's two largest newspapers, for example, each have one staff food writer.

So lately I've found my attention shifting to the United States, to publications like *The Counter*, *Eater*, the *San Francisco Chronicle*, and the *LA Times*, which have placed the stories of workers, immigrant entrepreneurs, and neighborhood gentrification ahead of top-ten lists of rainbow bagels. The 2019 package of stories in the *New York Times* connecting climate change and food, the various ethical questions we all face as eaters framed as a sort of interactive choose-your-own-adventure, is often cited as a contemporary gold standard in food coverage.[10]

Over the past two years, the *LA Times* food section has completely remade itself. For a long time, the paper had critic Jonathan Gold, who eschewed fine dining restaurants in favor of the bold flavors he hunted down across LA's expanse of culinary diasporas embedded in strip malls. Gold was a huge deal in Los Angeles, credited with almost single-handedly raising the city's status as a food town, not through lionizing pedigreed chefs or promulgating the expansions of global food brands, but by finding, eating, and promoting the diversity of cuisine in the sprawling metropolis. Translation: Gold ate where white people weren't going and told us how good it was. He was everyone's favorite restaurant critic. Yet other than Gold, the paper's food coverage had dwindled to a couple pages in the Saturday section.

And then, in 2018, two unexpected things happened, one good and one terrible. First, the paper was bought by billionaire Patrick Soon-Shiong, who cares deeply about food and was a big fan of Gold. The plan, to build food coverage as a tent pole of the paper, thrilled managing editor Kimi Yoshino, who had grown up near Modesto, in California's Central Valley, one of the most productive agricultural regions in the world. Her grandparents owned a vineyard, which friendly neighbors took care of during World War II, when Yoshino's family had been interned. So the farm was still in the family when Yoshino was growing up, she and her cousins splashing in the water while the grapes were being irrigated. With the sale of the paper finalized in June 2018 to a foodie billionaire willing to invest in hiring, Yoshino could build the food section of her dreams.

And then Jonathan Gold died. In July of that year, Gold was diagnosed with pancreatic cancer. Within a few weeks, he passed away.

A week after his death, on what would have been Gold's fifty-eighth birthday, landmarks around the city—the Natural History Museum,

Los Angeles City Hall, Union Station, the Wilshire Grand Center, Pasadena City Hall, pylons at LAX, and the Pacific Wheel on the Santa Monica Pier—were lit in gold to mourn his passing. "From the time we knew he was sick to the time he died was a matter of weeks. It was devastating," recalls Yoshino, who thought she was going to be constructing the food section around the acclaimed writer. "And suddenly I was tasked to find a replacement for this beloved figure in our city, the only restaurant critic to ever win a Pulitzer. I think we thought it would be a little unfair to burden a single restaurant critic with having to follow in Jonathan's footsteps."

At the time, Patricia Escárcega wasn't thinking about Los Angeles. Three years earlier, she had answered an ad in the *Phoenix New Times*, which was seeking a freelance food writer. Suddenly, she was a critic, with a dining budget of $200 per review. "My editor told me you have to go three times." That is not a lot of money if you're trying to uphold the *New York Times'* standard of three meals in order to give a restaurant as many chances as possible to do their best, to make sure one bad meal isn't an off night for them.

After a few months, Escárcega's budget went down further. Much of the time she was paying out of her own pocket. "It shaped my coverage. But I didn't feel bad about not being able to cover the four-star places. They were the only thing being written about in local papers." At the same time, she saw a cultural shift happening, one popularized by beloved writers like Gold and Anthony Bourdain, a focus on small restaurants and the first- and second-generation immigrants who often owned them. "These were the places to write about without going way over budget."

Escárcega had been raised in Southern California. Her parents were agricultural workers who picked citrus. This was the food she grew up eating, and she had not seen it exalted as much as fancy chef restaurants. After building a reputation at the *Phoenix New Times*, she moved on to the *Arizona Republic*. In the summer of 2018, Bill Addison, who had already been hired as one half of Gold's replacement, was in Arizona finishing up an assignment for *Eater*. The two ate dinner together, and soon Addison was singing Escárcega's praises to Yoshino, who had stalled on her search for a second critic. "I had read everything from every critic at every major publication," recalls Yoshino. "Nobody was clicking. When I looked at her clips, I was immediately impressed."

Escárcega's writing was different, particularly a piece about her search for *pajarete*, a rural cocktail of instant coffee, tequila, and milk pulled directly from the cow's udder into the cup, resulting in a milk-shake-like froth, at once extremely working class yet, by nature of the farm ingredients, utterly exclusive. "It was such a great piece. It said a lot about her and her sense of exploration, her curiosity. She was a gem."

Yoshino traveled to Phoenix to meet with Escárcega. Over dinner, the two found they had much in common. "She had a connection to the land and to food and the history of Southern California that I just loved," says Yoshino. "She reminded me so much of Jonathan Gold. He was similarly a deep thinker and student. I found her super appealing. So smart and passionate."

With new critics signed on, and a budget to build, the food team quadrupled, from three to twelve, the section developing into a forum that truly served readers. Yes, there were restaurant reviews and recipes and updates on the careers of notable chefs. There was also a renewed zeal for the lives of the people who produce food. Unfortunately, there was also what sounds like a poisonous work environment cultivated by the paper's new food editor, Peter Meehan, which would erupt in a midpandemic reckoning.

Though the *LA Times* has a policy against staffers attending media dinners, Escárcega could see the money being spent to ensure a restaurant's name shows up in social media. "I can almost organize the city's dining ecosystems into two categories. They either have a public relations person or they don't," says Escárcega. "In my work I'm trying to make sure that what we write about doesn't fall into one of those categories all the time. Because that has been a central failing of publications. We go to the people that give us easy access."

For almost two years, she met that challenge, highlighting restaurants serving everything from manchamanteles "tablecloth stainer" mole in Paramount and modern French in Orange County to mapo tofu lasagna downtown. Then came March 2020.

At first, there was no conversation about how Escárcega's duties, or anyone in the section's, had officially been redefined. The pandemic was the story of the day and likely the generation. Everyone just jumped to the task at hand, updating each other when they could.

Overnight, Escárcega went from dining critic to feature reporter. Immediately, she was speaking with restaurant people, listening to them cry, hearing about their hopes, aspirations, and dreams being dashed. Her work switched from recommending restaurants to informing readers about the health and safety of the people who work in them.

Since the beginning of the pandemic, the precariousness of restaurants workers has become a lot more widely understood. Considering that awareness, I'm curious if or when there will be much appetite for reviews in the future.

Escárcega believes the genre will be back. "I think there's a reason why the restaurant review is still here, even though there are varied ways to learn about a restaurant before you go out to eat. Yelp has been around for at least a decade. Yet we still have restaurant reviews. There's something about the form that persists."

There will be fewer zingers, Escárcega predicts of post-COVID reviews, with the tone shifting dramatically, allowing space to weigh what the pandemic has done to the restaurant world. The uncertainty, which is bound to be part of our lives for some time, will work its way into restaurant reviews. Like any hardwired narrative structure—genius detective mystery, giant monster, teenage romance—though the popularity of the genre may rise and fall, it's too familiar not to return.

The restaurant review, no matter what form it takes, comes with its own perfect story components baked in. I discovered this early in my career. While it's a challenge to make reviews fresh and captivating, they all start with the same ingredients—a critic eats at a restaurant and decides if it's good. Even if the story and its themes can go in so many directions, the tool kit comes with a protagonist, an antagonist, and a clearly defined conflict. People know what a review is. It needs no setup or backstory unless the writer (who can be both the hero and the villain of the piece) decides it's important to expand on those details. The restaurant review is, like a whodunit, elemental.

The aesthetics of the food will just have to give way to economics and a holistic look at the industry. "We'll have to talk more about the people who run the restaurant," says Escárcega, adding, "I think restaurant reviews were running that way anyways."

It'll be hard to write a negative review of a restaurant that has survived the Ragnarok of COVID-19. Yoshino says the prototypical review needs to be rethought. As Escárcega sees it, her job is to be honest, and at the very least not to varnish and make restaurants sound better than they are. "We get paid to tell the truth. And when I say tell the truth, I mean be completely honest and not try to avoid saying something that could be uncomfortable. I'm hoping to build a relationship with people who read my reviews, where they know I'm not hiding anything or trying to make something sound better than it is."

Still, I worry that readers, even those particularly interested in food, don't make a distinction between costly food journalism and a collection of brunch dishes pulled from Instagram. "I would hope with publications like the *LA Times*, they understand that we're not taking part in that type of journalism," says Yoshino. "But honestly, I don't know that readers would understand."

Escárcega is more nuanced, though less generous. "My impression is that readers are becoming increasingly siloed into their own universes. My sense is that we have some readers who are extremely savvy, and they understand the difference between something that was fact-checked and researched. And there are other readers who don't put as much weight to who is telling them the news. And I don't see a lot of overlap these days."

Though during our conversation Escárcega had nothing but praise for the *LA Times*, she was quietly waiting on a decision from the pay-discrimination claim filed through her union. This was separate from the 240 Black, Latino, and women journalists who settled their class action against the paper for paying them less than white male peers. In November 2020 she received a memo rejecting her request for equal payment with her cocritic, who she says makes a third more than her despite doing the same job. A statement from the *LA Times* argued that Addison is paid more than Escárcega due to his experience and that he has "won one of the most significant awards in food journalism."[11] It didn't mention the frequency of white people winning those awards. With every step forward, two steps back.

While newspaper food sections are tied to both the self-selected political audience and the fortunes of the rest of the paper, new media presents opportunities for new voices and different business models that allow a direct relationship between audiences and funding.

One of the criticisms of food media is the chumminess with chefs and thereby a reluctance to report on their failings. In my experience, any serious editor is eager to publish evidence of an abusive chef if backed up by thorough reporting. But the threshold for publishing these kinds of stories responsibly—number of on-the-record sources, documentation of abuse or illegal activity—is always high. One unexpected upside to the pandemic was that restaurant workers, furloughed, bored, and frustrated, began talking shit publicly. In the spring of 2020, social media accounts began popping up, calling out all manner of restaurant impropriety, from racism to sexism to classism. Movements like this may be a symptom of a broken system rather than a solution for one. In the absence of the legal variety, it's natural for us to gravitate to mob justice. "A big part of this current moment of racial reckoning is also a reckoning for institutions that, while supposedly meant to protect all people, often fail at doing just that. If those methods don't serve your interests, why not bypass them?" asked Ho, in her year-end *Chronicle* column.[12]

But borrowing from the language of restorative justice, the action of lobbing accusations, however much we believe them, is limited by the scope of social media, Ho finds. "All we have to go on are one-sided accusations and hurt feelings—a gossip rag with a veneer of radical politics," writes Ho. "In a similar vein, that's why, on paper at least, people have the right to face their accusers in a court of law, and why the ethics of journalism require reporters to try to corroborate claims and ask for comment from the accused (as admittedly flawed as these institutions are). But on Instagram, we're currently playing a game of whack-a-mole, waiting for the next bad manager or restaurant owner to be exposed and publicly shamed before moving our attention to the next one. Actual change—a bone-deep shift that will last beyond a single person's tenure at her café—will require more than demanding accountability on a platform primarily oriented toward entertainment."

Not all of this amateur journalism is anonymous or drive-by. Sometimes it is thorough, enabling legacy media to pick up the story without being exposed to a libel suit. For example, when I read the LA Times' exposé of problems at Sqirl restaurant—theft of creative credit for creative work, indifference to gentrification, and, most prominently, moldy jam—the story cited Joe Rosenthal as its main source. Owner Jessica Koslow released a statement that she shared credit whenever possible. She also cited mycologist and fungal expert Dr. Patrick Hickey as a mentor for her safety protocols in jam production, which included the scraping off of mold. Hickey not only disagreed with Koslow's methods, he claimed not to know her or her restaurant.[13]

Rosenthal is not a journalist. He is a Minnesota PhD mathematician with a background in biological modeling of Alzheimer's disease. He works for a nonprofit, building systems to improve cancer detection. An enthusiastic home cook, Rosenthal put a lot of creativity into his social media food content, before going a step further, practicing investigative journalism in his spare time, conducting extensive interviews to write and publish about the problematic behavior of restaurateurs.

Upton Sinclair was said to be disappointed that the public's takeaway from his investigative novel The Jungle was shock at the book's exposé of the hygiene problems in early-twentieth-century meat production, rather than the treatment of workers. When Rosenthal first started reporting about the problems at Sqirl, he posted under an Instagram story called "The Fungal." Beyond the literary reference, Rosenthal suspected that, like *The Jungle*, the moldy jam would be what most people cared about. "I kind of knew the mold would be the smoking gun that got everyone's attention," says Rosenthal, who nonetheless tried to use the outrageousness of that detail to steer people back to the subject of food media's failings and its problematic obsession with building up chefs. "These proposals to fix the restaurant industry and food media . . . people are proposing that journalists need to talk to restaurant workers," says Rosenthal. His Sqirl story had forty-one sources, including twenty-six past and present employees. A piece on pizza consultant Anthony Falco took months of work. "It takes a lot to get them to talk," Rosenthal adds. "With the Falco story it was a lot of Roberta's employees past and present. That was a particularly hard nut to crack." Having cracked that nut myself, I know that it's not as simple as telling writers, "Go talk to workers" (though that's a start).

Thanks to my background in cooking, I was able to write a column for which I spent a day each week cooking in a different restaurant kitchen. After a few ten- or twelve-hour shifts, cooks started loosening up around me, talking about wages and treatment. You can't tell a writer of top-ten lists to go out and do that. Publications that do have to invest the time and resources necessary. Rosenthal invested his own time in the project. There are hardly any publications with the kind of investigation team of a *Boston Globe* or *Washington Post*. While those crews will spend months working on a single story, food sections are expected to crank out material every day. It's incredibly uncommon for an editor to assign a reporter to spend two weeks looking into allegations about moldy jam. And it will happen only in cases where the suspect is sufficiently famous.

I don't want to be making excuses. Because I would love it if things were different. That's my dream: newspapers with budgets to sink into deep reporting on food issues. "If you want to write outside the lifestyle food sphere, there are very few places for food politics writing. And when there are, they are dry and policy driven," says food writer Alicia

Kennedy. "Food writing is understood to be light and happy and to occupy a space of distraction and entertainment. There's this real disconnect between what's going on in the world, economically, ecologically, politically, culturally, and what is written about in the food world."

Tired of waiting for food publications to change, the Puerto Rico–based Kennedy started writing for more generalist magazines while publishing her own newsletter. When the pandemic hit, she decided to take her newsletter more seriously and was pleased to find an audience for her type of cultural criticism. Unintentionally, she enacted the payment option on the newsletter software, a happy accident that led to a discovery—her readers were willing to pay for her writing. The income is the equivalent of a part-time job. For any freelancer, an anchor gig, the guarantee of some regular income, is essential.

Since finding success on her own terms, Kennedy has had more editors eager to work with her. But while some high-profile people have lost their jobs recently, she doesn't see the caste dynamic dying out. "You can change who the people are, but the system remains the same," says Kennedy. "I think the industry is able to adjust itself in terms of representation regarding racial and gender diversity. But socioeconomic diversity, unless it's free to go to college and we have Medicare coverage for all, I don't think you change who's going to have these editorial jobs."

Even if traditional food media is beyond reform, here are two things any publication can do differently without spending one extra dime—decolonize mastheads and stop deifying chefs.

To start, stop putting people like me, or who look like me, in positions of power. Nobody needs me, another white male, to explain or examine what some people call "cancel culture" and what others call "literally describing the horrible behavior of powerful people with the hopes that they will be held accountable for the first time." For example, after speaking with Escárcega, I wanted to hear from her bosses about the decision to hire her. In the two days between the moment Peter Meehan agreed to speak with me and the time we actually set up an interview, the food editor was outed as what, from descriptions, sounds like a tyrant whose behavior mimicked the high-end chefs who demand too much and then scream at employees when they're disappointed, with a touch of alleged racism and sexually inappropriate behavior thrown in.

Like the Sqirl story, information about Meehan came out not through a traditional publication but on social media. Earlier in the summer, wine writer Tammie Teclemariam had posted a photo of *Bon Appétit* editor in chief Adam Rapoport in a Halloween costume that appears to be based on stereotypes about Puerto Ricans, which got employees talking about Rapoport's allegedly horrible behavior; by the end of the day, he resigned.[14] A few weeks later, Teclemariam repeated the feat with a series of tweets about Meehan. Similar to the moldy jam, the smoking gun was not Meehan's alleged abuse of employees. It was living in New York while being handsomely paid to lead a high-profile section of an LA paper. These departures are another opportunity to replace the figureheads of our industries, not just with new figureheads, editors, and chefs who are just as likely to turn out to be deeply flawed human beings, but with principles, like promising to give a voice to the voiceless more often than a platform for the powerful.

Building people up makes it that much more likely that they will be torn down by lack of the perfection we demand from idols. Or, as with characters like Meehan or Koslow, it imbues them with power, which insulates them from criticism. It detracts from what matters, which is the work.

In 2020 *Eater* replaced their "Young Guns" annual list of up-and-coming chefs with the "New Guard," a list of people helping to change the industry, expanding the criteria to include "community organizers, people engaged in mutual aid, non-profit workers, artists, provocateurs, farmers and advocates for a more sustainable food supply and community health."[15]

Love it. Great start. Let's acknowledge the group rather than laud the individual. Let's focus on the work, the ideas, the food, and the experience and do away with the narrative crutch that there must be one person at the center of every story, someone who deserves to get leveled up, to be placed on a pedestal until such time that they can be torn down. Maybe that's un-American. That's okay. I'm Canadian. I grew up with free health care, ketchup chips, and the episode of *Degrassi Junior High* where Erica definitely gets an abortion (the US edit left it ambiguous).

The dining public can play a major role in solving the problems in food media. It's as easy as identifying food media of value versus junk media, paying for what we can, and ignoring the carnies.

In recent years, we've started to see more quality food journalism on the market. New publications like *Whetstone* and *Meal Magazine* are carving out a niche. *Eater* is leading the conversation on ethical issues in restaurants, while *The Counter* does a fantastic job covering agriculture, supermarkets, and policy. And some big newspapers are putting their money where their mouth is, by staffing food sections with reporters.

So even if our city doesn't have a great food section, there are reliable outlets to follow the national dialogue about restaurants. Locally, we can pop the balloon of PR-driven, overhyped restaurants and the chefs who run them simply by not paying attention. These places will all be back. Eventually, as the economy recovers, people with money will want to spend it. A horde of shiny, new gastronomic temples will rise up to serve them, outspending each other in their attempts to create that It Spot feeling of unmissable newness and nowness.

The next time this comes up, when your friends ask you to check out the new It Spot, remind them of a restaurant where you all shared a wonderful, memorable evening. Remember that dinner and how good a time you had. Suggest going back there, now that it's safe to dine in again. They deserve your patronage. They've worked for it.

Not only can I guarantee you'll have a better time at a good restaurant, rather than a new restaurant; you know it too.

· 4 ·

The Immigrant Restaurant

Stocks may rise and fall. Utilities and transportation systems may collapse. People are no damn good. But they
will always need land and they will pay through the nose
to get it.

—LEX LUTHOR, business leader and philanthropist

Market rate is a made-up number. And it's bullshit.

—GEETIKA AGRAWAL

NO ONE COMES TO OUR HOME THESE DAYS. SO THREE MONTHS
into the pandemic lockdown, when I hear the soft knock on the front
door, it's like sensing the hooves of Santa's reindeer on the roof. I rush
downstairs to receive the delivery of Sri Lankan lamprais, kothu roti,
and kochikadai rice. It's June 2020, my first Father's Day as a new dad.
My wife has insisted that I not cook dinner.

Victoria likes my cooking. I like my cooking. Our daughter, Scarlett, if we can divine meaning from her happy gurgles as she mashes soft
yams and hunks of couscous against her lips and one tooth, likes my
cooking. But you remember the summer of 2020. Confined indoors for

three months, unable to visit a friend's home or get together in a restaurant, we miss other people's cooking. So for my Father's Day treat, we order from Cucini, an underground Sri Lankan restaurant, one of the food services businesses birthed by the pandemic, many of quasi-legal status.

With Scarlett tucked safely into bed, we spread our goodies over the coffee table, kneeling close, bandits licking our lips over our illicit loot. "FNAP!" goes a plastic container as I unseal the lid, releasing a steam perfumed by cumin and curry leaves. The kothu roti—a hash of the soft flatbread, fistfuls of garlic, ginger, shallots, and chilies, fried on a flattop, usually prepared on a giant griddle, using plaster scrapers to chop and toss, bound together with egg and sauced with curry—is so nose-twitchingly spicy it makes Nashville hot chicken seem like a stick of peppermint gum. It's heaven. With all due respect to the childhood comfort of bagels with cream cheese, this dish is my favorite thing to eat. It is a dish not found too frequently around Toronto, yet a staple among the group that is the city's number-one source of immigrant restaurant labor.

To believe that restaurants exist without immigrants is like imagining lakes existing without rivers. Without workers from Central and South America specifically, frequently undocumented, treated poorly and paid less than American-born peers, the restaurants and agricultural fields of the United States would grind to a halt. Canada is not much different. Instead of undocumented workers, here there are documented-but-temporary ones: the country flies in people from Mexico and the Caribbean to plant, tend, and harvest produce and then sends them back home at the end of the growing season. Neither this Temporary Foreign Workers Program nor America's H-2A guest-worker program grants migrant workers any pathway to citizenship. They spend eight months a year in the country, many of them for decades on end, earning minimum wage, with limited access to health care.

Separated as Canada and Mexico are by a sixteen-hundred-mile drive over a landmass known as the United States of America, there are only 128,485 people of Mexican origin in Canada, compared to

36 million in the United States.[1] So while Mexican immigrants are the biggest group in the United States, the immigrants that Canadian restaurants depend on come from other countries. For the past few decades, a major point of origin has been Sri Lanka.

In a 1983 pogrom that would become known as Black July, orchestrated mob violence by Sri Lanka's Sinhalese majority against the Tamil minority killed thousands. Homes were destroyed, people were burned alive in the streets, and the country was plunged into a civil war that lasted until 2009.

Refugees from Sri Lanka began arriving in Canada in 1986, first in a boat containing 155 half-starved people found floating off the shore of Newfoundland. I once heard a survivor of this boat describe the experience, testifying that "we did not eat or shit for three days." Today Canada is home to the largest Sri Lankan diaspora in the world, about 150,000, three times as many as the United States.[2] And the highest concentration is in Toronto.

Washing dishes has long been one of the most accessible jobs for recent immigrants who haven't yet learned the local language. Every restaurant I cooked in had a Sri Lankan dishwasher. Some only knew the word *pans*, the single-syllable request most frequently and impatiently shouted at them. Those who mastered English moved on to prep cooking, which enabled them to work graveyard shifts, simmering sauces and chopping onions until the sun rose, before heading to their day jobs in factories. Most had two jobs, sending money home and saving as much as they could to bring over their wives, sisters, brothers, parents, and children.

In one restaurant, I used to make lunch for the dishwashers, based on instructions from a coworker. Each time, I'd add more chili. With every iteration, Jaya, Prapa, and Mogan told me that it was better than the last. I didn't grasp their appetite for heat until I tasted real Sri Lankan food.

It was early evening on June 1, 2012, the night of a rain so heavy that it flooded train stations. My friend Suresh Doss planned to meet me and a couple friends in midtown and drive to a suburban restaurant called Hopper Hut. Doss's mission in life is to find delicious food in the kinds of strip-mall places that never appear in glossy food magazines, eat it, and share it with as many people as possible. If you have dinner plans with Doss, you're going to eat something great. Do not cancel because of rain. Even a flood.

Shortly after seven, Doss pulled up in his black Acura. Three of us ran from the subway station to the car. Within seconds, we were soaked through, our wet clothes slapping against the seats of the air-conditioned vehicle.

When we pulled up to the strip-mall restaurant, we made another dash, before huddling, shivering, in our booth. Like a lot of family-run immigrant restaurants, Hopper Hut features a quick-service counter at the front, food in warming trays to serve takeout, with tables in the back. As the only diners that night, we got the best seat in the house, under the wall art that reads, "Sky Is the Limit," though the fluorescent lighting is the same in each booth.

Doss ordered for us. If you know someone like Doss, always let them order for you. Soon the table was covered in hoppers (cup-shaped rice-flour crepes) filled with egg, coconut milk, and lunumiris (a paste of chili, onion, and maldive fish). There was crab curry, eggplant curry, and kothu roti with mutton. That first forkful, a firecracker of saucy, copper-colored, fiery bread, was a Keyser Söze moment, making me realize that the daily meal I'd made for my Sri Lankan coworkers, that seemingly random stir-fry I'd been given instructions on how to make, was a copy of a facsimile of a replica of a bastardized version of kothu roti, cobbled together from available ingredients.

Within minutes of tasting the crab, coated in a blazing paste, I was asking for more napkins. Not just a few. I inherited the sweat glands of my grandfather Irving, who would sprinkle chili flakes over everything and then mop his brow as he ate. I needed a stack to dam the torrent bursting from my head. I kept going anyway, tearing and slurping at the crab leg, sucking the fragrant sauce off its shell, while wiping my forehead with the wad of paper.

What I realized that night is not just that I love Sri Lankan cuisine, but that the best food in my hometown was far from where I lived, outside what used to be the boundaries of the city.

Trips to the suburbs, to Mustafa for Turkish pide (small pizzas covered in roasted lamb or spinach), Lion City for Malaysian char kway teow (noodles, smoky from the wok's breath, coated in pork fat), or Argavi for Georgian khachapuri (cheese-filled bread baked with a soft egg in the center), became all I cared about eating. The latest downtown restaurant, with its million-dollar renovation and dynastically certified chef, seemed so pale, pompous, and unimportant by comparison.

Whether we're talking about first- or second-generation immigrants, we all understand this genre of restaurant: predominantly family operated, immigrant owned, and, due to the high expense of urban real estate, pushed to the fringes of our cities. They're referred to as "mom-and-pop" restaurants when run by white people. I debated over what to call them for this chapter—until I spoke with the founders of a Washington restaurant. "We are proud to be immigrants and how we contribute in a culinary aspect to this country," says Enrique Limardo, the co-owner of Immigrant Food. The Venezuelan-born chef has worked in Spain, Barbados, Doha, Hong Kong, and Bangkok, bringing all of those influences to dishes, which the menu identifies by immigrant group.

When we speak, Limardo and his partner, Peter Schechter, politely explain that America has been a little racist lately. As if that news had not traveled to Canada, which is also founded on the attempted genocide of Indigenous peoples and home to all the same problems of police violence and anti-immigration political factions.

Schechter worked for a long time as a political consultant, including in a think tank where he published "ten-thousand-word think pieces read only by a few people." Wanting to reach a broader audience, he and Limardo created Immigrant Food, with the dining room available for immigrant advocacy groups to hold meetings, an engagement menu that connects diners with volunteer opportunities (giving tours of the DC metro system, practicing mock interviews with Immigration and Customs Enforcement, detention visits, and so forth), and partnerships with five immigration-centered nongovernmental organizations (NGOs). "We wanted to reflect the fact that immigrants have been, are, and will continue to be, in the future, critical to the well-being, growth, and culinary diversity of the United States," adds Schechter. "We wanted to do that not only by the amazing food we serve but making the name reflect the amazing pride of immigrants."

Eaters don't have to live in Washington to support immigrant restaurants. We can make that dining choice anywhere. It helps to know someone like Doss, who can point you toward the best of everything (which is what he does for a living, on the radio, in writing, and through social media and guided tours). Anyone with a car is capable of his process:

1. Cruise strip malls for good things to eat.
2. Keep notes.
3. Bring back friends when you strike gold.

It's admittedly more challenging for folks without cars, and who live in cities—which, unfortunately, is most of them—that don't have reliable and fast transit running to these suburban havens of deliciousness. Navigating downtown Toronto on foot or a bike, as I'd always done, is easy. Like in any city, without leaving the downtown core, I had quick access to cold-brew coffee, fifteen-ingredient cocktails, housemade ketchup, and $185 wagyu sandwiches. For the really good food, though, I had to head to the outskirts. And I didn't own a car. If I wanted to get at the mountains of Cambodian, Nigerian, or Indian cuisine the city has to offer, I had to rely on the kindness of friends like Suresh. Unlike New York, with its intricate web of subways, where you can hop on in Park Slope, Brooklyn, and exit at the insane food court of the New World Shopping Center mall in Flushing, Queens, Toronto effectively stopped building underground transit in the 1970s.

Its two subway lines, which cross in the middle, failing to keep up with an exploding population, leave much of the city inaccessible.

It's the same all over. As long as mayors need to be reelected, public transportation needs, fed by property-tax increases, pretty much never keep pace with urban sprawl. As real-estate costs displace restaurateurs further and further from downtown, immigrant enclaves become more segregated. "Our transportation system is even worse than Toronto," says San Francisco food writer April Chan. "That's why Uber and Lyft were born, out of necessity."

Chan finds the same problems in her city, the most interesting restaurants inaccessible to the majority of the population, who live in the densest part of town. "San Francisco is shaped like your right thumb. All the good food is not on your thumbnail," says Chan. "The best Chinese stuff is no longer within proper city limits. It's down the trunk of your thumb." Chan, who regularly visits Toronto to see family, has never eaten south of midtown.

Searching out good food takes effort. But it is a journey worth taking. When I think about a postpandemic dining culture, I want every dollar I spend to have purpose. It's become obvious how much a single great restaurant can do for a community. You don't have to be a food writer to find these places. You just have to look.

After going to college and getting married in California, Danielle Lehman wanted to live somewhere more affordable. It felt too late for towns like Austin or Portland, which had already become too costly. So she and her husband moved to Kansas City, Missouri, closer to Lehman's family.

The city had all the building blocks—ethnic diversity, affordable housing, a barbecue tradition—of a rich food scene. It also had a lot of segregation, including a historic racial divide on either side of Troost Avenue. "When I moved here, my white aunt said, 'Never go east of Troost. It's not safe,'" recalls Lehman. "I don't think that's true. But that is the sentiment from a lot of people who've lived here a long time."

KC is also spread out. Public transportation isn't great. Even among those who own a car, Lehman sensed people's reluctance to leave their comfort zones, hearing that a twenty-minute drive was too far to try a new cuisine. "That's usually a cover for the fact that they're afraid to try it. I heard someone say recently, 'Don't mess with my pecan pie.' This was in Arkansas. But I think there is a Midwest sentiment of 'I know what kind of food I like. I know what kind of restaurant I want to go to. And I'm not racist, but I don't want to go to a Middle Eastern restaurant. Because I don't know what that food is, and I feel uncomfortable there.' The thing I hear people say here, which I think is thinly veiled racism, is, 'I'm more of a meat-and-potatoes kind of person.'"

Searching for a sense of accomplishment beyond her day job in marketing, interested in food, and frustrated with the cultural climate in KC, Lehman started a podcast to promote immigrant restaurants in her community. Successive seasons of *Open Belly* have gone beyond KC, the focus always on immigrant restaurant owners, their struggles coming to America, as well as the quest to serve their food without compromises.

I had an ulterior motive for speaking with Lehman. My wife had been advocating for us to move to Winnipeg, for similar reasons: her parents, both retired educators, were available and eager to help us with child care. And I wanted to know what it's like to relocate somewhere smaller when eating well is one of your prime concerns. I knew I would be giving up walkability if we left Toronto. I didn't want to give up eatability, too.

But KC is even smaller than Winnipeg. As of 2015, immigrants (composed mainly of people from Mexico, India, Vietnam, and the Philippines) made up just 7 percent of the population there, half the national average.[3] In Winnipeg, nearly 10 percent of the city is Filipino.

Deeper into small towns and suburbs, farther away from urban centers, ethnic culinary diversity diminishes. There are still immigrants, not far away from wherever you are in America, making and selling amazing food. "Cities you wouldn't expect to have really diverse scenes will often surprise," says Andrew Lim, director of quantitative research for the New American Economy, an advocacy organization aimed at smarter federal, state, and local immigration policies. "I think people are often siloed. It doesn't occur to them. Because they're not reading about it, or they may not know people who have been to those restaurants." Lim rattles off a list of seemingly disparate cities—Toledo, Anchorage, El Paso, Lubbock, Salt Lake City, Fargo, and Sioux Falls. "These are places seeing more immigrants in the last fifteen years. So just the idea of their communities as international communities is something that most people haven't become aware of yet."

How, then, does a person become aware, if they're not a member of a particular community? If you're going to ignore those lists of "best restaurants" and "best new restaurants," how do you do your research about where to eat out instead? Let's say, after my hectoring about media dinners, that we've torn up those old lists. That's half the battle. Knowing where to eat is the other half. It's also the fun half.

Once you get the hang of it, this kind of research gets pretty easy. Lehman suggests finding local publications, blogs, or Instagram accounts that focus on inclusivity. I just did this. The top Google hit for my city plus "food" and "inclusivity" takes me to an Instagram page dedicated to advocacy for people with intellectual disabilities. One scroll down the screen lands on mention of a sponsor, an Indian restaurant run by an immigrant family who have been supporting local charities for years. For my next meal out, why wouldn't I want to try this restaurant? This research effort took one minute.

"When you start venturing out," says Lehman, "I'd suggest asking the owners of the smaller shops what places they recommend. When I go into a new place to order, instead of looking on the menu for something that feels familiar, I usually ask the owners which dishes are traditional or maybe even family recipes that I should try."

THE TWO RESTAURANT WORLDS

A major obstruction to diners is that, though the borders are unofficial and blurry, America's restaurants exist in two almost entirely separate realms. One is populated by hardworking cooks from all over the world who speak fluent English and have trained in at least one European style of cuisine, or the food of a country that was colonized and therefore influenced by the British, French, Spanish, or Portuguese. These people are accessible to food writers. We can always reach them for a quote or a recipe. Staff at these establishments hop from restaurant to restaurant, in search of new skills (or better tips), sharing knowledge along the trail. These cooks tend to move around every couple years, in order to learn butchery, bread making, or management.

The other restaurant realm is staffed by equally hardworking cooks from all over the globe who don't always speak English and have typically been trained in a non-European style of cuisine. Children of the owners often work in the restaurants, translating for locals who don't read Cantonese, Vietnamese, Hindi, or Tamil. Cooking-school students don't come to apprentice. Though the restaurant may sponsor visas to bring experienced cooks directly from the old country, the culinary techniques don't cross-pollinate around the urban core's trendy restaurants. This can have a silo effect on recent immigrants. From Portland to Miami, you'll find a Little Cambodia or Little Haiti where whole communities and economies still speak only their native languages. There's a beauty to that. It's also limiting. I've been in Korean, Chinese, and Indian kitchens where the cooks have stayed ten, twenty, even thirty years. That lack of mobility (and often a protectionist attitude about recipes) can help preserve culture. It can also stifle creativity.

Language is a real barrier in reporting on this side of the restaurant world. For the food writer looking for a recipe, these restaurants often require an interpreter. That's how I came to be seated in the subterranean, neon-lit restaurant Chinese Traditional Bun with owner Gaoliang Ma, requesting the recipe for one of the great loves of my life, his dandan noodles. My colleague Jennifer Yang, a health reporter, translated between Mandarin and English.

After 9/11, the former engineer Ma lost his job repairing Russian airplanes and came to Canada with his wife and young daughter. His cuisine is northern Chinese, with a dominant influence from Shaanxi Province.

In the kitchen, Ma had arranged the ingredients for the first of two sauces that form the complex basis of the dish's flavors. Showing me the packages for roots and herbs I'd never seen before—fruit of villous amomum, root of angelica dahurica, rhizome of galanga resurrection lily—he toasted them in the oven and then ground them in a blender, combining them with chili powder and hot oil steeped with onions, dunking a handful of sesame seeds for a minute before fishing them out.

Wok frying demands high temperature adjusted with split-second timing. The control dial for Ma's stove was at hip level. With one hand on the wok and the other stirring, using his knee to adjust the dial, sending flames shooting up two feet in the air, he fried bamboo shoots, garlic, ginger, chilies, and ground pork. Before adding them to the wok, he showed me the containers for black vinegar and doubanjiang (the paste of fermented broad beans and chilies that gives mapo tofu its distinctive flavor) so I could find them later.

Ma's chef prepared the noodles. The man was sixty-four and told me he'd been making them since he was seventeen. Using only flour, water, and oil, his process had more steps than any Italian kitchen I've been in, producing a ropy noodle of intentionally irregular consistency. "Some of these things look so simple because it's been passed down many, many times over many generations. Some of these things are a thousand years old," Ma told me. "This is your job, to communicate."

Finding the ingredients to prepare the dish myself meant a special afternoon wandering around Chinatown to dried-goods stores, showing them pictures on my phone and Yang's notes in Mandarin. The shopkeepers laughed at my requests, as if I were a child asking for a sip of wine. I still found everything.

After learning to make the two sauces, the real lesson I learned was that it was a crime for Ma to only charge $7.99 for the dish (in Canadian currency, just over 6 bucks American). His modest restaurant survived multiple emergency closures. There was the 2003 SARS outbreak, which hit Toronto's Chinatown particularly hard. Then there was road construction that cut off business for months. In December 2011, a cook stabbed a manager, who died of her injuries, the cook eventually convicted of manslaughter.[4] The restaurant chugged along through all of that. Eventually, the elderly chef returned to China to visit family. He never came back, and a couple years after my kitchen visit, Ma sold the restaurant.

That recipe was not just regional. It was family specific. I'll never have it again (while I can make Ma's sauce, his chewy noodles are beyond my skill). But my hunger for it remains. I'll follow any tip, order anything called dandan, searching for that high. We all have a dish like that. Sometimes we can't remember the name of the restaurant or how we got there. But the scent of the food has its hooks in us forever.

One day in Winnipeg, someone told me to check out the dandan at a south-side restaurant. I drove my mother-in-law's car thirty minutes, ordered a bowl, and then sat on the curb outside, disappointed in the routine mix of chili and peanuts.

But as I sat there, fiddling with the noodles, I watched a half dozen people come in and out of the Indian restaurant next door. I struck up a conversation with a waiting patron, who recommended the parathas. I ordered a couple. While they cooked, I grilled him for more tips, furiously typing into my phone's note app. The parathas were outstanding, fatty and spongy in all the right ways, perfect for mopping up a bit of lime pickle, pungent with fenugreek. The rest of his picks were good, too. Plus they led me to a part of town where, unless I were shopping for a diesel truck, I would have had little reason to go.

That's how it's done. Being a curious eater is no different from being a curious journalist or an open-minded tourist. You follow your inquisitiveness, walk into new spaces, seek out people with more information than you, write down what they say, and repeat the process. Sometimes it's amazing what you find just by passing through a door.

Don't be afraid to look stupid or to ask questions that may seem obvious. It helps to let go of the assumption that you know how things like menus or ordering systems work. Also don't be afraid to end up with food you don't like. If ordering a tripe stew you don't want to finish is the worst thing that happens to you today, you're leading a charmed life.

Everyone loves sharing recommendations. If you really like your treadmill, socks, a Vietnamese restaurant, or the plastic gizmo you used to babyproof your kitchen cabinets, it's a pleasure to share the information with others. It's never nosy to ask. We all want to share a positive experience. Even better when it means supporting a small business that may not survive without the community's help.

And don't be shy to walk up to a stranger's table and inquire what they've ordered. It's not like asking someone to the prom. People almost never say no. When you're staring at a hundred-item menu, or dealing with a server who may recommend only what they think outsiders will like, this is the easiest way to cut through the noise.

RACIAL BIAS IN MENU PRICING

Unfortunately, when many of us do encounter these immigrant restaurants without intentionally seeking them out, it's through another kind of list, often described as "cheap and cheerful." That's food-media shorthand (one that's dying out, I hope) for the explicit expectation that certain cuisines are meant to be inexpensive. Long denigrated under the umbrella term *ethnic*, the immigrant restaurateur is probably the most unfairly treated of all the entrepreneurs in hospitality.

Though 14 percent of all US companies are founded by immigrants, in the restaurant field it's 29 percent. Immigrants are twice as likely to start a business as US-born citizens. These account for a quarter of all new businesses started in the United States.[5]

Because opening a restaurant requires capital but no special degree, hospitality is a popular vocation for immigrants, whose education or certification in other professions isn't often recognized here (I know a Syrian geologist who makes dynamite shawarma and fattet hummus). Immigrant restaurants are an engine of family-wealth creation and often a pathway to citizenship. Many act as job centers for incoming family members.

Despite being nothing but good for the economy, immigrant restaurateurs are burdened by the prejudiced assumption that there are cuisines the public is ready to pay good money for and "other" cuisines we expect to be cheap. Generations of food culture have fueled this problem by segregating lists—the best restaurants versus the best cheap eats.

The racist assumption that handmade tortillas or Asian noodles are literally worth less than fresh Italian pasta or artisanal sourdough bread has no basis in fact: in terms of the labor and expertise involved, there is nothing simpler or cheaper about making them. But for generations in North America and Europe, this has been the case: diners just haven't been willing to pay as much for certain kinds of cuisine, relegating entire foodways, without reason, to the discount aisle. This marginalizing of cuisines, no matter how much work is involved, or how costly it is to source ingredients, pushes these restaurants out of urban centers, where higher menu prices are needed to cover higher rent. Diners, who post on Yelp that they could get the same tacos on the street in Mexico for fifty cents, seem unaware that a portion of every bill they see Stateside is paying for real-estate costs or that there's a discrepancy in operating costs between a street cart in Oaxaca and a full-service restaurant in Atlanta.

When an editor asks me to contribute to these lists, I'll suggest that if we're going to call one "cheap," let's call the other "expensive." This never goes over well. Their usual response is to combine the two, pretend the divide doesn't exist, and quietly decide not to hire me again.

Diners may not do this consciously; however, there is a fairly well-established racial bias in restaurant menu-pricing expectations. For his 2016 book, *The Ethnic Restaurateur*, New York University associate professor of food studies Krishnendu Ray looked at menu prices and found a huge disparity between average check sizes at French ($66.45) or Japanese ($68.94) versus Mexican ($40.41) or Thai ($32.50) restaurants. "We can see the patterns clearly when we consider the price of a meal as a proxy for prestige and value," Ray told me at the time. Japanese cuisine, for example, rose above the second-class status with which other Asian culinary traditions were treated as the country became an economic superpower in the 1980s.

So the change has to start with us, the eaters, in how we value people's work. Why will we accept a $24 bowl of handmade linguini carbonara, but breaking the $10 ceiling for noodles in a Szechuan restaurant makes us say it's overpriced? What happens when economically marginalized cuisines attempt to charge what they are actually worth? And how do customers react to a nonsanitized version of what they consider "ethnic" food?

When the health inspector showed up at Favorites, a Toronto Thai restaurant, the owners chuckled. It's usually terrifying when an inspector walks in. They don't give warning, and suddenly you're worried if every fridge has a thermometer, if any food has been left out, if everything in the dry storage is at least six inches off the ground. But these were experienced owners with a half dozen restaurants between them. This was something else. The inspector was following up on complaints of food poisoning here, a dozen in the first four months, more than all the rest of their restaurants combined.

The health inspector found no problems. The owners were not surprised. They knew they ran a clean shop. The reason for the inspection, however, was troubling. Customers, the same ones who frequent the owners' other restaurants—a bistro, two pizza joints, two more "accessible" Thai restaurants, and a late-night snack bar—couldn't stomach real Thai food.

"I don't think I'm saying anything crazy by saying that more or less all the Thai restaurants in Toronto are green, yellow, red curry, pad thai, khao soi restaurants," says Favorites chef Haan Palcu-Chang. "They're seriously skewed to a Western palate. Which means that a lot of stuff is way too sweet, not acidic enough, not spicy enough, missing a lot of the intense fermented fish sauce and shrimp paste that are ubiquitous in Thailand."

Palcu-Chang helped open Vancouver's celebrated Thai restaurant Maenam. After that he continued to cook aggressively flavored Thai food in Copenhagen, at the Michelin-starred Kiin Kiin, and in Paris, as chef de cuisine of Le Mary Celeste. After that he traveled through Asia, consulting, hosting pop-ups, and continuing to learn.

One of Favorites' partners, Monte Wan, had established himself through his Thai restaurants Khao San Road, Nana, and quick-service restaurant (QSR) concept Bangkok Buri. He'll be the first to tell you that he has to cater to local tastes. About five years ago, I was interviewing Wan when I had the opportunity to eat the staff meal with his cooks. In the kitchen with chef Top Srisomphan, sitting on an overturned plastic bucket, I had a som tam (papaya salad) that was the most spicy, fishy, limey thing I'd ever eaten. Srisomphan shared her recipe, which included the clear amber fish sauce nam pla, plus pla ra, a cloudy, unfiltered, "cask-strength" fish sauce (if you're shopping, also keep an eye for bottles with the Vietnamese names nuoc man and mam nem). Though Wan was happy that I'd enjoyed the salad, he said that he could never serve a dish this way in his restaurants. His customers would revolt.

The situation at Favorites proved him right. While the restaurant was busy enough from its launch, the frequently hostile complaints from many diners—not real Thai food, no pad Thai on the menu, portions too small—caught the restaurateurs by surprise.

These attitudes and assumptions, along with the differences in price tolerance, are all extensions of colonial power. The Europeans that colonized this continent exalted their own cuisines above all others. Those attitudes persist today. It's got nothing to do with a rational valuation of the ingredients or labor involved. Mexican moles, Vietnamese bun bo hue, or tiraditos from Peru, though they require many ingredients, spices pounded by hand, layered in at different stages of cooking to create subtle ripples on the tongue, are still subject to the ghettoization of menu pricing.

When Allen Shi opened YiPing, a San Ramon, California, restaurant serving local and organic ingredients in Szechuan dishes, he found that there is a ceiling on what white people will pay for non-white cuisines, that diners seeking organic weren't including this in their expectations. Even the customers who did, he told food writer April Chan, still complained about prices and portion size. "The marginalization of a cuisine is reliably proportional to the marginalization of its people," Chan puts it.[6]

Iberico ham from Spain or prosciutto di Parma from Italy can get away with being displayed on a bar top, sliced and weighed by the gram to be sold for luxury prices. But how would a health inspector react if they walked into a Chinese barbecue establishment and saw unrefrigerated ducks hanging in the window? Actually, I know the answer to this one. Jim Chan, the retired manager of food safety for Toronto Public Health (who checked my fridge with a thermometer when he came to dinner), told me that he had to lean on his degree in microbiology to educate health inspectors who were too quick to hand out tickets based on their cultural assumptions rather than food-safety knowledge.

Another manifestation of our prejudice in dining is where we point the finger when we think we've gotten food poisoning. The perception that Asian kitchens are unclean is such a classic bit of bigotry that it was common for mid-twentieth-century Chinese restaurant menus to include declarations of the kitchen's hygiene practices. "The new dishwasher sterilizes with water at 180°, and the refrigeration chamber is equipped with 'sterilizer' ray lamps protecting foods from all bacteria" reads a menu from the era. "All these new machines result in the most perfect cleanliness in the handling and cooking of foods."[7]

The complaints and inspection still took Palcu-Chang by surprise. "The type of restaurants I've worked in, Michelin-star restaurants, there's a level of cleanliness we maintain," he says. "My standards have not dropped. And our kitchen is completely open."

What a lot of diners don't realize is that the harmful microorganisms (including bacteria, viruses, and parasites) that cause food-borne illnesses can take days to gestate. For example, symptoms of campylobacter can take between three to five days to develop, while norovirus is typically between twelve to forty-eight hours. Food poisoning can just as easily originate from risotto kept in an uncovered steam table or a salad prepared on a contaminated cutting board, leading to cross-contamination from a different food product, as it can from gumbo. Yet diners are prone to blame the last meal they ate, disproportionately pointing the finger at seafood dishes or cuisines outside their cultural boundaries.

The real issue, says Palcu-Chang, is customers who consider themselves more worldly than they are. "It's people not used to eating spicy food, not used to eating some curries that are rich in coconut fat, or some fermented fish products, and, to put it crassly, probably pooping a bit after their dinner. But instead of going, 'Maybe that's because my body isn't used to eating that type of food,' [they think] 'It's a dirty Asian restaurant, and I got food poisoning.'"

It's okay to not like something. That doesn't mean it's bad or that you don't have sophisticated taste. That philosophy may be out of step with our current cultural climate, in which any television show, food, politician, or celebrity is either the best thing ever or a symbol of everything that's wrong in the world.

However, a person can like both fluffy New York–style bagels and chewy Montreal-style bagels. It's even conceivable to prefer one without denigrating the other and tribalizing the difference. Or to choose one version of pizza without declaring that all the others are "not real pizza."

I'm usually not big on tendon. That's why, when eating at my usual dim sum place with a couple of young cooks, I take their ordering suggestions and try it. The dish is fantastic, like a beef-flavored Jell-O. I'd eat that for breakfast, over a bowl of congee, any day. I doubt I would ever have ordered it on my own. And so what if I hadn't liked it? That's why you need a crew. There's nothing like going somewhere in a gang of six (prevaccine, which still seems like a glorious fantasy) and ordering as much of the menu as you think you can eat. When you've got a good-size collection of friends, you tend to push beyond the handful of dishes you think are sure bets and start making riskier menu choices.

The first step is getting out and exploring our cities with an open mind, heading to places with informal names on the map, like "Little India" or "Koreatown," and even less formalized ethnic enclaves, an intersection where one strip mall features an Afghanistan bakery, Syrian pastry shop, Hakka restaurant, and a Lebanese dry-goods store, surrounded by a half dozen shops, all selling cell-phone cases.

PATHWAY OF IMMIGRANT RESTAURANTS

These informal agglomerations aren't there by chance. There's a pattern that most of them, though not all, have followed. "The people that move here, they bring with them the brain trust in culinary knowledge," says Doss, the strip-mall restaurant maven. "It could be that they owned a roti shop somewhere or maybe they come from a really food-rich family. They move here for a better life, no intention of opening their own place. But through the journey of getting a passport, a driver's license, a job here, they get a sense of the culinary landscape and they see that something is missing."

Nobody else, someone realizes, is serving a specific food from back home. And they know how to make it really well. The lightbulb goes off, and they look into how they can open a restaurant, researching budgeting, planning, financing, and licensing. Which, to be clear, is hard enough on its own. "There's a language barrier," Doss says, "So they don't know how to navigate the public health system and policies." Between writing a business plan and securing the proper licensing, everything is daunting. "These families are immediately thrown off downtown because of rent. So they tend to gravitate to micro neighborhoods where there's already a built-in audience."

In the past five years, the cost of a brick-and-mortar restaurant has become nearly too high a barrier to entry. "It's impossible to find affordable rent anywhere. Even in places like Scarborough."

Everyone wants to open downtown. But a Vietnamese family will have better odds where they live because they know there are enough Vietnamese families around the corner who would appreciate their oxtail pho without having to filter the recipe for a wider audience. "That's how most of the immigrant food businesses open. This is a prevailing story. Over and over."

Arrival City author Doug Saunders lists the many names—slums, favelas, bustees, bidonvilles, ashwaiyyat, shantytowns, kampongs, barrios, immigrant neighborhoods, ethnic districts, banlieues difficiles, Plattenbau developments, Chinatowns, Little Indias, Hispanic quarters—for the same global phenomenon of rural populations leaving hopeless poverty to live in slightly improved squalor at the edge of urban centers, in exchange for the opportunity to better their economic fortunes in other countries. These American neighborhoods where you'll find an emerging collection of ethnically linked businesses, which have sprung up in just about every North American and European city, are one of the next steps in that physical and socioeconomic progression. More than just a place of business, the immigrant restaurant is a cultural consulate for communities undertaking that worldwide migration.

It's a very difficult life: for those who are fleeing war, oppression, famine, and poverty and are unable to immigrate through legal means, wages are even lower than the typically low restaurant world, with little workplace protections or access to social services. An estimated 20 percent of America's restaurant cooks are undocumented, living in fear of deportation.[8] The mission for most is to work hard, spend little, and send as much back home as possible. The goal is to eventually bring family over, to provide them with the safety, education, and economic opportunity unavailable back home.

When this works, and when clusters of a diaspora are large enough that there's demand for food from the old country, this eventually shifts the fortunes of the family and the community from working class to middle class, leading to more jobs and increased home ownership, while also contributing to the local tax base and culinary diversity.

Not that every immigrant restaurateur is poor. After the second or third generation of this pattern, immigrants from these countries no longer need to live in the most economically depressed part of town or near the factories and restaurants where their few employment prospects lie. They begin cultivating larger, more affluent communities, usually in suburbs with larger homes, leaving their initial landing pads, the crumbling apartment buildings with poor access to services, for the latest wave of newcomers.

The immigrants who established Chinatowns in San Francisco, New York, and Toronto in the early twentieth century were poor and deliberately marginalized by racist immigration policies. In large cities, successive waves have carved out second and third Chinatowns. More recent generations of immigrants have been from a very different economic class. Since 1997, when governance of Hong Kong reverted from Britain to mainland China, wealthy Chinese have been getting their money out of the country, investing in property, and moving families abroad. Around them, successive generations of businesses have built up, catering to the more well-off clientele.

When I lived in Toronto's original Chinatown, friends who grew up in Markham, the suburb populated by later waves of wealthier Chinese, disdained my neighborhood's restaurants as substandard, dated, and insufficiently gourmet. The restaurants of Markham are bright and glitzy. The dim sum is noticeably better, with higher prices. None are down a flight of stairs or leave a mop bucket parked in the bathroom.

Some of the markers of this economic status are hidden from plain sight. Needing to be many things to many customers, different levels of service are available in ways not obvious to Western diners. Cutting the line at dim sum is sometimes possible by paying dues to an unofficial club, regular tipping to both front and back of house via cash stuffed into red envelopes, handed to the host, bussers, and cooks. That's how you get a quick table when everyone else is standing in line. "It's a huge underground thing," says Chan, whose family does this regularly. "We know we're going to get a seat. They bring out the good hot sauce, with the dried scallops. We don't just get the stuff you scoop out of a jar." She tries never to flaunt this special treatment in front of other customers. It's just part of their dining ritual.

Even without excessive tipping (or bribery, if you want to call it that), being a regular customer anywhere is a pathway to a special type of service. "Welcome back" is about the best thing you can hear from a restaurant host.

So let's say we jump in our cars or buses, find great food, maybe get to know the owners (without prying about the potentially painful circumstances that brought them here), tip as well as we can, and share what we learn widely. That's a reasonable contribution toward a more equitable dining culture. But as win-win as those practices are, immigrant restaurateurs need more and better ways to launch businesses in the first place.

"It's a nice thing. And there'll always be consumers that'll do it," says Geetika Agrawal. "But I think the reality is you need to create good opportunities. How do we develop spaces and places where everybody has an opportunity to participate? It's not our country's strength."

Agrawal is the program director of La Cocina, a business incubator for food entrepreneurs, primarily low-income women of color and immigrants who are already cooking and selling through an informal platform, like online or street markets—not yet legal, and ready to scale up.

Ofelia Barajas had been selling tamales in San Francisco's Mission District for a decade. Though she'd done well enough to bring her daughter, Reyna, to the States, Barajas was tired of getting fined for illegally selling food in the streets and, as the city gentrified, not having as many vendors to sell beside. Ready to formalize and grow the business, Barajas came to La Cocina, which has helped develop and launch more than thirty restaurants and other food businesses since 2005, including the celebrated Besharam, El Huarache Loco, Minnie Bell's Soul Movement, Nyum Bai, and Reem's.

The stewardship extends beyond providing business development and assistance and constitutes something like a mutual-aid network. When the pandemic shut down four out of their six Onigilly locations, Aki and Koji Kanematsu (the ghost-kitchen entrepreneurs from Chapter 1) received free legal aid from La Cocina's lawyers to help negotiate rent reduction. This is thirteen years after graduating from the program into their own shop. Partnering with law firm Gibson Dunn, twenty lawyers worked across twenty-three leases, La Cocina in communication with all of them, sharing best practices and strategies. "It's taken months to get those agreements in place," says Agrawal, disheartened at the feeling that La Cocina's graduates getting any shot at rent forgiveness was a rarity among independent San Francisco restaurants.

Influential nonprofits like La Cocina don't spring up overnight. The seed of the organization was a 1999 study conducted by local economic development organizations such as the Women's Initiative for Self-Employment. The purpose was to understand why women who had enrolled in business programs and written plans for food businesses weren't actually launching enterprises. The culprit was lack of affordable commercial kitchen space.

Over the next six years, an anonymous donor gave La Cocina the shell of a building, which includes a twenty-two-hundred-square-foot kitchen. Then the organization fundraised $1 million to build out the space with a hood system, ovens, stoves, a walk-in and freezer, and so on. In addition to fundraising through foundations, corporate sponsors, and individual donors, they still have to raise a percentage of the growing operating budget each year.

Thanks to the success of the program, and the federal government closing the post office on Hyde Street in the Tenderloin, enabling the city to redevelop the property, La Cocina has been able to expand into retail by building the Municipal Marketplace food hall—another genre of eatery, effectively upscale food courts populated by smaller nonfranchise restaurants, often with fancy cocktails).

Since its inception, La Cocina's budget has risen from $500,000 to $3 million, largely due to the expansion. Given the amount of jobs (and deliciousness) created, that doesn't seem like a lot of money for a city the size of San Francisco. In 2018, for example, Chicago spent $113 million just on police-misconduct lawsuits.[9] While La Cocina is a grassroots organization, imagine if cities invested in such programs.

"What would it mean if every mayor thought that they should have a La Cocina in their city?" asks Agrawal. "Not our organization. But something like La Cocina. And actually wanted to set aside land for that?" There are similar organizations—FoodtoEat in New York,

Comal Kitchen in Denver, Sanctuary Kitchen in New Haven—but they are too few and far between.

Immigrants are a key element in the growth of cities. Dedicating space for incubator kitchens, and providing tax breaks and land grants in order to foster the sort of economic and cultural benefits these small businesses bring, costs peanuts compared to the obscene incentives offered to companies like Google or Facebook whenever the tech giants dangle the opportunity for a new office location. Or the sweetheart deals struck with private sponsors of publicly funded sport stadiums. Or the generous tax credits that states use to attract film production. "From an economic development perspective," says Lim, "business incubators like La Cocina are a smart way to boost local economic activity and, more importantly, spur new business creation and additional job growth."

On a smaller scale, cities attract and foster entrepreneurial immigrants by providing technical assistance, training, low-interest loans, classes on financial literacy, and programs that help establish new businesses. This is all quantifiable, according to Lim's organization, New American Economy. The NAE publishes an index of US cities, scoring them in categories of government leadership (establishing or maintaining offices for immigrant services, hiring immigrants and members of immigrant ethnic groups as municipal employees), economic empowerment (anti-wage-theft and minimum-wage laws, professional licensing), inclusivity (materials translated into non-English, housing or zoning ordinances in response to immigration), community (partnering with local organizations to provide services, providing funding for immigrant organizations and activities), and legal support (separating local law enforcement from federal immigration enforcement, legal aid for immigrants facing deportation). The most recent top ten include some predictable cities, like New York and San Francisco, as well as some less known for these qualities, like Chula Vista, Baltimore, and Newark.

While La Cocina provides training, legal assistance, and kitchen space to participants, the focus is on mentorship and providing access to markets. Helping find locations and negotiate leases is a huge part of that, because one of the ways in which immigrant entrepreneurs are denied opportunity is the outrageous "market value" of commercial real estate in our urban centers.

In an earlier time, explicitly racist policies obstructed immigrant entrepreneurs. For the various Chinatowns in North American cities, the isolation was more implicit, imposed by white landowners who refused to rent based on race, nationality, or religion. These days, the market value of real estate in our cities' densest land makes our downtowns inaccessible to newcomer restaurateurs, whether they're arriving from Syria, the Philippines, or Vietnam. And it pushes these amazing cuisines to the fringes of our urban environments.

Every big city has a financial district (Wall Street in New York, the Skyline District in Houston, the Loop in Chicago), an area where banks, law firms, and real estate offices are headquartered and where a lot of their employees live, work, and play. In the early twentieth century, when these neighborhoods were more affordable, they were dotted with delis and diners run by immigrants from Germany or Greece, sometimes adjacent to Chinatowns that sprang up before urban property values became so polarized. But this concentration of density and disposable income is like steroids for commercial real-estate values.

Restaurant rents are priced by the square foot. In Manhattan, rents range from $75 to $200 a foot, and they can go up from there, for desirable attributes like corner locations.

Hady Kfoury, the Naya founder we met in Chapter 1, pays New York rents that range from $14,000 to $33,000 per month. He estimates the cost of build-out (renovating a space for a full-service restaurant), essential for creating something glitzy enough to attract the status-obsessed modern clientele, at $1 million. That is far beyond the reach of the average immigrant restaurateur. Even if they have the money, Agrawal points to the additional layer of bureaucracy demanded by ground-level locations in new developments. Few independents can hire their own architect, engineer, and contractor, whose skills are needed to integrate a restaurant's needs (ventilation, floor plan, exits, and so on) with a condo tower. That's why the dining options at the base of these buildings are corporate chains, fast-food franchisees, and the high-end restaurants that operate as de facto cafeterias for CEOs.

This isn't just a problem at the ground floor. In order to maximize tiny spaces in urban cores, condo developers in these markets build units without functional kitchens, forcing urbanites to use restaurants as their dining and living rooms. Dining prices reflect (or subsidize, if you want to see it that way) these runaway land values. Enrico Moretti, an economist at the University of California, Berkeley, estimates that when housing prices rise by 10 percent, the cost of local services, including restaurants, rises by 6 percent.[10] The price of a taco in a sought-after neighborhood is not gouging. It's the canary in the coal mine of our unsustainable urban housing situation.

That's why the wonderful downtown neighborhood where you live has such lousy restaurants (alternately, you may live in a suburban area with scarcely any restaurants or exclusively chain restaurants). It's why a developer just announced that they're knocking down a whole block of Chinatown to build condos or why a beloved deli, despite being packed every day, is closing after eighty years of operation. It's why risk-taking restaurateurs move into economically depressed neighborhoods that they can afford, creating the type of dining options that real-estate agents then use to lure home buyers, which in time gentrifies the area, drives up property value, and, by the end of their ten-year lease, forces out those same restaurants.

Because of this dynamic, the lease is the single most important document of a restaurant's success. At a later date, you can always change the menu, the chef, or the style of service. You can paint the walls and switch from oysters to burgers. But you cannot renegotiate a lease until it comes up for renewal. At that point, if your restaurant has helped create a more vibrant neighborhood, you'll be rewarded by a doubled or tripled rent increase.

I knew one landlord who was eager to rent commercial space to community-minded businesses well below the going price point. Later

I found out he had a terminal disease and was trying to do one last good thing. For the most part, landlords, in a behavior that drives Agrawal crazy, usually define "market rate" as what Starbucks or a bank would pay. "Market rate is a made-up number. And it's bullshit," says Agrawal. "It's an arbitrary statement."

This is why part of La Cocina's business mentorship includes steering participants (tenants and landlords) toward establishing rent as a percentage of total business revenue, something that many restaurateurs tell me must be the future of restaurant rent pricing—seeing the astronomical prices as no longer justified, some tell me they'll never sign a new lease that isn't based on this structure. "Rent needs to be a percentage of your total revenue and a healthy indicator," says Agrawal. "A good partner will say, 'Let's talk about what sort of business model you're demanding if you want $10,000 in rent.' That's a conversation you have with the businesses. And we can often have with the landlord. I wish, at a policy level, we can think about that. Because it's no surprise to me that the city has in the last fifteen years really shifted, since there's been such an increase in investor speculation. It's no shock that there's so much empty ground-floor retail in San Francisco. Or what does get built is either an investor-backed company or a Starbucks or some variant."

THE G WORD

High property values limit interesting dining options, prompting us to leave our glittering cities in search of something good to eat. What happens when that process continues, unabated? What does our dining culture look like at the end of that runaway real-estate market?

In the *San Francisco Chronicle*, Justin Phillips has been writing what seems like an ongoing elegy for Black-owned restaurants, the type that used to dominate the Fillmore District in his city. He and his colleagues paint a picture of what seems the very late stages of the city's march toward unaffordability for all but a few. I'd felt the same thing happening for years in Toronto, the Manhattanization of the downtown into a playground for the wealthy. Skyrocketing real estate keeps moving the goalposts not just for immigrant food entrepreneurs but also for first-time home buyers and generally making young people feel like they can afford to live there only for the first few years of their careers or until starting a family.

Food is the perfect prism through which to observe the processes of gentrification. Developers use restaurants to attract new residents, driving up property values. In the process, the food of a poor neighborhood gets gentrified as well, with boutique versions of the cuisines that once made an area desirable displacing the original businesses. On a long-enough timeline, this is the story of just about every neighborhood in every town. Unless you're already rich (nobody buys mansions to turn them into condos) or the land is so unlivable (can't build a Starbucks on a garbage dump), it's just a question of where your home is on the march toward capitalist enhancement. "The pattern of gentrification is common across the country, across North American culture," says Agrawal. "It's how we colonize. This is how white Western culture has built their wealth. This is what they know how to do. It's what we did to Indigenous people of this land. We were like, 'We like your shit. We'll take it. You move to the less good place. Thank you very much.'"

Gentrification seems to follow a consistent pattern, at least in urban spaces. First come the early adopters, the immigrants, the artists, and the entrepreneurs whose only access to commercial real estate is an economically depressed area. They open coffee shops, small bars and restaurants, design firms, micro boutiques. These things are neat and interesting and start attracting interest. Within a few years, the changed streetscape draws larger businesses, hundred-seat restaurants, and gyms, business owners recognizing the potential of the area and able to invest in costly renovations for big spaces. The last stage, which *Eater* writer Vince Dixon defines as "it's too late," is when developers arrive, buying up blocks and building condos. It's possibly naive to think of this as a last stage. As our uptowns, downtowns, east sides, and west sides gentrify, condo developments rolling toward neighborhoods with lower property values the way water travels downhill, available storefronts and strip malls, just small enough for first-time restaurateurs, are disappearing.

If land, like in Manhattan, is desirable enough, there's always the potential for homes to become just another collection of properties in an oligarch's portfolio, formerly lively neighborhoods emptied of residents, reduced to part-time playgrounds for the super-wealthy. "Capitalization and commodification are very strong forces," observes Agrawal.

THE GRAY MARKET

The socioeconomic divide that separates immigrants from prosperity gives way to a geographical one. As cities grow, they spread. The ethnic enclaves that used to jostle up against each other, a block-to-block transition from Little Portugal to Chinatown to the Jewish deli, all within walking distance of the entertainment district, grow farther apart and less accessible to each other.

Suresh Doss mentions a collection of blocks on the east side of Toronto, right on the subway line but not a prime commercial district. A couple years ago, half of these storefronts were empty. Just north of the strip, affordable housing that had been predominantly Sri Lankan has become overwhelmingly Punjab and Bangladeshi. Lately, as rents for restaurant spaces have reached beyond the scope of first-time operators, Doss has seen these smaller lots, traditionally used to sell jewelry and a variety of other goods, repurposed for food businesses. "That stretch has become Bangla Town and Biryani Row in two years. There are places so tiny, if you walk in there, you can't put your arms down. Smaller than shipping containers. You have to slide in, order your biryani, and then slide out. No white person is going there because they don't know it's there. There's no signage."

The micro market won't last long. Within five years, as houses and apartments change hands and chains and franchises knock down walls to expand storefronts, this part of town will be unrecognizable. Because of this, Doss has recently noticed a divergence in the pathway of immigrant restaurateurs, as the latest stage of real-estate pricing shifts these businesses off the street altogether. "Now you meet this South Indian couple that has moved from Madras, about seven months ago. He cooks. She cooks. They both come from a very food-rich family. They live [far away from downtown] in Scarborough, in an apartment building, finding that nobody is doing the food that they want." Like their predecessors, the couple researches the idea of opening a restaurant. "They look at prices downtown. That's not going to happen. They look at prices in Little India. That's not gonna happen. They look for places in Scarborough, and even that they can't afford. Because they just got here a year ago. They have no capital. So what they will do is resort to cooking out of their apartment and serving food using social media as a conduit to tap into their audience."

Recently, this gray market has exploded, expanding tremendously in the couple of years before the pandemic, then exponentially as a result of pandemic conditions. Often this starts without the intention of growing a business. "Let's say this woman's name is Anita. She makes South Indian food for her neighbor who's babysitting her daughter. Her neighbor says, 'This is great—you should open a restaurant.' Anita says, 'I can't do that.' The neighbor tells her neighbor. The next day there's a knock on the door. You multiply that by ten or a hundred. Now the entire apartment building is aware of Anita's food. Everyone's knocking on her door every day. She can't handle this."

What she does next, a step that was technologically unavailable until recently, is direct traffic within the building through a WhatsApp group or a more public listing on Facebook marketplace. "If you go on Facebook Marketplace and you type in the city and the type of food," says Doss, "you'll be astonished at the number of people that are doing this."

I just tried this. I found people nearby selling dosa batter, Hyderabadi biryani, jollof rice, and ayamase, a Nigerian stew of tripe, crayfish, and scotch-bonnet chilies. "There is an audience for this regardless of cliquey food people in the city. And this has all happened in the last twelve to eighteen months."

Given the limits that these entrepreneurs will be willing to drive to deliver an order, this type of food is mostly found in urban centers. At the moment, as much as I want to support immigrant restaurateurs, I'm not sure buying from these gray market operators is as vital as prioritizing established independent restaurants that I hope will stay in business. I have a friend who told me she is not cooking until the end of the pandemic, that all of her discretionary food budget is allocated toward keeping her local restaurants alive. Other people I know are jumping at the opportunity to buy from every new food business they see on social media, which is often just as much about the hunger for newness as it is about supporting furloughed workers. We all juggle this a different way.

Most of the merchants Doss has spoken to see no difference between what they're doing and selling a secondhand phone on eBay. So long as they're not selling out of a storefront, they believe, they're not operating a business and not subject to local rules for food service. "People are strapped for capital and options. It is completely operating in the gray market." But ignorance of the law has never been a good defense. The term *gray market* obfuscates the reality that this type of business is clearly not within the margins of laws governing preparation or serving of food.

It isn't quite like selling your old phone. There's clearly a big difference in terms of public safety. You're not likely to make anyone sick by selling them a used gadget. Whether it's a ham sandwich, cabbage rolls, or oxtail gravy on rice, there's a risk. As a diner, I don't care. I've been to plenty of underground food operations over the years. They're all covered by the same principle: Caveat emptor. "Let the buyer beware." The diner, rather than the bylaw officer who makes surprise inspections, is responsible for assessing and deciding what is safe to eat. If I get food poisoning from someone's home-cooked food, the responsibility is mine for having taken the gamble. At the risk of a false equivalency, I know restaurants and bakeries that are constantly cited for health-code infractions—lack of handwashing stations, food stored on the floor or at improper temperatures, infestation. Despite the requirement in many jurisdictions that food-service businesses display the results of recent inspections, this never seems to diminish customer eagerness for a popular spot.

The rules change from place to place, but generally in America you cannot make and sell food out of your home. However, it is possible to decriminalize this practice. Since 2018, under AB-626, "microenterprise home kitchen operations" are legal in the state of California. As of this writing, Riverside has been the only county to make use of the new legislation, letting home owners turn their backyards into restaurant patios.[11] But others must (or should) be eyeing this regulatory tool for unleashing culinary diversity and stimulating local economies, particularly at a time with so many people out of work.

What about the rest of us? If we don't live somewhere with legislation that helps create a more equitable environment, where more people have the ability to legally support themselves with their cooking, what can we do to foster immigrant food businesses?

The one thing we can all do is spend. I absolutely want my dining dollars to go toward the least-privileged members of the hospitality industry. The restaurateurs who can pay for the downtown rent, million-dollar renovations, and publicity machine will do fine without me. I'd rather be devoting my food spending to immigrants, women, and people of color. I want to see their businesses grow. That's what made our dining choice for Father's Day, which was about more than just my hunger for kothu roti, so easy. I crave Popeye's chicken too. But I wanted Sanjeev Yogeswaran to have our money more than 3G Capital, the Brazilian investment firm that owns the chicken franchise (along with Burger King and Tim Hortons).

In 1999 Yogeswaran came to Canada as a refugee. He was fifteen years old, and his family had paid almost $40,000 to get him out of Sri Lanka. At age sixteen he began working at Pizza Hut; within a few years, he was working at five Pizza Huts, putting in up to eighty hours a week. Except for a brief period when he co-owned a pub, Yogeswaran had spent the majority of his twenty-year restaurant career working for other people. Then the pandemic hit.

It was a Thursday afternoon in March. The restaurants Yogeswaran managed had closed. Two weeks without working was the longest vacation he'd had in two decades. His sister Mirna Yogeswaran, a financial analyst, had been casually catering for years, cooking for friends' parties. The siblings discussed renting a kitchen for two days a week and posting a small selection of dishes for sale, which they would deliver themselves near their homes, in the suburban Ajax and Pickering areas outside of Toronto. With little planning, just that quick conversation, they shared a menu on WhatsApp, telling family and friends that they were offering kochikadai biryani (a rice dish in which a basic dough is used to seal the pot lid so no steam escapes), rice with devil chicken (fried chicken chunks tossed in a vinegar, soy, and sweet sauce with peppers, onions, and chilies), yellow rice with goat curry, and eggplant curry. "Within two minutes we started getting orders," recalls Yogeswaran. "We hadn't started cooking."

They didn't even have the kitchen yet. Cooking out of Yogeswaran's home, that Saturday they delivered twenty orders. In the second week they made lamprais: rice with mutton curry, eggplant moju (pickle), fish croquette, boiled egg, and blachan (a chili shrimp paste), all bundled in a banana leaf. A lot of work and ideal for delivery. By the third week they were packing a hundred orders. They rented a commercial kitchen from 3:00 to 9:00 a.m., when it would otherwise have been closed, and hired one of Yogeswaran's laid-off cooks. By the summer they were cooking and delivering five days a week, with a menu that kept expanding. Requests from customers in farther municipalities prompted them to schedule drop-offs in parking lots with a one-hour window for pickup. By November, Yogeswaran signed a lease on a brick-and-mortar location.

"There are a lot of Tamil cooks in this city," says Doss, who is also from Sri Lanka. "And this pandemic has kind of whipped their ass into shape, in terms of the rogue pop-ups and the Facebook and Instagram ghost-kitchening. There are more Tamil cooks doing something now than ever before."

Though perhaps not intending to, Yogeswaran has merged the gray market with the ghost kitchen. Is it even necessary that his model reverts to the traditional restaurant? At the very least, I think many restaurateurs, for the next couple years, will be betting on this strategy: a brick-and-mortar location optimized for off-premises dining.

In the Bay Area, Agrawal has seen the same dynamic playing out against the catastrophic backdrop of the pandemic. She's observed everything: more immigrant restaurateurs promoting their home-cooked food on Facebook Marketplace; a baker switching from catering cakes for tech companies to Indonesian snacks; a fresh foraged sea urchin sold on Instagram; a group of Black entrepreneurs collaborating on a bake-sale box, or a group of Asian women (all part of the La Cocina program) putting together a snack box; a wine bar partnering with a bagel maker; and so on.

Some of these people are treading water, trying to pay their rent by replacing a portion of the revenue lost from catering work. In some cases this dynamic has been a chrysalis that has given rise to the creation of businesses that wouldn't have existed otherwise, collaborations and creativity born out of necessity.

"For a lot of Americans, who have been here for generations, the market is kind of stable," says Yong Zhao, the founder of junzi we met in our first chapter. "That gives you a feeling that the world is around you to work. One of the benefits of being an immigrant is you change your environment so dramatically. A lot of immigrants, the reasons for immigration is the distressed situation back in the home country. They know the world is never stable."

The lack of faith in institutions, the preparedness for disaster, argues Zhao, makes immigrant restaurateurs better suited to survive this extinction-level event. "Immigrants know you have to adapt to changes. That becomes instinct for changing. You have to fight for everything you have. The current is against you. If you don't swim forward, you get pushed back. That's part of what makes America work."

· 5 ·

The Fast-Food Restaurant, a.k.a. the QSR

> Would you buy a tomato if you knew
> it was picked by slaves?
>
> —GREG ASBED, human rights strategist

LOST IN FLORIDA

It takes a special type of fool to get lost while following GPS. Maybe I'm just used to riding my bike. Or maybe it's the long country roads in this part of southern Florida, the gravelly back lanes that lead to farmland just off of smooth highways. Some of these lines don't appear on my phone's map.

Whatever the reason, once I realize that I'm heading in the wrong direction, which was supposed to be down a short road bordered by tomato farms, the first place I find to turn off is the entry of what looks like a country club. I'd spotted another up the highway: a nicely paved road with a little bridge and a big sign that read Ave Marie. This one says Orangetree. I turn off the highway, into whatever Orangetree is.

Just down the path the landscape transitions from rural highway to suburban streets lined with wide sidewalks and four-bedroom houses. There's a gate, but it's open and there's no guard on duty. I've never seen a gated community before. Impulsively, instead of making my U-turn, I cruise around the streets of Orangetree for a few minutes. I see small children riding their bikes unaccompanied. There's a playground, a middle school, a high school, a men's clothing store, and a church. At the end of one street there are half-completed houses and next to that more land cleared with more foundations being laid. According to local real-estate searches, 36.6 percent of the population has at least a BA, 84 percent has health insurance, and the median household income is $79,502.[1] Not rich, certainly not by the standards of America. It counts as doing well based on national averages. More important, it's far better than how people live just down the road. This seems like a nice place to raise kids. I should probably leave before somebody calls security.

Twenty minutes later, as I get back to town, the sun is setting. I park in the lot of La Fiesta supermarket. Men and women stream in and out. Loud salsa plays out of huge speakers across the street in another lot where a less formal market is set up, a collection of trucks selling tacos, hot dogs, and chicken lo mein and tents loaded with secondhand clothing, suitcases, blenders, and hot plates. There's one guy just selling polo shirts. With no tall buildings to block the sound, the music is audible all over town. It's Friday night. People are already out having a good time, unwinding after a week of hard work. Some are showered, shaved, and decked out in collared shirts and fresh sneakers. Some still wear their long-sleeve jerseys from work, stained dark green at the elbows and chest from working among tall tomato plants. Some walk with six-packs of beer. Just as many carry Coca-Cola. Everyone has a plastic bag of something—chips, instant ramen, candy. Chickens strut across the parking lot. At one point, rooster fighting was popular here. After the county banned the practice, the gladiators were set loose. Their descendants now roam the streets, eating trash, occasionally fed bread or rice by locals.

In the back of a smaller grocer where the shelves are lined with ancho chilies, queso Olanchano, and Goya-brand everything, I buy a few tacos and sit on a bench in the parking lot. Pork fat drips down my chin as I watch buses, returning from the tomato fields, drop workers off in the lot. Some drift into the supermarket to shop for groceries, grab a bisteca torta, or line up to send money back home. Others go straight to sit at picnic tables, bone tired, to wait for buses that will take them back to the trailer parks where they live. Though the unincorporated town of Immokalee, governed by the same Collier County seat that oversees Orangetree, is not what you'd consider a hot real-estate market, the demand for places to sleep here, and shortage of actual housing, enables landlords to extort rent as high as $400 a week, for one-bathroom trailers that are often run-down, dirty, broken, infested, and shared by eight to twelve workers who cannot find or afford better accommodation. The poverty rate here is 44 percent.[2]

When we talk about fast food, or quick-service restaurants, as the food industry labels the sector, we tend to think about giant corporate brands like McDonald's and Burger King, focusing on understandably vital issues like the obesity epidemic and the fight for raising the minimum wage. We'll get to those. But before anyone can cook, serve, or eat fast food, there's the small matter of how these restaurants stock their freezers and pantries in the first place.

In the past one hundred years, as our population has urbanized, we have almost completely removed ourselves from the physical task of growing food. Because agricultural workers are some of the least visible members of our society, they are the most marginalized and brutalized. For every plate of sustainable halibut served over roasted heirloom beets, cooked and served by employees who share profits in an open-book management restaurant that delivers food by bicycle, Taco Bell sells a jillion Cheesy Gordita Crunches. No segment of the hospitality industry consumes a higher volume of raw ingredients than the QSR business. McDonald's is the world's largest buyer of beef, pork, potatoes, lettuce, and tomatoes.[3]

I don't eat a lot of fast food. My father never took us and I didn't play sports, so there were no baseball wins to celebrate with Whoppers or hockey losses to drown in honey mustard. My only tastes of this world came on Friday-night sleepovers at Jamie Nickerson's, where his parents let me watch R-rated action movies and fed me forbidden foods like McNuggets, Kraft Macaroni and Cheese, and, one time, fresh crab (I kept kosher until I was twelve).

But when we talk about restaurants in America, and who gets access to healthy food or good jobs, so much of our conversation revolves around fast food. Along with its sibling segment "fast casual" (which is just slightly fancier fast food, like Chipotle or Panera), this portion of the restaurant industry accounts for half of all sales. On any given day, 36 percent of adult Americans eat fast food, according to the Centers for Disease Control and Prevention. There's no more direct line into the darkest corners of our food system than the lives of the people who grow the tomatoes that end up in our fast food. And Florida produces about half of the fresh tomatoes grown in the United States.[4]

Immokalee is just seventeen miles down the road from the Orangetree gated community, one of several in the area. The residents here, primarily agricultural workers from Mexico, Guatemala, and Haiti, who produce about 90 percent of the country's winter tomatoes (those grown domestically between October and May), are as poor as anyone in America. There's a house around the corner from La Fiesta that looks like a lot of small-town bungalows. Inside this house, until 2007, lived the Navarrete family. Out in the yard they parked a twenty-four-foot truck, in which twelve people were held captive, beaten, and chained, left to urinate and defecate in the corners. The Navarretes transported them in the truck to work in the fields, every day, until one escaped. Six defendants were eventually convicted for these crimes. While this story might be an extreme example of terrifying conditions for agricultural workers, the Coalition of Immokalee Workers (CIW) website lists another eight prosecutions of slavery and forced labor during the same period, all relating to Florida's agricultural sector.[5] And it wasn't that long ago.

Until about ten years back, Immokalee was known as "ground zero for human trafficking in the United States." Then the people who plant, tend, and harvest tomatoes changed these conditions and reshaped the local industry. I'm here in Florida to learn how they did it.

About the same time that the Navarretes had people chained in their truck, Oscar Otzoy, who came here from Guatemala, would wake every morning around three and head to the parking lot in front of La Fiesta. To find work, you had to be there early. If a crew leader boarded a bus of thirty people and said they needed twenty, then ten would have to get off. Whether the drive to the farm was thirty minutes or two and a half hours, there was no pay for that time. Because tomatoes are wet early in the morning, and they should ideally be dry when picked, workers would often have to wait, sleeping or playing soccer, unpaid until it was time to start picking. "You're just losing those hours of your life," recalls Otzoy, sitting in an office at the CIW, directly across the street from the La Fiesta lot.

"And when you start working, you get a bucket like this one," he holds up a red bucket the size of a basketball net. "You hoist it onto your shoulder, fill it, run to get it on the truck, and turn in your tomatoes." Otzoy describes ten-hour days, plucking tomatoes, filling the bucket, and carrying it to be approved by the crew boss. Filled to the top, it weighed about thirty-two pounds. Crew bosses would routinely reject any bucket not "cupped," expecting tomatoes to be piled high above the rim, resulting in a heavier bucket, about thirty-eight pounds, with no extra pay. Whatever the weight, workers received around forty-five cents per bucket.

At every stage in our food system, there's a tension between what food actually costs to make and what people are willing to pay for it. Nearly everyone in the supply chain—restaurant owners, cooks, chefs, CEOs, wholesalers, even customers—has some ability to decide or negotiate what counts as fair value. At the least, we have the choice to walk away from a bad deal. Except for farmworkers. If they don't like the terms, their alternative is usually to not work, for their children to go hungry.

Getting paid for thirty-two pounds but being expected to pick thirty-eight is wage theft equal to 18.75 percent. For comparison, America's lowest earners spend 35 percent of their income on health care. What chance do they have to pay for insurance when they lose a fifth of their earnings from wage theft?[6]

As human rights strategist Greg Asbed describes it, back then if a worker brought a bucket that wasn't cupped, a boss would throw it back, saying it wasn't full. He doesn't mean metaphorically: they'd toss a thirty-pound bucket of tomatoes, from a truck bed, down onto the worker who brought it in. It would bloody or break someone's nose, which would spark a fight; the workers inevitably would lose because the crew leaders had the law on their side. In the rare case that growers got hit with a fine, it was the cost of doing business.

Harassment and intimidation were constant. The demand of sex in exchange for work was common. "In those days the conditions were really ugly," says Sylvia Perez, who worked in the fields between 1993 and 2008. "No access to water, no bathrooms. Really difficult work. Sexual harassment was something you had to deal with from crew leaders."

During this period, an experience elsewhere with watermelons changed Otzoy's perception of what was possible in the fields when working together instead of as individuals. Taking a break from tomato picking, where workers crouch, carry, and are compensated independently, Otzoy joined a group that went to Georgia to harvest watermelon as a team. "When comparing it to tomatoes, watermelon is very different. You're not in a field with a boss who follows you around yelling at you or sitting in his truck with the AC on. You are working as a team. And you forget about everything else because you're so focused." The harvesting process had to be different: unlike tomatoes, which an individual worker can gather in some significant way, watermelons are large and heavy and require a collective effort to harvest. Working like an assembly line, each person would pass the heavy fruit to the worker next to them, who would pass it to the worker after that, and so on, the last one placing it on the truck. "When we were able to fill a whole bus of watermelons, that was a nice feeling, because we knew we would split the payment evenly between us."

During the 1990s, after years of facing these abuses, workers organized, forming the Coalition of Immokalee Workers. They held labor strikes, hunger strikes, and marches—all the things people usually do to bring their employers to the table. None of them succeeded because farmworkers are excluded from the right to form a union and other forms of power that other workers have in America. Nor do they have reliable access to social services, health care, or law enforcement protection: citizenship, language, and geographical barriers all make these workers vulnerable. It's hard to go see a lawyer in Fort Myers when your transportation is a bike you share with six roommates.

And then the *Packer*, a local trade publication, ran a story about the contractual relationship between local grower Six L's (now Lipman Family Farms) and Taco Bell. At a CIW meeting, workers discussing the article concluded that the actual power driving conditions down and keeping them poor resided not with their employers, but at the top of the food-industry chain, with the multibillion-dollar buyers who leverage their volume-purchasing capacity to drive prices at the farm gate down and down, creating the pressure that perpetuated their conditions.

After that, the CIW started organizing consumers to tell Taco Bell that they wanted the companies from which they bought their ingredients to improve farmworkers' lives at the bottom of their supply chain, rather than impoverish them. The specific ask was for Taco Bell to pay a penny more per pound of tomatoes, for that price increase to be passed directly to workers, and for the company to agree to buy only from growers who met new standards set out in a human rights–based code of conduct, which became known as the Fair Food Program (FFP). It took four years to achieve victory in the boycott against Taco Bell.

"We don't believe it's our place to get involved in another company's labor dispute," Yum! Brands senior vice president Jonathan Blum told the *New Yorker* at the onset of the boycott. "It's heinous, but I don't think it has anything to do with us." Four years later, he declared, "Human rights are universal," after giving in to all of the CIW's demands.[7]

In 2005 the CIW signed its first Fair Food Agreement with Taco Bell, including market consequences for growers who violated conditions. Over the next decade, thirteen more major retail food corporations would follow, including Taco Bell's fellow Yum! Brands subsidiaries Pizza Hut and KFC, along with restaurant chains McDonald's, Burger King, Subway, and Chipotle Mexican Grill; major retailers Whole Foods, Trader Joe's, and Walmart; and massive companies including Compass Group, Aramark, and Sodexo, which provide food service to hospitals, stadiums, prisons, and other institutional locations.

If an offense, such as forced labor, failure to fire a sexual predator, or unsafe conditions, is found, the power exists, through CIW's agreements, to suspend sales to participating buyers for ninety days. So in addition to maybe getting charged, possibly being prosecuted, and the slim chance of paying a fine, breaking the FFP rules means that farms are unable to sell to fourteen of America's biggest buyers for three months. For a lot of growers, that's their entire harvest cycle. So the impact for noncompliance poses a dire threat to the viability of their businesses. The commitment of purchasers not to buy from growers that break the FFP rules creates pressure for producers, and the crew bosses they employ, to follow the human rights guidelines put in place by the FFP.

The establishment of the FFP in 2011, with the participation of so many brands, was a major success for workers in Immokalee and for labor organizers everywhere, who were watching to see what happened next. Which is tricky. Because the CIW's system of monitoring, investigation, and implementation, which prevents slavery and sexual harassment in production of the tomatoes in our stuffed-crust pizza, while enjoying a symbiotic relationship with law enforcement, was (and is) entirely self-administered. And they had no one to run the organization.

JUDGE LAURA

We are standing under the harsh, fluorescent glare of fast-food lighting as we place our orders: me, retired New York judge Laura Safer Espinoza, and human rights strategist Greg Asbed. This is a rare place in America where dinner at McDonald's means eating locally. The cashier stares, wide-eyed, at the multicolored Canadian cash that spills from my pocket as I pay for my Quarter Pounder with Cheese Deluxe. Asbed asks for a burger, fries, and mango shake. Judge Espinoza gets a salad and, perhaps because she's human, some fries. Within ninety seconds, we have our food.

It's been a long day. Espinoza has come from a training session with farmers from Cambodia and the Philippines, who have come to learn how they can replicate the CIW's success. Asbed is missing his kid's basketball game to have dinner with me.

No one needs me to describe a Quarter Pounder with Cheese. You know what it looks like, how it smells and tastes. You probably know what it costs, on its own or as part of a combo meal, and if it leaves you feeling hungry, full, or bloated. I keep wishing it was a McDLT.

In the 1980s, the big McDonald's campaign was for the launch of McDLT, not so much a new menu item as an innovation of packaging; a double-size Styrofoam container that allowed the two halves of the hamburger to remain separate until you ate them. The patty and sauce were on one side, fresh lettuce and tomato on the other. Though I know childhood memories distort perception (my grandfather Ben was not ten feet tall), it seemed like an event of importance at the time. Maybe because my TV schedule exposed me to a heavy rotation of the commercial, featuring Jason Alexander singing about how the McDLT keeps the hot side hot and the cool side cool, as if warm lettuce or slightly cooled beef were America's biggest problem of the age, or even the biggest problem with McDonald's hamburgers. "Hey! You say you're getting tired of lettuce and tomato hamburgers that don't quite make it?" Alexander asked the viewer. "Then look at McDonald's new McDLT." Then he began singing with dancers behind him. "I'm talking quarter pounder beef on the hot-hot side. The new McDLT. Hot! Hot! Crisp lettuce and tomato on the cool-cool side. The new McDLT! Cool! Crisp! The beef stays hot. The cool stays crisp. Put it together, you can't resist."

Like "New Coke," another innovation launched in 1985, the product sought to solve a consumer problem that did not exist. No one was unhappy with the existing Coca-Cola flavor and no one ever requested a deconstructed burger. Nevertheless, McDonald's, the world's largest restaurant chain, once prioritized the creation and promotion of this useless change in their product line, including the creation of new packaging, twice as bad for the environment, to keep burger lettuce at room temperature for the brief moment between purchase and consumption. These days, the corporation sources all of the Alaskan pollack for Filet-O-Fish from fisheries certified by the Marine Stewardship Council (MSC), a global sustainability organization. The company buys all of its tomatoes from FFP-approved farms. These choices have a tremendous, positive impact on the lives of millions of people.

Unless you're familiar with seafood-sustainability certification bodies and antislavery activism, you wouldn't have heard a peep about them. McDonald's doesn't allocate the kind of marketing budget to promote these choices that they do for Shamrock Shakes. The seafood sourcing gets a mention on their website's sustainability page. The anti-slavery initiative goes unheralded.

Before taking a bite of my burger, I crack it open and dredge through the swamp of ketchup, mustard, and mayonnaise to find the three slices of pickle and three slices of roma tomato. I lift out one of the tomato slices and hold it up to the light, this sad, anemic thing drawing us all to this place.

As detailed extensively in Barry Estabrook's 2011 book *Tomato-land*, Florida is just about the least hospitable environment to the crop. The soil is too sandy. Threats from insects, which breed in the humid climate, demand a terrifying cocktail of pesticides. Retired New Yorkers belong in Florida more than tomatoes do.

When Judge Espinoza moved here in 2010, she had been retired for all of five minutes. "I'm not good at golf or tennis," she tells me, stabbing at her salad with a fork. While still working as a New York superior court judge, Espinoza had spent part of her time in Latin America, teaching judges, prosecutors, and defense attorneys to conduct oral trials (they were transitioning from the inquisitorial system, in which everything was done in writing, to an adversarial system with spoken trials). As soon as she retired to Fort Myers, to be close to her daughter, she found herself doing this full-time, traveling to lead teams of teachers.

One morning, as she sat in her kitchen listening to the radio, she heard about an area close to her new home that was "known to prosecutors as ground zero for modern-day slavery." Appalled, she began looking around to learn who, if anybody, was doing anything about this. A search that quickly brought her into the orbit of the CIW. "I was very aware of those conditions as a young person. In my teens and twenties, my generation experienced the news from California with grape and lettuce boycotts and the United Farm Workers union effort to better conditions for the people who harvest the food we eat. And I think I made some assumptions that things would have gotten better in the interim thirty-some-odd years. But that was simply not the case. And particularly [with] the kind of forced-labor cases that CIW was servicing, like people chained up in box trucks and held against their will. Networks of three and four hundred workers held in these isolated camps and being patrolled by people with weapons. It seemed like something from another time and place."

Without getting directly involved, Espinoza kept in touch with people at the CIW for several months, learning more about their work, until they had achieved all these FFP agreements with purchasers, including a key one with the Florida Tomato Growers Exchange, a collective of farm owners that had put up a robust opposition. Knowing that they would need help implementing such a far-reaching program, which needed to include workers, growers, and buyers from multinational corporations, but expecting that there was some sort of board set up to facilitate this, Espinoza contacted the CIW, figuring she would volunteer a few hours a week.

They told her that they'd been working twenty years to better conditions for farmworkers in this area and were on the precipice of actually being able to do something completely transformational. However, if not done and implemented properly, it would be worse than if they never started. The workers would be disillusioned. The growers would be angry. The buyers would likely walk away from their commitments. All their efforts would have been dismissed if the FFP didn't succeed in securing the rights it was intended to. It would have been near impossible to convince workers to stand up for their rights again.

"And I said, yeah, I get that. And I'm willing to lend a few hours a week. But I'm really not looking for full-time work."

The CIW had hired a few investigators but hadn't been able to find a director, someone they felt they could trust and that they believed all the different stakeholders in the program—workers, growers, buyers—would feel comfortable with. Who could be better than the retired superior court judge who had just come knocking on their door, asking how she could help?

"They said, 'Here's the thing. You may not realize it, but the entire thirty years of your legal career were just destined for this one moment when you would come across our path.' How are you going to resist that?" Espinoza has been working seven days a week ever since. "They're excellent organizers, and they organized me right out of retirement."

These days, Perez and Otzoy work in the CIW office, fielding complaint calls from workers. They don't hear about the types of abuses they endured anymore. The most common call now is from workers who haven't been paid in a month. If the grower works under the FFP (almost all of Florida's tomato farms do), the CIW will send the complaint to the council that oversees the FFP and investigates complaints. Half of cases are now resolved in less than two weeks, and close to 80 percent in under a month.

Does the success of the FFP mean that McDonald's is a 100 per-cent ethical corporation and I should eat all my meals there with a clean conscience? I don't think it's reasonable to believe there is any such thing. But when I get the craving for a fast-food burger, it makes an easy choice between one of the FFP's partner restaurants and a place like Wendy's, a holdout that is still refusing to pay that penny a pound. I did not receive a response from the company. A spokesper-son did comment to the *New York Times* for a 2019 story, stating that they require tomato suppliers to "submit to third-party reviews of their human rights and labor practices."[8]

The FFP is also evidence that boycotts and grassroots organizing can be effective. So can individual consumers, when we hear about and support those kinds of efforts. After the initial boycott, corporate restaurant partners started signing on without additional pickets. They saw how it would affect their bottom line if they didn't. The change cost Taco Bell, which at the time was buying ten million pounds of Florida tomatoes a year, only an additional $100,000.

Paying a penny more per pound, which the CIW estimates has so far cost these companies $35 million, is nothing to the combined forces of McDonald's, Subway, and so on.[9] They spend that much on ink cartridges. Split between the fourteen participating buyers, that's about $2.5 million each, spread over a decade. It seems like the FFP has made it less expensive to do the right thing than to get caught do-ing the wrong thing.

I know some people who work in crisis communications. That's a wing of the PR business in which a client hires a firm to strategize their response to a scandal. Sometimes this happens after a misdeed goes public. More often, companies retain a firm to create a crisis comms plan in advance, to prepare for the mere possibility of a scandal.

Curious about this hunch, that a penny a pound costs these giant food companies less than crisis communications would, I call some-one who works for one of these PR firms. She tells me that the plan-ning alone doesn't cost too much, maybe $50,000. Keeping a big firm on retainer will run about five figures a month. If some disreputable action becomes public and the plan needs to get implemented, that requires that bodies are thrown at the problem. Account directors bill at $200 per hour and lawyers at double that; maybe a couple of senior VPs at $700 an hour get thrown into the mix as well, clusters of them going into all-day meetings. This can start adding up to hundreds of thousands a month. If it's a global issue, the work could be spread and duplicated between different firms across continents. Never mind the potential for lost sales following bad press.

How far would the CIW have gotten if diners had said that they didn't care about slavery in tomato production? Despite the pessimism that our consumer decisions or votes don't mean anything, they do. Collective action means a lot of individual action.

The strategy hasn't stopped at Florida tomatoes. The FFP has now spread to cover other crops (including peppers, cut flowers, and squash) and to other states: first when Walmart applied FFP's standards to their tomato suppliers in New Jersey, Georgia, South Carolina, Virginia, and Maryland, and then to still more states, including Tennessee and most recently California. Labor activists from other industries, like film production in California and clothing manufacturing in India, plus farmworkers from all over the world, have reached out to learn how they can reshape their industries with this model. Every agricultural product and region needs and deserves a version of the FFP. When they try to achieve it, starting with boycotts, that's when they need our direct support and voice.

"Would you buy a tomato," Asbed asks me as I eat my burger, "if you knew it was picked by slaves?" Most of us, given the informed choice, would not. But outside of Florida, across fields in the United States and Mexico, the conditions that the CIW worked to eliminate are still rampant. There's no fast-food restaurant with a clean supply chain. Chipotle does a little better than most. But they've also been sued in New York for violating the city's Fair Workweek Law (they say they are working with the city to be in compliance) and fined $1.3 million in Massachusetts for more than thirteen thousand child-labor violations.[10] Nobody is perfect.

Unless we pay the premium at a nice restaurant or a farmers market, we're probably eating produce picked by people in horrendous situations. Even then it's not guaranteed.

COVID-19 only reinforced this point. Across America, middle-class office workers transitioned to doing their jobs remotely. People like software engineers, politicians, and food writers were able to restructure their professional realities. Fast-food workers, caught between low wages and a lack of paid sick days, still had to go strain deep fryers and mop floors in person. It was always a danger to workers that there are no federal legal requirements for paid sick leave.[11] COVID-19 made that a public health crisis.

Labeled "essential" and expected to show up on time to assemble burgers for minimum wage, fast-food employees had little choice but to work in arguably unsafe environments. Consider the range of pandemic job loss: from college graduates (1.7 percent) to those with some college education (9 percent), high school graduates (14 percent), and those without a high school diploma (25 percent).[12] In the absence of a coordinated federal response, and with a patchwork of policies at state levels, worker safety was left to the discretion of employers.

With millions of people out of work, America wasted time and resources pushing businesses to reopen, in some states forcing employers to report those employees who wouldn't return to work. We've been desperately, and fatally, trying to patch cracks in the foundation of our economy—in which poor people are the stones and low wages the mortar—instead of concluding that it is beyond repair and needs to be repoured as a new concrete foundation.

From California to Illinois to Florida, fast-food workers were told not to wear masks (for fear of scaring customers) and then forced to make their own out of hair nets. Complaints of workers not informed by management that coworkers had tested positive for COVID-19 became frequent.[13]

In April 2020, workers from a variety of fast-food companies began staging strikes, asking only that they be provided with protective equipment—masks, soap, gloves—and paid sick days. Burger

King employees went on strike following the COVID-related death of Angela Martinez Gomez, who was allowed to keep working for a week while she displayed symptoms.[14] Coworkers allege that managers told them that Gomez, who was trans, died as a result of hormone injections.

In Immokalee, where the privilege of self-quarantine is not available to workers who share a trailer, the CIW attempted to prepare for COVID-19, imploring the state to set up a field hospital. "These people can't self-isolate. And they can't work remotely," says Lisette Morales, a photographer who teaches art to children in the community. The labor of growing America's food, and the danger to those who do it, does not stop. "And when day care closed down, someone had to stay home with the kids." Morales went to take photos at a public testing event and found it sparsely attended. Workers, she believes, were afraid that if they tested positive, they would be ostracized, unable to work and pay their bills. By June international relief groups Doctors Without Borders and Global Response were active in Immokalee, where about 5.5 percent of the total population tested positive.[15]

WHAT IS A FAIR WAGE?

When our meal is cheap, it costs us somewhere else. Probably it's bad for our body, and we pay with poor health outcomes, which cost us all. Mostly, cheap food comes at the price of exploitation of workers, animals, and the environment. What possible dining choices can we make when eating fast food to offset that?

On March 15, 2020, the day America's restaurants started closing dine-in service, President Trump got on a call to discuss the impact of COVID-19 with leaders from McDonald's, Domino's, Chick-fil-A, Subway, Papa John's, Wendy's, RBI (Popeye's, Burger King, Tim Hortons), Raising Cane's, Yum! Brands (Taco Bell, KFC, Pizza Hut), Darden (Olive Garden), and Bloomin' Brands (Outback Steakhouse).[16] Amid all the closings and job losses, you don't have to worry for these companies. These are some of the main funders of the National Restaurant Association, the lobbying arm of the chain restaurant industry, known as "the other NRA."

In the second quarter of 2020, when independents were closing by the tens of thousands, Papa John's, Domino's, and Wingstop tripled their online business.[17] In the third quarter, they reported double-digit same-store sales growth.

While independent restaurant owners clutched at any life raft available to stave off closure, at the other end of the market fast-food brands like Dunkin' Donuts (now just known as Dunkin') and Chipotle have been transparent about how these closures are real-estate opportunities for them. In August 2020, a collective of executives from chains like Ruby Tuesday, &pizza, and Qdoba Mexican Grill formed FAST Acquisition Corp. to take advantage of the desperation among independent restaurateurs.[18]

QSR was more prepared, and fared far better, than any other format of restaurant during the pandemic. Food made to be eaten off-premise and served through a minimal interaction with the diner needed only a few tweaks to adapt to the pandemic. Even with these advantages, prioritizing employee health by providing protective equipment and paid sick days was asking too much of these companies.

The other NRA was singled out by the National Council for Occupational Safety and Health as one of the country's top offenders at failing to protect workers from the spread of COVID-19. "A key method to slow the deadly coronavirus is for those who become sick to stay home to prevent the spread of infection," reads the report. "This life-saving strategy is difficult to implement in the United States, the only developed country in the world that does not provide paid sick leave for all workers. Why is the U.S. so far behind other countries? One reason is a years-long lobbying effort by the National Restaurant Association."[19]

In 2016 the NRA spent $3,930,000 on lobbying and $1,188,888 on direct campaign contributions.[20] When everyone else was asked to shelter in place, fast-food and meat-processing workers were told that they were needed. It wasn't because the country didn't have other sources of food, but because the supply chain dare not be interrupted and the leaders of these industries had a president who prioritized business over public safety.

As of 2020, there were 4.2 million fast-food workers in America. Their median yearly salary hovers around $23,000, and as of 2013 one-fifth of them lived below the poverty line.[21] Unable to afford time off, and lacking paid sick leave thanks in part to the NRA's lobbying, fast-food workers were backed into a dangerous corner.

While many of us get our start in the workforce at fast-food restaurants, these jobs are not summer gigs for teenagers. The majority of employees are adults who need these jobs to make a living. (What kind of business model would it be if all the employees were short term?) Yet the tip from McDonald's to its own employees, during the short reign of its McResource page, intended for employee health and financial advice, was "Breaking food into pieces often results in eating less and still feeling full" (a spokesperson said the suggestion was taken out of context). A 2015 study by the Berkeley Center for Labor Research and Education found that 52 percent of fast-food workers rely on some form of public assistance programs. That's not just tragic and unfair. It also means that the low wages these private enterprises provide are subsidized by tax dollars, to the tune of $152.8 billion a year.[22]

Since 2012 fast-food workers have been organizing under the Fight for $15 banner. These are people working for the major chain restaurant brands, usually paid the minimum wage, or a subminimum wage, having income stolen from them through unclocked work hours, pay tied to tips that rarely materialize, or overtime hours rolled into the coming week to avoid paying time and a half.

Despite the reality that everyone's rent goes up every year, federal minimum wage has not increased in more than a decade; it has been stuck at $7.25 since 2009.[23] One of the first executive orders President Joseph Biden signed after taking office raised the minimum wage for federal contractors to $15, a potential first salvo in a broader effort. As of this writing, based on inflation, fast-food workers are making less now than when there were only four *Fast & Furious* movies (there were eight when I started this book, and nine at present, not counting the spin-off *Fast & Furious Presents: Hobbs & Shaw*).

So far, the wage campaign has been quite successful at municipal and state levels. New York, San Francisco, and Seattle, cities where the cost of living is far higher than the national average, have all raised their local minimum wages to $15. California, Connecticut, Illinois, Maryland, Massachusetts, New Jersey, and New York have passed legislation that will gradually do the same.

Introduced to Congress at the beginning of 2019, the Raise the Wage Act (HR 582) would have increased the stagnated federal minimum wage to $8.55 within a year and to $15 within five years, and thereafter to keep pace with inflation. It would have also phased out the subminimum wage, that lower-than-minimum wage that can apply to workers with disabilities, workers under twenty years old, and tipped workers.[24]

As an issue fairly split along party lines, the Raise the Wage Act passed a Democrat-controlled Congress and was sent for approval to the Republican-controlled Senate, where it was expected to die, barring a reversal of political fortunes. Following the 2020 election and the runoff elections that changed the balance of power in the Senate, the bill came into play again, tacked on to the $1.9 trillion stimulus package aimed at rescuing the economy from the ravages of the pandemic. Then, between a parliamentarian (a bipartisan referee of the Senate) ruling against the wage-increase inclusion and lack of unified Democrat support (seven party members voted against it), the federal $15 wage fell back down to earth for now.[25]

The other NRA, when they're not seemingly obstructing fast-food employees' rights to a safe working environment, or connecting burger magnates with policy makers, puts a tremendous effort into opposing local and federal attempts to raise the minimum wage and paid-sick-leave benefits. Over the years, it seems they've been pretty successful at it. The basic strategy is fear: they argue that raising the minimum wage will hurt small businesses and eliminating the subminimum wage will hurt employees and erode service.

"The tip credit allows tipped-employees to earn far more than the minimum wage, while helping to reduce labor costs for restaurants and others that operate on thin profit margins," wrote Shannon Meade, the NRA's vice president of Public Policy and Legal Advocacy, in a statement to Congress. "Tipping creates major earning potential for tipped employees and fuels the high-quality guest service that is a hallmark of the restaurant industry."[26]

Yes, the verb *fuel* is doing a lot of work in that sentence. And no, we're not going to get dragged back into the tipping debate from Chapter 1.

Depending on which economist you ask, they will tell you either that raising the minimum wage will reduce poverty or that it will cost jobs. Sometimes, like when the Congressional Budget Office assessed raising the minimum to $15 by 2025, they predict both, with the CBO forecasting that it would lift 1.3 million Americans above the poverty threshold, while another 1.3 million Americans would become jobless. Whatever your economic point of view, if you cherry-pick evidence, you'll find what you need to support it. Ordinary noneconomist diners are similarly inconsistent. When asked, we tend to be in favor of paying people better. But when it's reflected through higher prices, like the 4 percent surcharge on restaurant bills for Healthy San Francisco (to subsidize medical costs for employees), we complain.

In 2015, Seattle began rapidly raising its minimum wage, from $9.47 to $11. It hit $13 in 2016 and at the start of 2021 went to $15 (or $16.69 for companies with more than five hundred employees). Dueling studies—one from the University of California, the other from the University of Washington—declared the change wonderful and terrible, respectively. The first found that the raise had had no discernible effect on employment, while the second found a loss of earnings due to employees being offered fewer workable hours. Are both right? Are both wrong? In my home province of Ontario, the minimum wage went through a similarly long-delayed jump from $11.25 in 2015 to $15 in 2019 (this is in Canadian dollars, and Ontario ended up stopping at $14). The province saw a 4.5 percent year-over-year job loss, mostly in the fifteen- to twenty-four-year-old worker range.[27] Over the same period, in "an era of sluggish wage growth," the same age group experienced a wage increase of 18.24 percent.

Behind closed doors, I had cooks tell me that when the minimum wage went up, their chef-restaurant bosses immediately switched them from hourly pay to day rates—a set compensation amount no matter how many hours you wind up working. What we saw publicly, rather than massive job loss, were streamlined menus and job stagnation. More little restaurants focusing on producing one thing well, like the sudden preponderance of shops only making fried chicken sandwiches. (This was also a reaction to rising beef prices, a result of a drought-induced spike in the cost of hay and increased beef export demand from an expanding middle class in China.)

It might seem like too much at once for the Raise the Wage Act to take on the elimination of the subminimum wage on top of increasing the minimum wage. But the subminimum wage is the basis for a time-honored form of wage theft in the restaurant business: reclassifying nontipped workers (such as checkout-counter staff) as tipped workers in order to pay them less.

Reclassifying is something I've been bumping up against more often in recent years. Though it's not like businesses advertise this. You may have noticed lately that, when you settle up at bakeries and other food shops, the payment terminal has started asking if you'd like to tip on your purchase. Which, on its face, is confusing: Isn't tipping supposed to be in compensation for service, like the attention of waitstaff at a sit-down restaurant? In theory, yes. But this categorization is starting to erode. When I encounter this tipping prompt now at someplace like a bakery, I ask the person behind the counter (always with respect and never if there is a line behind me): Do you get paid a living wage? Or is this tip because the business gets away with paying you a subminimum wage?

"We've already seen this grow," says Saru Jayaraman, the labor activist we met in Chapter 2, describing tip creep beyond the expected venues of nail salons, car washes, hairdressers, and airport valets. "We're now seeing it grow to retail and tech. You walk into a retail outfit, they turn Apple Pay around, and you're asked to tip at a flower shop or when you're getting bottled water at a coffee shop. And suddenly that worker can be classified as a tipped worker and be paid two dollars. As long as there is a two-tiered wage system, you'll have companies do everything they can to utilize that subminimum wage because it's cheaper having nontipped work, including what's traditionally done by back of house, done by tipped workers. And you'll see other industries start to say, hey, if they get to pay two dollars, we should too."

When workers are paid the subminimum wage, employers are expected to top off the federal minimum, to bring earnings up to the state minimum, if it's not reached by tips. That tip credit system is full of holes. "The solicitor general, under Obama, said it's impossible to enforce," says Jayaraman. "When they were engaged in their best enforcement, they found an 84 percent violation rate with regards to complying with that two-tiered system. And under Trump, they've basically revoked all protections. The Department of Labor reported that we are the industry with the highest rates of wage- and tip-theft violations. And it is compounded by our absurd two-tier based system, which is a legacy of slavery."

There is some reason to hope that the Biden administration will be more labor-friendly and willing to scrutinize wage and tip theft. It's early, though. I'll believe it when I see it.

Legislation isn't even the biggest hurdle: tips are probably harder to get rid of culturally than legally. Tipping is like cigarettes, a product that would never be proposed, much less approved, by government regulators today. It's grandfathered in as part of our expected behavior. We can, however, eliminate the subminimum wage, installing a floor under the earnings of tipped workers. And we should.

If tipping is truly a fair and voluntary practice, it can continue to exist on its own, as a choice made by employers, employees, and consumers. Then tips can genuinely become what the propaganda tells us they are: a reward for outstanding service.

The subminimum wage is a legal mechanism that forces that choice on everyone. The legislation is already there. It needs public support to stand up to its opposition—lobbying by the NRA.

Jayaraman's organization, One Fair Wage, has been campaigning to eliminate the subminimum wage in the forty-three states that haven't already done so. Following the pandemic, Jayaraman says she's been approached by more than two hundred restaurants from across the country wanting to transition to a full, livable minimum wage.[28] "There is a tremendous momentum to shift toward the elimination of the subminimum wage, to have what California and quite frankly some other countries have, a full minimum wage and tips on top. That is a stepping-stone toward ultimately livable, professional wages in the industry."

RISE OF THE BURGER BOTS

The final cruelty of this long fight for livable wages is that by the time it's won, fast-food jobs may be gone.

If you've been to Creator in San Francisco, and seen the robot cooking burgers, you may have also begun to question how much longer humans will be needed to make Whoppers at all. The elegant mass of machinery, suavely color-coordinated in white, copper, and blonde wood, provokes some important unanswered questions about how automation will reshape the dining industry. Before we address that, let's be real about Creator restaurant and its burger-making machine. If, by the time this is published, my species has been crushed under the heel of its metallic oppressors, I will regret saying this, but the burger robot is cool as hell.

Unlike the automated woks at Spyce in Boston, which fry up presliced and preportioned ingredients, the machine at Creator is fed whole brisket and chuck, pickles, tomatoes, and all the other fixings. Never mind that it slices garnishes; it bisects, toasts, and butters buns;

it grinds and sears beef and squeezes out doses of ketchup measured to the milliliter. Creator's ridiculously perfectionist machinery can churn out a "loosely packed" and "vertically aligned" bite, as promulgated by Heston Blumenthal's television show *In Search of Perfection*, meaning that the grain of the burger will run in the same direction as your teeth so "you're biting down onto the fibers and not biting across them."[29] I've eaten a lot of burgers in my life, and I've never found the alignment of the grains to be an impediment. Like the supervillain who thinks that the solution to a resource shortage is using a magic glove to kill half of everyone in the universe, the advanced-idea mechanics of grain alignment borders on self-parody. With so many problems orbiting the nucleus of the fast-food burger, this was not the one I wanted our best engineering minds to solve. Still, if only for its capacity to grind beef to order—a genuine culinary benefit—the machine is an impressive feat of innovation and a sign of things to come.

The savings in labor costs, according to Creator's messaging, allows the restaurant to reallocate spending on higher-quality, more sustainable ingredients and offer better working conditions for the staff it does have.[30]

Take one glance at this marvel of the modern age cooking the most popular food item in America and your first question is: Will the country's biggest purveyor of hamburgers, McDonald's, which has already been pursuing automation in various aspects of restaurant operation, buy Creator out or attempt to replicate its technology? Founder Alex Vardakostas insists that he is not looking to sell to the highest bidder. "Should Creator partner with other restaurants in the future, these partners would need to hold shared values and principles in ingredient sourcing and producer partnerships," he says, listing sustainability of operations, carbon-footprint consciousness, transparency in food preparation, and worker growth opportunities.

The restaurant sources pasture-raised beef from Country Natural Beef, a co-op of family-run cattle ranches. Salad greens are produced by Plenty, an indoor, pesticide-free vertical farm. Their packaging is compostable. Staff start at sixteen dollars an hour and are entitled to unusual perks like book budgets and paid breaks for reading.

Vardakostas's position is that Creator's machines will do the dirty work of cooking so that humans can develop other skills. The belief that automation will free us up to pursue more cerebral activities is a classic argument of technocrats. In some areas of our lives, like out-of-office email replies, that's true. But if you believe that manual-labor robots are just here to help, without disrupting our job market, talk to an autoworker.

Don't expect the Terminator to be recommending wine pairings the next time you go out to a high-end restaurant. In the full-service mid-range, R2-D2 isn't going to be inspired to concoct a lunch special from the zucchini blossoms growing in your neighborhood bistro's rooftop garden. However, at the fast-food level, where profitability has always been about sourcing the cheapest ingredients or finding efficiencies in the repetitive assembly-line cooking, automation will displace jobs as soon as it is cost-effective to do so.

As far as technological capability, we're not talking about the distant future. "I think for sure at Starbucks, within five years, you could have a robotics system that would be able to replace at least 80 percent of what a barista does," says Nima Fazeli, an assistant professor with the Robotics Institute and the Mechanical Engineering Department at the University of Michigan, Ann Arbor. "The hard part is where it has to interact with people. The random human element is really hard to predict as a roboticist."

Fazeli works on inference, modeling, control, and learning algorithms applied to robotic manipulation—in other words, the science and art of robots interacting with the physical world. He says that taking a customer's order, grinding beans, steaming milk, even spelling your name wrong: these are tasks a machine will do just fine. But what happens when a customer jumps over the counter, or tries to pay with foreign currency, or any number of variables for which engineers have not provided contingencies?

"The traditional, old-school way of robotics is rule-based systems, in which you have this deterministic set of rules and the robot looks up which rule applies where and executes something," says Fazeli. "And that works great as long as the engineer who designed those rules is able to anticipate all the things that are going to happen. The issue with real-world robotic deployment, especially in unstructured environments, where it's very difficult to anticipate all this variation, is that you just cannot come up with enough rules. A robot eventually gets confused."

These technicalities aside, the larger issue is financial viability, for which we have to consider the capital investment versus profit. "I don't think people realize that there's this huge back-end cost, not only of engineers' time, but also of R&D that goes into this. Many of these things are possible. It's just that a lot of them are not economical."

Now that Fazeli brings it up, let's talk about cost. Yes, if I somehow get Will Smith to star in my movie, it will make money. Now, however, it has to make enough to cover the enormous expense of hiring one of the world's highest-paid actors.

A cooking robot, like a wood-burning pizza oven or a marble floor, is an upfront cost that has to be amortized over a long period. I don't know how much it costs to develop a headline-grabbing burger-making robot, but I know it isn't cheap. Creator declined to comment on how much they have invested in R&D or how long it will take them to balance their sunk costs. Looking at the pedigree of their consultants— engineers, roboticists, designers, chefs, and restaurateurs formerly of Tesla, NASA, Apple, Walt Disney Imagineering, Chez Panisse, Momofuku, The Fat Duck—and a reported minimum of $18 million invested in development, I think it's fair to say the $6.07 burger won't turn a profit.[31] Not without Creator growing to a lot of locations or selling the technology. "If you have gifted engineers that are able to do these things, fine," says Fazeli. "The question is whether that's economically viable. It depends on the company. For Amazon it's worth it because they're so big that these systems are going to save money for them."

Pizza, if you're doing it right, can be one of the most delicious, satisfying meals to eat. Even when you're using imported 00 flour and San Marzano tomatoes, it's one of the most profitable foods to sell. I spoke with a couple people in the pizza business about the possibility of automated labor. One, who runs a group of full-service pizza restaurants, says he's been looking into it. For dough making, portioning, and stretching, he thinks we're nearly there. There was a company in California, Zume, that got some buzz for delivering pizza made in a roving kitchen, which was installed in a truck packed with automations rather than workers. They've already folded their robot pizza plans and rebranded as a food-packaging company.[32] Another pizza impresario, one who operates more than two hundred franchise locations, tells me it won't matter how good the tech is, until the cost comes down. These robots won't be feasible for his operation until they cost less than $200,000 and can be maintained by someone with a high school education, he says.

Though Vardakostas insists that his goal is to build a company, rather than sell his technology, and says that he would partner only with companies that share his values, the big players have to be sniffing around.[33] The QSR chains are too scared by minimum-wage hikes to not consider replacing workers with machines. They've already done it successfully with ordering kiosks and app purchasing, a movement to eliminate cashiers that the pandemic has sped along.

Automation in fast-food cooking is inevitable. If you can create a machine to cook burgers, you can do it with burritos, ramen, and soy lattes.

No, fast-food cooking jobs are not the best jobs, certainly not the middle-class, secure union jobs tens of thousands had in car manufacturing, until they were displaced by automation and free trade. But before the pandemic, there were 4.2 million Americans employed this way. They are some of the most accessible jobs in America, and they pay horribly. As movements like Fight for $15 gain momentum in their campaign for livable wages, automation will become an even more appealing alternative to corporate shareholders, compared to their nightmare scenario of paying employees fairly for their work.

The fast-food sector's convergence of technological advances and rising wages pushes us toward an automation disruption that will affect many workers' lives. The only question is the time line. Which means we can do something more than force workers to make Filets-O-Fish for $7.25 an hour until their jobs evaporate. We can and must plan to create new and better opportunities.

In their 2019 paper, "Automation and a Changing Economy," Alastair Fitzpayne, Conor McKay, and Ethan Pollack of the Aspen Institute identify policy initiatives to manage the transition from an increased automation disruption.[34] The focus of their advice is reskilling, as outlined in a four-part strategy that includes worker-training tax credits for employers, government investment in wage subsidies and education subsidies (because it costs less to help people get jobs than to let them slide into poverty), better unemployment payments and services, and targeted investment in business development for areas hit hardest by automation.

Even before the pandemic, the paper's authors saw this investment necessitated by a decline in employee training. The researchers found that between 1996 to 2008, the percentage of US workers receiving employer-sponsored or on-the-job training fell from 42 percent to 36 percent. Suggesting that this will continue to decline, they cite a recent Accenture survey of twelve hundred business leaders in which 74 percent said that they intend to use artificial intelligence to automate tasks in their workplace over the next three years, but only 3 percent plan to significantly increase investments in training over the same time period. That leaves a hole you could drive a truck full of burger robots through. So what happens to those workers? Where is the National Restaurant Association, currently decrying public health lockdowns as unfair, writing letters to Congress, when it comes to the long-term job losses that workers in their field are facing?[35]

There is currently legislation similar to Fitzpayne, McKay, and Pollack's recommendations being proposed. The Investing in American Workers Act was introduced in the Senate in 2017, followed by a companion bill in the House of Representatives in 2018.[36]

None of this detracts from the burgerbot looking neat, and doubtlessly making precision, quality, delicious burgers (with grain alignment!). While I don't think fast-food jobs will evaporate overnight, a ten-year time line is a realistic projection for how long it will take for automation to take over the sector. It also offers a real opportunity for us to plan for that job loss and the reskilling necessary to offset it.

FOOD DESERTS WERE NO ACCIDENT

One thing that's unlikely to change no matter how our burgers get made is what they do to our bodies. If the labor-automation crisis is five to ten years down the road, what about the health crisis today and how it is exacerbated by fast food? Before counting obesity and diabetes, heart disease alone kills 655,000 Americans every year.[37] Poor nutrition and lack of exercise are primary causes. And the fast-food sector, though it generates much-needed employment, also provides an abundance of cheap, unhealthy food.

Another problem is that as kids we are inundated with junk-food ads. By the time we reach school age, we're seeing a dozen food ads a day, mostly emphasizing toys and movie tie-ins. Yet by the time we graduate high school, public education hasn't taught us so much as how to cook broccoli. Learning where food comes from, how it's grown, how to cook it and make it taste good, and how to meal plan, grocery shop, and budget are a necessary part of any solution to our diet-related health problems, as is making healthy food widely available and affordable.

As a cardiologist once told me, on an individual patient level, we're not big on prevention. We'd rather roll the dice with surgery next year than eat salad today. On a societal level, we choose to incur the financial burden of cardiovascular diseases (CVD), rather than teach cooking skills in grade school beyond the fleeting weeks some sixth graders spend on "home economics." In my grade 7 home-ec class, we sewed a stuffed animal and made tomato sauce and a cake—apparently that was all the life prep we needed.

First, let me give you some great news. We're not dying from CVD as frequently as we were a few decades ago. Between 1980 and 2007, thanks largely to the decline of smoking, plus advances in medicine, the mortality rate from CVD decreased from 544 per 100,000 to 251 per 100,000. It's continued to drop, down to 198.8 per 100,000 by 2017.[38]

The bad news is that we're not preventing these illnesses, merely living with them. That both detracts from quality of life and is expensive. Between medical costs and lost productivity, the United States spends $219 billion a year on cardiovascular disease. That's the budget of 1,095 Marvel movies. Here's some more bad news: Almost half of US adults have some form of CVD. It kills more people than cancer. It's the number-one cause of death in America and accounts for 17 percent of medical spending.[39]

When I purchase a ten-piece of lemon-pepper boneless wings from Wingstop, even if I make it a combo with fries and a twenty-ounce drink, am I making poor children sick? No. But I can't ignore the impact of this industry on overall public health.

Wouldn't it be great if there was a fast-food choice that made a positive impact on America's obesity epidemic? It would. And many well-intentioned entrepreneurs have tried to scale that mountain.

Yes, there are businesses operating in the QSR segment aiming to combat the model of serving unhealthy food as cheaply as possible. Though finding a fast-food restaurant with a progressive eye toward health outcomes is even harder than finding one with good labor practices.

José Andrés, who formed World Central Kitchen in response to the 2010 Haiti earthquake, has spent a lot of the past decade feeding people in crisis situations, in the Dominican Republic, Peru, Uganda, and Cambodia. More recently, WCK began doing this on American soil, producing meals to feed Americans dealing with food insecurity as a result of Hurricane Maria in Puerto Rico and then the pandemic. Andrés's restaurant company, ThinkFoodGroup, has even been able to make progress in the QSR space, with the Washington-based Beefsteak restaurants, which replace environment-destroying beef patties with good tomatoes served inside soft brioche buns with some crunch from pickled onions and sprouts and gooeyness from caper mayo. All menu items are under ten dollars. It's vegetable focused, with chicken sausage available as an option. The menu skews toward healthier fast food, with nothing fried. If you live near one of the locations, great.

Everytable in LA has a similar approach (bowls and wraps with no deep frying) and price point, mostly from grab-and-go display fridges in their nine locations. Plus they have a unique twist: those prices vary by location. In communities that are generally underserved by grocery stores and where fresh food is hard to come by, like Watts and Compton, all menu items have one price of five dollars; in affluent communities like Brentwood, it's eight dollars. Wealthier clientele pay a premium for healthy fast food in order to subsidize the same product in areas that don't have as many good options.

The most ambitious enterprise of this nature was probably Locol, a collaboration between restaurateurs Roy Choi and Daniel Patterson. The idea was to create a QSR brand in the poorest neighborhoods featuring healthier versions of fast-food staples. Locations started shutting down within two years. It's unclear what went wrong. It could have been the well-known chefs parachuting into a neighborhood that was not theirs, instead of partnering with local talent, and addressing lack of healthy food options as a failure of the market rather than the direct impact of institutional racism. It could have been the food, the target of a zero-star review by Pete Wells in the *New York Times*. The founders won't talk about it.

Kitchenette, a similar concept to Everytable, where locally sourced fast food was available for under five dollars, also quickly fizzled.

For most of us, the utopian ideal of fast food that tastes great, is healthy, and is also affordable, just isn't available. It's really hard for merchants and consumers to upend the paradigm of the fast-food industry—not while the production of corn, soybeans, and wheat (for use as livestock feed, corn syrup, and in refined carbohydrates) is so heavily subsidized and growing fruits and vegetables is not. What would it look like if farm subsidies were used to prioritize nutrition instead of profit?

It's important to keep in mind that our fast-food health problems didn't arise by accident, and they won't be solved without action.

Nor are they equitably distributed: communities of color are the hardest hit by diet-related health problems. Welcome to the hostile realm of food deserts: geographic areas, generally low-income neighborhoods, that are underserviced by grocery stores and frequently by public transportation—where it is harder, in short, to go buy fresh fruits and vegetables. Within food deserts, fast food is often the dominant food option, contributing to poor health outcomes. As of 2016, the highest rates of CVD were among Black females (57.1 percent) and Black males (60.1 percent).[40]

The relationship between food deserts and the QSR sector is not a coincidence. It is a result of a collaborative effort by private enterprise and government. "The contemporary health crisis among black Americans—like all of our society's most pressing problems—has a history," recounts historian Marcia Chatelain in her 2020 book, *Franchise: The Golden Arches in Black America*.[41] Chatelain connects the latter days of the civil rights era with the rise of fast-food franchising in urban centers, starting with the late 1960s uprisings in major cities, which put pressure on McDonald's to divest ownership by white franchisees in predominantly Black neighborhoods.

In the early days of McDonald's, the company's success lay in its appeal to a mostly white, suburban car-driving clientele. Then, when the corporation saw that the National Black McDonald's Operators Association, founded by their first African American franchisee, Herman Petty, outsold white suburban areas, the company doubled down by recruiting more Black franchisees, who tended to service communities where there were few other food options and where most people didn't own cars. With postriot property values dropping 30 percent in these neighborhoods, it was also cheaper to buy the land. "We are not basically in the food business," Harry J. Sonneborn, the first president of McDonald's, once told investors. "We are in the real estate business. The only reason we sell 15 cent hamburgers is because they are the greatest producer of revenue from which our tenants can pay us rent."[42]

In places without the social infrastructure of good jobs, healthy food, and safe places for children to play, Chatelain concludes, a fast-food restaurant becomes the de facto community hub. While federal aid programs were largely inaccessible to the independently owned barbershops, family restaurants, and grocers that made up the retail streetscape of these neighborhoods, the fast-food corporations, backed by an army of lawyers and lobbyists, knew how to take advantage. "Feds promoted franchising to budding black entrepreneurs who wanted to help revitalize neighborhoods ravaged by economic decline and the domestic rebellions of the 60s that destroyed parts of Watts, Chicago and Newark," writes Chatelain. "Beginning with Nixon's support for black capitalism, the federal government would prop up and underwrite the expansion of fast food restaurants in black neighborhoods for decades." This created what today we call food deserts. According to Chatelain:

> Government support for fast food franchising has imperiled black health, but our societal vigilance should take us beyond that. In addition to government assistance, the fast food industry relies on indefinable, but palpable, emotional appeals to black consumer citizenship, the extension of the mid-century march for civil rights toward the marketplace, and calls for racial solidarity under the expansive umbrellas of "black capitalism," and later "black empowerment." The origins of the urban food crisis reveal the ways that various actors—politicians, civil rights activists, business executives, advertising agencies, community organizers, and market researchers—aligned to use the symbols, language and strategies of black freedom movements to sell scores of hamburgers, myriad buckets of fried chicken, and gallons of soda.

It worked. Today, we need to look at policy efforts aimed at undoing the harm.

It often feels like America loves to equate personal freedom with consumer choice. Poor people aren't sick because they lack healthy food, according to this line of thinking, but because they choose unhealthy food.

"A large part of our culture, especially from a policy maker's side," says Dr. Monica Wang, associate professor of community health sciences at Boston University's School of Public Health, is that "most of the chronic diseases related to diet are still viewed as individual responsibility." As a result, policies that combat the health fallouts from fast-food diets with taxes on sugary beverages have been no less controversial than raising the minimum wage. Opponents of this legislation have positioned these "soda taxes" as an assault on personal freedom by out-of-touch, overreaching politicians, successfully obscuring the intent of and reasoning behind the strategy.

Working at the local level, Wang conducted a study of 110 mayors (unlike Washington legislators, mayors at least live in the places they represent), who named obesity as their number-one issue, ahead of even opioids. "[Health problems arising from obesity] are costing cities and states and the country hundreds of billions annually," says Wang. "They're also highly preventable."

The goal of sugar taxes, with rates tied to sugar content, is not to generate government revenue but to change consumer behavior, which they have. Following the introduction of soda taxes in Philadelphia, San Francisco, Oakland, Berkley, and Mexico, water consumption increased and sugary beverage consumption decreased.[43] The other purpose is to encourage industry to reformulate their recipes so there is less sugar in their beverages in the first place. To win over the public, however, it's important to connect the taxes with services the community needs, like funding prekindergarten programs and building public parks, the very kinds of social infrastructure spaces that fast-food restaurants usurped. "That was something the voters cared about," Wang says of Philadelphia. "They saw the benefits of their money in a pretty short amount of time. They saw the expansion of their pre-K and investments in new parks and recreation centers in cities that were underserved. So when the opportunity came to repeal the tax, voters did not want to do that because they saw that the money was going to something they wanted."

Based on these successes, Wang has been working on a sugary drink tax for Massachusetts, which, if passed, would be the first initiative of its kind on the statewide level. It was scheduled to be brought to session in the winter of 2020, before COVID-19 disrupted everything.

I'm not immune to the charms of a McGriddle, but I'm privileged enough to be able to afford healthy food, have the training to produce nutritious meals for my family, and my dietary choices aren't limited by where I live. The fact that these are, right now, accurately described as privileges is the problem. These are the basics, and everyone should have them. Access to nutritious food is a human right.

While I commend the corporate partners that have signed on to the Fair Food Program, I don't think I'm doing much to actively support farmworkers when I buy a vegan salad bowl at Chipotle. On the other hand, I wouldn't set foot in a Wendy's until they sign on to the FFP. With so many places to get a burger, going out of my way to visit one of the major holdouts to paying farmworkers an extra penny seems intentionally unhelpful. What probably matters most about our dining choices in the fast-food sphere is supporting boycotts and strikes.

❋

THE FIRST TIME I saw there was a show called *American Pickers*, I was awed that there were twenty-one seasons of a program documenting the lives of agricultural workers. It turns out that, no, it's a show about evaluating antiques from the collectors and hoarders who own ridiculous volumes of vintage coin-operated cigarette dispensers and motorcycles. America, like every other country in the world, ignores the people who pick its food. The plight of fast-food workers is only marginally more visible and only then because we share the same space. If the other NRA could somehow have every McDonald's employee doing their work in a field, one hundred miles from any city, they wouldn't have to spend a dime lobbying against minimum-wage raises.

When we see people picketing outside of a restaurant, it's for a reason. No one gives up work and pay and risks being fired to stand out in the cold, chanting, because they're bored. People take to the streets when they are out of options. As diners, we have a ridiculous number of options. The least we can do is avoid giving our money to identifiably bad operators. Recently, I saw employees at a QSR franchise picketing in the January weather. Curious about the dispute, I asked what their issue was. They were negotiating for a thirty-cent hourly raise, and the owner would only go to twenty. They were striking over ten cents.

Compared to other restaurant genres, it may seem that there is less good to be done here as eaters. Quite the opposite. The hero myths we grew up on taught us that one person can save the day. The truth is more complex.

Within and around the sphere of fast food, there are established campaigns afoot, organizations (many more than discussed here, and all findable on social media) fighting to change the lives of restaurant and agricultural workers. Strikes and boycotts are part of their arsenal. Those already in the fight have boots on the ground, and they are dug in. The biggest difference we can make is to stand with them. When we hear about an organized action against a fast-food restaurant, we can talk to workers, learn what people are fighting for, and support them by boycotting the business and amplifying their voices.

The victories of the Coalition of Immokalee Workers were based on getting people to give a damn. That's what grassroots movements need from us.

The Chain Restaurant

More matter, less art.

—Gertrude, queen of Denmark

IT ANNOYED THE TOYOTA SALESPEOPLE THAT I BOUGHT A CAR over the phone.

I didn't get my license until I was thirty-seven. And only then because my niece had been texting me about how she was going to turn sixteen and beat me to it. In Toronto, my wife and I walked to restaurants and to our friends' homes for dinner, biked to pick up groceries, and took the subway if something was really far. We never needed a car. But as the city kept becoming less affordable, and our daughter neared her first birthday, we were ready for a change.

So now we find ourselves in Winnipeg—a new town for me—with new restaurants, new friends, and newly close-by family. Winnipeg is a spread-out prairie town, even less traversable by public transit. A car here is essential for us.

But I have no desire to learn about cars. So rather than research Chevy versus Honda, Nissan versus Ford, my wife and I did the easy thing. Staying with her family as we looked for a house, driving her mother's car every day, we said, let's get one of those. I called the dealership. We made a deal. I was glad when it was over.

While the car is a necessity here—we need to be able to drop our daughter off at her Baba and Dido's on weekday mornings—it's a luxury, too. I've only ever been able to shop for what I could carry or would fit in my bike basket or backpack. A trunk feels like a penthouse suite.

I've also found myself lured by the siren call of the newly accessible drive-thru. If you are like most North Americans, you know what it's like to turn into a drive-thru, shout your order into a faceless mic/speaker, pay, and get a sausage-and-egg McMuffin in just a few minutes, without getting out of the car. If you, like me, have walked and cycled your whole adult life, let me tell you, it's pretty neat! The convenience is mind-blowing. Since buying the car, I've indulged in a Double Quarter Pounder with Cheese and even a Cheesy Gordita Crunch. After hearing devoted fans gush about the "CGC," I learn it is a hard-shell taco wrapped in a soft-shell taco. A great premise, the bundling of chewy and crispy, if slightly underserved by each component of the dish being the lowest common denominator. Not quite the joy of getting a Jamaican beef patty wrapped in the pillow of a coco-bread bun. My drive-thru indulgences were all fun, if closer to the experience of doing recreational drugs than consuming a meal. After eating breakfast from McDonald's, I don't feel so much satiated as high. Somehow it's still legal to drive under the influence of a Whopper. These were what my wife calls "cheat meals" and what Cookie Monster deems "sometimes food." I can't eat like this all the time. It gets old quickly. I'm hungry for real food, and I finally have my own vehicle to go fetch it.

My in-laws' house is in the suburbs. Living with them is the longest I've spent outside of a major city in almost thirty years. I miss the huge array of food choices that used to be available to me. I crave handmade noodles coated in Sichuan chilies. I'm desperate to locate a Sri Lankan place to get my kothu roti fix. I can't wait to start cruising for food in the first car I've ever owned.

But as soon as I'm behind the wheel, the first thing that hits me is the sameness of the restaurants from the vantage of the driver's seat. I'm not sure what I expected to see. When I begin looking left and right for where I might eat, it's all Applebee's, Red Lobster, Golden Corral, Fatburger, Taco Bell, Olive Garden. As the sea of strip malls whizzes past me, each with its own anchor tenant, a utility like a grocery store, pharmacy, or gas station, I think about how much prime real estate these cookie-cutter restaurant chains take up and how difficult that makes it for independents. How block after block of identical plazas with identical food choices, the endless repetition of chain restaurants, not only is depressing but crowds out opportunity for actual restaurants.

When we talk about how many restaurants will never reopen in a postvaccine world, a figure that varies between 20 percent and 85 percent, the loss of jobs, to people who need those jobs, is crushing. While we will lose so many great places to eat, so many special kitchens and dining rooms that helped nourish communities and provided spaces for people to gather, it's not like we will lack places to eat. Because we started off with so many.

As of 2018, there were 329 million people in America and 660,755 restaurants.[1] That's one restaurant for every 497 people. If that seems like plenty of customers per business, consider that the average full-service franchise has 225 seats. They're open for lunch and dinner. Typical franchise agreements don't allow franchisees to close early because even if one person comes in at eleven and orders a burger and a beer, the franchisor gets their 6 percent. All this means that an average Applebee's on its own has enough restaurant capacity to feed every single person nearby, every single day. So where does that leave every other restaurateur in the area?

"We have too many restaurants, open too many hours, spreading the labor pool thin," says Bruce McAdams, hospitality professor at the University of Guelph. "This idea that restaurants have slim margins. It's BS. I worked in independent restaurants. I worked in corporate restaurants. Restaurants don't [innately] have slim margins. They have slim margins because we have so many restaurants that are losing money. So many franchise restaurants. That's what brings the average down." Before moving on to academia, McAdams worked for Darden—the parent company of Olive Garden—which, even after its sale of Red Lobster in 2014, was the world's largest full-service chain restaurant company.

McAdams echoes what I see on the highways. Chain restaurants constantly need to grow, which means opening new restaurants, which is why we have way too many. "That saturation has a huge impact. You'll go into an area that should have seven restaurants, and there are ten. And four of them are franchises and two are losing money."

When considering the glut of chains, it's helpful to think of these restaurants in a kind of tiered system. Fast-food restaurants like Mc-Donald's and Taco Bell prioritize price. That's one tier. The next tier, fast-casual restaurants like Chipotle and Panera, prioritizes quality. And the third tier, full-service chains like Applebee's and Olive Garden, prioritizes portion size. In cooking school, they called this "perception of value," like stacking food high so it looks like more.

When we talk about chain restaurants, we can divide them into so many subsets: franchised versus company owned, public versus private, counter service versus full service. What they all have in common is the priority of presenting that perception of value to the consumer. That's why, as the Venn diagram of this chapter overlaps occasionally with the previous one, you'll see examples of QSR groups.

For example, franchises operate at each of these tiers. The structure of a franchise operation is pretty simple. The franchisor sells the concept, infrastructure, systems, and marketing support to people who want to open specific storefront locations. They charge an upfront fee to the franchisee (generally in the $10,000 to $50,000 range), requiring a certain amount of start-up capital (somewhere between $250,000 and $2,000,000), and take between 5 and 7 percent of gross sales. In theory, the restaurant is a proven concept—franchisees benefit from its branding and name recognition. The systems, training, and support guarantee efficiency. Marketing/branding brings in customers (this assumes that the franchisee runs a tight ship and that the location is not so chock-a-block with other similar food options). And this setup is why a would-be restaurateur might choose to open a Huddle House rather than their own independent diner. Often there is a prerequisite that franchisees have some minimum level of liquid assets (franchisors don't want overleveraged operators to damage their brands by closing due to personal debt). No matter how much investment they have to start, some franchisees don't succeed but don't close. Their slim profits are part of what drives down the average.

"These people are coming in with capital investments. They're paying for their fees, and their losses are draining their capital," says McAdams. "They're allowed to exist as a franchisee. As a corporate restaurant, they'd never exist. They would be closed because they'd never be successful given the hours that they run. And they won't allow them to alter the hours or modify the menu."

While Howard Johnson is sometimes credited with creating the franchise model in the 1930s, the concept can be traced back to the Middle Ages, when the Catholic Church allowed tax collectors to keep a percentage of the money they collected from citizens. While the last thing I need to do is to absolve the church of anything, it was a much more recent and a much more obscure culprit who sowed the seeds of our oversaturated restaurant field.

As with so many of our greatest villains, this was another dude who thought he was just doing his job. With all due respect to Doctor Octopus or the Green Goblin, the actual main nemesis of Spider-Man has always been J. Jonah Jameson: publisher of the *Daily Bugle*, a terrible journalist bent on smearing Spidey at every opportunity and a guy convinced he was serving the public.

To find the true archvillain of modern American restaurants, we have to look past the usual suspects. We are familiar with Mario Batali, Chick-fil-A, Paula Deen, and the rainbow bagel. But who is Michael Jensen?

You won't find Jensen on this year's list of canceled or problematic food personalities. He's not an abusive celebrity chef, bad-boy restaurateur, racist food editor, or corrupt influencer. He didn't find a way to combine popular pastries, like the cronut, the cruffin, or the donug (a chicken nugget/donut hybrid that, no matter how many questions its existence demands, will not divert our attention here). He didn't invent the tornado style of beer drinking. Jensen is an economist.

If we're looking at what is wrong with American dining, examining why every second restaurant is a part of a homogenous chain, we have to look back at our economic history and discuss some of the trends he helped steer.

Jensen, whose ideas of how CEOs should be compensated would go on to reshape much of our society, was influenced by Milton Friedman, as was a whole generation of economists. Friedman, the free-market absolutist, believed that it was immoral for corporate leaders to make decisions for the purpose of benefiting the public rather than the company. "The businessmen believe that they are defending free enterprise when they declaim that business is not concerned 'merely' with profit but also with promoting desirable 'social' ends; that business has a 'social conscience' and takes seriously its responsibilities for providing employment, eliminating discrimination, avoiding pollution and whatever else may be the catchwords of the contemporary crop of reformers," wrote Friedman in a 1970 *New York Times* opinion piece, "The Social Responsibility of Business Is to Increase Profits." "They are preaching pure and unadulterated socialism. Businessmen who talk this way are unwitting puppets of the intellectual forces that have been undermining the basis of a free society these last decades."[2]

Friedman was a brilliant speaker and debater who managed to sound sweet and grandfatherly (which some might read as paternalistic and condescending) while scolding his opponents. In his ten-part 1980 PBS series, *Free to Choose*, he sells the idea that workers in a Hong Kong plastic toy factory enjoy the freedom to decide their hours or move to other jobs with the folksiness of telling you that lemonade is a nice treat on a hot day. All of this stuff is on YouTube. I really recommend watching at least a little of it. Because even if I disagree with Friedman's main theories, beyond his obvious intelligence he is so incredibly charismatic. It helps to understand how influential he was. He always seems sincere in his belief in the undisputed badness of regulation and the cosmic goodness found in unbound competition. As an adviser to President Ronald Reagan and Prime Minister Margaret Thatcher (who loved his free-market economic philosophies, not so much his opposition to medical licenses and the War on Drugs), though, Friedman's theories inspired policies that did incalculable damage to our world.

I don't think the free market exists—not the way Friedman talked about it, with the invisible hand correcting wrongs we foolish mortals might be impelled to fix with laws. All the talk about how eliminating tariffs will stimulate trade, spur innovation, and eventually balance wages on a global scale seems like so much hot air. The handful of duopolies (Amazon and Alibaba, Facebook and Twitter, Apple and Microsoft, Republican and Democrat) that have come to rule our environment—in which anyone with a good idea and solid work ethic is supposed to be able to prosper—are testimony to a larger truth: once people or companies amass power, they use it to prevent others from ever gaining it.

The politicians who championed Friedman's free-market dogma in the 1980s have either retired, died, or rebranded. Some have done what comic-book readers call retconning (short for *retroactive continuity*). Jean Grey, after destroying an inhabited planet, didn't die in *X-Men 137*. We later learned that she had been replicated by the alien entity Phoenix during the shuttle crash in *X-Men 101* and had for several years been asleep in a cocoon at the bottom of Jamaica Bay. This means she couldn't be held responsible for the atrocities committed by Phoenix in her guise. This is also known as the Shaggy defense: "It wasn't me." Friedman's political heirs have explained, patiently, that they were always antiregulation and stood against the Democratic conspiracy known as "globalism." There never was an economic policy known as free trade, you see. So they couldn't have supported it.

Okay. So what does this have to do with why there are 1,635 locations of Denny's and 660 Cracker Barrels?[3] How did we get more chain restaurants than we could possibly need or want?

In 1976 Jensen took Friedman's ideology a step further. Along with William Meckling (a student of Friedman), Jensen cowrote *Theory of the Firm: Managerial Behavior, Agency Costs and Ownership Structure*, in which, according to the *Harvard Business Review*, the authors argued that shareholders are the true owners of a corporation (a concept advanced by economist Ronald Coase a quarter century earlier), that they delegate decision-making authority to managers who, as "agents," are obliged to prioritize the interests of shareholders, which is to maximize economic returns. In 1990's "CEO Incentives: It's Not How Much You Pay, but How," he urged companies to directly tie CEO compensation to stock performance. This became a popular idea. In line with this thinking, over the 1970s through the 1990s, economists and financial leaders put more and more focus on pay, options, and tools to try to more closely align the interests of stockholders/shareholders and managers. The most important example of this has been the heavy use of stock options as compensation for senior executives. Between 1992 and 2000, average CEO compensation at Fortune 500 companies went from $2.7 million to $14 million, ushering in our current age of short-term thinking.[4] Incentivized to prioritize the next financial quarter, leaders focused on keeping their job another three months and earning the biggest bonus possible through constant growth, which became more important than the long-term welfare of the company, its employees, or the world they inhabit.

A BETTER BURGER AND A 3.7-INCH FRY

Consider In-N-Out Burger and McDonald's. While they both started more or less the same way—selling hamburgers, fries, and shakes to Southern California drivers in the 1940s—one is privately owned and operated and the other is publicly traded and franchised. "Corporate structure and ownership of restaurants . . . those two questions are going to determine their whole approach to business," says McAdams.

If you live in the Great Lakes region, you can get a great burger at Smashburger; ditto at CaliBurger in Shanghai, or the Burger's Priest in Toronto, or Shake Shack in pretty much any global city. If you live in California, Nevada, Arizona, Utah, Texas, or Oregon, you go to the restaurant that they all copied, In-N-Out Burger.

In addition to making a burger recognized as the best in its class, In-N-Out is known for being an exemplary employer. They pay workers above minimum wage, and store managers average $160,000, triple the industry average. This, in addition to health benefits and 401(k) contributions, results in long-term employee retention. "We strive to create an atmosphere that is upbeat and enthusiastic and always customer-focused," VP of operations Denny Warnick tells me over email. "A higher pay structure is helpful in making that happen but it is only part of our approach."

So it's clearly possible to make burgers well, sell them cheaply, and still take care of your workers. Part of why In-N-Out is able to pay people fairly and also make a profit is because they keep their menu limited. Every time you add something to a menu, either your existing employees need to do new tasks, or you need to increase the number of people you employ (and pay them less, if you want to maintain profitability). In-N-Out just makes burgers, fries, and shakes (with a few variations on their widely disseminated "secret" menu). The current McDonald's menu has more than three dozen items, before even counting drinks and desserts. Part of the reason In-N-Out is able to keep their menu so streamlined is that they don't have stockholders or a board of directors demanding both top-line growth (the company's overall revenue) by opening more stores and continuous growth in same-store sales, which many chains try to achieve through expansion of their menus or operating hours.

Not all QSR chains are franchised. Starbucks, Chipotle, White Castle, In-N-Out, and Panda Express, for example, are all company owned. And not all franchises are publicly traded. But it's fairly common among national brands to be publicly traded or part of the portfolio of a much larger cabal that is. Like the previously mentioned Darden (Olive Garden, LongHorn Steakhouse, Cheddar's Scratch Kitchen, and more); Brinker International, Inc. (Chili's Grill & Bar, Maggiano's Little Italy); Yum! Brands (the parent company of KFC, Taco Bell, and Pizza Hut); RBI (Burger King, Popeyes, Tim Hortons); Bloomin' Brands, Inc. (Outback Steakhouse, Bonefish Grill, and more); and so on.

Conversely, privately held companies (like Roark Capital, which owns Dunkin' Donuts, Arby's, Carvel, Jimmy John's, and plenty more) are not immune to these pressures. However, in the case of a publicly traded firm, the CEO must constantly generate growth and increase profitability or risk getting fired. In addition to increasing sales at existing locations, growth comes from opening more stores, regardless of whether anyone needs them. It is usually achieved by paying people poorly, using the cheapest possible ingredients (which means paying agricultural workers poorly), constantly adding menu items to attract new customers, or using the company lawyers to take advantage of tax breaks, sometimes going too far, like when a Subway franchisee tried to nab a tax exemption for their bread under Ireland's Value-Added Tax Act, only to have the country's supreme court rule that the base of their sandwiches contained five times the legal limit of sugar to be classified as bread.[5]

In-N-Out has remained in family hands since its founding by Harry and Esther Snyder in 1948. Their granddaughter, Lynsi Synder, is now the president of a company with 358 locations, all company owned, with no franchises. "Slow and controlled growth has always been part of our strategy at In-N-Out Burger. We only promote restaurant managers from within," explains Warnick. "Each of our managers was hired as an hourly Associate, learning everything from peeling potatoes and cleaning tables to operating the business the In-N-Out way. This approach definitely isn't the quickest way to grow, but we feel that it is the best way to maintain our strong values and company culture."

During the rise of third-party delivery apps, while the bigger QSR operations expanded their reach by using their market clout to negotiate preferred terms, In-N-Out resisted the temptation to have someone else serve their food to customers. In 2015, when DoorDash started listing In-N-Out for delivery, without permission, In-N-Out sued. Following a confidential settlement, according to a lawyer who represented the burger chain, In-N-Out doesn't show up on Door-Dash anymore.[6]

Though lesser known nationally, Tennessee-based Pal's Sudden Service follows a similar ethos. "We get a constant stream of requests to franchise," CEO Thomas Crosby tells me. "But our vision is to be the best, not the biggest. Not to grow with other people's money. So, by being able to stay with a really simple menu, a simple business structure and service mode, maintain company control over all operations, we don't owe people money."

Most restaurant chains have head offices where executives, needing to justify their salaries, look for ways to grow sales or cut costs. Out of 1,350 Pal's employees, only Crosby and two others work in leadership roles outside of a restaurant. "We don't lease land. We buy land. So we have zero debt. We don't have the burden of a public company, where you're having to try to appease stockholders and then figure out how to appease customers. We can be laser focused on the only obsession we have—to delight customers in a way that creates loyalty."

Employees are regularly quizzed on product knowledge and company procedure, with 100 percent being the only passing grade. If they don't know that the average Pal's French fry is 3.7 inches, they're scheduled for more testing or training. The menu, only slightly longer than In-N-Out's, makes it possible for workers to know everything about the product. That's not possible when you've got thirty-six items. Instead of a voice-box ordering kiosk, a human face greets customers at the drive-thru order windows. Because of this, says Crosby, they find only one mistake per thirty-six hundred orders, versus the QSR standard of one in twenty-five. Except for general managers, staff are paid hourly. The lowest starting wage (depending on experience) is $8.75, with a company average of $13. Not a fortune. Still, it's high above Tennessee's state minimum wage of $7.25.

Meanwhile, franchised chains are constantly expanding into new markets, from Milan to Minsk, their ever-ballooning menus necessitating contributions to the NRA, which lobbies to suppress wages (as recently as 2021, when they sent a letter to congressional leaders opposing a $15 minimum wage), because the more bodies you need, the less you can afford to pay them.[7]

Some chain operators are serial franchisees. Others have no hospitality experience, dentists and real-estate developers who have identified that there are enough customers at the intersection of Main Street and Offramp Boulevard to support another Pizza Hut, Denny's, or Huddle House. When franchises close, it's usually because of local market conditions, a franchisor's failure of due diligence in advance (wrong neighborhood, poor visibility, limited vehicle access, too much competition), or a massive economic downturn, as we're experiencing now. In a nonpandemic economy, far more franchises open than close. The closure rate is hotly debated (those who want to sell you a franchise have an interest in perpetuating the myth of their guaranteed success), but drive anywhere in America and you can see the market saturation by chains and franchises with your own eyes. This makes the odds so stacked against the kind of independent restaurateurs we love to champion.

A massive chain wants each franchisee to generate more and more same-store sales. So franchisors push discounts, specials, longer operating hours, and lower-priced items to get consumers in the door. These discounts are less profitable, or even lose money for the franchisees. "Go back to *Theory of the Firm* by Michael Jensen, where he started linking CEO pay to corporate performance," says McAdams. "Before that, CEOs used to just get a salary. Jensen said their pay should be based on performance. So we went down this road of short-term gain. That's why there are so many mergers and acquisitions and downsizing and short-term moves to grease numbers. All so CEOs can keep their job for another three months."

For their engines to continue running, large chains and franchises eat up the majority of dining clientele. Chains, operated by corporations whose boards of directors expect constant expansion, keep growing.

When COVID-19 hit, some QSR chains (Wendy's, Dunkin' Donuts, and Chipotle) struggled.[8] But most are doing a gangbuster business. Takeaway food, with its demand for high efficiency, is what they excel at. Full-service chains, already competing in a glutted market, unable to capitalize on their physically expansive spaces and menus that offer something for everyone, have struggled. California Pizza Kitchen and Chuck E. Cheese filed for bankruptcy. The Cheesecake Factory found itself unable to pay rent. By the summer, 12 percent of full-service chains were closed, possibly for good. The downturn for these chains wasn't entirely pandemic related. Many were already in rough shape.

Who reports on the chains and franchises, all those restaurants that are maybe less sexy than the chefs and taco trucks that dominate our food media, yet actually make up the bulk of businesses? That would be Jonathan Maze, executive editor of *Restaurant Business* magazine. He had no doubts, prepandemic, that the entire restaurant space has been oversaturated for at least the past four years. "There's been an expanding economy. Within that you have sectors that are performing better than others. And those sectors that are performing better are fast food, within a chain space. The reason why is consumers don't spend as much time eating inside restaurants as they used to."

There's no debate there. While the twenty-nine thousand full-service franchise restaurants in the United States had grown 13 percent since 2013 to thirty-three thousand in 2020, everyone I've spoken to in recent years has pointed to revenue percentages leaning toward online, takeout, and delivery sales.[9] "You could make an argument that it is the full-service chain space that is oversaturated," adds Maze. "But I would argue that there is not a whole lot of growth available in the fast-food chain, without taking business from someone else. All of the sectors are oversaturated."

Yes, our dining-out budgets have exceeded our grocery budgets in recent years. But chains can't count on demand increasing to keep pace with their growth, certainly not with household spending likely to decline postpandemic. At a certain point, chains are chasing not growth but each other's customers. "If Wendy's adds breakfast to its six thousand United States restaurants, to do that it is going to have to take breakfast business from somebody else," says Maze. "Theoretically, it might get some consumers to eat breakfast at a restaurant more often than they would have otherwise, but that consumer might not go to lunch at Wendy's later on in the week. So it might take business from itself. Or it might take business from McDonald's, which is the market leader in QSR breakfast by a mile. Or it could take business from Burger King, its closer rival. Or Taco Bell." If only chains could convince diners to eat a fourth meal every day.

Instead, what we've been seeing is chains buying growth. When the head office can't entice one more customer with a Triple Crunch Decker Beyond Beef Quesadilla, or locate another available empty storefront and someone to operate it, when they can't grow sales, they buy sales. That means corporate mergers and acquisitions. "It is increasingly difficult for chains to grow, to add units," explains Maze. "Say you're Olive Garden, or you're Darden Restaurants, which owns Olive Garden. And Olive Garden only has so many places it can grow. And you'd really like to get to a 10 percent growth level. But realistically, through same-store sales and unit growth, you can only grow 5 to 6 percent. So to get to that 10 percent you find another company that you think promises unit growth in the future."

Until 2020, the chain industry was acquisition hungry. For example, in 2017, Darden paid $780 million for the 165-location chain Cheddar's. Darden CEO Gene Lee described Cheddar's as a great fit with the company's portfolio, a complement to their existing brands, promising the addition would enable Darden to further strengthen their most competitive advantages: "our significant scale and our extensive data and insights."

In a similar deal, in 2019 Cracker Barrel bought the twenty-eight-unit Maple Street Biscuit Company for $36 million as well as a minority stake in Punch Bowl Social (which they rescinded in March 2020 to focus on their core business).[10] "You're going to see more consolidation," says Maze. "That's a broad, long-term trend."

As I speak with Maze, I get frightened about what was clearly happening before the pandemic and now feels inevitable as independent neighborhood restaurants fall like flies. As with many unpleasant changes in our culture, it has been turbocharged by this crisis. The shift toward consolidation is about more than just the need for growth in revenue, Maze points out. It is also based on the rise of delivery (for which the third-party tech companies give better deals to bigger brands) or the investment in technology for these restaurants to develop their own ordering and delivery streams.

But the main motivation, bringing us back to Michael Jensen and the impact of his executive incentive philosophy, is the constant hunger for growth. "The big pressure on saturation is coming from private-equity investors that have spent the past decade pumping money into small-growth chains and then demanding that they add new units," says Maze. "In many cases, they made compromises in terms of locations or lease percentages. They've driven unit growth at all costs."

LONG-TERMISM

Not all chains operate like this.

For twenty years as a public company, Panera Bread was the best-performing restaurant stock in the United States. From 1997 until the company's acquisition in 2017 by JAB Holding Company (owner of Krispy Kreme, Pret A Manger, Keurig, Dr. Pepper, Snapple, and others), Panera boasted a shareholder return of 9,753 percent.[11] Founder Ron Shaich credits this to avoiding the short-term leadership that has plagued America's chain restaurants (and companies in general). "I think increasingly, larger companies financed by private equity, in the public markets, are under such pressure for profitability, such pressure for short-term profitability, that the very things that often would allow these companies to create better experience aren't able to do that."

The morning we speak, my daughter is still not sleeping through the night. Victoria and I wake every three hours to feed her. That, says Shaich, is a perfect example of long-termism. "You'll find out with your daughter. Sleep is a short-term pleasure. But you're up in the night making a long-term commitment to her health and well-being. We're making these decisions all the time, between the short, medium, and long term. Big private companies can have the same issues. And when you're optimizing short term, about all you can do is deal with costs. Thinking long term, that's where value is created."

Shaich divides the two sides of management into what he calls *discovery* and *delivery*, terms we might interchange with *creativity* and *logistics*. Some chains begin as deeply funded big business, like Chuck E. Cheese, created in 1977 by Atari founder Nolan Bushnell, flush with cash and seeking a way to capitalize on the lifetime revenue of the arcade games his company made. At a trade show, he spotted what he thought was a coyote mascot costume, perfect for the Coyote Pizza concept he was developing. It wasn't until some employees saw what Bushnell bought that he learned it was a rat. When his marketing department rejected the idea that they change the name to Rick Rat's Pizza, Charles Entertainment Cheese was born.[12] And then they figured out the minor details of making pizza and developed the business into America's favorite place for children's birthday parties, with more than six hundred locations.

A lot of chains start like that: an existing, successful business developing a hospitality brand intended to be duplicated for expansion. Just as many start as someone's small business. Applebee's began as one location of T. J. Applebee's Rx for Edibles & Elixirs in Decatur, Georgia. Before it became Subway, with more than forty thousand locations, there was just Pete's Super Submarines in Bridgeport, Connecticut. Many of our massive chains, even if the owners were dreaming big, launched with a single restaurant. Every rookie food entrepreneur has been warned how risky the business is. When they start, says Shaich, success seems so far out of reach. Unless you're launching with limitless family money, the business has no scale, no economics, no customers. You've got to do such a better job than everyone else to get customers to choose you. Occasionally, people make it. That's likely because they've created a better experience.

Maybe this grows to five restaurants, or ten or twenty. The business starts to attract capital, people who believe you know the secret to making money. "And now you've got investors. And they start to say, 'We love all this discovery. But we need to bring delivery to bear.'" By delivery, Shaich means consistently serving the product that your customers want and expect. To achieve this, you start to adopt the kind of management tools that make the company more disciplined. And though margins improve, discipline drives out creative thinking. "What ends up happening is these companies get to be a billion dollars, and they have all delivery and no discovery."

Once, on a road trip, Shaich and his twenty-one-year-old son made a sport of stopping in and assessing ten different restaurants. They found the same thing I did when I first got in my car. "They all were offering exactly the same product." The only difference they saw was price. "Does anybody understand that the sea of sameness, selling on price, is not how to win at this for the consumer? But they're all under so much pressure that they're looking sideways, and they get into this pattern."

Doing the exact same thing as your competitors doesn't seem like the way to get ahead. But consider the attitude of the contemporary investor. Fifty years ago, the average shareholder in a public company held their stock for five years. Today, it's between four and eight months.[13] "They're renting that stock for an inflection point," says Shaich. "They're not investing in the company. It's all informed by an ideology that came out roughly in the '70s. I got out of business school in '78. I can remember when the role of corporate leadership was to serve not just shareholders but guests, team members, employees, the communities in which we live. Increasingly, in the '70s, '80s, '90s, 2000s, the idea was that shareholder value was preeminent. Shareholders own the company, and as management we work for the shareholder. You had an obligation to maximize their return. The problem is, not all shareholders are the same. Short-term shareholders are people day trading."

Shaich advocates for something called the Long-Term Stock Exchange, an idea supported at the federal level by Senator Elizabeth Warren. In simplified terms, the LTSE (approved by US regulators in 2019) encourages long-term investing by providing differential voting rights based on how long stock is held. That means investors can't buy a stock just to apply pressure to make changes that will generate short-term earnings but hobble the company's future—their influence over a company would only grow over time.

For me, franchising had always been a bit of an enigma. Probably because I came through cooking school, where every student fantasizes about food from what Shaich would call a discovery perspective (whether they have any creativity to express or not), it always seemed strange to me that anyone would take on the burden of owning and running a restaurant without the fun of getting to make their own artistic decisions.

But for first-timers, maybe it's worth it to pay the upfront franchise fees and 5 percent of gross sales to buy a predeveloped concept. Though we can't peg the exact rate at which franchised locations close, they seem like a much less risky investment than going it alone. Twenty or thirty years ago, before our streets became so clogged by the same restaurants, franchises might have been gold mines for investors.

The importance of long-termism goes well beyond having better chain restaurants. Or even better restaurants. It's about climate change. It's about having any future at all. It's about redirecting a system that currently incentivizes business leaders to destroy life on earth in order to generate a bonus in the next financial quarter.

But for restaurants, the end result of our short-termism is that the chain sector is full. There are no real undeveloped pockets left. If you're looking for a region to expand your portfolio of Cici's Pizza or Beef 'O' Brady's locations, you'll have to look beyond America.

†

WHEN CHRIS WYNNE arrived in Russia, he wasn't thinking about pizza. After studying engineering and economics, Wynne had moved to DC to work for a company that handled satellite operations for the Pentagon. After earning a master's in international relations, with a specialty in international security, having his application to the Central Intelligence Agency rejected, and botching a second attempt, he hopped on a plane to Russia. This was 2007. "I knew nothing about pizza," says Wynne, who now operates 220 locations of Papa John's Pizza in Russia. "Even when we bought the business, I knew very little."

Instead of the spy game, he got into the mortgage business, trying to create a Russian version of Fanny Mae. At the same time, he had bought some real estate and was leasing it to the local Papa John's franchisee (international franchising is usually done via "master franchisers" who secure the rights to large territories). They were going under and couldn't pay the rent. So Wynne effectively traded the debt for 51 percent of the business. He didn't get involved in its operation at all until the next year, when the 2008 mortgage crisis put an end to his financial firm and forced him to learn the pizza business.

When he made the initial deal, there were only four hundred restaurants delivering pizza in Moscow, a city of fifteen million people. Street food was either hot dogs or baked potatoes (garnished with cheese, butter, salmon, dill, or chives), monopolized by a chain called Kroshka-Kartoshka. "Delivery was a completely new concept. No one understood the concept of delivery."

Wynne estimates that local restaurants were barely meeting 20 to 30 percent of demand for delivery. Unlike in every American city, with its endless supply of delivery options, there was a huge opportunity.

Today, the Moscow market is pretty much clogged as well. Wynne's metric for saturation is the number of stores relative to the consumer purchasing power of the population. Since the 1950s, Americans have had disposable income to spend on dining out. Until the fall of the Soviet Union in the '90s, this wasn't much of a thing in Russia, where outside of Moscow, eating out was still considered a luxury. ("Moscow is a different country than Russia," says Wynne.) Suddenly, the Russian people had disposable income, enabling Wynne to grow Papa John's to about two hundred locations in Russia, Poland, Belarus, and Germany, split almost evenly between company owned and franchised. In April 2020 Moscow went into a lockdown. With nothing like the federal support for small businesses seen in the United States and Canada, it was a retail Armageddon. Only about 30 percent of Wynne's sales were dine in, so he was able to make the transition. Plus the situation presented an opportunity to cut fixed costs by renegotiating rent, which in Moscow is about five times the price as most US cities.

Large restaurant companies like Wynne's have access to capital along with departments dedicated to strategic planning, marketing, and business development. In a time of flux, this can be a great advantage. Smaller restaurants share a bond with their customers and have loyalty in their communities that chains often do not. As several industry analysts have pointed out to me, while people will rally to save their local bistro, no community is going to fundraise on behalf of Applebee's or Papa John's. However, despite the emotional ties that many independents maintain, they've traditionally been too lean to plan for emergencies and have little in the way of savings.

Our postpandemic restaurant landscape is likely to be even more dominated by chains than before. Most will be smaller in a number of ways: fewer brick-and-mortar locations, with smaller footprints. While the future isn't written yet, everyone predicts fewer of the restaurants we want and more of the ones we don't. That bums me out. Particularly as I now live in a city that's less international and not a nexus of ambitious cooking or immigration. I can feel the uniformity of food options closing in on me.

A RESTAURANT STREET WITHOUT CHAINS

Is it possible to prevent chains from scooping up all the best restaurant real estate? Of course it is. It's a lesson we can learn from a town like Louisville, which is coincidentally home to both the global headquarters of Papa John's (technically in Jeffersontown, a suburb that maintained independence when the city amalgamated with Jefferson County in 2003) and a major strip of urban real estate with zero chain-restaurant presence.

A decade ago I met Marty Rosen on my one and only press junket. That's when a company with money forks out to send journalists on a trip (often fancy) in exchange for the hope or promise of media coverage in return. (For reasons discussed in Chapter 3, I never did this again.) The tour, of bourbon distilleries, was financed by the liquor lobby. The restaurants they took us to, a reflection of their collaboration with local tourism boards, were uninteresting. So once they sprang us for the night in Louisville, I got in touch with Rosen, who was then the critic for the *Courier-Journal*. (Remember: local food writers love to share.) He told me that if I was in town for one night, I had to eat at Shirley Mae's Café. The only caveat was that the kitchen didn't open until 10:00 p.m., and if I really wanted to get the experience of the community, I shouldn't show up earlier than 11:00. The concierge at our hotel pretty much refused to call a taxi when I told him where I was headed. He used a lot of nonspecific language to imply that I might not feel comfortable or safe, which I later understood to mean that I was going to a neighborhood where Black people live. Incensed, Rosen insisted on driving me. The evening at Shirley Mae's, the owner's warm hospitality, the piles of ribs, green beans, chitterlings, mac and cheese, sweet potatoes, and hot-water cornbread, everything swimming in lard, somehow segueing into drinking and dancing at a bar across the street, the sort adorned with Polaroids of regulars, was one of my all-time favorite dining experiences.

Rosen, who now edits *Food & Dining*, knows his city. For an example of a commercial area thick with restaurants yet absent of chains, he points me toward Crescent Hill. "This stretch has developed into the most interesting restaurant row in the city," says Rosen. "There are about three dozen places that serve food along that strip, and not a single chain or drive-thru. Everything is locally owned."

Over about three miles of Frankfort Avenue, running through Crescent Hill, you'll find pizza, sushi, gumbo, craft beer, coffee, and every other edible delight you'd expect in a lively urban area, with no trace of an Applebee's, Subway, or Starbucks. Not even a Papa John's. "How many strips with dining density like Frankfort Ave. don't have a chain outpost?" asks Rosen. "Business abhors a vacuum. There has to be a cause."

So why does a stretch of road in Louisville have so much independent entrepreneurship, versus the chains found everywhere else? Are locals doing something differently? Is there a unique form of road design? Influence of zoning laws on architecture? As New Yorkers would have you believe of their bagels, or Kentuckians of their bourbon, is there something in the water? I propose all these as explanations of this bulwark against the homogenizing tide of chain restaurants to Dr. Tom Owen. "Double-dog yes," answers the archivist for the University of Louisville and former member of the city council. It's all of them.

To understand how this culinary oasis developed, Owen takes me back to the nineteenth century (suddenly I'm not such a pedant for my forty-year digression about Jensen), when both Frankfort and Bardstown Road (another commercial corridor with a strong, independent restaurant presence) were turnpikes, private toll roads beyond the limits of the old city. Back then there were taverns and inns along the turnpikes, which provided access to the rural hinterlands of Kentucky.

Starting in 1870, streetcars carried people over these roads, mule drawn at first, later replaced by electric trolleys. This transportation hub enabled the first subdivisions in Louisville, transforming farmland along the turnpikes into housing. These were comfortable, middle-class suburbs, made all the more desirable in 1899, when the government acquired the private roads, eliminating tolls.

During the trolley's tenure, commerce had cemented along the turnpikes—grocery, variety, hardware, and so forth—particularly at the intersections where the streetcars stopped. This in turn increased density along these corridors.

By 1948 the city had traded streetcars for buses. From the 1950s to the 1980s, Louisville experienced declining population and economic disaster, the flight to the suburbs common to most North American cities. This was less pronounced on the Frankfort and Bardstown corridors, which bounced back quickly and, by the 1970s, were gentrifying. "Beginning in the '70s and '80s, there got to be a mystique among younger people, for older neighborhoods," recalls Owen. "These are older Victorian neighborhoods, with storied architecture, stained-glass windows, and front porches."

Along with gentrification came even more density and commerce, so much so that by the 1970s people in the area were opening businesses in their front yards, transforming private homes, built in the 1910s, into restaurants. All of this helped Frankfort (and, not far away, Bardstown) become a regional dining destination.

Along the way, culture and policy have evolved to protect what is distinct and desirable about this neighborhood. Since 1990 municipal rules have required any substantial renovation on Bardstown to conform to traditional design. On Frankfort, though the city didn't implement the same regulations, it invested in parking spaces, sidewalks, and streetscaping. The vibrancy of the area, enjoyed by locals, regional visitors, and tourists, has spurred residents to fight to protect it. "Well, people get in a pissing contest every time there's construction," says Owen, who represented Bardstown during this period. "The neighborhood wins some, and the developer wins some. I would say that Bardstown Road and Frankfort Avenue have been at least 75 percent successful in preserving key aspects."

Frankfort today has an enviable mix of commercial and residential uses, with beautiful houses nestled between businesses like the Champagnery, Hilltop Tavern, or Boujie Biscuit. Most cities have a neighborhood with a story like this. The challenge anywhere, for residents who want to encourage this kind of independent restaurant culture, is in how to go about it.

If we want to foster these kinds of desirable neighborhoods, we might have to consider using that annoying bane of every antiregulatory ideologue's existence: *laws*.

Years ago, in what seems like a dream when I hosted dinner parties for a living, I had over Jennifer Keesmaat, who at the time was the chief planner for the city of Toronto. I reached out to Keesmaat, always an advocate for smart design and walkable communities, to ask how we as citizens can create or preserve conditions for the sort of neighborhood restaurants we want. "Often we think that the type of commerce we see on a corridor happens somehow organically," says Keesmaat. "But it's often deeply embedded in policy. Whether or not you get a chain that has a very large footprint or a small mom-and-pop shop has a lot to do with the underlying zoning." For example, to stop large companies from buying up multiple storefronts and knocking down walls to build giant stores, local governments can pass zoning regulations that prohibit the assemblage of retail properties. This obstructs big-box stores from buying neighboring storefronts to create one much larger retail site. Cities can prioritize small businesses through tax exemptions. Design-overlay district (it's called a heritage-preservation district where I come from, but the intent is the same) rules can limit the height of buildings, or prevent developers from extending stores to the edge of the sidewalk, in order to preserve a traditional esthetic.

Zoning laws and their names vary between countries and municipalities. The strategies and intentions are mostly the same. Keesmaat cites Melbourne as a useful example. "You'll find a lot of restaurants in Melbourne with twenty seats. There might be five seats indoors and another fifteen in the middle of the laneway. Everything is on a much smaller scale, and it's very entrepreneurial." Again, this did not happen by coincidence. "One of the reasons why this emerged in the culture of Melbourne twenty years ago was because an urban designer looked at the laneways and said that the building codes didn't allow restaurants because you were required to have fire access, washrooms." So the city changed the code, and it built public washrooms, eliminating the need for each business to provide one, which in turn enabled small cafés and restaurants to flourish. "You don't get chains in this type of environment, because it's not appealing to them. Chains run based on a formula, best delivered at scale."

Keesmaat emphasizes that this type of urban environment happens only by intention and through design, that population density, absent small business policies, equals chain retail. "Planners have spent the past twenty years talking about the importance of Main Street retail to neighborhood vitality. And I think there's an opportunity to flip the switch and to talk about food as a community-building device. You don't achieve that by accident. You need policy. If you're not intentional about having small-scale retail and as a result you have policies in place that enable a larger-scale retail, you'll get the larger-scale chain. Because they will find that market."

The problem with some of these policies is that they legislate costs, like setbacks and bike spaces, that can only be passed on to consumers through higher prices in affluent neighborhoods. "From a planning perspective and as a practitioner of planning, I think one big issue that we need to do is to have local ordinances that speak to gentrification," says Faisal Roble, chief equity officer of LA's planning department.

Borrowing from other fields, like restorative justice (in which victim and offender work together to repair the harm done) and sustainability checklists for development (factors to evaluate projects based on issues like vegetation, recycling, roof angles, and more), Roble is in the process of crafting a development checklist that addresses impact on the community and prevents that dreaded sea of sameness. "All the chain businesses are formula based. They duplicate themselves without any variety. I think we need a checklist of equity so when a project comes, we may compare whether it enhances the pace of gentrification and displacement."

Factors to consider might be what has existed at the location, what is being replaced, and what public benefits the project creates, such as affordable housing or jobs. "What people eat is beyond planning," says Roble. "But we can create the environment that enhances and encourages the type of food establishment we want to flourish. You can encourage some and discourage others." For example, chains prefer parking in the front. We can make a rule so it has to be in the back. Or that windows have to be 50 percent of the street wall, which contradicts the rigid design format for chain stores. We can tie square footage to the dining area or place a maximum on square footage. These conditions are ideal for small, six-hundred-square-foot family-owned restaurants. But they are abhorrent to chains, which require space that conforms to their formulas. "Restaurants like Pizza Hut and Denny's would not like to come to that area."

GO BIG OR GO HOME

For those of us not on planning committees or zoning boards, we don't have to wait until a local politician knocks on our door and asks for our vote. An infallible way to oppose chains is to not go give them our business. In theory, this should not be a hard choice, because big chain restaurants, in addition to their negative impact on the market, are also not good and not cheap. At $16.99, the chicken alfredo at Olive Garden isn't something you eat because it's all you can afford.

Value is highly subjective. To a billionaire, the difference between a $10 meal and a $100 meal is statistically insignificant. To most of us diners, moderate price jumps make all the difference in our choices. With fast food so ubiquitously available, if we're deciding to spend anything above the minimum, we demand something additional for our money. We want better food, or we want more food. It will come as no surprise to anyone who has ever eaten the Admiral's Feast at Red Lobster, provolone-stuffed meatballs with fettuccine at Applebee's, or Grandpa's Country Fried Breakfast at Cracker Barrel that these restaurants prioritize volume. At chain restaurants, the perception of value is about making people feel like they got their money's worth.

Outside of competitive athletes, no one should be served portions this large. When we are, the food ends up in one of three places. We take extras home (absolutely reasonable best-case scenario), we eat more than we need or want (contributing to our diet-related health crisis), or we let some of each plate go in the garbage (contributing to our shameful problem of wasting half the food we produce). The giant portions don't change the check size. That's because the price point of a typical big chain, where mains average $12 to $25, is no different from an independent, chef-driven restaurant. Since they can't compete with fast food for price, or good restaurants for quality, they pile low-quality food high, with an ever-expanding menu to ensure that there is "something for everyone."

That's why menu size becomes as important as portion size. That's why you get the 197-item menu at the Cheesecake Factory, which includes 14 snacks, 22 appetizers, 11 salads, 4 "super" foods, 7 flatbread pizzas, 17 "Glamburgers" and sandwiches, 18 pastas, 15 meats and seafoods, 29 "specialties" (including Thai coconut lime chicken, truffle honey chicken, and Baja chicken tacos), 28 "SkinnyLicious" items, 8 eggs, 13 breakfast items, and 11 kids dishes. That's not counting drinks and desserts.[14]

Try as we might, chains are often unavoidable. We end up there after Little League games, or at conferences, because they have private rooms we can book for fifty guests or we've got a diverse crowd of picky eaters and the expansive menu promises options for people on paleo, keto, vegan, or other restrictive diets. The goal of their broad menus is to offer more on the plate, and more variety than anyone else, in order to cast the widest possible net to ensure that when you're looking for a space to host your postgame/retirement/book-club lunch, you have no reason to say no. Or we end up there because we live somewhere that is mostly serviced by big chains.

SUSTAINABILITY BS DETECTOR

So if we have to eat at a big-box chain restaurant, how do we pick the lesser of evils? As far as labor goes, conditions aren't much different from other parts of the industry. I worked with a chef who had spent years at a roast-chicken chain, where she had been a unionized employee with benefits. I mistakenly thought that was the norm at big chains. It's not. Cooks and servers in the machine of chain restaurants are the weakest link. To maintain prices, staff wages are the most easily pressed upon.

What about the food? Do any of these companies care about, or do a better job than others, sourcing their ingredients? And how can we as diners tell the difference?

To the fast-food industry, food is a utility. McDonald's, for example, is the single largest beef purchaser in the United States. Subway is one of the top buyers of tuna in the world. This means raw ingredients have to cost as little as possible. It also means these companies have more potential to effect change if they're motivated to do so by consumer demand. The buying power they wield, which can influence working conditions in agriculture (see: Fair Food Program), is available to be used toward environmental sustainability.

Some do use this power. Though you may not have heard of it, Cheesecake Factory sources palm oil that does not come from deforestation. Who would have guessed that 77 percent of their produce suppliers have a biodiversity plan in place or have conducted biodiversity projects (or both), such as creating riparian buffers, crop rotations, and invasive species management? It's not in their TV ads, which focus on the size of the menu.

These companies, the ones not being steered by nihilistic day traders, would like to exist ten or twenty years from now. They won't if we run out of meat and seafood, as predicted by the World Health Organization's assessment of a global, rising middle-class appetite for animal protein. When McDonald's, which has used their incredible market power to switch entirely to Alaskan pollack for their Filet-O-

Fish sandwiches, moves toward sustainability certification, it may not be because customers demand it, but because they're beginning to realize that if they don't, they'll run out of fish.

Plant-based meats (a component of Asian cuisines long before their recent trendiness) have seen huge strides, gaining a solid foothold in food service, through partnerships with cheffy restaurants first, then branching out to fast-food chains, before launching onto supermarket shelves. Though the retail price of those products has dropped, the Impossible or Beyond burgers are still double the cost of beef. As traditional meat companies like Tyson and Cargill enter the market, that price will continue to decrease. I think that cell-grown meat (actual animal tissue, generated from animal DNA, grown in a lab instead of inside a mammal) is on its way too. As of 2017, pioneer Memphis Meats had gotten the price of their cell-grown beef down to $1,700 a pound. It'll be a while before this is an affordable option for chain restaurants.

In some circles, there's been hype about how we're going to transition to eating insects. In addition to the apparent marketing challenges, breeding them for food still uses too much energy. The solution narrative of insects as a panacea for health, resource, or climate challenges will only lead us to the same monoculture mistakes we made with crops like soy, which was also predicted as an agricultural cure-all and in practice has become just another industrialized food.

Within full-service chain restaurants, there's enough demand or expectation for sustainability from middle-class consumers. There's just not much wiggle room to raise menu prices to account for ethically sourced ingredients. The menu size creates an additional challenge. Because McDonald's sells only one type of fish, it's conceivable for them to work with suppliers and a certification body like the Marine Stewardship Council to provide a consistent, sustainable supply of the product they need. For a chain like Olive Garden, which offers shrimp, salmon, and calamari, any effort at seafood sustainability requires change (and in a corporation, change equals conflict) on multiple fronts. It's harder to make commitments across a wider portfolio.

It's not impossible, though. J D Wetherspoon, an operator with almost nine hundred pubs in the United Kingdom, sources their cod, haddock, skipjack tuna, scampi, farmed salmon, and prawns (a.k.a. shrimp) from separate certified suppliers.[15]

I asked one seafood expert if there was any full-service chain known for doing a best-in-class job on the sustainability front, and they cited the Cheesecake Factory. But how would you or I know this?

These days, every corporate restaurant's website has a page dedicated to their sourcing policies. The verticals go by various names; sustainability, community, or corporate social responsibility (CSR). A decade ago this information wasn't there at all. Today it's still cryptic at best. Reading these pages usually feels like studying Shakespeare in junior high: at the end of every sourcing claim, I can hear my eighth grade teacher asking, "What do we think the author means by this phrase?" Technically, they're written in English, though they usually require a code to translate the hidden intent of each sentence. For example, under the heading "Our Values," here is everything that Applebee's page says:

TRUST
  You can count on us
INCLUSION
  All are welcome
COMMUNITY
  We give back
INTEGRITY
  We do what's right
EXCELLENCE
  Always expect us at our best
INNOVATION
  We're always improving
ACCOUNTABILITY
  We take responsibility[16]

That reads more like a corporate tone poem than an explanation of their policies.

Olive Garden has a "community" page that lists their charitable activities. Parent company Darden has extensive web content devoted to "citizenship," with separate pages for "people," "planet," and "plate," describing their efforts to reduce waste as well as water and energy consumption.[17] While their Olive Garden online material doesn't list any specific initiatives, another Darden brand, LongHorn Steakhouse, goes into more detail, explaining that every location has a sustainability team and uses energy-efficient lightbulbs. The stuff about meat sourcing is a little less specific. "LongHorn is also concerned about the environmental impact of beef production. We believe it's important to advance sustainability not only in our restaurants, but also in the foods we serve. There are more than 700,000 family farms and ranches in the U.S. That's where our beef production starts. . . . LongHorn and our parent company Darden Restaurants are committed to helping find solutions that reduce the environmental impact of beef production and support the livelihoods of beef producers. We are engaging with our key suppliers and partnering with organizations such as the National Cattlemen's Beef Association, the U.S. Sustainable Beef Coalition, and the Global Roundtable on Sustainable Beef to support research and promote improved practices." What does any of that word salad mean? If your child tells you that they are concerned about homework and are working with industry trade groups to explore what can be done about the homework problem, does that mean they've done their homework? Either way, the CSR statement is no longer visible on LongHorn's website.

"Traceable. Sustainable. Responsible." Red Lobster makes big claims in this territory. "These are more than just words on our menu— it's our promise that all of the seafood we serve is sourced to the highest standards. Because, as one of the world's largest seafood purchasers, we believe it's our responsibility to protect and preserve our oceans and marine life for generations to come."[18]

What do these pages and claims mean? And how do we decode them? How do we separate legitimate sourcing commitments from PR bullshit?

Shortly after the turn of this century, within the chef-driven sector, there was a move toward supporting local, sustainable agriculture. We started to see the names of the individual farmers who'd raised the chickens or cultivated the heirloom tomatoes that appeared on menus, and after a little while we grew to expect that any restaurant within this sphere was on the up and up. As Laura Reiley uncovered in "Farm to Fable," her fantastic investigative piece for the *Tampa Bay Times*, fraud is rampant on these menus because food is sold mostly on a trust-based system. "How do you know the Dover sole on your plate is Dover sole? Only that the restaurateur said so," wrote Reiley. "Your purchases are unverifiable unless you drive to that farm or track back through a restaurant's distributors and ask for invoices. I did." Reiley even sent fish samples to be DNA tested. She found tilapia sold as grouper and canned jumbo lump crab from the Indian Ocean or West Pacific Ocean sold as Florida blue crab.[19]

A few years ago, after the *Guardian* published their investigation into slavery in the shrimp business, I contacted ten restaurants in my town and asked them where they got their shrimp. Then I called their suppliers (except for Red Lobster, from which I got no reply to repeated requests) to confirm what they told me. No diner has time to do that. I did because it's my job. But that's supposed to be what these sustainability pages are for, to offer some transparency to the sourcing process. They can't do that if they're written in Orwellian double-speak.

To learn the codes, I spoke with a few people working with sustainability certification organizations, in the United States, Canada, and the United Kingdom. The common thread behind the scenes with these brands is a reluctance to be too public about the effort and positive gains they're making, because they don't want to be criticized for what they haven't achieved yet. Telling diners that you're only using close-containment shrimp in the seafood paella exposes you to questions about where the beef is coming from. "Some are nervous about putting their head above the parapet and drawing attention to the good work that they're doing, for fear that someone might point out the bad work they're doing," says George Clark, senior commercial manager for MSC. "I think that's paranoid or naive."

Because it's harder to make commitments across a wider portfolio, a lot of these companies either don't try or don't want to be too vocal about what they are doing.

Here are some tips I learned from Clark and others for deciphering the language of corporate sustainability claims.

Watch for weasel words.

This is a common term among journalists and English teachers, meaning word choices that diminish the commitment expressed in a sentence. It's the difference between "I'll meet you at noon" and "I'll try to meet you around noon." In the first one, you know I'm leaving on time to meet you at noon. In the second, you don't really trust that I'll be there at all.

Let's look at an example from Cracker Barrel's "Food with Care" page: "At Cracker Barrel, we are dedicated to animal welfare and encourage our suppliers to lead the way in adopting the best animal welfare practices. Cracker Barrel is committed to transitioning 100% of its Grade A egg supply to be cage-free by 2026."[20] Did you spot it? The word *encourage* completely defangs the word *dedicated*. Encouragement is the level of involvement I had when my daughter developed sufficient motor control to grasp a kernel of corn. It's not how you effect major changes in the supply chain. If the company was dedicated, they would use the word *require*. However, in the very next sentence, we see a solid example of clarity, the word *committed* attached to a deadline for a specific policy on cage-free eggs. This is the kind of language we look for. It's a good sign of the company's actual intentions.

Some chains make this decoding simple by being transparent about how little they are doing. Of all the CSR pages I've read, this one by Buffalo Wild Wings is the boldest in what I perceive as its public-facing "whaddaya gonna do" shrug to slavery:

> Buffalo Wild Wings, Inc. ("BWW") provides this statement about its obligations under the Calif. Transparency in Supply Chains Act of 2010. The Act requires BWW to disclose its efforts to eradicate slavery and human trafficking from its direct supply chain. At BWW we believe in doing the right thing. As stated in our Code of Ethics and Business Conduct, BWW expects its suppliers to respect applicable laws and to behave in an ethical manner. While BWW does not presently engage in verification of its product supply chain, audit its suppliers or require certifications regarding the supplies that it receives, we expect our suppliers to conduct their activities in compliance with all applicable laws including those that require them to treat workers fairly, respect human rights and provide a safe and healthy work environment. In coming years, BWW intends to evaluate the ways that it may reduce the risk of slavery and human trafficking in its direct supply chain which may include developing internal accountability standards and providing training to those who have direct responsibility for supply chain management regarding mitigating the risk of slavery and human trafficking in BWW's supply chain.[21]

You don't need to be a professor to translate that one. It seems to me that they don't know and don't care. But in the future, it sounds like they intend to look into it, at which point doing something is not entirely out of the realm of possibility.

That was on their website in the summer of 2020, though, before we knew that forced labor was a bad thing. By the start of 2021, BWW has updated their transparency statement. While it is somewhat more guarded, it is still shockingly dismissive of responsibility: "If we determine that our employees or suppliers are engaged in slavery or human trafficking, our employees will be disciplined, up to and including termination, and we maintain the right to set forth corrective actions with our suppliers and/or terminate the business relationship." Is it too radical to suggest that slavery is beyond the sort of workplace malfeasances for which one gets reprimanded? Seems like a fireable offense.

Conversely, the Cheesecake Factory publishes an annual corporate social responsibility report with an extensive section devoted to sourcing that starts with a flow chart illustrating the company's process for auditing its purchasing agreements.[22] Each group of ingredients lists a stated 2025 objective, like eliminating pesticides in a particular category of produce classified as type 1a or 1b by the World Health Organization or lowering the stocking density (that's how many animals per area) of broiler chickens equal to or less than six pounds per square foot. There's a listing of current progress thus far (50 percent of the pesticides eliminated so far, 30 percent reduction in chicken stocking density), as well as notes on insights and challenges and things they've learned along the way, so diners can contextualize some of what is involved. That kind of specificity is how you earn trust.

I have to confess that when I started to examine these sustainability pages, I wasn't expecting to find anything as seemingly flagrantly dismissive of accountability as Buffalo Wild Wings, but I also didn't dream of anything as helpful and clear as the Cheesecake Factory.

Avoid self-certification.

"We believe in and support efforts within our industry for responsible sourcing and improving the welfare of farm animals," reads the International House of Pancakes' CSR page. "When creating policies and practices related to farm animals we consider impacts on animal health and well-being, the environment, food safety, worker health and safety, consumer preferences and food affordability. We also rely on animal welfare experts to guide our policies." It then goes on to list two professors, and their credentials and university affiliations, advising them on animal-welfare issues, before adding the caveat, "All commitments are dependent on supplier capabilities."[23]

First, that addendum mitigates anything that preceded it. If my wife said that she promises not to murder me so long as I keep the cupboard stocked with the Italian vanilla wafer cookies she likes while adding, "All commitments are dependent on supplier capabilities," there would already be a Lifetime movie about my death called *The Cookie Killer*. In a later passage, they add that their commitment to sourcing cage-free eggs from Latin America is conditioned not just on supplier availability but also on "consumer affordability." So they'll try. But if it's expensive, they may not do it.

Second, beware any restaurant chain touting their own experts or internal policies. The whole purpose of sustainability NGOs is to develop systems for protecting our environment based on research, not profit. The reason for their existence is that the gap between what governments will allow and what business will get away with is too wide. For all our sakes, there need to be higher standards. The MSC and its counterparts (Seafood Watch from the Monterey Bay Aquarium and Oceanwise from the Vancouver Aquarium) are not infallible. For now, they are the best way we have, as consumers, to speedily identify which species can be sustainably consumed. They are inherently more trustworthy than the consultants that chain restaurants retain.

In one particularly striking case of adding insult to injury, IHOP adds a last line to their CSR page, seemingly for the purpose of letting us know they don't believe in the efficacy of any of their actions: "IHOP accounts for only a small fraction of the animal-based products purchased each year, making our ability to impact industry-wide practices somewhat limited. Regardless, we will continue to explore opportunities to improve the treatment of farm animals within the context of our business and the industry." This company, which seems not to believe their actions leave a significant footprint, has 1,831 locations and uses 214 million eggs a year. It was the fifth-highest-grossing full-service chain in 2020 (after Olive Garden, Applebee's, Buffalo Wild Wings, and Chili's).[24]

Ask for the names of suppliers.

We don't have to be well versed in the difference between grain- and grass-fed beef or farmed and wild salmon to ask our restaurant server if they can tell us something about where our food comes from. Knowing or caring about that answer at all is the bare minimum.

As you'll recall from the legendary "Is it local?" Portlandia sketch described in the Introduction, asking where your chicken comes from is often thought of as the height of urban, bourgeoisie elitism. Yet what could be more supportive of rural communities than wanting food to come from independent, rather than industrial, farmers? The question of where food comes from should stand as a reflection not of the diner but of the merchant. If they can't answer the question, do they deserve our business?

In case you're wondering, I do actually ask these questions when I go to restaurants, even chain restaurants. I've gotten a lot of different kinds of answers. Any given server, who is frequently just another underpaid employee of these large corporations, is often in way over their head when trying to account for policies they may have no knowledge of or control over. I try to be respectful of their role and its constraints. Here, from most desirable to least, is the full list of responses I've encountered.

- I don't have to ask: I find the answers to all of my questions clearly displayed on the restaurant's menu or website.

- When I inquire, my server proudly describes the names and locations of producers as well as their agricultural practices with all the detail and passion of a museum docent.

- The server is able to provide clear information about some, if not all, food sources.

- The server displays some awareness of the restaurant's sourcing practices and promises to return with more information from a manager or chef.

- The server admits they don't know the answers to my questions but offers, if I'd like, to ask the chef.

- The server admits they don't know the answers to my questions and shows absolutely no interest in chasing them down.

- The server suggests, "Maybe it's on our website?"

- The server asks, "Why do you want to know?"

- The server admits that no one in the restaurant knows or cares.

- The server delivers a completely fake answer.

I was once on a judging panel for a chowder competition at a sustainable-seafood event. We heard all the answers on this list. The chef next to me, who grilled each contestant thoroughly, reminded me that these are all teachable moments, that if we don't hold restaurants accountable, we're saying it doesn't matter. But always use a please and a thank-you. It's never rude to ask, though the way we ask certainly can be.

Some chains may have good sourcing practices but poor training and education for staff, though I find that there's usually a relationship between caring and knowing. If a company is concerned enough to make environmental commitments in sourcing, it will probably be reflected in the staff's awareness of some of those policies.

That last one on the list, a fake answer, is sometimes hard to detect. If a server told me, "It's from Steranko Farms," I wouldn't know if that were true or not. Deception of this sort is far from rare, as "Farm to Fable" uncovered. If someone's going to lie to you, it's going to take work to uncover that fact. It happened to me: one of the restaurateurs whom I asked about shrimp sourcing made false claims to me, easily disproved when I called his supplier.

Few of us, as diners, are able to invest in that type of legwork, especially in the few hungry minutes while we decide what to order. Restaurants willing to lie to us will likely go undetected. I salute them, in the way that I must concede some grudging respect for con artists, cult leaders, grifters, flimflammers, and others of their kind. If you'll permit a generalization, scammers are usually, by their nature, greedy. Yet they rarely get found out. The exposure of high-profile liars, such as drug-enhanced cyclist Lance Armstrong or the seven tobacco CEOs who testified to Congress that they believed nicotine was not addictive, happens only once or twice a decade.

Cost is one proxy for doing the detective work: if a menu item is really unexpectedly cheap, that's usually an indication of questionable sourcing. The method is far from infallible, but especially if you pay consistent attention to prices you'll start to notice more patterns. Mussels, for example, are a very sustainable choice in seafood and affordable too. Shrimp, on the other hand, *should* be expensive: most are farmed in environmentally destructive conditions, and many are harvested by modern-day indentured workers and in some cases by enslaved labor. The warning sign you're looking for is a dish that seems like a bargain given the specific kind of food it is.

It's not possible to entirely resolve the mystery of where a restaurant's food comes from through amateur sleuthing. These tools, however, are a good way to get a better sense of how serious they are about their environmental commitments and a good entry point to a conversation about it.

So what I'm saying is, give yourself permission to be that person. Don't be afraid to ask questions. It should not be embarrassing, to you or your friends. Actually, quite the opposite. It helps. When more of us ask, it demonstrates a consumer demand for the type of food choices and changes we want to see in restaurants.

There are better operators in the chain space, both in QSR and in full service, like In-N-Out, Pal's, and the Cheesecake Factory. It takes asking around to find them. In general, I think we'd do well to stay away from chains altogether. None of these restaurants need our business—not in the way that a locally owned small restaurant does. If we're going to frequent them, it may as well be as activist shareholders, using our minuscule investment as a platform to voice our desire for the type of company we want them to be.

· 7 ·

The Grocerant

The advent of supermarkets changed household
purchasing habits, but not in the direction
advertisers would like us to think they did.

—Ruth Schwartz Cowan

When I saw those shelves crammed with hundreds,
thousands of cans, cartons and goods of every possible
sort, for the first time I felt quite frankly sick with despair
for the Soviet people. Even the Politburo doesn't
have this choice. Not even Mr. Gorbachev.

—Boris Yeltsin, upon visiting Randall's,
an American supermarket, in 1989

We have no idea who grew the food or where it was
grown. We don't have cultural rules around those foods
to help us determine our choices.

—Dr. Sarah Fessenden, anthropologist

AFTER CRUISING THE AISLES OF LUCKY'S MARKET, I PULL UP
a stool at the ramen bar in the center of the store and ask for a bowl

of spicy tonkotsu. The cook starts assembling my order: a small ladle of tare (the concentrated sauce that flavors the broth), squirt of sriracha hot sauce thinned out with boiling water (or the clearest chicken stock I've ever seen), a few slices of char siu, pickled cabbage, jalapeno slices, jiggly noodles, and a near-runny boiled egg. As far as ramen I've had, it's not the worst. Compared to other meals I've eaten inside a supermarket, where the usual options are deli sandwiches on cold bread, mushy potato wedges, and desiccated lasagna, it's easily the best.

It's Saturday morning in Naples, Florida, and I'm hungry. I wolf down the bowl of salty, fatty spiciness, wipe my sweaty brow, and then head over to the store's café, which offers an assortment of fancy coffees, cold brew, tea, chai, kombucha, and more. They've got maple bacon donuts made in-house, a community corkboard with nothing pinned to it, plus two-dollar beer and three-dollar wine. The fluffy donut disappears down my throat between two sips of espresso. Then, as advised by the "sip and stroll" sign, I get a plastic cup of red wine to drink while I check out the selection of organic apples and wild salmon burgers.

Lucky's is located, to paraphrase newscaster Ted Koppel, thirty miles and billions of dollars west of Immokalee, where tomato pickers live six to a trailer. Thanks to a handful of billionaire residents in a town with fewer than four hundred thousand people, Naples is one of the richest cities in America, with a cost of living 20 percent above the national average.[1] And Lucky's, a sort of red-state Whole Foods that focuses on organic produce and hormone-free meat, where the pharmacy section is labeled "apothecary," is correspondingly posh.

The chain grew out of Boulder, Colorado, in the early 2000s, where the original store's shopping carts had cup holders for beer. In 2016, after expanding the brand to Missouri, Montana, Kentucky, Michigan, Wyoming, Indiana, Iowa, and Georgia, the company sold a majority interest to Kroger, America's second-largest food retailer, which quickly expanded Lucky's from seventeen locations to thirty-nine. However, in 2019, Kroger divested their stake. By January 21, 2020, four days before I stop by for my ramen, the company announced that they would close twenty of their twenty-one Florida stores. Two days later, Lucky's filed for bankruptcy.[2] Given that the company is selling off hundreds of millions in assets, I feel the sale on organic chicken stock ought to be better than two for six dollars.

If anyone is watching me on the security camera, they must wonder what the hell I'm up to. Who goes to a supermarket just to eat? After my soup, donut, and coffee, I've just wandered the store drinking, with no shopping basket, before finally getting in line at the cashier just to buy saltwater taffy. The taffy is for my wife. I'm here to see how supermarkets are fighting for their survival in a digital era—which, it turns out, involves getting into the restaurant game.

It's January 25, 2020. So I don't yet know the separation we'll all feel soon, when we can no longer stroll, safely, and carefree, around these cathedrals of food and mercantilism. I don't know that soon we'll be wearing masks when we shop and that supermarket employees will become frontline essential workers, expected to risk their lives but told to wait their turn for vaccinations, that they'll receive bonus hazard pay for a few months, before having it taken away by just about every supermarket chain except for Costco and Trader Joe's.[3] It's still the Before Times. Just barely.

For the past decade, grocery stores have been trying to outrun extinction from the same forces that put them on top of the food business—convenience and price. They are under attack from two fronts: they can't beat Walmart (the nation's grocery leader by a wide margin) on pricing, and they can't beat Amazon for convenience. So, while trying to still compete on those levels, investing in technology in the desperate race to catch up to their digital opponents, they've also been developing in-store experiences intended to attract customers and keep them shopping in person.

That's where the grocerant, the restaurant inside the grocery store, comes from. Yeah, it's a dumb name—possibly the worst portmanteau since *bromance*. Even a good idea can have a bad name.

FAFH VERSUS FAH: WHEN TITANS CLASH!

Well before they felt the encroachment of retailer Walmart or saw the threat of e-commerce on the horizon, supermarkets were feeling the pinch as American spending on food away from home (FAFH) rose to match spending on food at home (FAH). Dining out comprised only a quarter of our household food budgets in the postwar years. But it kept inching upward, more or less equalizing until June through August 2018, when dining budgets exceeded groceries for three straight months.[4]

In the 1990s and well into the 2000s, grocery stores were convinced that they should stick with the strategy of competing on commodity pricing, even as Walmart, then Google and Amazon, made that impossible. "Fifteen years ago, I had a hard time getting them to experiment," says supermarket designer Kevin Kelley, speaking shortly after my visit to Lucky's. "Now they're desperate. They're willing to let go of the shackles of their industry. Certain players, local and regional, are much more willing to go for broke. Because they are going broke."

The son of an advertiser and an architect by training, Kelley understands that design influences behavior. At the beginning of his career, in the early 1990s, Kelley's firm was approached by North Carolina grocer Harris Teeter. Supermarket owners were already nervous about the shifting food dollars of Americans and were tempted to incorporate food service. The store redesign was successful. It put Kelley's firm, Shook Kelley, on the map, leading to work with Whole Foods, Kroger, and smaller chains like Hy-Vee, Freson Bros., Save Mart, Gelson's, and more.

Given their shared interest in food, you'd think that at a certain level, restaurant and grocery company executives would have a similar mindset. Kelley, whose work fuses the two worlds, found that they couldn't be further apart in their thinking. Compared to the experimental eagerness of restaurateurs, leaders in grocery are terrified of making a single mistake, obsessed with not being inefficient for a second. Thomas Crosby, Pal's CEO, tells me that if the company has an idea to test, they'll try it out at three locations: prioritizing one manager who loves the idea, one who hates it, and one who is indifferent. The business results then dictate further action.

Food service within supermarkets mostly goes after a subsection of customers: those who enjoy shopping and are willing to incorporate eating into the experience. Catering to them runs against the temptation, in the modern era, to be all things to all customers. The "Macy's model," says Kelley, is the fatal error that department stores made—and supermarkets have been replicating it. The only way for most supermarkets to survive, not counting the national or global chains that have at least a chance of developing e-commerce streams to compete with Amazon, is to specialize, to pick some key factor at which they can excel. "The sad reality is the grocery store business model, as it was, no longer works. Amazon will invade every small corner, every small town. There's nowhere to hide. That doesn't mean physical stores don't work."

At the time, Kelley predicted smaller, more focused stores, aiming to appeal to our desire to enjoy our food-shopping experience. A huge part of that is food service.

Capturing that FAFH spending was key to the survival of supermarkets. If busy shoppers were going to leave the grocery store and stop at the drive-thru on their way home, why not capture those dollars before they stepped out the door by giving them a grocery-plus-dining experience under one roof? It worked. From 2008 to 2015, in-store and prepared food sales in supermarkets grew 30 percent, amounting to a $29 billion bite taken directly out of QSRs' lunch.[5]

Kroger launched their own brand of in-store restaurants, Kitchen 1883, plus a food hall in their hometown of Cincinnati. Hy-Vee supermarkets began featuring Market Grille, a restaurant where you could enjoy shrimp tacos or biscuits and gravy with a bottle of wine. Gelson's in LA offered "sip and shop," allowing customers to hand off their shopping list and sit down for a meal in the "noshing & imbibing" area while letting staff pick up their groceries. As grocery stores began featuring dim sum stands, pierogi bars, and wood-fired pizzas, eating became an increasing part of the food-shopping experience. This happened only when supermarkets found themselves hopelessly under attack, their old tactics having proven ineffective against modern adversaries.

Getting a grocery store to cook food doesn't seem all that hard. They've got flour, cheese, and tomatoes. They've got thousands of square feet for ovens. Making pizza should be in their wheelhouse. "I've sat in grocery store meetings with companies that are in big trouble, close to bankruptcy," Kelley says. "They'll put their head in their hand and almost cry and say, 'We can't make a good slice of pizza.'"

The problem is that supermarkets, even smaller regional chains, are such large ships that they're almost impossible to turn. There is always internal opposition to change—and particularly to doing anything incrementally, such as making really good pizza at only one location. Companies with more than one hundred stores are so committed to executing everything at scale that anything requiring finesse inflicts decision paralysis. "What grocery loves to do is fifty to a hundred things on a mediocre level. And what we try to get them to do is six to eight things on a stellar level. And that is probably the hardest battle we ever fight." Kelley's clients all want to make changes across the board, in one or two hundred units. And they can't. Altering the lighting, rearranging how the aisles flow into each other, and constructing a place for diners to sit within a stadium of food retail space are major projects. "So what I have to get them to do is do one store. Success perpetuates success."

The grocerant strategy is about changing what a supermarket means to its customers. While there are people, like me (disclosure: I got married in a grocery store; but we'll get to that), who do enjoy shopping, and even feel a deep, personal connection to grocery shopping and even to particular stores, for many of us grocery stores have long been utilitarian depots—places you pop in and out of to acquire the milk and toilet paper you need and don't think about once you're out the door.

For retailers, the grocerant "gets people on the lot," as car dealerships describe the most crucial element of sales. The supermarket with those tri-tip sandwiches inside the store offers an incentive to choose one shop over another. Eating at the supermarket may also be an impulse purchase. We're already there and short on time. Why not kill two birds with one stone? If we don't have to make another stop for dinner, we can keep shopping. And the longer we shop, the more we spend. Or, to use another retail phrase, the longer we spend in the store, the larger our "basket size."

That's why, in recent years, supermarkets were developing restaurants inside their buildings, to get customers to want to stay, to hang out, to relax. It was working. While Costco, which loses money on their $1.50 hot dog and soda combo, is willing to take a hit on food service just to satisfy customers, most grocerants have been making money.

By 2019, in-store food service constituted 5.3 percent of supermarket revenue, continuing the growth of 8.2 percent a year.[6] And then you-know-what happened.

TWO MONTHS LATER

We all remember the horror of grocery stores in March 2020. "Like a zombie movie" was how a lot of people described the panic buying of toilet paper and frozen vegetables, coupled with the eerie quality of empty streets. The zombie genre is just a proxy for what everyday life is like for displaced people all over the world. More canny observers noted that the supermarket experience of the early pandemic, the visual of long lines and empty shelves, the dread of uncertainty, was for more privileged shoppers their first visceral experience with the concept of food insecurity.

This wasn't actual scarcity. Society wasn't going to run short of food or cleaning products. This was more like when people say it's impossible to get a reservation at a restaurant because they tried and failed to land one for 7:30 p.m. on a Friday. The restaurant has plenty of seats, available at different times or different days. We just can't all consume the same commodity at the same time. A supermarket shelf can only hold so many cans of beans. When everyone tries to buy everything at once, the suddenly short-staffed store cannot restock the shelves fast enough to maintain the label-forward appearance of order.

If you've ever been in a warehouse or food terminal, you know that retail shelves are a minuscule fraction of stock. Collectively, we had plenty of meat, cheese, and lettuce. Despite the weakness of a too-consolidated supply chain, we had a federal government willing to label workers in meat plants and agricultural fields as essential, to put their health at risk so we didn't run out. Production kept rolling.

This was our worst instincts at play—some of us hoarding more than we needed at the expense of others having enough. I understand and share the anxiety. North Americans are not accustomed to seeing empty shelves. In a society where we have instant access to everything all the time, the thought of eating beans and peas, because there is no beef or broccoli on the shelf today, is repellent. It's a psychological threat to our culture's perception of abundance.

It was no surprise that many of us panicked. If you're looking for a species that reacts to calamity in a calm, organized fashion, uniting for their common interest, I'm sure there are many episodes of *Star Trek: The Next Generation* that fulfill that fantasy. But we're twenty-first-century humans; panicky shortsightedness is our brand.

And this was in the early days, when people believed that social isolation lockdowns would be a matter of only weeks. We had yet to see the mass layoffs widening the gaps in our weak social safety net that would push so many people into actual food insecurity.

At least temporarily, pandemic conditions reversed the trend in food spending. In 2019 FAFH (eating out) reached 54.8 percent of America's total $1.77 trillion food spending. That dropped 20 percent in March 2020, then another 34 percent in April, while FAH spending increased by 26 percent.[7] And certainly, nobody was taking a break from their toilet-paper hoarding to lounge in the store with a tray of grocery-store sushi before getting home.

Though grocery executives knew it wouldn't last, suddenly they were dealing with Thanksgiving- and Christmas-level volumes every day. Their stores became necessary to the maintenance of society, with employees forced to work in impossible environments. Overnight, they hired additional staff to keep up with restocking, hustled to erect

Plexiglas shields between cashiers and customers, to place markers on the floor indicating how far apart we should be standing. But as we grappled to understand the transmission factors of COVID-19, and to implement the necessary safety precautions, the political conspiracy side of our culture was busy doing what it does, aided by a president who fueled the fire by denying the severity of this health crisis and the measures needed to combat it. Retail employees soon found themselves under physical threat from customers who wouldn't adhere to mask-wearing requests or requirements. All over the country, minimum-wage workers were subjected to insults, threats, and assault by customers. At the beginning of May, in Flint, Michigan, Family Dollar security guard Calvin Munerlyn was shot in the back of the head, murdered for asking a customer to put on a mask. In addition to a contagious disease, other shoppers had become a lethal threat as well.

By late spring, though it would be inaccurate to say tension had lessened, most of us had figured out a new pattern for food purchasing, based on our personal formula of risk tolerance, compassion for workers and businesses, local availability, and what we could afford. The days of cruising the aisles, pausing to compare prices between two packages of couscous or find a sugar-free breakfast cereal, were replaced by following directional arrows on the floor and keeping as much distance from each other as possible. We planned our supermarket visits in advance and wore masks and gloves, getting in and out as quickly as possible. We ordered online, for click-and-collect or delivery. We supported restaurants and catering companies pivoting to food retail, picking up bread or cheese from a local bistro. Some of us bought directly from local farmers and subscribed to community-supported agriculture food boxes.

What had changed in the process, probably forever, is our relationship with physical grocery stores, something that had already been happening in every other part of our lives as consumers. Prepandemic, America's nearly forty thousand supermarkets were a major holdout in the shift to online sales. E-commerce accounts for only 3 percent of grocery sales, compared to the massive uptake in other retail fields like toys, fashion, furniture, and electronics, where online business already constituted as much as a quarter of all sales.[8]

Globally, e-commerce's chunk of total retail had doubled from 7.4 percent in 2015 to a projected 15.5 percent in 2020. At the same time, the adoption of online grocery ordering in North America was well behind countries like South Korea, Japan, and China, though every industry analyst predicted it to grow, with the Food Marketing Institute estimating 20 percent of grocery sales to be digital by 2025.[9]

COVID-19 changed that. Our old reasons for preferring the physical shopping experience—the desire to squeeze a lemon or be around people—were rendered irrelevant by the necessity of safety concerns. Almost overnight, Walmart's e-commerce sales were up 74 percent (half of Walmart's revenue is from food). Kroger was up 92 percent.[10] The volume of purchases wouldn't last. But the acceleration toward online food shopping, something many customers were still uncomfortable with, would be irreversible. People finally had a compelling reason to get over their prudishness about buying a peach online. Even postvaccine, grocery businesses are likely to reconfigure both digital strategy and store design, out of fear of another pandemic as much as new expectations in communal hygiene.

As our lives streamlined during the early lockdowns, so did our conversations. I found myself repeating the same talking points with every friend: lack of child care, walks around an empty downtown, the viability of restaurant delivery, concern for people around us, fear of infection, and Zoom bar mitzvahs. But the most common thing we talked about was how much food shopping had changed. We talked about our trips to the supermarket like they were mountain-climbing expeditions. We asked each other what grocery channels (in-store, delivery, community-supported-agriculture box, direct from farmers) we were using, how much rice we had, and how long we thought the situation would last. It frustrated me how much we were thinking in the present, when the massive supply chain and experience of food purchasing needed to change so much more than installing plastic shields.

We were all just guessing. So I looked for someone who actually knows the business.

Having the foresight to launch supermarketguru.com in 1994, Phil Lempert has been America's grocery maven for the past twenty-five years. "Going through the COVID-19 retail shopping experience has turned off a lot of people," says Lempert. Customers, he says, can no longer enjoy the act of shopping. Also, stores have increased costs from sanitation, Plexiglas, masks, and so on. "We can't make money on the current system of delivery or even click-and-collect. It's too labor intensive. We have to reimagine what retail is and what it's gonna look like."

Lempert's first prediction is that the grocerant is dead. The room the food-service stations take up, and the lousy experience of socially distanced dining, defeats their purpose. Also deceased is the forty-thousand-square-foot warehouse-style store, filled with tens of thousands of items, that we're supposed to explore until we find the twenty-five things on our list.

Lempert envisions a new hybrid, with the big-box store divided in half. The front half has all the fresh, experiential food with which we want to interact: the vibrant produce bins, the butcher counter, the toasty smell from the bakery, along with the human staff to help us, to smile and say hello. In the back half would be all the cans, jars, and boxes, the products we need but feel less emotional attachment to, with fulfillment executed by automation.

Lempert says that we'll order these things online, either manually or by auto-replenishment, and then make an appointment to go shopping at the front part of the store, enabling the business to control the number of shoppers at any one time in the store and the number of employees needed to assist them. "And after I'm done with my fresh-food shopping, I'm going to pick up my groceries that are packed and waiting for me and walk out the door. That back end of the store is fully robotic." I'm in no position to doubt Lempert's expertise, though the long-term future of supermarkets is still unwritten. What seems indisputable at this point is that supermarkets must change.

Otherwise, local grocery stores and regional chains are just waiting as Walmart chips away at their profits, with acquisition by Amazon as their only salvation.

As long as they're adapting, we should too. Now that we've all experienced how it feels to stand in line for food, let's think about changing how we buy it. If supermarkets have to go through a transformation to continue their existence, we should reconsider our shopping habits, who we buy from, how much we buy, and why we buy it.

Before we reimagine the act of food shopping, we need to understand how much it has already changed in our lifetimes, how the grocery business is always changing. Rather than shed a tear for supermarkets, let's remember that they were the Amazon of their era, the price and convenience juggernaut that put a generation of butchers, bakers, fishmongers, and greengrocers out of business. To question the grocery experience of the future, we have to understand its past.

SUPERMARKETS, THE AMAZON OF THE 1930s

They may seem like they've always been part of our lives, an unconsidered but essential utility like roads or plumbing. However, supermarkets, the disruptors of their day, were invented less than a century ago. Escalators, neon lights, and airplanes have been around longer.

In the nineteenth century, public food markets were erected in every major city. Dealing in both retail and wholesale, this was a model borrowed from Europe, where towns constructed markets on public land. These buildings provided centralized space for merchants, and an easy way for local officials to inspect and regulate shops, ensuring fair business practices and food safety. The concept got federal support in America after the Civil War, by Commissioner of Agriculture Horace Capron, who pushed for the development of public markets as a way to connect farmers with their growing urban consumers.

Many cities had multiple markets. Baltimore, for example, had the Wholesale Fish Market, the Produce Market, Hollins Market, Broadway Market, Cross Street Market, Belair Market, Northeast Market, Lafayette Market, and Lexington Market.

Thanks to this agglomeration of food businesses, markets were hubs where ordinary people encountered food items far beyond their own inherited cuisines. "More than just places to buy and sell fresh food, these buildings and spaces created a dynamic, open environment that encouraged the transmission, exchange, and introduction, of new tastes and ingredients," writes Helen Tangires, author of *Public Markets and Civic Culture in Nineteenth-Century America*.[11]

As cities grew, merchants expanded outside of these markets, opening independent stores on busy streets. But even by the twentieth century, there was no such thing as a one-stop shop for food. Every aisle we're now familiar with in the supermarket corresponds to a separate type of store that was common back then. You'd go out in the morning to the dry-goods store, for canned goods and bulk items, for instance, and speak with a shopkeeper to make your requests. They filled your order behind the counter, weighing out beans or flour from barrels and sacks. After that, as a next step in this daily ritual, you'd stop at a butcher, fishmonger, greengrocer, and bakery for the goods they provided. These small stores, maybe a thousand square feet or less, were everywhere in our cities. Catering mostly to their own neighborhoods, shop staff and customers would know each other by name.

In the late nineteenth century, an entrepreneur named Bernard Kroger had four of these smaller grocery stores called the Great Western Tea Company, until he bought out his partner and eventually gave the business his own name. In 1901 he added a bakery to the company, merging what had previously been two separate kinds of businesses and enabling the Cincinnati stores to supply bread at cost. By 1902 Kroger had opened forty locations.[12] By the 1920s, most smaller shops made forays into this diversification of products—a little bread at the greengrocer, a little produce at the butcher shop—diluting each store's specialty or expertise.

The next major innovation was self-service, with store owners stocking items on shelves in the front of their shops instead of the back, so customers could help themselves. This shift, pioneered in Memphis by the first Piggly Wiggly in 1916, was a big convenience, as customers didn't have to wait for someone to fill another customer's order before obtaining their own items.[13] This also removed the need to form a direct relationship with shopkeepers—an early step down a long road of depersonalization.

As regional chains expanded, gradually carrying a wider variety of goods, they were able to copy Kroger's move, buying related businesses like bakeries and canneries, effectively becoming their own suppliers in a business strategy known as vertical integration. This allowed them to sell at lower prices, fueling a competitive edge over smaller grocers.[14]

It would be another decade before someone put together the whole supermarket idea.

In the 1920s, Michael Cullen was a regional manager for Kroger, overseeing ninety-four small stores in Illinois. Cullen had a vision for retailing all food products under one large roof, offering more prepackaged food with less weighing and serving, surrounded by ample room for cars. He pitched this idea, of a monstrously sized store with a lot of parking and 80 percent self-service, in a letter to his bosses. "Can you imagine how the public would respond to a store of this kind? I would have to call out the police and let the public in so many at a time," his proposal boasted. "I would lead the public out of the high-priced houses of bondage into the low prices of the house of the promised land."[15]

Possibly hampered by his biblical writing style, Cullen was ignored. But he was determined. Quitting his job with Kroger, in 1930 Cullen realized his dream when he opened King Kullen, a six-thousand-square-foot store in Queens, New York.[16]

His proto-supermarket didn't just carry a little of this and that. When you went to King Kullen, there was no need for a trip to another store. It sold everything, and at cheaper prices, thanks to the scope of its buying power, a huge advantage for a retailer at any time, but especially as the Depression made customers ever more price conscious.[17]

For customers, the early supermarkets—a term first used by the Albers Super Market, launched by a former Kroger VP in 1933—were major innovations, no less radical than online shopping or dating apps seemed at the dawn of the twenty-first century.

Those first supermarkets looked very different from the grid layout of aisles, familiar to shoppers today. Clarence Saunders, founder of Piggly Wiggly, patented a system in which customers entered a channel at the front door, a zigzagging aisleway that escorted them through all the sections, before arriving at the cash register at the end. The maze was similar to Ikea's design, minus the shortcuts. Saunders expanded Piggly Wiggly to 1,260 locations (there are 530 today), generating $100 million a year, before losing a stock battle for control of his company in 1923. He started another chain, which fell victim to the Depression. He then spent a decade developing another futuristic concept way ahead of its time, Keedoozle, an automated grocery where products were behind glass, accessed by keys also used to add up bills. "In five years," Saunders told *Life* magazine in 1949, "there will be a thousand Keedoozles throughout the U.S., selling $5 billion worth of goods."[18]

It didn't work out that way. Still, at the time of his death in 1953, undaunted by the failure of Keedoozle, he was working on another automated grocery idea, this one called Foodelectric.[19] Saunders was a grocery visionary. (A second disclosure: my daughter currently sleeps with a stuffed animal named Piggly Wiggly, who also answers to Clarence Saunders.) He was a half century early with his ideas, trying to execute a concept suited to the digital age using analog tools. Keedoozle was basically a steampunk version of the automated bodegas and cashier-free groceries being pioneered by tech companies today. Like Howard Stark, Saunders had envisioned the future, but was limited by the technology of his time.

Around the same period when Saunders was trying to mad scientist the grocery industry, a less ambitious innovation found a more welcome embrace with shoppers. As distinct from more contained shops where you're making a limited number of purchases at any one time, larger stores with many items required a new way of collecting your goods. Baskets were no longer big enough for the scope of shopping: people filled them to the brim and they were too heavy. Sylvan Goldman came up with the solution to put them on wheels.

The shopping cart, created in 1937 for Goldman's Oklahoma City chain of stores, Humpty Dumpty, was at first rejected by men as too effeminate and similar to a baby carriage. After the store hired models to walk around pushing the carts, however, they took off and became a standard part of the shopping experience. Now customers could buy more than they could carry.[20] In the spring of 2020, we demanded that retailers create Plexiglas barriers overnight, to contend with a pandemic we hadn't heard of yesterday. So seven years seems like a long time between the first supermarket and the first shopping cart.

But perhaps the biggest technological innovation that enabled people to adopt supermarkets was the fridge. Developed and patented in the late nineteenth century, early refrigerators used toxic gases—methyl chloride, ammonia, and sulfur dioxide—as coolants. Accidents pushed fridge companies to develop chlorofluorocarbons and facilitated the creation of larger, safer, and cheaper fridges. In 1911 General Electric sold a wooden model, the Audiffren, for $1,000—twice the cost of a car at the time. The all-steel Monitor Top refrigerator, introduced by GE in 1927, was a comparative steal at $525. By the end of the decade, the majority of Americans owned a fridge. Until this era, most people had used iceboxes, which were essentially large, wooden coolers, the interiors lined with zinc and filled with ice.[21] These were small, had to be washed out regularly, and were not conducive to long-term food storage. There had simply been no point in filling the icebox with a week's worth of meat or fish because things wouldn't stay fresh that long: back then, daily shopping wasn't a lifestyle choice but a necessity. The prevalence of electric refrigerators meant that people could safely store food for longer, and we gradually shifted to the concept of a weekly shop.

Not all these developments were met with pure enthusiasm. As grocery chains expanded, and the Depression worsened, a popular and legal resistance to them mounted. Much of this stemmed from what were seen as the new chains' monopolistic practices.[22] "As the grocery chains got bigger, they bought directly from manufacturers, often demanding volume discounts, rather than through wholesalers," explains Marc Levinson, author of *The Great A&P and the Struggle for Small Business in America*. Wholesalers did not appreciate being cut out, and their opposition to the new supermarkets culminated in a victorious 1946 antitrust suit against A&P, which succeeded in partially breaking the company up. As the economy rebounded after the war, however, public pressure waned. Under a more business-friendly Eisenhower administration in the 1950s, the Department of Justice dropped the campaign to dismantle the growing power of chain supermarkets.[23]

With no legal impediments in their way, the rise of car culture empowered supermarkets to dominate our food shopping. In the 1950s, fueled by a postwar boom in the economy and population, we built suburbs with bigger houses and highways leading to them; populations transitioned to the habit of driving everywhere. Cars and their spacious trunks additionally favored the weekly shop at the supermarket over daily trips to multiple stores. The suburban supermarket, with its parking, variety, and price, took precedence over the old-fashioned, smaller shop's quality, expertise, and personalized service. The trend perpetuated itself, with chains building ever-bigger stores and ever-bigger parking lots to accommodate them.[24]

It was billed as a time saver, a boon for shoppers—which, then as now, primarily meant women. While it might seem that purchasing all of our food in one location would reduce domestic labor, it had the opposite effect. "The advent of supermarkets changed household purchasing habits, but not in the direction advertisers would like us to think they did," says Ruth Schwartz Cowan, historian and author of *More Work for Mother: The Ironies of Household Technology from the Open Hearth to the Microwave*. The new supermarkets provided everything under one roof while offloading the work of buying food to individual shoppers. "After World War 2, the spread of automobile ownership and the growth of the suburbs led to the cessation of retail delivery services."[25] Those smaller local shops required you to make multiple stops, but those stops were all in your neighborhood. Also, many of the shops had delivered.

As supermarkets continued to develop, they found technologies to save on in-store labor, as well. In June 1964, inside a Marsh supermarket in Troy, Ohio, a pack of Wrigley's chewing gum passed over a glass plate, exposing the bar code on the package to a helium-neon laser beam. The beam, detected by a photo-diode, relayed the data to a computerized cash register. That gum, with the aid of a Spectra Physics–model price scanner that now lives in the Smithsonian, became the Neil Armstrong of groceries, the first item to be scanned and sold, transforming the analog systems of inventory control, until then managed by paper, pencils, and human memory. Before then, packages each needed a price sticker, which would have to be modified if the price changed.[26] Universal product codes (a.k.a. bar codes), pushed by companies like Kmart and Walmart, didn't become standard until the 1980s. Eventually, though, they eliminated much drudgery. They also laid the groundwork for the automated and self-service checkout options we are starting to see today—the ones free of human cashiers entirely.

The jobs these innovations displaced were done by people like Babe Secoli, the supermarket checker featured in Studs Terkel's 1974 book, *Working: People Talk About What They Do All Day and How They Feel About What They Do.* "On the register is a list of some prices, that's for part-time girls. I never look at it. I don't have to look at the keys on my register," said Secoli, who professed an intuitive ability to spot shoplifters, describing her wizardry with the cash register.

> I use my three fingers—my thumb, my index finger, and my middle finger. The right hand. And my left hand is on the groceries. . . . I got my hips pushin' on the button and it rolls around on the counter. When I feel I have enough groceries in front of me, I let go of my hip. I'm just movin'—the hips, the hand, and the register. You just keep goin', one two, one two. If you've got that rhythm, you're a fast checker. Your feet are flat on the floor and you're turning your head

back and forth. . . . If someone interrupts to ask me a price, I'll answer while I'm movin'. Like playin' a piano. . . . I love my job. I've got very nice bosses. And the pay is terrific. I automatically get a raise because of the union.[27]

Like the people who grow our tomatoes, supermarket cashiers are classified as unskilled labor, an insult to workers who find artistry in efficiency. As with most businesses around the world, supermarkets spent the latter half of the twentieth century consolidating and finding ways to get rid of people like Secoli. Chains bought smaller chains, were in turn gobbled by larger chains, or merged with competitors. The innovation of the 1970s, driven by economic inflation and price wars, was supermarkets buying or creating alternate brands, discount variations, convenience stores, and pharmacies.[28] "That's when you start seeing a lot of chains opening discount branches with different names to distinguish them from the parent company," supermarket historian David Gwynn tells me. For example, Kroger's current roster of 2,752 stores includes the banners of Dillons (with its subsidiaries Baker's and Gerbes), Fred Meyer (including Ralphs), Harris Teeter, Roundy's (a.k.a. Metro Market, a.k.a. Pick 'n Save) and Smith's. Over the years they've owned a dozen more: Barney's, Hook's, Krambo, Loaf 'N Jug, Quik Stop, Turkey Hill, and so on.

Transformed by a childhood visit to an old A&P, University of North Carolina librarian Gwynn has devoted himself to the history of supermarkets. He maintains Groceteria.com, a database of US and Canadian supermarkets past and present. Want to know when the Bettendorf-Rapp on Hampton in St. Louis became a Schnuk's? When Skaggs Alpha Beta on Buffalo Gap Road in Abilene became an Albertsons? The years that the Winnipeg Piggly Wiggly on Academy Road turned into a Shop-Easy and then later a Tom Boy? Gwynn has answers. His vacations always include visits to older stores, ancient Walgreens and Pay'n Takit outlets treated like temples.

As larger chains bought up smaller regional players, Gwynn explains, this shuffling of the deck, rebranding, and shift to franchising, allowed supermarket companies to lower labor costs by eliminating unionized jobs. "On the plus side, it allowed them to stay in neighborhoods where they might have not otherwise stayed and just push the risk off to someone else. But it also was a response to unionization. A lot of the big chains in the US and Canada started these discount chains in the '70s and '80s. Because they were officially subsidiaries they could start from the ground up without union workers. Under new ownership, the union contract is gone. It was a way for a struggling company to offload unionized stores but still maintain control over them."

This focus on price led to the next big shift, into the era of the superstore, known in some parts as a big-box store or hypermarket (a term I very much like, as it approximates the anxiety I feel in such a large space surrounded by so much merchandise). Most superstores are about two hundred thousand square feet (the size of five supermarkets), with space to sell food as well as clothing, furniture, eyeglasses, flowers, and electronics. Selling in ever-larger volumes, these stores are able to leverage their purchasing power into ever-lower prices. Most major retailers are gradually evolving toward this in some way or other. Walmart expanded from its origins as a discount department store to add groceries, while Kroger merged with superstore Fred Meyers—the biggest players finding a way to sell everything to everyone.[29]

Though it's taken a century, there's a straight line from Kroger's shops starting to bake their own bread to the shopping cart and the superstore and beyond to e-commerce, which to the analog dinosaurs of this sector who are unable to develop digitally, is a blazing comet in the sky, headed in their direction.

The most talked-about grocery news in the past decade was the 2017 purchase of upscale supermarket chain Whole Foods for $13.7 billion by Amazon, which signaled that the online behemoth was embarking on a major push into food retail.[30] For several years, everyone expected Amazon was coming for groceries. It wasn't until the sudden acquisition of 465 retail locations, now turbocharged by Amazon's data, logistics, and delivery expertise, that the stakes were raised faster than anyone predicted.

Amazon's Chinese counterpart, Alibaba, already has 150 locations of Hema, a high-tech supermarket that features facial-recognition software, real-time pricing (digital price tags that adjust based on supply and demand), thirty-minute delivery, app payment, and automatic checkout.[31] The service is so efficient that even prepandemic, 60 percent of their customers were already ordering online.

A couple years ago, I took a bus to an airport convention center to hear Walter Robb, curious what the former CEO of Whole Foods had to say about the future of groceries. "We know that 45 percent of customers think that shopping is boring or a chore," said Robb, pausing during a presentation filled with buzzwords like *connectivity* and *curation* to assure the crowd of retail executives that "physical stores still matter." The sale of Whole Foods to Amazon was necessary, Robb said, in order to pursue the two-tiered shopping experience of the future: competitive digital sales and delivery bolstered by an enriched retail experience, which includes food service. The winners, he predicted, needed to excel on both fronts. Without the partnership of Amazon, Whole Foods wasn't going to get there.[32] While its in-store experience was tops, the company was never going to catch up on the digital side. Robb praised the Hema stores in China as the best integrated retailing he'd seen anywhere in the world. This is the future that Whole Foods needed to achieve, he said, a genuine marriage of digital and corporeal.

Prepandemic, there were a host of other experimental efforts to streamline the shopping experience for consumers—7Fresh (no cash), Amazon Go (no staff), and a horde of delivery meal-kit companies (no shopping). Walgreens and Kroger have been experimenting with facial-recognition software that could target in-store ads at you based on age, gender, race, or mood. In the fall of 2019, Walmart began offering grocery delivery with an annual membership of $98, while Amazon made delivery free (within delivery zones) for Prime members, which costs about the same. By the end of the year, Amazon sold $6.13 billion of food, 23.7 percent of the grocery e-commerce sector.

Uber has been dipping its toe in the grocery business too, through its 2019 acquisition of delivery start-up Cornershop. It'll be interesting to see what they have cooking. Supermarkets aren't the weak prey that restaurants and cabbies were. The autonomy that restaurant entrepreneurs wielded is what made them vulnerable to being muscled out of their turf by tech companies that were smart enough, or ruthless enough, to figure out how to get in between the business and the customer. America's top three supermarkets—Walmart, Kroger, and Albertsons—control more than 40 percent of the total market.[33] They're not going to let some tech start-up from Silicon Valley steal their customers and ransom them back for a 30 percent commission.

While all of these experiments are playing out, the way we get our food keeps changing. The industry, which generates approximately $835 billion and employs 2.7 million people, has been in an arms race to modernize with the digital era, in which more and more customers expect the convenience of thinking far less about their groceries, and working less hard to get them, than they ever have before.[34]

The obstacle in the face of all this progress is that, at least prepandemic, many of us just still enjoy shopping for groceries. According to a 2017 Morgan Stanley study, 85 percent of consumers cited the need to see and choose food as the reason for the preference for physical rather than digital shopping.[35]

Our attachment to shopping is personal, not logistical. Despite the insistence on touching and feeling an apple before buying it, professionals who work with produce every day can probably do a better job of selecting fruits and vegetables. If we feed all of our social, economic, and moral priorities into a computer, an algorithm could likely make more accurate choices for products to suit our needs: a peanut butter that matches our preference for creaminess, a breaded fish stick that aligns with our commitment to sustainability but falls within the parameters of our budget. Facebook probably understands which mustard we'll pick off the shelf, and why, better than our conscious brains. Not that things actually work this way. When we order on-line, the produce manager doesn't select our peaches. It's an employee with no specialty, who roams the whole store, filling six baskets at once. They're not going to decide, as we would, to skip the cauliflower be-cause it all looks spotty this week. And marketing algorithms are not programmed to suit our needs. Their purpose is to sell us stuff we don't need. They don't analyze our buying habits to suggest products custom-ized to our tastes or moral compass. They note that we bought ketchup and then promote every product in the Heinz catalog. The tech is still in the hands of the sort of people who think that after I've bought an engagement ring, I'm likely to continue buying diamond rings.

BACK TO THE KITCHEN

For better and worse, the pandemic has forced us into the kitchen. What seemed clear from day one is that when this is all over, some of us will emerge with new cooking skills, greater confidence, and the ability to menu plan and preserve meals, producing less waste and spending more time at the table with the people we love. And some of us will swear to whatever higher power we believe in that if we get out of this jam, we will never cook again so long as we live.

Some of us were already cooking more, following directions from popular recipe writers or tutorials through social media. I am, indicted by words already written, obviously in one camp (since our interview, I got Nik Sharma's recent book and have been cooking the hell out of it). More people cooking is better for our health, for our rates of dia-betes and cardiovascular diseases, for the $219 billion America spends treating them annually.

This needs to happen in our educational systems, at as young an age as possible. Yes, we include the basics of nutrition in our public school curriculums. Without teaching cooking skills, it's useless. With-out the physical aspect of cooking, no child is going to care about nu-trition or meal planning. If you spent a term teaching the rules, science, and history of baseball, yet never went out to the diamond with a bat, ball, and glove, how many students would you expect to ever see hitting or catching a ball? Now imagine that baseball is essential to their long-term health.

Currently, cooking is treated as an extracurricular in school or folded in as a footnote to existing classes like social studies, phys ed, or health. There's always one teacher in every school district, or one non-profit group, rolling the boulder up the hill, doing something tremendous and inspiring with a cooking class or student garden. They are always understaffed, underresourced, and up against administrative cultural resistance to anything seen as a subtraction from time students are expected to be focusing on math and science units. "We've had bighearted teachers reach out and try to get a pilot," says Sasha Bernstein, cofounder of the Cooking Project, who teaches kitchen skills to at-risk youth in the Bay Area. "And then the school won't let us use the space."

The tragedy of this attitude is that cooking is not time away from academics. The kitchen is the perfect vehicle for lessons on history, language, culture, geography, science, nature, and math. Look, I'm not going to evangelize to the unconverted. No one has to cook or to like cooking. If you don't enjoy preparing food and can afford to pay others to do it for you, while maintaining a reasonably healthy diet, I salute you.

However, we all had a moment, in the spring of 2020, when we were told that it was unsafe to go to the grocery store more often than necessary. Once every two weeks, we were advised. We did some quick calculations, adding up how long perishables like fresh fruit and meat last in the fridge, how much storage space we had for rice and beans. A lot of us developed newfound frugality, or skills at budgeting and planning. The most financially stable among us rediscovered important lessons about not wasting a broccoli stem or the end slice on a loaf of bread. Food waste, long a necessary preoccupation of folks on a budget and environmentalists wanting to conserve, broke into wider public consciousness.

This historical blip aside, America still wastes half of the food it produces. Half of that happens between the farm, the food terminal, and the supermarket, due to conditions beyond our control. But half of our food waste happens in our own homes. We own that failure. We buy more than we need, all but ensuring we won't eat it. Because the package of six romaine heads seems so economical, we take home an amount of lettuce that would take us two weeks to eat, but will rot in half that time. We scrape leftovers into the trash because we barely have time to eat the new food we've bought. We let expiration dates tell us that yogurt has become inedible rather than trust our senses of sight and smell. Part of the blame can be shifted back on an educational system that didn't train us to have confidence in the senses evolution gave us for this purpose. Disconnected from our food, we fear a spot of mold on cheese that can easily be sliced away. Our default, when in doubt, is to trash the contents of our fridge. We toss out slightly wilted but still perfectly good and nutritious vegetables because our fridges are packed tighter than an airplane's overhead compartment, with rows of hot sauces that are more collection than food source. Somehow a limp zucchini goes straight in the bin, yet we cannot imagine parting with the three bottles of Worcestershire sauce that we will never consume in our lifetime unless we start a Caesar-salad business.

What all of us can do is never forget how many of us felt for the first time at the onset of the pandemic—worrying that we might not have enough to eat—and to carry that respect for food into the way we menu plan, shop, cook, preserve, and store it. I'm not saying we all have to bake sourdough and cure salami. It's just that this is an opportunity to redefine our relationship with food waste. "The best way to get people to not waste food is for them to feel the preciousness and dearness of food, whether it's through economic measures or scarcity itself," says Jonathan Bloom, author of *American Wasteland: How America Throws Away Nearly Half of Its Food (and What We Can Do About It)*.[36] "I would never wish that on anyone, but as we're trying to find a silver lining to this pandemic, maybe that is one."

I don't want to fall into the trap of blaming individuals instead of the system, the kind of greenwashing that has flanked the recycling conversation. We shouldn't guilt each other for a failure to rinse out a peanut butter jar while letting corporate polluters evade any meaning-ful regulation. Six states have bans on food in landfills, Bloom tells me, citing Vermont as the gold standard because theirs applies to single-family households, while most states only limit action at the institu-tional and commercial level. Which is hugely important. No food in landfills means more composting. These policies prompt people and businesses to donate food, too. States and cities can also encourage food redistribution through tax incentives.

On a personal level, Bloom has some tips for how we can all reduce our food waste. They are mostly simple steps.

1. Shop smarter. Take inventory first. Don't buy too much.

   I used to enjoy finding something interesting at the butcher shop and then figuring out a meal to make of it. Now, with a small child and less free time, I sit down during her Sunday-morning nap and plan our menu for the week, adding to our grocery list. By the time I hit the supermarket, I'm not guessing about vol-umes or impulse buying.

2. Store properly, avoid clutter, and freeze excess.

   In another holdover from my kitchen days, the only Tupper-ware I own are deli cups. These are just plastic containers that come in three sizes. What makes them a key to organizing my fridge, pantry, and freezer is that they are clear and a uniform cylindrical shape. Rather than the Jenga tower of opaque con-tainers, random squares and rectangles holding leftover roast chicken or grated carrots, everything is stacked neatly and I can see it all at a glance. Nothing gets pushed to the back and for-gotten. It makes a huge difference.

3. Be wise about portion size.

   This takes practice. By default we always will risk making too much rather than too little. There's no reason for a house-hold of four to make enough food for six every night. Unless you're building in extra for tomorrow's lunches.

4. Love leftovers.

Eating leftovers doesn't need to be merely reheating the meal that was. There's a phrase, "the continuous kitchen," credited to cookbook author Barbara Kafka, which expresses a philosophy of seeing your ingredients, both new and already used, as part of an ongoing process. "It seems to me that less cooking is done today than used to be and that when it is done, it is so much more work because we have lost the habit of the continuous kitchen," wrote Kafka. "We start each meal from scratch with fresh shopping and a brand-new independent recipe. Our predecessors didn't, and we can save ourselves a great deal of work and have better, more economical food with greater depth of flavor by seeing cooking as an ongoing process."[37]

The carcass from last night's chicken turns into chicken stock, which becomes soup. Leftover roasted vegetables go into a salad. This applies to delivery leftovers too. The last of the fried rice that we almost threw out can get a second life with some of the pulled pork from two nights ago, plus whatever vegetables are in the crisper. Why not throw the remaining broth from that extra-large order of pho into the blender with frozen spinach to make a healthy soup? It's not just economical—it's fun. It's how we discover new flavor combinations. This goes for ingredients, too. The half a squash left over from one recipe can quickly become food waste if we don't look at it as the basis for a new meal.

5. Never landfill food—reuse, give away, feed animals, compost.

Depending on where you live and how much space you have, this one can be trickier. Yes, you can make stock from leftover shrimp shells, but eventually you have to do something with the inedible physical matter that remains. We just moved from a city that, for ten years, has had a fairly robust residential composting pickup program. Because I got so used to having the composting available, it's now shocking to place even an apple core in the garbage bin. This is a new challenge for me. I've started looking into alternatives, and so far my options here are a worm compost in my yard or paying for private compost pickup. We don't have enough land for the one, and the other feels elitist and impractical. I suspect I will settle for the private option as a short-term solution until we can find something better (update: as the snow melts, I just discovered a compost device in my backyard).

It's a challenge for any of us to change these habits. Prepandemic, food shopping was such a routine experience that it barely registered as an experience and so ubiquitous as to be nearly universal. To rewire that is to question what it means to us as individuals. Is the act of gathering food—seeing it and smelling it and touching it, cruising the aisles without purpose, adjusting our shopping list as we go because the apricots look particularly nice or the celery disappointingly wilted, buying taffy on a whim—an essential aspect of human life? Or are supermarkets, where we made physical and social contact with food and people in a giant room filled with twenty-eight thousand different products, a quaint twentieth-century anachronism, like vinyl or democracy?[38]

WHAT DOES FOOD SHOPPING MEAN TO US?

The answers to those questions, it turns out, have to do with a lot more than just food. As the pandemic reminded us: it kind of sucks to be on our own all the time. Despite how annoying other human beings can be—clipping their nails on the subway, calling instead of texting, disrespecting the unwritten rule that the middle seat on a plane gets armrest preference—we need each other. Forced isolation has proved that to all but the most misanthropic of us. Autonomy, while often an empowering feeling, comes at a price. More than ever, after being trapped inside, we like getting out of the house, being in a large and expansive space, the visual stimulation of all that abundance on the shelves, the discovery of new foods, saying "Excuse me" to fellow patrons as we reach for our favorite brand of peanut butter, even the game of choosing the right checkout aisle, the one with the fastest cashier—these are all shared experiences, ways to not be alone.

We may no longer depend on our personal bonds to help us find a good restaurant, raise a barn, or defend ourselves from tigers, but even if a physical trip to a grocery store is not the most efficient way to get our food, we like it. Some would even say that on a basic human level, we need it.

Sarah Fessenden, at Kwantlen Polytechnic University in British Columbia, is a sociocultural anthropologist. I got in touch with her to better understand what the alignment of business development and cultural shifts has to do with the social evolution of our species. She tells me that the trend we're following, our gradual removal from our sources of food, goes a lot further back than a mere century. The current tech innovations in supermarkets, she suggests, are just the latest microdevelopment in a much longer history that starts about ten thousand years ago with the twin advents of agriculture and markets. "What we know is central are the myriad relationships that are built around and attached to food-getting strategies. Food-getting strategies are always more than just food. Foodways are the cultural and social interconnections that surround food acquisition or production. So social relationships, political relationships, economic relationships, religious relationships—those are all built in and around food."

Before agriculture, humans were foragers. We tended to share the food we collected. That changed as we started planting and harvesting crops. "When we get agricultural societies, they're producing so much food that not everyone has to produce food anymore," Fessenden says, pointing to the social hierarchies that emerged at the same time as early agriculture, severing the connection between people and their food sources. "We have no idea who grew the food or where it was grown. We don't have cultural rules around those foods to help us determine our choices. When you buy food at supermarkets, it's often already packaged and processed. It increases our situation of feeling isolated, alienated, and distanced—an increasing lack of social connections.

We're not building relationships around food with one other. We're not spending time with people. We're not learning from them. From an anthropological perspective, it's clear how important food is. So when you start losing it, it's kind of like losing a language."

One of the elements of our new postvaccine world will be less physical grocery shopping. But that continuing disconnection from our food source, with e-commerce just being the latest stage, was already the path we were on and have been for ten millennia.

Many of us don't want to lose that connection. We like physical shopping (or farming, foraging, and hunting). That's all supermarkets were trying to do with grocerants. Or in-store classes and cooking demonstrations. They were for business purposes, yes—to get us in the store, keep us there, and keep us spending. But the effect, when these things work well, is also to get us to enjoy shopping more, to make it mean something more than a purely transactional act to us. Smaller stores are better at personalizing the experience, through the care they put into stocking items, the knowledge of the butcher, with aisles devoted to kosher, halal, Mexican, Filipino, or whatever kind of food the community needs. It's hard to do at scale.

❦

I USED TO live on the same street as the grocery store where I did all my food shopping, in a Toronto neighborhood called Kensington Market.

At the beginning of the twentieth century, Jews from "the ward," a ghetto for immigrants from all over, began operating street carts in the nearby Kensington area. Gradually, they transformed the ground floors of row houses into shops and bought homes, transitioning the area into a Jewish neighborhood. Because they were my people, I can say in plain English that they were poor immigrants who worked hard and succeeded in their aspiration to raise their socioeconomic standing by buying the homes that an earlier immigrant group had outgrown.

At the time, my great-grandfather Herschel Litvak was a black-smith. I still have a cleaver that he forged. Sometimes I use it to take the head off a chicken or rabbit. Primarily, it's for chopping frozen lemongrass and slicing pizza.

Eventually, the ward was annexed to make way for city hall. Herschel sold his land, now a bus station, to the city. He pooled his money with others to buy a house to use as a synagogue, followed by an adjacent house as the congregation grew, in 1927 knocking them both down to build the Kiever Shul. It still stands today, preserved by heritage status, at the edge of a Kensington park shared by children playing on swings and stoners on drums. But it has no congregation and sits empty most days.

By the 1980s, the neighborhood had changed hands so much that it was equal parts Portuguese, Jamaican, Vietnamese, and so on, with a few Jewish owners. My mother, when she was on welfare, lived in a third-floor apartment there lousy with cockroaches. As a kid I visited her, amazed by a streetscape like no other. Each block held multiple butchers, fishmongers, grocers, and bakeries. Until 1983, when the practice was banned by the city, you could still buy a live chicken.

By the time I moved into a place of my own in the neighborhood as an adult, it was a shell of its former self. The multigenerational households of an earlier era, the families who bought cabbage or tomatoes by the case, to make cabbage rolls or sauce, sustaining small grocers in the process, were gone. Between condo developments and Airbnb ghost hotels, visitors began to outnumber residents. Where once there were dozens of complementary food businesses, five butchers and ten fishmongers, now there was one, maybe two, of each. Between each food-retail shop grew the new face of Kensington; cafés, tattoo parlors, and trendy snack shops catering to tourists who were unaware that the neighborhood they came to see was being displaced by the very activity of tourism.

Still, the surviving shops were outstanding. I knew everybody by name. I could leave my apartment and, within an area of about four square blocks, buy bacon from Peter, cheddar from Frankie, a little mackerel from Dan and Kristen, some romaine from Pots, and feel like a king.

Potsothy "Pots" Sallapa grew up on a farm in Sri Lanka, never making a connection between his health and the insecticides he used to spray the field, until he was diagnosed, years later, with non-Hodgkin's lymphoma. After quitting his job and pursuing treatment, he opened up the shop, 4 Life Natural Organics, a five-thousand-foot space filled with vibrant produce and other delicacies.

Unlike most supermarkets, or even the most hippie health food co-ops, which are always lit as brightly as airports, it was dark in 4 Life. Romantic, I'd call it. When I told Pots I was getting married, he insisted I have the wedding in the store. Victoria laughed at the idea, declaring that she would not be getting married in front of a box of Corn Flakes. However, understanding that food has been the central preoccupation of my adult life, she agreed to at least give the space a fresh look with open eyes. As we toured the high-ceilinged store, with its antique wood beams, the underlighting of the ice-cream freezer dancing on our chins, Saturday-morning crowds stocking up on grapes and granola, asking about the Pfennings Farm kale, I could see on her face that she saw too this wasn't just a place people went to acquire toilet paper, that this space was vital to our community. To my surprise, she agreed. A few months later, we walked down the grocery aisle and got married between the cash register, the root-vegetable display table, a group of our friends and family, and a stack of maple syrup jars. Until we left Toronto, I went there once a week, just to stand on the spot, near the potatoes, where Victoria and I exchanged our vows.

When we started to make plans to leave town, I was afraid of losing a lot of things. Friends and family, for a start. My walkable neighborhood. Five minutes to three grocery stores, two parks, the subway, or a friend's house. I'd miss the restaurants, sure—maybe not all six thousand of them, but the variety and quality and some very special places that made me feel like I was out of the house for more than a meal. Mostly I was going to miss Kensington Market. As we got closer to making our decision to leave, it became clear that Kensington was already gone—that soon there would be nothing to miss. So yeah, you could say that the act of buying food is personal to me.

Until recently, I enjoyed the luxury of a neighborhood where I could shop for food the same way people did a hundred years ago—on foot, visiting individual stores to buy from merchants who each sold only one product. Now I live like the majority of the population. I've got a kid and a car, and I feel the pull to buy everything I need from one store. Now that it's no longer convenient or easy, my desire to shop for food from specialists is put to the test.

After the initial culture shock, I became enthralled by the supermarket. Bread and cheese in the same store? Filling up a basket with vegetables, milk, and toilet paper, and paying in one installment, instead of a half dozen exchanges, coming home with only what I can carry in my hands or bike basket? What a world. It's easy to imagine how the first visitors to King Kullen felt. Not that I'm locked into a relationship with a single food provider.

And yet . . . After moving to a new city, quarantining with my sister-in-law for two weeks, and then living with my wife's parents for three months, we are just now getting into our new home. Following months of stasis, I can finally begin to stock my own fridge again. Though this is a smaller town, just as Kansas City has at least one great Thai restaurant, Winnipeg has good places to buy food. It's a strange experience, after years of walking into Pots's shop and asking "What's good today?" to start over fresh. Doubly so in a pandemic, when every visit to a store contains a level of risk and precaution, and wearing a mask makes it awkward to introduce myself. It's hard, though not impossible, to find merchants I trust.

When we shop for food, we're assaulted by messaging, most of it impossible to decipher. The best we can do as buyers is to develop a relationship with our sellers. This is swimming backward in history a bit. I believe it's worth it.

Staff at the little Polish butcher shop around the corner that sells exemplary bacon is only too eager to tell me the origin of their pork. I've walked into the nearby bakery and said, "Hi, I'm Corey. I just moved into the neighborhood. I've heard great things about your bread. Can you tell me where your flour comes from?" At an Asian supermarket on Pembina, I found an aisle with nearly everything Mr. Ma sent me to find in Chinatown medicine shops, all neatly labeled here in multiple languages. When I finally had space for a forty-pound bag of basmati rice and was stymied by the options at the Indian spice shop, I introduced myself and found the owner eager to make a recommendation and a connection.

Maybe that sounds weird, conditioned as we are to treat staff as mere labor and shopping as a chore. The wonderful surprise of people is, once you start talking, information flows. You begin to learn about the policies of workplaces and why you might support them and advocate for others to do so too. After starting a conversation at the bakery, it was less awkward to ask about the tip prompt on the payment terminal—and refreshing to learn that employees kept 100 percent of tips.

Even in a modern supermarket, it's possible to introduce yourself to the person arranging stacks of brussels sprouts or slicing the deli meats. They have names. And you'll get along better when you know them. If a retailer has high standards, they'll do the legwork of answering all your questions and solving your ingredient challenges when they arise. You are entitled to ask your fishmonger: When did this fish come in? Is it fresh or frozen? Farmed or wild? Can I smell it? This is not rude. It's how professionals buy seafood.

Anybody can build these kinds of relationships. Supermarket staff may not have the product knowledge of a specialist. But they likely know more than us. If they don't, we can find somewhere new to shop.

I'm aware that this ethical consumption is a reflection of my socioeconomic status. I look for local tomatoes, grass-fed beef, shrimp that's harvested by workers who are paid appropriately. These choices take some work on my part. They also cost about 40 percent more and are not available at all in many neighborhoods.

And for almost everyone, there are limits; creativity is always required. In my new city, there aren't multiple butcher shops specializing in naturally raised animals, where I can put my trust in the sourcing policies. For some foods, that means I have to find local farmers and buy directly.

I cannot get cavolo nero (a.k.a. black kale) here. Maybe I'll try growing it this summer. There are no fishmongers dedicated to sustainable fishing. So I have to figure out which species I should be eating and where to get them. It makes for less variety too, primarily mussels from the East Coast and locally caught pickerel (a.k.a. walleye). The free app Sweat and Toil makes it easy to look up child and forced labor in international commodity products. That helped me say yes to frozen shrimp from Ecuador at the Vietnamese grocery.

This is very different from the days when I went to my fishmonger, who had direct relationships with fisheries, where I simply trusted that everything in the shop was sourced to the highest standards. Like everyone else's, my relationship with food shopping is going to continue to change, just as food shopping has for at least the past century. Maybe the big chains will take another run at grocerants. Not that ramen counter at the Lucky's in Naples, though. That's gone. But some form of in-store dining that synchronizes with and complements our evolving hygiene needs.

New ways of choosing where to eat, what to look for, who to support, and what questions to ask may seem like a big change in a process that was previously curated for us. But the spring of 2020 is still fresh for us, the suddenness with which we all reacted, for good or ill, to a radically altered state of affairs. Overnight, people who still had a steady income and the ability to work remotely set up video calls with relatives and Googled local farms to see which ones brought their produce into our cities.

Supermarkets respond to, and influence, consumer demand. Let's make them earn our business. These are spaces for us to advocate for the food we want.

Not only are we capable of change. We can do it much more quickly than expected, if we're motivated. For me, adapting to a new home, finding a new way to connect with my food purveyors has to be part of that change.

The nature and size of supermarkets—thousands of square feet, cathedral-high ceilings, dozens of employees—make us feel like our interaction has to be impersonal. Like all organizations, though, they are made up of individuals. They likely care about doing a good job. More important, everyone likes recognition. If you're looking to start this kind of conversation at your local store, start with a compliment. Tell them how impressive the deli section is before asking specific questions about all the sliced-turkey options. Tell people your name. Yes, it is an old sales schtick. But you're not selling anything. All you are searching for, within an overlit, dehumanizing retail environment, is trust. And trust can only be built on a sincere, human connection, which starts by being a person with a name, just like in the old days.

· 8 ·

The Virtuous Restaurant

If we had just kept our mouths shut and ran
Mission Chinese Food, we would be rich..

— Karen Liebowitz

Achilles, without his heel,
you wouldn't even know his name today.

—Stan Lee

"There is one thing worse than a business going no-tipping and then closing because they couldn't afford to do it or didn't plan accordingly," says Claire Sprouse. "That is the business going no-tipping and reverting back."

In July 2020, as New York restaurants began to get their engines running again and Danny Meyers's Union Square Hospitality Group abandoned its "hospitality included" policy, Sprouse reopened her Brooklyn all-day café, restaurant, and cocktail bar, Hunky Dory, eliminating tipping at the same time.[1] The choice, one of many Sprouse has made or hopes to make in her fledgling business, feels to her just one step on a path to a better kind of hospitality.

Paying attention to food waste in the cocktail arena, Hunky Dory's mai tais don't use orgeat, the almond syrup typically found in bars (almonds are a huge source of water use), but rather an in-house syrup made from sunflower seeds. Citrus peels, which cocktail bars usually throw away in heaps, are transformed into oleo saccharum, the sweetened citrus oil that forms a base for many cocktails.

Her staff takes two half-hour breaks per shift. That shouldn't be as rare as it is. Sprouse says it's the least she can do. After closing down in March, she sold cocktails online and pushed a cart around the neighborhood to deliver them. As her hospitality friends sought ways to make money, she hosted pop-ups for them in the dormant space. When outdoor dining resumed, she sat customers on her large patio, turning the interior into a retail space to sell sustainable goods, with a focus on Indigenous producers.

If people could quickly get used to wearing masks and ordering through a QR code, she figures they'll adjust to no tipping. Succeed or fail, she's happy to be a guinea pig others can learn from. "It's great that we do these things that lean toward being more sustainable. But at the end of the day, we're just one little drop in the bucket. So we need other people, other businesses, to take up these fights too."

⚜

THE DAY SUZANNE Barr opened her first restaurant, Saturday Dinette, she received the unexpected news that she was pregnant. Self-employed in an industry with no wiggle room for child care, she and her husband, Johnny, raised their son in the restaurant. She breastfed between food prep and occasionally let diners hold the baby while the new parents cooked and served tables. Barr quickly incorporated a training program for young women into her kitchen structure. In 2019 she launched another restaurant, True True Diner, this one without tipping. In July 2020, though Barr wanted to continue through the pandemic, her partners, who owned the building, decided to close.

When I reach Barr by phone, she's planning a move from Toronto to Florida, to be close to family, to buy a home, to escape a city that feels economically constrictive.

The future of restaurants she sees has less fine dining and more concepts generated by social responsibility, furthered by transparency and an ongoing conversation with customers. "We can have that dialogue and start to see some fundamental things changing. But it has to start with the abolishment of tipping. Because it's a part of an archaic, broken system that hasn't worked. It doesn't see me. It doesn't see any person of color. In particular a woman of color."

A research paper coauthored by Michael Lynn concluded that not only did restaurant customers tip Black people less, but the adverse impact might make the use of tipping to compensate employees a violation of employment discrimination law in the United States.[2]

Educating customers and changing minds, about tipping or any other part of the restaurant experience one is attempting to change, are part of the restaurateur's responsibility, says Barr, while conceding that you can only do so much. "At the end of the day, they come in with their own expectations. They are going to choose not to come back to your establishment or to go on to Yelp and complain. And they will do that regardless. Because that's just human instinct when you walk with so much entitlement. And then that entitlement is coupled with privilege. And that coupling is tied with race."

At the moment, restaurant owners are terrified of "getting canceled," losing popular support due to public awareness of formerly discreet practices such as discrimination, exploitation, and other business decisions that in recent years have become more visible while less socially acceptable. Instead of listening to employees and diners, many owners are hiring consultants with the hopes of developing a policy statement that indemnifies them from criticism. The key, Barr says, is to remember that if there is a recipe for how to make a restaurant, it is a living document and it's always going to continue to change. "Every decision you make as a business owner, you have to be accountable for it. Everyone now is so concerned about their best practices as a business. Bringing in consultants and experts, telling them how to build out codes of conduct. Because they have former staff calling them out on social media. Yes, this is a call-out culture. And it is uncomfortable for so many people. And it is about being honest and direct and confronting it and taking it on as a business owner and saying, 'I fucked up.' I think we are seeing that the accountability part of it all has to be in the forefront. Because you're the only one making that decision. And you have to be accountable."

⚹

VANCOUVER'S EAST HASTINGS, like San Francisco's Tenderloin District, is riddled with epidemic levels of poverty, homelessness, and drug abuse, surrounded by some of the most expensive real estate and the glossiest retail in the country. Rather than create another outpost of gentrification locals can't afford, the restaurant Save On Meats now prepares a thousand meals a day that are distributed to a variety of organizations, primarily for women and children fleeing violence. For a few dollars, tokens can be bought and handed out in the community to be redeemed for sandwiches (the program is on hold during the pandemic). For eight years, Save On lost money operating a butchery side of the business that bought meat at the rail price (the whole cow, by the pound) direct from farmers, which would be used for their burger and sausage meat while returning the prime cuts (ribeye, striploin) to the farmer, enabling them to get a better price by selling it elsewhere. During the second half of 2020, Save On Meats rescued ten tons of food from grocery stores, which would have gone to landfill, and redirected it toward shelters.

The social enterprise sets a goal of having 60 percent of its kitchen employees come through various agencies aimed at job placement for people with barriers to employment (physical or mental health impairments, criminal records, and so on).

They're not alone in this. From Minneapolis (All Square) to LA (Homegirl Café), from Columbus (Hot Chicken Takeover) to Cleveland (EDWINS), there is a growing number of kitchens organized around the mission of creating professional opportunities for the formerly incarcerated who are obstructed from meaningful employment at every turn.

GOOD WORK IS NEVER DONE

Restaurants conceived for, and devoted to, social good? Food businesses founded on the premise of contributing to the community more than profiting from it? Sign me up. Problem solved. Let's only dine with these heroes, hang a "MISSION: ACCOMPLISHED" banner, pat ourselves on the back, and head home.

Unfortunately, altruistic restaurants have a habit of going out of business. Like Rooster, an extension of the Philadelphia restaurant empire of Steve Cook and Mike Solomonov. Using the carcasses from their fried chicken restaurant to make stock, Rooster was a soup-focused restaurant, with all of the profits funneled to Broad Street Ministry's Hospitality Collaborative, a charity that helps feed the city's most vulnerable. In 2019, after two years of operation, the restaurant closed.

Finding alternate sources of meat, seafood, and grains, with a surcharge on beef and lamb dishes going toward carbon offsets, the Perennial in San Francisco was a high-water mark for environmental sustainability. The expectation that the location, across the street from a new Twitter headquarters, would provide them with steady customers, proved a fatal mistake. Big tech companies provide in-house dining options so workers don't leave the office. After three years, the doors closed. They lasted longer than their peers, other new, high-profile restaurants in the Mid-Market area (Oro, Cadence, Bon Marché, Volta) that all closed in 2016, in what *Eater* dubbed the "Mid-Market Massacre."

Not far away, Krystin Rubin and Karen Heisler's Mission Pie, a community-focused bakery and café, a no-WiFi haven dedicated to equity and fair pay, called it quits at about the same time as Rooster and the Perennial. Even as the bakery got busier, the rising cost of the city pushed the business into the red.

Another Bay Area restaurant group, Alta, took aim at systemic racial bias in employment. Following the success of an initial Alta in 2013, working with Restaurant Opportunities Centers United on the launch of a second location, founder Daniel Patterson initiated a pilot for a racial equity program aimed at dismantling bias in hiring, training, and professional advancement. "If you look at the restaurant industry, and especially fine dining, from a critical perspective, and ask how we got to be where we are, a lot of it has to do with gatekeeper issues," Patterson told me in 2018. "People with money, people who control who gets hired, how they get trained, and who gets promoted—it's white people and mostly men in the most visible and highly paid positions. This is a systemic issue. It's not specific to restaurants, but it manifests in restaurants." Since then, however, chefs of color at Alta restaurants Besharam (Heena Patel), Dyafa (Reem Assil, whom we met in Chapter 1), and Kaya (Nigel Jones) have left the company, citing lack of control and tokenism, that rather than being treated as partners, they were exploited for their social capital. "I pushed for partnerships in a rushed way, and I did not spend enough time on communication," Patterson told *Eater*. "I take responsibility for how these mistakes impacted the businesses and I am sorry for that."[3]

Locol, in which Patterson was partnered with LA restaurateur Roy Choi, was probably the most visible of these well-meaning disappointments. Meant to challenge the supremacy of unhealthy fast-food and create employment opportunities in poor neighborhoods, Locol lasted barely two years. "We're going to tackle the fast-food industry," Choi promised at the time. "We're going to build a concept that will have the ideology and heart and science of a chef but the relevance of McDonald's. And we're going to do it in America."

The launch in Watts drew hundreds. But Locol didn't attract locals. What happened? Is it not possible to do good and do well at the same time?

Of course it is. Look at José Andrés. In 2020 his organization, World Central Kitchen, activated shuttered restaurants in the United

States, transforming them into production kitchens to provide meals for people falling through the widening gaps in the social safety net and offering free meals to Americans waiting in long lines to vote.

Before the pandemic, Alma Cocina Latina in Baltimore had worked with Mera Kitchen Collective, an organization that employs mostly refugee women. When COVID-19 hit, Alma switched to take-out, to ensure work for the many employees who would be unable to access unemployment benefits. Soon they were supported with funds from WCK to produce meals for people suddenly in more desperate need—immigrants, schools, and laid-off workers from Johns Hopkins medical school. "The needs are vast in the city," says owner Irena Stein. With a budget of ten dollars per meal, Alma was able to keep staff while serving the nutritional needs of the community. Though a challenge to keep food costs at 30 percent, Alma found the change transformational. "I love doing this. I love participating in this combination of food and social engagement." Stein envisions a postpandemic future in which the restaurant still serves a full dinner but dedicates its mornings to community programs. Though she is unsure where the money would come from (the city, state, nonprofits?), the pandemic has been too much of a catalyst to go back to how things were before.

By the start of 2021, Alma merged with Mera. With the day split in thirds, the kitchen produces community meals (ninety thousand so far), then catering by refugee women, then dinner (still takeout) for the restaurant. Between grants and a donation base, they've got six months of run time. "I see this as the long term. I love the idea of taking this opportunity of the crisis to make profound changes. For us and the city. We're all thinking in five-year terms. Not just what we're doing now so we're able to reopen. We have to think of reinventing ourselves right now."

Part of what makes altruistic work like this sustainable is building on the foundation of a large, well-oiled, for-profit business. While WCK is funded by donations, foundations, and businesses, Think-FoodGroup had been operating for thirteen years before Andrés devoted so much of his energies to relief work. It helps that Andrés has a tremendous celebrity credibility that he is willing and able to leverage to secure funding and partnerships.

It's harder when you start out trying to help the world and turn a profit at the same time. Good intentions don't always translate into immediate success. It's difficult to persevere if you don't have the infrastructural or financial runway. However, success and failure should not be seen as binary options. Success is not the sole evidence for an idea being good or bad. When ideas don't work, what matters is that we learn from them—that the people behind them don't just give up and go away.

Take Karen Leibowitz and Anthony Myint. In 2008, with full-time jobs and hopes of running a restaurant like a hobby, they rented a taco truck from a Guatemalan couple, using the restaurant where Myint cooked as a prep kitchen. On Thursday nights, they served "PB&J" (pork belly and jicama on flatbread with cilantro mayo, Myint correctly reasoning that people are more likely to try food that at least sounds familiar) to a rapidly and surprisingly growing audience in San Francisco's Mission District. Soon they graduated to a similar deal with the owners of nearby Lung Shan, "a remarkably unpopular and pretty run-down Chinese restaurant," and started giving their profits to a local food bank. The Great Recession was also the dawn of the pop-up. It didn't take long for the couple's restaurant within a restaurant, featuring rotating guest chefs, to grow into a phenomenon, including a cookbook.

The success of Mission Street Food (which became Mission Chinese Food) led to an expansion, to New York, along with partners. While the compromises of partnership obstructed them from running the business according to their environmental beliefs, Liebowitz and Myint (who weren't involved in the New York operation) put that energy into the Perennial. Bread was made from kernza, a lab-developed grain that returns carbon to the soil. The restaurant operated an offsite aquaponic farming system utilizing food scraps from the restaurant as feed for fish and plants. Rather than banish beef and lamb from the menu, the Perennial sourced from regenerative ranches whose pastures sequestered more greenhouse gases than their animals emitted (as measured by scientists at nearby UC Berkeley). The presence of meat at such a self-consciously sustainable restaurant created a conversation about the animal proteins and how our dining choices relate to climate change. The list of sustainability choices goes on and on. In the end, despite San Francisco's supply of wealthy diners and the city's enthusiasm for liberal causes, the restaurant lasted three years. "If we had just kept our mouths shut and ran Mission Chinese Food, we would be rich," laughs Liebowitz. "We could be in every airport. But the food would not be very good. Instead, we're totally in debt. Because we wanted to save the world."

But here's what's important. They didn't stop. Leibowitz and Myint could have fallen back on consulting work. They could have developed a fried chicken sandwich QSR brand. Instead, they moved their focus on sustainable hospitality from within their own restaurants to all restaurants.

Their organization, Zero Foodprint (ZFP), formerly the Perennial Farming Initiative, named Humanitarian of the Year by the James Beard Awards, and its Restore California program channel money from restaurants into regenerative agriculture projects. As a public-private collaboration (with the California Department of Food and Agriculture and the California Air Resources Board), they have signed up dozens of restaurants to commit to an optional bill line—a 1 percent charge that goes to soil plans on farms and ranches. It's voluntary. So diners can opt out. Dozens more restaurants are pledged, though the pandemic naturally halted much of this progress. It's hard to calculate your carbon footprint when you're struggling to stay in business every day. That just shifts their work, for now, to cultivating political will. "One thing I'm hearing is that regional and local governments are already thinking about recovery and how to make the recovery correspond to their climate goals," says Leibowitz. "A lot of regions want the reopening of the restaurant sector to not be going back to how it was before. But to develop something more equitable. More resilient economically and in terms of climate."

So far, ZFP has a few dozen participating restaurants. The labor of coordinating farms, streamlining the grant-application process (essay questions were an impediment to people whose first language isn't English), onboarding restaurants, and working with legislators to get governments to match grant funding has so many moving parts. While as an individual restaurant the Perennial was an achievement in environmentally sustainable hospitality, there was only so much Leibowitz and Myint could do while also needing to think about reservations, ordering, paying invoices, and staff scheduling every day.

By letting go of the trappings of dining, they are able to accomplish so much more. Hospitality, when done well, is both art and science. Restaurants with a mission beyond hospitality—nutrition, immigration, climate, sustainability, employing marginalized groups, and more—are admirable and deserving of all the positive attention they create. There will also likely be a new generation of young chefs who take over distressed properties, with smaller staff, smaller menus, and smaller footprints. As followed the Great Recession, many will cook more of the food they want rather than following trends or catering to the broadest audience. Possibly many will do away with service and shift entirely to takeout or experiment with co-ops and profit sharing for staff. The risk takers will get plenty of attention. I hope they will inspire change. Finding these places and supporting the hell out of them, as loudly as possible so that others support them too, feels right. That's the kind of eater I want to be. The more I talk to restaurateurs about the truly fantastic choices they've made, to align their business with the well-being of workers or the planet, the more I think that what's important about these restaurants is not merely what they achieve on their own, but their capacity to inspire larger cultural shifts.

These restaurants need to instigate a bigger change than what happens between their walls. "There's a limit to what you can do when you're trying to vote with your fork," Barry Lynn tells me. "If you want real change, you've got to vote with your vote." Lynn, the executive director of the think tank Open Markets Institute and author of several books (most recently 2020's *Liberty from All Masters: The New American Autocracy vs. the Will of the People*), studies the ways in which monopolies threaten our personal and political freedoms.[4]

Instead of finding restaurants that serve some higher purpose, should I instead be campaigning for ballot initiatives while eating all the Wendy's baconator fries I want? Has my focus on the details of restaurant operation left me with a myopic view, omitting the kind of change that happens only on a legislative level? I'm hoping Lynn can help me take a step back and understand the big picture. Because from Whoppers to kothu roti to tasting menus, I want the dining choices I make to mean something. I want the money I spend to go to the kinds of businesses I hope to see more of. I can and do advocate for these restaurants. I believe, I have to believe, that our choices as individuals make a difference, that the smallest ripples matter. Everything I do, from teaching my daughter the golden rule to practicing it myself, has an impact on the world around me.

THE LIMITS OF VOTING WITH YOUR FORK

I'm haunted by a line from a Gene Hackman movie, about which every other detail has been deleted from my memory. "There's only one rule. The golden rule. The rest is just conversation." As individuals, that's as good and simple a guiding principle as any. Yet what is the extent of the change we can hope to accomplish through our personal consumer choices?

So many of my conversations about how to fix restaurants wind up in larger issues about the way our society and the economy is structured—obstacles that often seem insurmountable. What good does it do to raise the minimum wage if people don't have access to nutritious food or affordable housing? If we had a real investment in public health care, transportation, education, and other basic services, would I be looking at restaurant owners to fix problems, which are frequently symptoms of a far more institutionalized inequality, in their shops?

I once spoke with a Dutch economist who helped establish Fair Trade certification standards back in the '80s. It was a whirlwind morning for me, a few hours during which I also interviewed an astronaut and an evolutionary biologist. I was struck by something the economist told me: that in any of the commodities his organization tracks (beef, sugar, coffee, gold, and so forth), ethical consumption caps out around 3 to 5 percent of the market. While that's a huge leap from the 0 percent of thirty years ago, that's hardly enough to alter the foundations of our food and restaurant industries. It won't incrementally grow to 5 percent, 10 percent, or 15 percent by the momentum of our purchasing decisions alone. "The idea that people are gonna eat consciously, they're gonna use their eating dollars to try to change the world?" says Lynn. "Let's just call it 5 percent to be generous."

That 5 percent, Lynn clarifies, is people who can afford to be conscious shoppers and diners. People with the time, the desire, the knowledge, the money. But there are plenty of towns where Walmart is the only place to shop and Olive Garden is the only place to eat. So the difference we're trying to make with ethical dining choices mostly happens at the margins.

If people want to effect change, at some point consumer choice needs to level up to policy action. "The only way to make real change is to vote rules that are fairly applied to all," says Lynn. As for nongovernmental action, the nonprofits and certification bodies that get private companies to agree to voluntary standards? That sort of thing is "great when it works," he says. "But those kinds of agreements are not written in law, and pretty much the first time a corporation runs into any kind of problem—it could be because it's just not as nimble as it used to be or because there's a larger crack-up in the economy—they'll abandon it. So it's not worth a damn thing. When Walmart says it will source sustainable fish, it ain't worth a damn thing." So far, the pandemic (which certainly qualifies as a crack-up) has not resulted in any of the Fair Food Program's partner companies rescinding their commitments. However, I take Lynn's point.

That doesn't mean that between elections our consumer actions don't matter. Rather, they matter all the more because they are micro-votes we get to cast all the time. Yes, there's a limit to the good we can do with our choice of where to eat. It's a cop-out to say I voted and that's the end of my social responsibility. I can eat all the slave shrimp I want while it's up to those bozos in Congress to do something about it. In between federal elections there are roughly 4,380 meals. That's a lot of opportunities to choose the kinds of restaurants, and the kind of restaurant industry, we want to exist.

If there is a lesson in the harsh times we live in, it's that our societal failures are reminders of the purpose of laws. Because we are now truly seeing and feeling the full results of the antiregulation bootstrap-ism of the Reagan and Thatcher era, the downstream impact of free trade and cutting rules for employers, public health, advertising, pollution, and voting, Lynn says that we are all just now rediscovering the need for government. Even Canadians, who Lynn feels never became nearly as libertarian as Americans (though we had our own economic conservative leader in the '80s, Brian Mulroney, whose son went on to host *Canadian Idol*). "It's great around the edges to support little restaurants and support your farmers market, to keep those arts and practices alive. But if you're going to scale those arts and practices, you can only do it with law. This is a purely political challenge."

HOW A CARROT BECOMES A LAW

What does that look like? How does a community-driven business choice translate to political action? How does it scale up, and who do you have to know to get that done? Is there any connection between running or supporting an ethical business and the large-scale impact achieved only at the policy level?

Michel Nischan learned the answers to those questions when he set out to make a difference with his restaurant. Nischan began cooking in the late 1970s. Both of his parents were farmers. Or they were until post–World War II policy (commodity support payments, export subsidies, and more) shifted the focus from the kind of midsize farm his grandparents had operated in Missouri and Kentucky to the type of industrial manufacturing credited with helping to win the war. His grandfather held on to his land, but he had to sell off portions of it to survive. Until the age of seventeen, Nischan spent summers working the farm. It was a fully diversified, mixed-used farm operation (though Nischan didn't know those terms back then): there were goats, pigs, chickens, and a vegetable plot for the family, with a money crop of watermelons and sweet corn.

When he started cooking in Chicago's top-of-the-line French restaurants of the era—L'Escargot, Le Francais, Le Perroquet—Nischan was astonished to see perfectly round, pink greenhouse tomatoes coming in the back door in February. Once he became a chef and had some power over whom he bought from, Nischan drove to the countryside, looking for farmers who were growing the type of food his grandfather had grown. The farmers he encountered produced conventional cereal and oil-seed crops. Nischan convinced some of them—by paying in advance and bringing his kitchen crew at harvest time because the farm was busy with picking corn, soy, and oats—to plant specialty crops for his kitchen.

Then, in the late 1990s, his son was diagnosed with diabetes, and the endocrinologist explained that changing his diet would have the biggest impact on his health. So Nischan poured his chef energy into studying, quickly realizing that what he was feeding his family and his customers was not great for their long-term health. Even though it was local, organic, sustainable, it was cream, butter, and foie gras. It was apple-smoked bacon fat, all-purpose flour, and refined cornstarch, which the science of the time said you shouldn't be eating if you have diabetes. Nischan, on his way to some fame as a young, rising star chef, felt he had to completely change the way he cooked.

That would have been impossible at Miche Mache, the Norwalk, Connecticut, restaurant he had at the time. Then Nischan met Drew Nieporent, of the Myriad Restaurant Group, which operates Nobu and Tribeca Grill, among others. Nieporent, who at that point was dealing with his own diet-related issues, asked Nischan to collaborate on a restaurant called Heartbeat. It would be local, organic, sustainable, but also no butter, dairy, all-purpose flour, or sugar. Meeting the challenge of making sauce without butter and dessert without sugar, Heartbeat earned critical acclaim from the *New York Times* and zero stars from the *New York Post*, along with an accusation of being the "food police." The attention got Nischan invited to think tanks and public health conferences; America was just breaking the seal on the phrase *obesity epidemic*, and the conversation around the government's role in public health, central in the fight to regulate cigarettes, was starting to migrate to food.

Nischan, anomalous at the time for cooking fancy food that was healthy, found himself in high demand. It seemed that his cooking was at the vanguard of something his country needed, which, for a moment, appeared beneficial for his career. "At first I thought this was a great opportunity," he says, believing that Heartbeat was "the perfect restaurant for this particular time."

Until, that is, he learned about the social determinants of health and that the majority of people who struggle with type 2 diabetes, and need the access to a healthy diet to prevent it, better manage it, or (in the early stages) actually reverse it, live at income levels so low that they couldn't afford to change their lifestyles. "I remember going back to Heartbeat and looking at the tablecloths and thinking, 'I can only do this because people can come here and afford thirty dollars for an entrée,'" says Nischan. "A single parent with three children and three part-time jobs to equal a full-time job, they run out of federal food assistance in the middle of the month. And they have two dollars for all four people for dinner tonight. A plateful of vegetables is impossible." Even more depressing, there was no business solution that he could implement. He knew there was no model for a for-profit restaurant that produces healthy food sold at prices affordable for someone who has two dollars to spend on dinner for four.

And then he was introduced to Gus Schumacher, who at the time was undersecretary for farm and foreign agricultural services for the

US Department of Agriculture (USDA). This is where the opportunity of attending think tanks and conferences imparts the privilege of connections. "When I met Gus, he was dealing with milk in Afghanistan and soy in the Amazon and deforestation and all the pressures of that. But he was simultaneously working on things like federal food assistance for pregnant women and children under the age of five."

A colleague suggested that if Nischan wanted to do something about healthy food access, he should start a nonprofit or find a way to collaborate with one working on those issues. "At the time food banks were getting a lot of crap from the public health movement, that everything they were giving people was highly processed. That there should be more fruits and vegetables in food pantries, which is very expensive. You have to build a refrigerator. You have to fill it with produce, which is a perishable product. And if you can't distribute the produce, you throw it away. Grocery stores won't donate produce because it's a high-margin profit center for them. But it's at the most risk because it's highly perishable. By the time you're passing the sell-by date, you've got a week to use it before it's pretty gacky and you've got to throw it away. So by the time a grocery store will donate produce to you, the underserved consumer is insulted by what they're getting because it's not fresh."

I cooked in a homeless shelter for a couple years. Though we always did our best to turn supermarket-donated produce into nutritious meals that tasted good, it was awful to see the degraded quality of food given away by supermarkets, slimy green beans or spotty peppers, knowing how much perfectly good food was left to sit until it got to this stage.

This problem, of how to get fresh produce to people who need it the most, gave birth to an idea—doubling food-stamp value for fruits and vegetables—and a nonprofit, Wholesome Wave, to service it. "There was this huge movement to restrict what food stamps could be used for, which was a form of cruel and unusual punishment. Why don't we find out what happens if you increase someone's affordability for what they can spend on fruits and vegetables? Will they choose it? If we can do something that's transactional, you put money in someone's hand,

and they make a personal choice, you can track that and measure it. You can measure the economic impact of it. You can prove that people got the fruit or the vegetable."

In the fall of 2007, the Double Value Coupon Program (DVCP) started at a couple farmers markets. By 2008 it was integrating with the Supplemental Nutrition Assistance Program (formerly food stamps) in several states. Four years later, the agencies at the USDA were talking to Wholesome Wave because the research was bearing positive results. The DVCP didn't make it onto the 2012 farm bill. But in 2014 it passed as part of the $100 million Food Insecurity and Nutrition Incentive Program (later renamed for Schumacher, after his passing), and in 2018 funding was increased to $250 million.[5] These were, like funding approval at any level of government (but particularly federal), divisive votes. This is why it matters whom we elect to represent us, who will be willing to carry the causes we believe in over the finish line.

From Nischan's impulse to change as a restaurateur, it took a decade for his effort to coalesce into political action. Then it took another six years of collaboration with so many people, developing and proving that idea, to become a law. None of the victories along the way, Nischan clarifies, were possible without donors, government networks, and community-based organizations throughout the country that do the real work on the ground. But an idea can grow into a movement. A personal choice can evolve into a matter of public policy. And our first step of individual action is as important as the finality of enacting laws.

We don't get to vote that often. It's not like we hold referendums on every matter of public policy. But our energies are always welcome and well put to use volunteering. Whatever political cause we believe in will welcome our time, money, or skills to canvas, phone bank, or conduct research. We do occasionally get to exercise our power at the ballot box more surgically, like when Philadelphia voted in a sugary drink tax and Washington State voted against it. Or that time the state of California voted against gig workers being treated as employees.

⁜

"I'VE SAID FOR years that if there were half as many restaurants in the United States and people saw them as luxuries, that would be a good thing," says Mark Bittman. In 2015 Bittman left his job as a food columnist at the *New York Times* to join a start-up company making vegan meal kits. He returned to journalism as editor in chief of the digital publication *Heated* (to which I was an occasional contributor) and the Bittman Project and is much more a proponent of home cooking than of restaurants. "As with all catastrophes, there's an opportunity here," says Bittman of our post-COVID-19 world. "There's also an opportunity to reestablish the status quo even more firmly. There are things about the status quo that people like." That's something I worry about, our individual and collective impulse to return to what we know as "normal." Even in good times, familiarity has a powerful gravitational pull; that effect is only magnified in tragedy.

During the sudden mass-unemployment period of COVID-19, restaurant workers found the time, energy, and will to voice their feelings of anger at a system that had treated them unfairly for a long time. With the return of dining, and jobs, will there be a sustained movement to change hospitality? Or will people be so desperate for work that they will accept conditions as they are?

"It's not a question of unemployment," says Bittman. "One of the things that really pissed me off at the beginning of COVID was restaurants saying, 'Oh, our workers.' Where were they when the workers were working and they were paying them $9 an hour? If you have a shitty job or two shitty jobs, and you're taking shitty public transportation to get from one to the other, and you're eating shitty food because you don't have time and money to cook, but you're not on the unemployment roll, it doesn't mean that your well-being is up there."

I don't want to see anyone out of work. I also don't want to see people crushed in a broken system. Which is worse, terrible jobs or no jobs? "Those aren't food issues. Those aren't restaurant issues. Those are social justice issues," argues Bittman. "Do you want to guarantee that your fellow citizens lead decent lives and everybody has good access to good food? If the answer to those two questions is yes, then it's a question of 'How do we balance priorities?' It's not a question of, 'Are there enough $9 an hour jobs for restaurants?'" It still seems inconceivable, because we are so used to the status quo. But what if the shitty jobs went away?

"EVERYBODY NEEDS MONEY. THAT'S WHY THEY CALL IT MONEY."

"Let it die," wrote chef and food activist Tunde Wey in an essay on our collective responsibility to not bail out the dining industry, titled "Don't Bail Out the Restaurant Industry," published on social media in the spring of 2020—a time when a lot of public conversation veered in the direction of how to save hospitality. "An industry where on the higher end is great food at fat prices in spaces that drive up real estate values, pushing property prices higher and poorer people further. And on the lower scale, working poor people, making barely enough to keep them going, serve low nutrition meals to other working poor people, who can't afford quality housing because of predatory development that supports new restaurants. Let it die."[6]

Wey is a firebrand, an activist known for challenging audiences to think about race in the context of food: at his 2018 lunch counter, Saartj, he charged white customers more than double what people of color had to pay.[7] It was not dissimilar from what Everytable does. Except Wey's purpose, in addition to filling bellies, is to use food to challenge people's thinking and force dialogue about topics many of us avoid.

I found myself nodding along as I read Wey's essay. Even though I had been thinking, and writing publicly, about the need for policy and financial support for the restaurant industry in the wake of the pandemic, we were committed to many of the same values, and his writing made me question my initial impulse to want to save the industry.

"I have a book I should be writing," says Wey, speaking to me from his home in New Orleans. I feel better about my deadlines already. I ask the unpleasant question that's been rattling around in my skull: What does Main Street, USA, look like with a bunch of boarded-up storefronts where there used to be restaurants? What happens, for example, when the mass disappearance of restaurants has a cascading effect on real-estate values everywhere? I'm kind of spinning out as I ramble through my questions. How much does this impact the price of homes and office spaces in places that used to be desirable, in part, because of all the restaurants? Which is worse, millions of people with crappy jobs or millions of people with no jobs?

A wise editor once told me, when I asked her how much of the chemical process of ceviche needed to be explained, that I could follow any story down to the microscopic level—though it may not serve the reader. At this point, my thinking about restaurants has taken me toward the opposite direction of macroeconomics.

Wey suggests we explore something economists call modern monetary theory (MMT), which, at the risk of gross oversimplification, is a belief that governments that control their own currency should spend and tax rather than tax and spend. Instead of collecting taxes and deciding how to allocate the revenues that come in, the view is that the federal government should create jobs and spend what it needs to reach the goals of a healthy society, like full employment and proper access to health care or education. As part of the Depression-era program the New Deal, Americans were put to work through a variety of public projects. Imagine the government using its access to capital to expand the mandate of organizations like WCK, paying hospitality professionals a living wage to cook nutritious meals for the growing number of Americans who are food insecure.

Opponents of MMT argue that government-created jobs equal socialism, which in our political climate is indistinguishable from communism (a scourge worse than death), and that printing money causes inflation, a boogeyman in political circles since the 1970s. Proponents say that a little inflation is tolerable, certainly more than mass unemployment, homelessness, and hunger. Remember, over half of fast-food workers require public assistance, so taxpayers are already subsidizing these lousy wages with $152.8 billion a year.

We're already doing the first part of MMT—intentionally or not. We have created money (which, as economist Stephanie Kelton, MMT's most visible proponent, reminds us, is not the same as printing money), trillions of dollars for bailout programs intended to prevent total economic collapse.[8] We did pay people to stay home. Why not pursue the second part and see something for our spending by putting people to work?

While I can't stop the direction that my thoughts and questions are propelling me, national work programs and economic controls take me high above the street-level decision making of where to eat. That gap between local politics and galactic intrigue is why Spider-Man and Thor team-ups don't work.

Are we going to nationalize Popeyes? Probably not. Could the United States develop a massive public works program that utilizes a dormant labor force to repair the country's aging infrastructure? As a society, we may still be a couple tweaks away from a complete overhaul, in which we restructure our world to prioritize things like physical and mental health, public education, and our impact on the planet, ahead of GDP.

As individuals, however, we are capable of fundamental change right now. I think it matters, particularly at a pivotal moment when we have the once-in-a-generation chance to completely alter big habits as fundamentally entrenched as how we eat in restaurants.

"For a long time, people who work on climate issues have been saying we're in a crisis," ZFP's Karen Leibowitz tells me. "And everyone has been like 'Yeah, yeah, yeah, but in the short term I don't want to be disrupted. Things just have to continue on. People have jobs they need to keep,' and so forth." And then COVID-19 did that anyway, undoing our social and economic fabric in a matter of weeks. "I remember in the first two weeks of the coronavirus crisis feeling so upset to have been right. To see how brittle our systems were. And not at all seeing the crisis as an opportunity." Painful as that is, this calamity has absolutely been an opening to reinvent ourselves.

Over the past year, a year without restaurants, I've had time to reflect on what they mean to me, what I want them to be, and where I want to eat when we all get out of this mess.

Coming down from the panic-attack altitude question of "How do we solve all of society's problems?" I'm glad I asked those questions. It's a direction worth going in and a conversation worth having. Back on earth, I have found real answers in my search for a better dining culture. Some of the prescriptions require serious effort. Others, like simply abandoning the precept that the customer is always right, take only a moment's action or a minor shift in the way we think about restaurants. In the myriad forms our dining choices can take—deleting our 3PD apps, obsessing a bit less over chefs and food-media hype, rethinking tipping, seeking out immigrant restaurateurs, and even taking political action—where and how we dine matters.

"While our individual food choices are not going to end hunger, poverty, and environmental destruction, it is my belief that collectively consumers have more power than is exercised," offers Lisa Holmes, founding board member of the Perennial Farming Initiative (now Zero Foodprint) and GreenWave (a regenerative ocean farming nonprofit). "Perhaps it's because I grew up in California in the 1960s and remember my mother boycotting grapes to support Cesar Chavez and what became the United Farm Workers. Especially now that a company's reputation is its currency, it is sharing (and shaming) through social media that has become a powerful tool for consumers." Yes, the bust of labor leader Chavez currently on display in the Oval Office is a symbolic prop. As symbols go, I'll take it over the president serving a table full of Wendy's to a victorious football team.

Holmes cites the work of the Coalition of Immokalee Workers (whom we met in Chapter 5), which began as community organizing of farmworkers in Florida and led to the building of a national consumer network that leveraged public awareness campaigns and boycotts to demand justice through corporate supply chains in supermarkets and fast-food restaurants. On the national level, she points to proposals like the Green New Deal and the Blue New Deal as signs for hope, as well as an increasing number of healthy soil bills being introduced in state legislatures. Closer to home, there is the creation of food-policy councils on state, local, and regional levels. Initiatives such as the Good Food Purchasing Program are making a measurable difference to local economies by changing procurement practices. From community-supported agriculture and fisheries to community land trusts, food co-ops, school gardens, community gardens, and composting programs, there is no shortage of "bottom-up" approaches that increase local food sovereignty and resilience. We are all needed as a part of that.

"Ideally," says Holmes, "we would have policies that support a just transition to regenerative agriculture on both land and sea to avoid climate catastrophe." But she notes that public and private leadership has been less than impressive on these fronts. So, as she puts it, "It is grass-roots organizing and consumer activism that currently provide a work-around to effect change in the absence of sound public policy. Until we step up as citizens and claim our political power, our wallets are unfortunately one of the most effective tools we have to effect change."

An integral component of how this happens is our support as diners for the restaurants, outliers though they are, that are forging a better path, demonstrating how to lead, and providing the tools to change. "On the individual level, the choices we all make as eaters on a daily basis do make a cumulative difference. There are many ways that we can engage, because we all eat and food is our most intimate and powerful connection to each other and to the earth."

THE NEXT SUPPER

Market-based solutions and policy solutions are not at odds or mutually exclusive. The problems of our tipping culture, for example, require work both from the bottom up, with individual restaurateurs changing their compensation structure, and from the top down, through legislation that prevents workers from being paid less than the minimum wage. Those aren't two trains traveling in opposite directions. They are headed to the same destination: the fair treatment of workers. Every link in the track is progress toward that goal. The unavoidable equation is that the level of dining experience to which we have become accustomed has to either simplify or become more expensive if we want everyone in the supply chain treated fairly.

When faced with a difficult task, people used to say, "We put a man on the moon." Their point was, compared to that, anything felt achievable. We've already done that in the dining industry. The moon landing of restaurants was the elimination of smoking.

When I was a kid and we entered a restaurant, the first question the host asked was, "Smoking or non?" If you said smoking, they brought you to a section of tables with ashtrays on them. If you said nonsmoking, they brought you to different tables, directly beside the smoking tables. Sometimes the smoking section was raised on a little platform, about eight inches higher than the floor. Or it was separated by something as permeable as a row of ferns or a paper screen. It seemed as insane then as it does now. While I have some misplaced nostalgia for going to dim sum and watching older diners who could hold chopsticks, a newspaper, and a lit cigarette at the same time, smoking in restaurants was always a disgusting practice.

It was also a public health problem, as secondhand smoke made nonsmoking customers and employees sick. Though we eventually passed legislation prohibiting smoking in restaurants, it was a ridiculously uphill battle, with a bloc of restaurant associations arguing, on behalf of the tobacco industry, that smoking bans would be a brutal blow to restaurants. It seemed inconceivable then that we would change what felt like such a fundamental aspect of dining out. When I saw, in movies from the 1950s, how people smoked in hospitals, I thought, "The olden times sure were crazy." Yet I never thought we'd be able to get rid of smoking in bars and restaurants. It seemed then that allowing people to enjoy a cigarette immediately following their meal was integral to the dining experience. It wasn't. It was banned in the majority of US states and cities, and the restaurant industry discovered that things were going to turn out just fine. Now when I watch a movie from the 1980s and see people smoking in restaurants, I realize that I grew up in olden times.

That was our moon landing. If we were able to get rid of smoking in restaurants, we can do a lot more, even if it might seem impossible.

Earlier today, before sitting down to write this, I had a minor medical procedure. As the nurse and doctor prepared to make a hole in me and poke around, they advised me to imagine myself in a peaceful place, like a beach. A screen above me played a slide show of farmhouses. Instead, I closed my eyes and pictured a steaming bowl of noodles. I could hear the sizzle as the kitchen fried more garlic, the glug glug of water glasses being filled, someone at a nearby table asking if the special could be made without pork, the rush of traffic whizzing by as new diners opened the front door. Inhaling, I breathed in a complex mist of fermented chili paste and wheat as familiar to me as my wife's perfume. This is my happy place. This is where I want to be.

I miss restaurants, from sloppy meals on the go to full-service evenings with candles and the whole shebang. The next time I sit down in any kind of restaurant for real—every time I sit down—regardless of what I'm eating, I want to feel good about it. All of it.

COVID-19 has been a nightmare for restaurants. The businesses that survive, and those that sprout in the soil after this calamity, must be better than what came before.

There is more to rethinking restaurants than online ordering, curbside pickup, and outdoor tables under heat lamps. That stuff got us through the short-term crisis. It also showed we can make big changes when we need to. The long term, with its potential for restaurants to redefine their relationship with workers, public health, the environment, and us, the diners, is unwritten.

I think there is a better future for restaurants. And we can be part of making that happen.

Acknowledgments

"LET'S GO FOR A SWIM AND THEN EAT NOODLES," SAID David Sax. He said this over and over again. And, as I always want to swim and eat noodles, I kept saying yes. After swimming twenty meager laps, then indulging in the bowls of spicy noodles our exercise had justified, Sax helped create this book with his interrogations about the ethics of dining.

Through Sax I met Ben Adams, my editor at PublicAffairs, and through Ben my agent, Lynn Johnston. Both of them unsquiggled my noodley ramblings into something lucid that sounded like a book.

Without Hamutal Dotan, I wouldn't have had the nerve to write a five-thousand-word feature, let alone the audacity for a book. She has repeatedly saved me from embarrassing myself, making sure this book is something I can be proud of.

I didn't go to school. So it's hard to imagine reaching this point in my career without the guidance of other passionate editors—Denise Balkissoon, Graeme Bayliss, Kim Honey, Alison Uncles, Christina Gonzales, Katie Gillmor Ellis—who taught me to care, steered me toward work that mattered, and demanded that I do better.

A few passages in this book originally appeared in stories written for the *Walrus*, the *Counter*, *TVO*, and *Heated* with Mark Bittman. I'm grateful to the publications that have enabled me, over the past couple years, to test out ideas for this book, and have been cool about my repurposing a few elements for this jigsaw puzzle of a project. Not only was this helpful in fleshing out theories and getting a head start on reporting, but listening to and learning from audience reaction was like a sonar beacon for what people knew about or cared about.

This type of journalistic nonfiction exists only because people like me have the gall to contact strangers and not only ask them for their time, but also intrude on their privacy. And those strangers have the graciousness to say yes. From their patiently explaining how franchising works to describing abuse at the hands of employers and diners, I owe my gratitude to the many people who spoke to me, sharing their knowledge, experience, and wisdom.

One person who deserves zero credit is my little Puddin', who at the beginning of this was still not born and who now jumps in puddles and eats pickles. And yet she is the center of our world. It is only out of the belief in her digital privacy that her apple-cheeked face, which calmed me down at the end of each day, is not on this book's cover. We would sell a jillion copies. I hope that by the time this sees print, she has gotten to play with another human child.

There's no possibility I could have finished writing if not for my wife's parents, Gord and Olga, who spend every day with our daughter so we can work. And I could not have gotten through this difficult year without my brother, Yonan, who supported me as a new dad, or my mother, who has watched her grandchild grow up over video calls at dinner.

Most of the interviews for this book were conducted over speakerphone, in the basement of my Toronto home, then Gord and Olga's basement in Winnipeg, and at the tail end of the process aboveground in the office of my new home.

My original intent was to travel, to spend time with people in Louisville, San Francisco, Boston, LA, and so on. But after my first trip, to visit tomato farmers in Florida (during which Victoria sleep-trained our daughter), the pandemic reshaped our lives. With the change went any plans to order pastrami on rye from a Manhattan ghost kitchen while waiting to see the latest Marvel movie (an event that seemed, until theaters shut down, evergreen for the first weekend in May), or traveling anywhere, meeting people face-to-face and gathering the sort of physical details that craft the introductory scenes in this type of book.

Many authors found themselves in the same position. My attitude was, to heck with it. While frustrating, it was no hardship compared to people unable to do their jobs, to earn money. I was disappointed not to be able to collect the sort of rich detail that comes only from immersing yourself in a place, its people, sounds, and smells. And I was bummed not to find transformative food experiences along the way. On the other hand, I was happy to do away with physical descriptions of interviewees. Conjuring images of curly hair, a crisply ironed shirt, a steely gaze, or all the other literal characteristics is something I've never felt entirely comfortable with. And I've always disliked the unwritten nonfiction rule that beautiful people get to be described based on their beauty, and everyone else by their personality quirks or clothing choices. A bit of backstory, biography, and qualifications is necessary for putting people's words in context. But instead of what they look like, I think that what they have to say means more. I hope you do too.

During this process, which was supposed to include a crisscross tour of America, but instead was just me in a basement, my wife, Victoria, brought me hugs and kisses and cookies and made sure I felt smart and handsome. Halfway through the book, and halfway through Vic's maternity leave, she fell and broke her foot. I put aside work, not knowing how long it would take for the foot to heal. It ended up being only three weeks, followed quickly by a global catastrophe that shut down everyone's lives and plans for the future. But those few weeks, pushing a stroller through snow-clogged streets to the library, cooking, cleaning, and looking after my ladies, were about the best three weeks of my life. And though I was happy for my wife's speedy recovery, I was a little sad when it was clear that she could walk and I headed back down to the basement.

This lousy pandemic, which has taken so much from so many, has brought us closer together. And though Vic has not gotten tired of my cooking, and I am always in the mood to make dinner, I am looking forward to restaurants like you wouldn't believe. I hope we can all soon go do the things we have been missing. For me that is swimming twenty laps and using it as an excuse to go for a spicy noodle lunch, talk shit with friends, and then write a book to justify that it was all part of my workday instead of goofing off.

Notes

INTRODUCTION

1. Ashwin Deshmukh (@ashwindeshmukh), "Just hit $100k of cancelled event business. Guess I have to go to med school after all," Twitter, March 11, 2020, https://twitter.com/ashwindeshmukh/status/1237822501587161093; Julia Moskin, "Le Bernardin, Daniel and Other Top New York Restaurants Temporarily Close," *New York Times*, March 13, 2020, www.nytimes.com/2020/03/13/dining/restaurant-closings-coronavirus.html?smid=tw-nytfood&smtyp=cur; "Coronavirus: Spain and France Announce Sweeping Restrictions," BBC, March 15, 2020, www.bbc.com/news/world-europe-51892477.

2. Peter Romeo, "Epidemic Will Cost Restaurants $225B Short-Term, National Restaurant Association Says," *Restaurant Business*, March 18, 2020, www.restaurantbusinessonline.com/operations/epidemic-will-cost-restaurants-225-billion-short-term-nra-says.

3. Jonathan Maze, "McDonald's to Close Seating Areas at Company Restaurants," *Restaurant Business*, March 16, 2020, www.restaurantbusinessonline.com/financing/mcdonalds-close-seating-areas-company-restaurants; Jonathan Maze, "A 'Meteor' Obliterates Restaurant Stocks as In-Store Dining Stops," *Restaurant Business*, March 17, 2020, www.restaurantbusinessonline.com/financing/meteor-obliterates-restaurant-stocks-store-dining-stops.

4. David Kamp, *United States of Arugula: How We Became a Gourmet Nation* (New York: Clarkson Potter, 2006).

5. Yewande Komolafe, "The Problems with Palm Oil Don't Start with My Recipes," *Heated*, June 19, 2020, https://heated.medium.com/the-problems-with-palm-oil-dont-start-with-my-recipes-1ce29f00bb4a#6f28.

6. Heather Haddon, "McDonald's, Chipotle and Domino's Are Booming During Coronavirus While Your Neighborhood Restaurant Struggles," *Wall Street Journal*, October 12, 2020, www.wsj.com/articles/mcdonalds-chipotle-and -dominos-are-feasting-during-coronavirus-while-your-neighborhood-restaurant -fasts-11602302431; Caleb Pershan, "The Ugly Legal Battle over Restaurant Insurance Has Begun," *Eater*, April 9, 2020, www.eater.com/2020/4/9/21214136 /restaurant-business-interruption-insurance-lawsuits-coronavirus-coverage.

7. Madeline Wells, "Line Cooks Are at the Highest Risk of Dying from COVID, Says UCSF Study," *SF Gate*, January 28, 2021, www.sfgate.com/food /article/Cooks-restaurant-workers-risk-death-COVID-UCSF-15905789.php.

8. Alexia Fernández Campbell, "The Problem with Amazon's Speedy Shipping, in One Graphic," *Vox*, October 18, 2019, www.vox.com/identities/2019 /10/18/20920717/amazon-shipping-workers-injuries; Annie Palmer, "Amazon Downplayed Rising Injury Rates at Its Warehouses, Investigation Finds," CNBC, September 29, 2020, www.cnbc.com/2020/09/29/amazon-reportedly -downplayed-rising-injury-rates-at-its-warehouses.html.

CHAPTER 1: THE VIRTUAL RESTAURANT

1. Gary He, "New Yorkers Are Overcrowding Carbone's Sidewalk, Forcing Police Action," *Eater*, March 23, 2020, https://ny.eater.com/2020/3/23 /21190803/carbone-crowds-nyc-delivery-takeout-coronavirus.

2. Michael Milken and Igor Tulchinsky, "How Technology Liberates Human Capital," *Wall Street Journal*, April 11, 2017, www.wsj.com/articles/how -technology-liberates-human-capital-1491946796.

3. Stefan Poser, "Leisure Time and Technology," Institute of European History, September 26, 2011, http://ieg-ego.eu/en/threads/crossroads/technified -environments/stefan-poser-leisure-time-and-technology#LeisureTimeMeaningful orDisruptive.

4. John Frazer, "How the Gig Economy Is Reshaping Careers for the Next Generation," *Forbes*, February 15, 2019, www.forbes.com/sites/johnfrazer1 /2019/02/15/how-the-gig-economy-is-reshaping-careers-for-the-next -generation/#4a34f10249ad; Bruce Feiler, "Overscheduled Children: How Big a Problem?," *New York Times*, October 11, 2013, www.nytimes.com/2013/10/13 /fashion/over-scheduled-children-how-big-a-problem.html; Maryam Shah, "$22/Hr Is Average Wage Needed to Afford a Two-Bedroom Apartment in Canada: Report," *Global News*, July 17, 2019, https://globalnews.ca/news/5510783 /minimum-wage-renting-canada/; Beth Elderkin, "The One Good Scene In: *Beneath the Planet of the Apes*," *Gizmodo*, September 22, 2020, https:// io9.gizmodo.com/the-one-good-scene-in-beneath-the-planet-of-the-apes -1845075716.

5. Jason Daley, "Recently Uncovered Thermopolium Reminds Us That Romans Loved Fast Food as Much as We Do," *Smithsonian Magazine*, April 3,

2019, www.smithsonianmag.com/smart-news/romans-loved-fast-food-much-we-do-180971845/.

6. Jan Whitaker, "Dinner to Go," *Restaurant-ing Through History*, May 3, 2020, https://restaurant-ingthroughhistory.com/tag/take-out/; Emelyn Rude, "What Take-Out Food Can Teach You About American History," *Time*, April 14, 2016, https://time.com/4291197/take-out-delivery-food-history/.

7. Sarah Pruitt, "The Post World War II Boom: How America Got into Gear," *History*, May 14, 2020, www.history.com/news/post-world-war-ii-boom-economy.

8. "Pizza Hut Celebrates 20th Anniversary of World's First Online Purchase with 50 Percent Off Online Deal for Hut Lovers Members," *Restaurantnews .com*, January 2, 2014, www.restaurantnews.com/pizza-hut-celebrates-20th-anniversary-of-worlds-first-online-purchase-with-50-percent-off-online-deal-for-hut-lovers-members/.

9. "Papa John's Launches Mobile Gift Card Ordering Site," *QSR Magazine*, January 20, 2014, www.qsrmagazine.com/news/papa-john-s-launches-mobile-gift-card-ordering-site; Shareen Pathak, "Domino's Is Now 'an E-commerce Company That Sells Pizza,'" *Digiday*, April 3, 2015, https://digiday.com/marketing/dominos-now-e-commerce-company-sells-pizza/.

10. Eric Newcomer and Selina Wang, "Square Said to Have Discussed Caviar Sale with Uber, GrubHub," *Business Insider*, October 11, 2016, www.bloomberg.com/news/articles/2016-10-11/square-said-to-have-discussed-caviar-sale-with-uber-grubhub.

11. Jason Aten, "Uber and Lyft Are Betting That Driverless Cars Will Help Them Finally Make Money. Here's Why It Won't Work," *Inc.*, August 13, 2019, www.inc.com/jason-aten/uber-lyft-are-betting-that-driverless-cars-will-help-them-finally-make-money-heres-why-it-wont-work.html; Marco della Cava, "It's Self-Driving or Bust for Uber CEO; the IPO Can Wait," *USA Today*, August 19, 2016, www.usatoday.com/story/tech/news/2016/08/19/s-self-driving-cars-uber-ceo-travis-kalanick-ipo/88967594/; Edward Ongweso Jr., "Uber Sells Off Sci-Fi Pipe Dreams. Exploiting Human Labor Is Its Only Plan," *Vice*, December 9, 2020, www.vice.com/en/article/93wq9y/uber-sells-off-sci-fi-pipe-dreams-exploiting-human-labor-is-its-only-plan.

12. Jacques Bughin and Jan Mischke, "Exploding Myths About the Gig Economy," McKinsey Global Institute, November 28, 2016, www.mckinsey.com/mgi/overview/in-the-news/exploding-myths-about-the-gig-economy.

13. Danny Klein, "Fighting for Share in the $16.6 Billion Delivery App Market," *QSR Magazine*, June 2019, www.qsrmagazine.com/technology/fighting-share-166-billion-delivery-app-market.

14. Ethan Baron, "DoorDash, Uber Eats, Grubhub, and Postmates Make Restaurant Meals Cost More: Lawsuit," *Mercury (CA) News*, April 14, 2020, www.mercurynews.com/2020/04/14/doordash-uber-eats-grubhub-and-postmates-make-restaurant-meals-cost-more-lawsuit/.

15. Heather Somerville, "Uber Posts $50 Billion in Annual Bookings as Profit Remains Elusive Ahead of IPO," Reuters, February 15, 2015, www .reuters.com/article/us-uber-results/uber-posts-50-billion-in-annual -bookings-as-profit-remains-elusive-ahead-of-ipo-idUSKCN1Q42CI; Erin Griffith, "DoorDash Faces Its Latest Challenge: Wooing Wall Street," *New York Times*, March 4, 2020, www.nytimes.com/2020/03/04/technology /doordash-ipo.html; Mike Stenger, "Is the DoorDash IPO Worth Investing In?," *Morning Money*, https://moneymorning.com/2020/09/09/is-the-doordash -ipo-worth-investing-in/; Levi Sumagaysay, "DoorDash Shares Sink as Revenue More than Triples but Loss More than Doubles," *MarketWatch*, February 25, 2021, www.marketwatch.com/story/doordash-shares-sink-as-revenue-more -than-triples-but-loss-more-than-doubles-11614289424.

16. Joe Guszkowski, "At Grubhub, Profits Remain Elusive Despite Sales Growth," *Restaurant Business*, February 4, 2021, www.restaurantbusinessonline .com/technology/grubhub-profits-remain-elusive-despite-sales-growth; "Grub-hub Reports First Quarter 2020 Results," *Grubhub*, May 6, 2020, https:// investors.grubhub.com/investors/press-releases/press-release-details/2020 /Grubhub-Reports-First-Quarter-2020-Results/default.aspx; Grubhub letter to shareholders, February 5, 2020, https://s2.q4cdn.com/772508021/files /doc_downloads/Documents/February-2020-Shareholder-Letter.pdf, 5.

17. Allison Robicelli, "Literally No One Is Profiting Off of Third-Party De-livery Apps," *Takeout*, June 6, 2020, https://thetakeout.com/literally-no-one-is -profiting-off-of-third-party-delive-1844180260; Erik Chan, "How Restau-rants Can Offer Delivery—and Make Money," *QSR Magazine*, May 2017, www .qsrmagazine.com/outside-insights/how-restaurants-can-offer-delivery-and -make-money.

18. Ilya Bañares, "Would You Live in a Condo Without an Oven? 162 Units in This Downtown Building Don't Have One," *Toronto Star*, June 11, 2019, www.thestar.com/news/gta/2019/06/10/would-you-live-in-a-condo-without -an-oven-162-units-in-this-downtown-building-dont-have-one.html.

19. SkipTheDishes courier application, https://couriers.skipthedishes.com /application; Cameron MacLean, "Skip the Dishes Could Face Class-Action Lawsuit over Treatment of Couriers," CBC, June 31, 2018, www.cbc.ca/news /canada/manitoba/skip-the-dishes-lawsuit-1.4768467.

20. Jeongmin Kim, "Why Young Koreans Love to Splurge," *Financial Post*, May 4, 2019, https://foreignpolicy.com/2019/07/04/why-young-koreans -love-to-splurge-shibal-biyong-millennial-fuck-it-expense/?utm_source=pocket -newtab.

21. Maria Yagoda, "These Are the 25 Most Popular Dishes of 2018, Ac-cording to Postmates," *Food & Wine*, December 11, 2018, www.foodandwine .com/news/popular-dishes-postmates-2018-orders.

22. Eric Newcomer, "Uber and Travis Kalanick Are in Business Again. This Time, as Competitors," *Bloomberg*, March 11, 2019, www.bloomberg.com/news

/articles/2019-03-11/uber-and-travis-kalanick-are-in-business-again-this
-time-as-competitors; Katie Canales, "Ousted Uber Cofounder Travis Kalanick
Has Reportedly Spent $130 Million on His Ghost Kitchen Startup. Here's What
It's Like Inside One of the Secretive Locations," *Business Insider*, October 20,
2020, www.businessinsider.com/cloud-kitchens-travis-kalanick-san-francisco
-location-address-pictures-2019-11?op=1.

23. Coral Murphy Marcos, "Ordering Food? Chuck E. Cheese's New
Pizza Place Is Confusing Some Online," *USA Today*, May 18, 2020, www
.usatoday.com/story/money/food/2020/05/18/chuck-e-cheese-operates
-pasquallys-pizza-wings-delivery-apps/5215475002/.

24. Chris Crowley, "Big Delivery Is Winning—Even If Everyone Hates It,"
Grub Street, February 24, 2021, www.grubstreet.com/2021/02/third-party
-delivery-platforms-are-winning.html.

25. Jonathan Shieber, "Serious Injuries at Amazon Fulfillment Centers
Topped 14,000, Despite the Company's Safety Claims," *TechCrunch*, September 29, 2020, https://techcrunch.com/2020/09/29/serious-injuries-at
-amazon-fulfillment-centers-topped-14000-despite-the-companys-safety
-claims/; Steven Greenhouse, "Is Your Grocery Delivery Worth a Worker's Life?,"
New York Times, March 30, 2020, www.nytimes.com/2020/03/30/opinion
/coronavirus-worker-strike.html.

26. Stuart Rudner and Ayesha Adamjee, "Are Uber Drivers 'Employees'?,"
Rudnerlaw.com, July 15, 2020, www.rudnerlaw.ca/uber-drivers-employees/.

27. "Canadian Union of Postal Workers v Foodora Inc. d.b.a. Foodora, 2020 CanLII 16750 (ON LRB)," CanLII, February 25, 2020, www
.canlii.org/en/on/onlrb/doc/2020/2020canlii16750/2020canlii16750
.html; Ryan White, "How the Ontario Labour Board Ruled Foodora Workers Are 'Employees' and Not Independent Contractors," Canadian Law of
Work Forum, March 5, 2020, http://lawofwork.ca/how-the-ontario-labour
-board-ruled-foodora-workers-are-employees/.

28. Johana Bhuiyan, "DoorDash's About-Face on Tipping Shows Customers Have More Clout than Workers," *LA Times*, July 25, 2019, www.latimes
.com/business/technology/story/2019-07-25/doordash-tipping-amazon
-flex-drivers.

CHAPTER 2: THE CHEF-DRIVEN RESTAURANT

1. Bill Addison, "Razed and Exposed, the Restaurant Industry Is Due for
Change," *Los Angeles Times*, September 17, 2020, www.latimes.com/food
/story/2020-09-17/los-angeles-restaurant-industry-2020-pandemic.

2. Janelle Bitker and Justin Phillips, "The Restaurant at Meadowood Pushed
Chefs for Brilliance—Some Say at a Human Cost," *San Francisco Chronicle*,
October 18, 2020, www.sfchronicle.com/restaurants/article/The-Restaurant
-at-Meadowood-pushed-chefs-for-15623434.php.

3. Killian Fox, "The Kitchen Apprentices: Have Knives, Will Travel," *Guardian*, November 15, 2015, www.theguardian.com/lifeandstyle/2015/nov/15/the-kitchen-apprentices-have-knives-will-travel-stagiaires; Lesley Bargar Suter, "I Staged at Noma and All I Got Was This Lousy Inspiration," *Los Angeles Magazine*, January 31, 2013, www.lamag.com/digestblog/i-staged-at-noma-and-all-i-got-was-this-lousy-inspiration/.

4. Robert Booth, "Michel Roux Jr Admits Restaurant Staff Get No Share of Service Charge," *Guardian*, December 15, 2016, www.theguardian.com/lifeandstyle/2016/dec/15/michel-roux-jr-restaurant-staff-no-share-service-charge-le-gavroche; Robert Booth, "TV Chef Michel Roux Jr. Paid Kitchen Staff Below Minimum Wage," *Guardian*, November 17, 2016, www.theguardian.com/money/2016/nov/17/tv-chef-michel-roux-jr-paid-kitchen-staff-below-minimum-wage.

5. Ben Schneiders and Royce Millar, "Heston Blumenthal, the Tax Havens and the Ripped-Off Workers," *Sydney Morning Herald*, December 9, 2018, www.smh.com.au/business/workplace/heston-blumenthal-the-tax-havens-and-the-ripped-off-workers-20181207-p50ksz.html.

6. Irene Jiang, "85% of Independent Restaurants May Go Out of Business by the End of 2020, According to the Independent Restaurant Coalition," *Business Insider*, July 14, 2020, www.businessinsider.com/85-of-independent-restaurants-could-permanently-close-in-2020-report-2020-6.

7. Laura Testino, "Fact check: Tipping Began amid Slavery, Then Helped Keep Former Black Slaves' Wages Low," *USA Today*, December 16, 2020, www.usatoday.com/story/news/factcheck/2020/12/16/fact-check-tipping-kept-wages-low-formerly-enslaved-black-workers/3896620001/; "Tip Credit and Tip Pooling Provisions of the Fair Labor Standards Act," Congressional Research Service, June 27, 2018, https://fas.org/sgp/crs/misc/IF10917.pdf.

8. Fiona W. Ong, "DOL Provides Clarification on FLSA Tip Pooling Amendments," Shaw Rosenthal LLP, April 9, 2018, www.laboremploymentreport.com/2018/04/09/dol-provides-clarification-on-flsa-tip-pooling-amendments/; Glenn Blain, "Per Se Restaurant Must Pay $500K to Workers in Settlement over Tips," *New York Daily News*, July 2, 2015, www.nydailynews.com/new-york/se-restaurant-pay-500k-workers-settlement-article-1.2279349; Amanda Kludt, "Mario Batali Settles $5 Million Class Action Lawsuit," *Eater*, March 7, 2012, https://ny.eater.com/2012/3/7/6607651/mario-batali-settles-5-million-class-action-lawsuit; Kathryn Vasel, "Pricey Manhattan Restaurant Owes Staff $500,000 for Unpaid Tips," *CNN Money*, July 2, 2015, https://money.cnn.com/2015/07/02/pf/per-se-fine-tipping/index.html.

9. Nikita Richardson, "Every Chef and Restaurant Owner Accused of Sexual Misconduct in the #MeToo Era," *GrubStreet*, March 14, 2019, www.grubstreet.com/2018/10/how-chefs-and-restaurateurs-are-faring-post-metoo.html; Kim Severson and Ben Berke, "Mario Batali Appears in Court

to Deny Charges of Indecent Assault," *New York Times*, May 24, 2019, www
.nytimes.com/2019/05/24/dining/mario-batali-arraignment.html; Warren
Rojas, "Mike Isabella Settles Lawsuit Alleging Sexual Harassment at His Restaurant Group," *Eater*, May 7, 2018, https://dc.eater.com/2018/5/7/17326298
/mike-isabella-chloe-caras-lawsuit-settlement.

10. Nikita Richardson, "Why Tips Won. They're Outdated. They're Discriminatory. And They Aren't Going Anywhere," *Grubstreet*, December 6, 2018,
www.grubstreet.com/2018/12/restaurant-tipping-returns.html.

11. "Minimum Wages for Tipped Employees," U.S. Department of Labor,
January 1, 2021, www.dol.gov/agencies/whd/state/minimum-wage/tipped;
"The Separate Tipped Minimum Wage Should Be Eliminated," Economic Policy Institute, July 10, 2014, www.epi.org/press/separate-tipped-minimum-wage
-eliminated/.

12. Michael Lynn and Zachary W. Brewster, "Racial and Ethnic Differences
in Tipping: The Role of Perceived Descriptive and Injunctive Tipping Norms,"
Cornell Hospitality Quarterly 56, no. 1 (2015): 68–79, https://static.secure
.website/wscfus/5261551/1619058/cq-2015-race-tipping-final.pdf; Zachary
Brewster and Michael Lynn, "Black-White Wage Gap Among Restaurant Servers:
A Replication, Extension, and Exploration of Consumer Racial Discrimination
in Tipping," *Sociological Inquiry* 84, no. 4 (2014): 545–569, https://static.secure
.website/wscfus/5261551/1619831/socinq-2014-earning-gap.pdf.

13. Elise Gould and David Cooper, "Seven Facts About Tipped Workers and
the Tipped Minimum Wage," Economic Policy Institute, May 31, 2018, www.epi
.org/blog/seven-facts-about-tipped-workers-and-the-tipped-minimum-wage/.

14. Emily Badger, "San Francisco Restaurants Can't Afford Waiters. So
They're Putting Diners to Work," *New York Times*, June 25, 2018, www.nytimes
.com/2018/06/25/dining/san-francisco-restaurants-service.html; Amelia Levin,
"5 Fine-Dining Chefs Changing Fast Casual," *QSR Magazine*, October 2016, www
.qsrmagazine.com/menu-innovations/5-fine-dining-chefs-changing-fast-casual.

15. Donna M. Bush and Rachel N. Lipari, "Substance Use and Substance
Use Disorder by Industry," *CBHSQ Report*, April 16, 2015, www.samhsa.gov
/data/sites/default/files/report_1959/ShortReport-1959.html.

16. Hannah Selinger, "Life Was Not a Peach," *Eater*, December 21, 2020,
www.eater.com/22193151/momofuku-david-chang-memoir-eat-a-peach
-review; Jonathan H. Kantor, "10 Wildest Contraptions Fantastic Four's Reed
Richards Invented (and 10 Most Dangerous)," *CBR*, January 18, 2019, www.cbr
.com/fantastic-four-wildest-dangerous-inventions/.

CHAPTER 3: THE INSTA-BAIT MEAL

1. Madeleine Davies, "*Bon Appétit* Editor-in-Chief Adam Rapoport Resigns Following Allegations of Racist Culture," *Eater*, June 8, 2020, www.eater

.com/2020/6/8/21284390/bon-appetit-adam-rapoport-resign-racism-brownface
-photo; Lisa Respers France, "Alison Roman Pens Apology to Chrissy Teigen and
Marie Kondo," CNN, May 12, 2020, www.cnn.com/2020/05/12/entertainment
/alison-roman-teigen-kondo-trnd/index.html; Farley Elliott, "Peter Meehan Resigns from *LA Times* Food Section After Allegations of Creating a Toxic Workplace Culture," *Eater*, July 1, 2020, https://la.eater.com/2020/7/1/21310294
/peter-meehan-resigns-los-angeles-times-food-editor-section-lucky-peach-news.

2. "FTC Staff Reminds Influencers and Brands to Clearly Disclose Relationship," Federal Trade Commission, April 19, 2017, www.ftc.gov/news
-events/press-releases/2017/04/ftc-staff-reminds-influencers-brands-clearly
-disclose; Food Insider (@FoodInsider), "This shop only makes peanut butter
and jelly," Twitter, August 29, 2020, https://twitter.com/InsiderFood/status
/1299815162006966272.

3. "People Lined Up for 10 Hours to Try Toronto's First Jollibee Restaurant," *Toronto Life*, April 2, 2018, https://torontolife.com/food/people-lined
-10-hours-try-torontos-first-jollibee-restaurant/.

4. Food Hype meme generator, https://food-hype.glitch.me/.

5. Chris Crowley, "The Nightmare Inside Mission Chinese Food," *Grubstreet*, October 22, 2020, www.grubstreet.com/2020/10/inside-mission-chinese
-food-report.html; Erika Adams and Tanay Warerkar, "Years-Long Mission
Chinese Leadership Conflict Is Back in the Spotlight After New Allegations Surface," *Eater*, September 22, 2020, https://ny.eater.com/2020/9/22/21445433
/mission-chinese-danny-bowien-angela-dimayuga-controversy.

6. Craig Silverman, "The Philippines Was a Test of Facebook's New Approach to Countering Disinformation. Things Got Worse," *BuzzFeed*, August,
7, 2019, www.buzzfeednews.com/article/craigsilverman/2020-philippines
-disinformation; Davey Alba, "How Duterte Used Facebook to Fuel the Philip-
pine Drug War," *BuzzFeed*, September 4, 2018, www.buzzfeednews.com/article
/daveyalba/facebook-philippines-dutertes-drug-war.

7. Sunny Jung Kim and Jeffrey T. Hancock, "How Advertorials Deactivate
Advertising Schema: MTurk-Based Experiments to Examine Persuasion Tactics and Outcomes in Health Advertisements," *Sage Journals*, April 25, 2016,
https://journals.sagepub.com/doi/abs/10.1177/0093650216644017.

8. Andrew Ellson, "'A Third of TripAdvisor Reviews Are Fake' as Cheats
Buy Five Stars," *Times*, September 22, 2018, www.thetimes.co.uk/article/hotel
-and-caf-cheats-are-caught-trying-to-buy-tripadvisor-stars-027fbcwc8; Diana
Hubbell, "The Complicated, Problematic Influence of TripAdvisor Restaurant
Reviews," *Eater*, December 5, 2019, https://ny.eater.com/2019/12/5/20978234
/tripadvisor-best-nyc-restaurant-rankings-scam.

9. "Facebook's Advertising Revenue Worldwide from 2009 to 2020," Statista,
February 5, 2021, www.statista.com/statistics/271258/facebooks-advertising
-revenue-worldwide/; Jasmine Enberg, "Global Digital Ad Spending 2019,"

eMarketer, March 28, 2019, www.emarketer.com/content/global-digital-ad -spending-2019.

10. Julia Moskin et al., "Your Questions About Food and Climate Change, Answered," *New York Times*, April 30, 2019, www.nytimes.com/interactive /2019/04/30/dining/climate-change-food-eating-habits.html.

11. Patricia Escárcega (@piescarcega), "Last night, after nearly 6 anxious months of being told 'the company will have a response for you shortly', my employer, @latimes, finally handed me a decision on the pay discrimination claim I filed through my union," *Twitter*, November 15, 2020, 1:35 p.m., https:// twitter.com/piescarcega/status/1328043858698137601; Mona Holmes, "*LA Times* Denies Restaurant Critic Patricia Escárcega's Request for Equal Pay," *Eater*, November 17, 2020, https://la.eater.com/2020/11/17/21571364/los-angeles -times-latina-food-critic-pay-discrimination-patricia-escarcega; Brittany Martin, "*L.A. Times* Food Critic Patricia Escárcega Accuses the Paper of Discrimination," *Los Angeles Magazine*, November 16, 2020, www.lamag.com/citythinkblog /patricia-escarcega-food-critic-los-angeles-times-discrimination/.

12. Soleil Ho, "The Restaurant Equity Revolution Will Not Be Instagrammed," *San Francisco Chronicle*, December 21, 2020, www.sfchronicle.com/restaurants /article/Restaurant-workers-filled-Instagram-with-outrage-15811744.php.

13. Garrett Snyder, "Sqirl Owner Jessica Koslow Addresses Moldy Jam and Food Safety Allegations as Former Employees Speak Out," *Los Angeles Times*, July 14, 2020, www.latimes.com/food/story/2020-07-14/sqirl-moldy -jam-safety-allegations.

14. Kim Severson, "Bon Appétit Editor Adam Rapoport Resigns," *New York Times*, June 8, 2020, www.nytimes.com/2020/06/08/dining/bon-appetit -adam-rapoport.html.

15. "New Guard" nomination form, *Eater*, October 21, 2020, www .eater.com/2020/10/21/21517981/eater-new-guard-2021-nominations-change makers?amp;amp;amp.

CHAPTER 4: THE IMMIGRANT RESTAURANT

1. Statistics Canada, Census Profile, 2016, www12.statcan.gc.ca/census -recensement/2016/dp-pd/prof/details/page.cfm?Lang=E&Geo1=PR &Code1=01&Geo2=PR&Code2=01&Data=Count&SearchText =Canada&SearchType=Begins&SearchPR=01&B1=Ethnic+origin&TABID =1; "Facts for Features: Hispanic Heritage Month, 2017," US Census Bureau, August 31, 2017, www.census.gov/newsroom/facts-for-features/2017/hispanic -heritage.html.

2. "Sinhalese Canadians," in *The Canadian Encyclopedia*, February 22, 2011, www.thecanadianencyclopedia.ca/en/article/sinhalese; "Place of Birth for the Foreign-Born Population in the United States," US Census Bureau, 2017,

https://archive.vn/20200213005436/https://factfinder.census.gov/bkmk/table/1.0/en/ACS/17_1YR/B05006/0100000US.

3. Randy Capps and Ariel G. Ruiz Soto, "Immigration to the Heartland: A Profile of Immigrants in the Kansas City Region," Migration Policy Institute, October 2016, www.migrationpolicy.org/sites/default/files/publications/KansasCity-FINAL.pdf.

4. Alyshah Hasham, "Man Who Stabbed Co-worker at Chinatown Restaurant Guilty of Manslaughter," Toronto Star, March 6, 2014, www.thestar.com/news/crime/2014/03/06/man_who_stabbed_coworker_at_chinatown_restaurant_guilty_of_manslaughter.html.

5. Dionne Wright-Bower, "Immigrants and the Restaurant Industry," New Mexico Restaurant Association, February 16, 2017, www.nmrestaurants.org/immigrants/; Dan Kosten, "Immigrants as Economic Contributors: Immigrant Entrepreneurs," National Immigration Forum, July 11, 2018, https://immigrationforum.org/article/immigrants-as-economic-contributors-immigrant-entrepreneurs/; Dinah Wisenberg Brin, "Immigrants Form 25% of New U.S. Businesses, Driving Entrepreneurship in 'Gateway' States," Forbes, July 31, 2018, www.forbes.com/sites/dinahwisenberg/2018/07/31/immigrant-entrepreneurs-form-25-of-new-u-s-business-researchers/?sh=30b2fb44713b; Michael Blanding, "One Quarter of Entrepreneurs in the United States Are Immigrants," Harvard Business School, August 31, 2016, https://hbswk.hbs.edu/item/one-quarter-of-entrepreneurs-in-the-united-states-are-immigrants.

6. April Chan, "How Chinese Restaurants Are Shut Out of the Organic Food Movement," San Francisco Chronicle, February 1, 2019, www.sfchronicle.com/food/article/How-the-organic-movement-makes-it-impossible-for-13578993.php.

7. Corey Mintz, "Here's What Happened When DaiLo Chef Nick Liu Cooked Chinese Food from a 119-Year-Old Menu," Toronto Life, November 2, 2017, https://torontolife.com/food/heres-happened-dailo-chef-nick-liu-cooked-chinese-food-119-year-old-menu/.

8. Helen Rosner, "If You Care About Food, You Need to Care About Immigration Policy," Eater, February 17, 2017, www.eater.com/2017/2/17/14649202/trump-immigration-policy-food.

9. Jonah Newman, "Chicago Spent More than $113 Million on Police Misconduct Lawsuits in 2018," Chicago Reporter, March 7, 2019, www.chicagoreporter.com/chicago-spent-more-than-113-million-on-police-misconduct-lawsuits-in-2018/.

10. Badger, "San Francisco Restaurants Can't Afford Waiters."

11. "AB-626 California Retail Food Code: Microenterprise Home Kitchen Operations," California Legislative Information, September 18, 2018, https://leginfo.legislature.ca.gov/faces/billNavClient.xhtml?bill_id=201720180AB626; Farley Elliott, "Riverside's Newly Legal Home Restaurants Look to Revolu-

tionize California's Food Scene," *Eater*, September 2, 2020, https://la.eater.com /2020/9/2/21418664/riverside-ab-626-home-restaurants-legal-california-chefs.

CHAPTER 5: THE FAST FOOD RESTAURANT, A.K.A. THE QSR

1. Orangetree, FL, https://livability.com/fl/orangetree.

2. Liz Freeman, "Immokalee's High Rate of COVID-19 Draws Reopening Warning from International Relief Group," *Naples (FL) Daily News*, June 10, 2020, www.naplesnews.com/story/news/coronavirus/2020/06/10/immokalee -sees-concerning-spike-covid-19-coronavirus-cases-shouldnt-reopen-relief-group -says/5320184002/.

3. Peter Nowak, "How McDonald's Has Shaped the Food Biz," CBC, May 14, 2015, www.cbc.ca/news/business/how-mcdonald-s-has-shaped-the -food-biz-1.3074081.

4. Matt Sena, "Fast Food Industry Analysis 2020—Cost & Trends," Franchise Help, 2020, www.franchisehelp.com/industry-reports/fast-food-industry -analysis-2020-cost-trends/; Cheryl D. Fryar et al., "Fast Food Consumption Among Adults in the United States, 2013–2016," *Centers for Disease Control and Prevention*, October 2018, www.cdc.gov/nchs/products/databriefs/db322 .htm; Florida Tomato Committee, www.floridatomatoes.org/tomato-101/.

5. Katrina vanden Heuvel, "The Nation: Florida's Modern Slavery . . . the Museum," NPR, March 29, 2010, www.npr.org/templates/story/story.php ?storyId=125296794; *United States v. Navarrete*, SHERLOC, December 19, 2012, https://sherloc.unodc.org/cld/case-law-doc/traffickingpersonscrimetype /usa/2008/united_states_v._navarrete.html; "Anti-Slavery Program," CIW, https://ciw-online.org/slavery/.

6. "How Much of Americans' Paychecks Go to Health Care, Charted," Advisory Board, May 2, 2019, www.advisory.com/daily-briefing/2019/05 /02/health-care-costs.

7. Eric Schlosser, "A Side Order of Human Rights," *New York Times*, April 6, 2005, www.nytimes.com/2005/04/06/opinion/a-side-order-of -human-rights.html.

8. Noam Scheiber, "Why Wendy's Is Facing Campus Protests (It's About the Tomatoes)," *New York Times*, March 7, 2019, www.nytimes.com/2019/03/07 /business/economy/wendys-farm-workers-tomatoes.html; "Oxfam Great Britain: Fair Food Program a 'Signpost for Good Practice,'" CIW, February, 2021, https://ciw-online.org/blog/2021/02/oxfam-signpost/.

9. Fair Food Program, www.fairfoodprogram.org/results/.

10. Michael Gold, "Workers Accuse Chipotle, the 'Food with Integrity' Company, of Abuses," *New York Times*, September 10, 2019, www.nytimes .com/2019/09/10/nyregion/chipotle-lawsuit-workers.html; Jordan Valinsky, "Chipotle Cited with 13,253 Child Labor Law Violations in Massachusetts,"

CNN, January 28, 2020, www.cnn.com/2020/01/28/business/chipotle-child
-labor-law-violations/index.html.

11. "Sick Leave," US Department of Labor, www.dol.gov/general/topic
/workhours/sickleave.

12. Michael Hicks, "COVID-19 and Economic Inequality," *Muncie (IN)
Star Press*, September 6, 2020, www.thestarpress.com/story/opinion/columnists
/2020/09/06/michael-hicks-covid-19-and-economic-inequality/3450718001/.

13. Dom Calicchio, "McDonald's Employees in California Told to Use Dog
Diapers, Coffee Filters as Face Masks: Lawsuit," Fox News, June 17, 2020, www
.foxnews.com/us/mcdonalds-employees-in-california-told-to-use-dog-diapers
-coffee-filters-as-face-masks-lawsuit; Andrew Chamings, "SF McDonald's
Workers Used Coffee Filters as Masks, Got Infected, per Complaint," *SF Gate*,
May 21, 2020, www.sfgate.com/bayarea/article/SF-McDonalds-workers
-ppe-coffee-filters-masks-15286829.php; Becky Dernbach, "McDonald's Workers File Complaints Demanding More Coronavirus Protections," *Mother Jones*,
April 10, 2020, www.motherjones.com/food/2020/04/mcdonalds-workers-file
-complaints-demanding-more-coronavirus-protections/.

14. Matthew Hall, "Burger King Employees Protest After Coworker
Dies," *Santa Monica (CA) Daily Press*, July 11, 2020, www.smdp.com/burger
-king-employees-protest-after-coworker-dies/194081.

15. "Tomato War Ends at Taco Bell," CBS, March 9, 2005, www
.cbsnews.com/news/tomato-war-ends-at-taco-bell/; Jacob Ogles, "South-
west Florida COVID-19 Cases Climb as First Vaccines Reach Coastal Hospitals," *Florida Politics*, December 23, 2020, https://floridapolitics.com/archives
/390519-southwest-florida-covid-19-cases-climb-as-first-vaccines-reach-coastal
-hospitals.

16. Monica Burton, "Trump's Restaurant Industry Conference Call Only
Included Major Chains," *Eater*, March 17, 2020, www.eater.com/2020/3/17
/21183535/trump-restaurant-industry-call-only-included-major-chains.

17. Heather Haddon, "McDonald's, Chipotle and Domino's Are Booming
During Coronavirus While Your Neighborhood Restaurant Struggles," *Wall
Street Journal*, October 12, 2020, www.wsj.com/articles/mcdonalds-chipotle
-and-dominos-are-feasting-during-coronavirus-while-your-neighborhood
-restaurant-fasts-11602302431.

18. Rachel King, "More than 110,000 Eating and Drinking Establishments
Closed in 2020," *Fortune*, January 26, 2021, https://fortune.com/2021/01/26
/restaurants-bars-closed-2020-jobs-lost-how-many-have-closed-us-covid
-pandemic-stimulus-unemployment/; Haddon, "McDonald's, Chipotle and
Domino's Are Booming"; Kate Taylor and Irene Jiang, "Fast-Food Giants Like
Dunkin' and Chipotle Are Using the Restaurant Apocalypse as a Chance to
'Swallow Up' Independent Restaurants That Are Struggling to Survive the Pandemic," *Business Insider*, August 25, 2020, www.businessinsider.com/pandemic
-paves-way-to-chains-to-swallow-up-independent-restaurants-2020-8;

Jaya Saxena, "Chains Are Using the Pandemic as an Opportunity to Buy Independent Restaurants," *Eater*, August 27, 2020, www.eater.com/2020/8/27/21403911/chains-find-opportunity-in-pandemic-to-buy-independent-restaurant-spaces.

19. Tara Nurin, "The National Restaurant Association Still Doesn't Want to Pay Sick Workers to Stay Home," *Forbes*, April 25, 2020, www.forbes.com/sites/taranurin/2020/04/25/the-national-restaurant-association-still-doesnt-want-to-pay-sick-workers-to-stay-home/?sh=1eb5edd21cbb.

20. "National Restaurant Association," Center for Responsive Politics, www.opensecrets.org/orgs/national-restaurant-assn/summary?toprecipcycle=2020&contribcycle=2020&lobcycle=2020&outspendcycle=2020&id=D000000150&topnumcycle=2016.

21. "Fast Food Restaurants in the US—Employment Statistics 2002–2027," IBISWorld, www.ibisworld.com/industry-statistics/employment/fast-food-restaurants-united-states; "Fast Food Worker Salary in the United States," Salary.com, www.salary.com/research/salary/benchmark/fast-food-worker-salary; Allison Linn, "Many Fast-Food Workers Are Living in Poverty: Report," CNBC, October 15, 2013, www.cnbc.com/2013/10/15/many-fast-food-workers-are-living-in-poverty-report.html.

22. Susanna Kim, "McDonald's Defends Telling Workers to 'Quit Complaining' to Reduce Stress," ABC, November 21, 2013, https://abcnews.go.com/Business/mcdonalds-defends-employee-tips-deemed-offensive-clueless-advocacy/story?id=20954354; Ken Jacobs, Ian Perry, and Jenifer MacGillvary, "The High Public Cost of Low Wages," UC Berkeley Center for Labor Research and Education, April 2015, https://laborcenter.berkeley.edu/pdf/2015/the-high-public-cost-of-low-wages.pdf, 3, 2.

23. Minimum Wage," US Department of Labor, www.dol.gov/general/topic/wages/minimumwage.

24. "H.R. 582—Raise the Wage Act," US Congress, January 16, 2019, www.congress.gov/bill/116th-congress/house-bill/582/text.

25. Emily Cochrane and Catie Edmondson, "Minimum Wage Increase Fails as 7 Democrats Vote Against the Measure," *New York Times*, March 5, 2021, www.nytimes.com/2021/03/05/us/minimum-wage-senate.html.

26. "National Restaurant Association Opposes H.R. 582, 'Raise the Wage Act,'" National Restaurant Association, March 5, 2019, https://restaurant.org/news/pressroom/press-releases/association-opposes-raise-the-wage-act.

27. Noam Scheiber, "How a Rising Minimum Wage Affects Jobs in Seattle," *New York Times*, June 26, 2017, www.nytimes.com/2017/06/26/business/economy/seattle-minimum-wage.html?_r=0; Paul Roberts, "Minimum-Wage Hike Jan. 1 Is Welcome Prospect for Workers, but Employers Are Divided," *Seattle Times*, December 31, 2020, www.seattletimes.com/business/economy/minimum-wage-hike-jan-1-a-welcome-prospect-for-workers-but-employers-are-divided/; Daniel Tercer, "Did Ontario's Minimum Wage Hike Kill Jobs?

A Look at the Numbers, 1 Year Later," *Huffington Post Canada*, February 9, 2019. www.huffingtonpost.ca/2019/02/09/ontario-minimum-wage-impact_a _23665531/.

28. Adele Peters, "David Chang and Other Chefs Say Now Is the Time to Fix the Restaurant Industry's Long-Standing Inequities," *Fast Company*, August 7, 2020, www.msn.com/en-us/news/us/david-chang-and-other-chefs-say-now -is-the-time-to-fix-the-restaurant-industry-e2-80-99s-long-standing-inequities /ar-BB17Hnjh.

29. "Heston Blumenthal: In Search of Perfection—Hamburger," BBC 2, 2006, www.youtube.com/watch?v=6WPq5jtW5J0.

30. Melia Robinson, "We Tried the World's First Robot-Made Burger Restaurant That's Backed by Google's Parent Company—Here's the Verdict," *Business Insider*, July 28, 2018, www.businessinsider.com/robot-made-burger -restaurant-creator-review-2018-7#guests-can-monitor-their-order-on-this-tablet -the-colored-dots-represent-each-stage-in-the-robots-preparation-process-19.

31. Melia Robinson, "This Robot-Powered Restaurant Is One Step Closer to Putting Fast-Food Workers Out of a Job," *Business Insider*, June 12, 2017, www .businessinsider.com/momentum-machines-funding-robot-burger-restaurant -2017-6.

32. Deirdre Bosa, "SoftBank-Backed Zume Is Laying Off Half Its Staff and Shuttering Its Pizza Delivery Business," CNBC, January 8, 2020, www.cnbc .com/2020/01/08/softbank-backed-zume-cuts-360-jobs-closes-pizza-delivery -business.html.

33. Josh Constine, "Taste Test: Burger Robot Startup Creator Opens First Restaurant; $6 of Algorithmic Deliciousness," TechCrunch, January 21, 2018, https://techcrunch.com/2018/06/21/creator-hamburger-robot/; Email state- ment via Emunah Hauser, "Should Creator partner with other restaurants in the future, these partners would need to hold shared values and principles in ingredient sourcing and producer partnerships; sustainability in operations; car- bon footprint consciousness (Creator is carbon neutral); transparency in food preparation; worker growth opportunities and an excellent work environment; and aligned intentions around the guest dining experience."

34. Alastair Fitzpayne, Conor McKay, and Ethan Pollack, "Automation and a Changing Economy: Policies for Shared Prosperity," Aspen Institute, April 2, 2019, www.aspeninstitute.org/publications/automation-and-a-changing -economy-policies-for-shared-prosperity/.

35. Letter to Governor Andrew Cuomo, National Restaurant Association, November 17, 2020, www.restaurant.org/downloads/pdfs/advocacy/letter -from-tom-bene-to-nga-chair-andrew-cuomo_11.

36. "S.2048—Investing in American Workers Act," US Congress, October 31, 2017, www.congress.gov/bill/115th-congress/senate-bill/2048.

37. "Heart Disease Facts," Centers for Disease Control, September 8, 2020, www.cdc.gov/heartdisease/facts.htm.

38. "Cardiovascular Disease Mortality in New York State," New York State Department of Health, 2008, www.health.ny.gov/diseases/cardiovascular/heart _disease/docs/cvd_mortality.pdf, 6; "National Vital Statistics Reports," Centers for Disease Control, June 24, 2019, www.cdc.gov/nchs/data/nvsr/nvsr68 /nvsr68_06-508.pdf, 17.

39. Joonseok Kim, "Healthcare Costs and Resource Utilization Based on Diabetes and Cardiovascular Risk Factor Profile," American College of Cardiology, June 29, 2017, www.acc.org/latest-in-cardiology/articles/2017/06/29/08/22 /healthcare-costs-and-resource-utilization-based-on-diabetes-and-cv-risk -factor-profile.

40. "Heart Disease and Stroke Statistics: 2019 at a Glance," American Heart Association, 2019, https://professional.heart.org/en/science-news/-/media /22cf5db5b1a21b38a135fcecb42d588b.ashx, 1.

41. Marcia Chatelain, *Franchise: The Golden Arches in Black America* (New York: Liveright, 2020), 15, 16, 21, 60, 66, 68–71, 77, 78, 86, 264.

42. Eric Schlosser, *Fast Food Nation: The Dark Side of the All-American Meal* (New York: Houghton Mifflin, 2001), 96.

43. Sarah A. Roache and Lawrence O. Gostin, "Untapped Power of Soda Taxes: Incentivizing Consumers, Generating Revenue, and Altering Corporate Behavior," US National Library of Medicine, June 14, 2017, www.ncbi.nlm.nih .gov/pmc/articles/PMC5582434/.

CHAPTER 6: THE CHAIN RESTAURANT

1. "Number of Restaurants in the United States from 2011 to 2018," Statista, November 4, 2020, www.statista.com/statistics/244616/number-of-qsr-fsr -chain-independent-restaurants-in-the-us/; US Census (website updates daily), www.census.gov/popclock/.

2. Milton Friedman, "A Friedman Doctrine: The Social Responsibility of Business Is to Increase Its Profits," *New York Times*, September 13, 1970, www.nytimes.com/1970/09/13/archives/a-friedman-doctrine-the-social -responsibility-of-business-is-to.html.

3. "Number of Denny's Restaurants Worldwide from 2007 to 2019, by Mode of Operation," Statista, February 25, 2020, www.statista.com/statistics /222818/number-of-dennys-restaurants/; "Cracker Barrel Annual Report," Cracker Barrel Old Country Store, 2019, https://investor.cbrlgroup.com/static -files/2cac2972-89a6-4932-bb5d-2daa8801660e, 5.

4. Joseph L. Bower and Lynn S. Paine, "The Error at the Heart of Corporate Leadership," *Harvard Business Review* (May–June 2017), https://hbr.org /2017/05/the-error-at-the-heart-of-corporate-leadership?ab=seriesnav -spotlight; Michael C. Jensen and Kevin J. Murphy, "CEO Incentives—It's Not How Much You Pay, but How," *Harvard Business Review* (May–June 1990): 4, www.researchgate.net/publication/13185791_CEO_incentives_its_not_how

_much_you_pay_but_how; Duff McDonald, "Harvard Business School and the Propagation of Immoral Profit Strategies," *Newsweek*, April 6, 2017, www .newsweek.com/2017/04/14/harvard-business-school-financial-crisis -economics-578378.html.

5. Jack Guy, "Irish Court Rules Subway Loaves Are Too Sugary to Be Called Bread," CNN, October 1, 2020, www.cnn.com/2020/10/01/business/subway -bread-ireland-ruling-scli-intl/index.html.

6. Ananya Bhattacharya, "In-N-Out Sues Delivery Service DoorDash," CNN Business, November 12, 2015, https://money.cnn.com/2015/11/12 /technology/in-n-out-doordash-delivery-lawsuit/index.html; Robert Chan-nick, "Suburban Restaurant in DoorDash Lawsuit: Stop Delivering Our Food," *Chicago Tribune*, January 10, 2018, www.chicagotribune.com/business/ct-biz -doordash-restaurant-food-delivery-lawsuit-20180109-story.html.

7. Paul Best, "As Congress Considers Minimum Wage Hike, National Restaurant Association Says It Would Kills Jobs and Increase Menu Prices," Fox News, February 16, 2021, www.foxbusiness.com/economy/national-restaurant -association-says-minimum-wage-hike-would-kills-jobs-and-increase-menu -prices.

8. Colman Andrews, "Coronavirus Effect: Here Are 50 Popular Restau-rants That Won't Reopen After the Pandemic Subsides," *USA Today*, Septem-ber 12, 2020, www.usatoday.com/story/money/2020/09/12/50-most-popular -restaurants-that-wont-reopen-after-the-pandemic/113707568/.

9. "Number of Full Service Restaurant (FSR) Franchise Establishments in the United States from 2013 to 2020," Statista, February 25, 2020, www .statista.com/statistics/217579/number-of-us—full-service-restaurant -franchise-establishments/.

10. Sara DiNatale, "Cracker Barrel Buys Maple Street Biscuit Co. in $36 Million Deal," *Tampa Bay Times*, October 14, 2019, www.tampabay.com/news /business/2019/10/14/cracker-barrel-buys-maple-street-biscuit-co-in-36-million -deal/; Joanna Fantozzi, "Punch Bowl Social Closes Two Locations in Wake of Cracker Barrel Divestment," *Nation's Restaurant News*, June 9, 2020, www.nrn .com/news/punch-bowl-social-closes-two-locations-wake-cracker-barrel -divestment.

11. Dan Schawbel, "Ron Shaich: Panera's Success Comes Down to These 3 Things," *Forbes*, September 25, 2017, www.forbes.com/sites/danschawbel /2017/09/25/ron-shaich-paneras-success-comes-down-to-these-3-things /?sh=357c51d35c18.

12. Alexis C. Madrigal, "Chuck E. Cheese's, Silicon Valley Startup: The Ori-gins of the Best Pizza Chain Ever," *Atlantic*, July 17, 2013, www.theatlantic.com /technology/archive/2013/07/chuck-e-cheeses-silicon-valley-startup-the-origins -of-the-best-pizza-chain-ever/277869/.

13. Warren Fiske, "Mark Warner Says Average Holding Time for Stocks Has Fallen to Four Months," *PolitiFact*, July 6, 2016, www.politifact

.com/factchecks/2016/jul/06/mark-warner/mark-warner-says-average-holding-time-stocks-has-f/.

14. "Menu," Cheesecake Factory, 2020, www.thecheesecakefactory.com/menu/.

15. "We Are Working with All of Our Fish Suppliers to Support Sustainable Fishing Practices," J D Wetherspoon, www.jdwetherspoon.com/food/food-provenance/our-fish.

16. "Our Values," Applebee's, www.applebees.com/en/about-us.

17. "Community," Olive Garden, www.olivegarden.com/about-us/community; "Citizenship," Darden, https://darden.com/citizenship/plate/sourcing.

18. "Seafood with Standards," Red Lobster, www.redlobster.com/our-story/seafood-with-standards/our-beliefs.

19. Laura Reiley, "At Tampa Bay Farm-to-Table Restaurants, You're Being Fed Fiction," *Tampa Bay Times*, April 13, 2016, https://projects.tampabay.com/projects/2016/food/farm-to-fable/restaurants/.

20. "Food with Care," Cracker Barrel, www.crackerbarrel.com/about/food-with-care.

21. "California Transparency in Supply Chains," Buffalo Wild Wings, www.buffalowildwings.com/en-ca/California-Transparency-in-Supply-Chain-Act/.

22. "Corporate Social Responsibility," Cheesecake Factory, www.thecheesecakefactory.com/corporate-social-responsibility/; "Corporate Social Responsibility Report," Cheesecake Factory, 2019, www.thecheesecakefactory.com/assets/pdf/2019-CSR-Report-The-Cheesecake-Factory.pdf.

23. "See What Social Responsibility Means to Us," IHOP, www.ihop.com/en/about-ihop/social-responsibility-program/environment.

24. Gloria Dawson, "IHOP Announces New Brand President," *Nation's Restaurant News*, June 03, 2019, www.nrn.com/family-dining/ihop-announces-new-brand-president; "IHOP Celebrates 55th Birthday with a 55-Cent Short Stack," *Chattanooga Times Free Press*, July 4, 2013, www.timesfreepress.com/news/chattanooganow/dining/story/2013/jul/04/get-a-55-cent-short-stack-monday-at-ihop-and-tell/112296/; Nicole Duncan, "Taking a Closer Look at the 50 Top-Grossing Full-Service Restaurants Within the U.S.," *FSR Magazine*, August 2020, www.fsrmagazine.com/2020-fsr-50.

CHAPTER 7: THE GROCERANT

1. "Places for Business and Careers, 2019," *Forbes*, October 2019, www.forbes.com/places/fl/naples/?sh=41c4c0461aff.

2. Ashley Nickle, "Kroger to Divest Its Interest in Lucky's Market," *Produce Market Guide*, December 5, 2019, www.producemarketguide.com/article/news-article/kroger-divest-its-interest-luckys-market; Ron Hurtibise, "Lucky's Market Closing All but One Florida Store," *South Florida Sun Sentinel*, January 21, 2020, www.sun-sentinel.com/business/fl-bz-luckys-closing-florida-20200121-jc5uva7oirg3nb2gp4oasgxusm-story.html; Lucas High, "Colorado-Based Grocery

Chain Lucky's Market Files for Bankruptcy," *Denver Post*, January 27, 2020, www.denverpost.com/2020/01/27/luckys-market-bankruptcy-colorado/.

3. Sapna Maheshwari and Michael Corkery, "'We Are Forgotten': Grocery Workers Hope for Higher Pay and Vaccinations," *New York Times*, February 8, 2021, www.nytimes.com/2021/02/08/business/grocery-workers-hero-pay -vaccines.html.

4. Derek Thompson, "Restaurants Are the New Factories," *Atlantic*, August 9, 2017, www.theatlantic.com/business/archive/2017/08/restaurant -jobs-boom/536244/; Eliana Zeballos, "U.S. Food-Away-from-Home Spending Continued to Outpace Food-at-Home Spending in 2019," US Department of Agriculture, June 15, 2020, www.ers.usda.gov/data-products/chart-gallery /gallery/chart-detail/?chartId=58364..

5. Bonnie Riggs, "Enter the Grocerant: Grocery Stores Winning at Foodservice," *NPD*, March, 2016, www.npd.com/wps/portal/npd/us/news/latest -reports/2016/enter-the-grocerant-grocery-stores-winning-at-foodservice/.

6. "Variety, Speed and Embracing Technology All Bolster the Power of Foodservice at Retail," *FMI*, September 4, 2019, www.fmi.org/newsroom/news -archive/view/2019/09/04/fmi-releases-annual-exploration-of-grocery-food service.

7. "Food Prices and Spending," USDA, www.ers.usda.gov/data-products /ag-and-food-statistics-charting-the-essentials/food-prices-and-spending/; Beth Kowitt and Lance Lambert, "The Coronavirus Pandemic Is Dramatically Changing the Way Americans Eat," *Fortune*, July 21, 2020, https://fortune.com /2020/07/21/us-consumer-spending-food-dining-out-restaurants-coronavirus -pandemic-lockdown/.

8. "Supermarket Facts," *FMI*, 2019, www.fmi.org/our-research/supermarket -facts; "How Many Grocery Stores Are There in the United States?" foodindustry.com, April 2019, www.foodindustry.com/articles/how-many -grocery-stores-are-there-in-the-united-states/.

9. "E-commerce Share of Total Global Retail Sales from 2015 to 2023," Statista, November 26, 2020, www.statista.com/statistics/534123/e-commerce -share-of-retail-sales-worldwide/; Pamela N. Danziger, "Online Grocery Sales to Reach $100 Billion in 2025; Amazon Is Current and Future Leader," *Forbes*, January 18, 2018, www.forbes.com/sites/pamdanziger/2018/01/18/online -grocery-sales-to-reach-100-billion-in-2025-amazon-set-to-be-market-share -leader/?sh=58b385fd62f3.

10. Shelley E. Kohan, "Walmart's Online Sales Have Surged 74% During the Pandemic," *Forbes*, May 19, 2020, www.forbes.com/sites/shelleykohan /2020/05/19/walmart-revenue-up-86-e-commerce-up-74/?sh=7e171a8466cc; Melissa Repko, "Kroger Stuns with 92% E-commerce Gain, but It Has to Prove It's Not a Coronavirus Blip," CNBC, June 18, 2020, www.cnbc.com/2020/06 /18/kroger-stuns-with-92percent-e-commerce-gain-but-it-has-to-prove-its -not-a-coronavirus-blip.html.

11. Helen Tangires, "Public Markets and the City: A Historical Perspective," *Project for Public Spaces*, October 29, 2005, www.pps.org/article/6thmktstangires.

12. Robert Lewis, "Kroger Co.," in *Britannica*, April 17, 2017, www.britannica.com/topic/Kroger-Co.

13. Kat Eschner, "The Bizarre Story of Piggly Wiggly, the First Self-Service Grocery Store," *Smithsonian Magazine*, September 6, 2017, www.smithsonianmag.com/smart-news/bizarre-story-piggly-wiggly-first-self-service-grocery-store-180964708/; "Who We Are," *Loblaw*, www.loblaw.ca/en/about-us/history.html.

14. "How the A&P Changed the Way We Shop," NPR, August 23, 2011, www.npr.org/2011/08/23/139761274/how-the-a-p-changed-the-way-we-shop.

15. Nicole Perlroth, "The Consumer's Temple," *Forbes*, May 1, 2009, www.forbes.com/2009/04/30/1930s-advertising-innovation-business-supermarket.html#bf3584d1437f.

16. "International Directory of Company Histories, Vol. 15," St. James Press, 1996, www.fundinguniverse.com/company-histories/king-kullen-grocery-co-inc-history/.

17. David Gwynne, "Cincinnati Area," Groceteria, July 2, 2018, www.groceteria.com/place/ohio/cincinnati/.

18. "Piggly Wiggly Floor Plan," Digital Archive of Memphis Libraries, 1920, https://memphislibrary.contentdm.oclc.org/digital/collection/p16108coll17/id/304/; "Saunders Is Sure Keedoozle Will Build His Third Fortune," *Life*, January 1949, https://books.google.ca/books?id=h0oEAAAAMBAJ&lpg=PA36&dq=Clarence+Saunders+Keedoozle&pg=PA36&hl=en&redir_esc=y#v=onepage&q=Clarence%20Saunders%20Keedoozle&f=false; "Keedoozler," *Time*, July 6, 1936, web.archive.org/web/20110529223313/http://205.188.238.109/time/magazine/article/0%2C9171%2C770289%2C00.html; "Saunders Is Sure Keedoozle Will Build His Third Fortune."

19. "About Us," Piggly Wiggly, www.pigglywiggly.com/about-us.

20. Kerstin Sjoden, "June 4, 1937: Humpty Dumpty and the Shopping Cart," *Wired*, June 4, 2009, www.wired.com/2009/06/dayintech-0604/; Charlie Sorrel, "How the Shopping Cart Shaped Our Buying Habits," *Fast Company*, March 8, 2016, www.fastcompany.com/3057306/how-the-shopping-cart-shaped-our-buying-habits.

21. "History of Refrigeration," Peak Mechanical Partnership, www.peakmechanical.ca/menu/resources/history-of-refrigeration.html; Carroll Gantz, *Design Chronicles: Significant Mass-Produced Designs of the 20th Century* (Atglen, PA: Schiffer, 2005), www.industrialdesignhistory.com/book/export/html/148; "GE Monitor—Top Refrigerator," Albany Institute of History & Art, albanyinstitute.org/ge-monitor-top-refrigerator.html; Rachel Ross, "Who Invented the Refrigerator?," *Livescience*, February 08, 2017, www.livescience.com/57797-refrigerator-history.html; "Background—Domestic Technology,"

Canada Science and Technology Museum, www.alcainc.com/wp-content/uploads /2016/02/Domestic_Technology2.pdf.

22. Richard Schragger, "The Anti–Chain Store Movement, Localist Ideology, and the Remnants of the Progressive Constitution, 1920–1940," SSRN, June 29, 2005, https://papers.ssrn.com/sol3/papers.cfm?abstract_id =749084.

23. Marc Levinson, email to the author; *United States v. New York Great A.&P. Tea Co.*, 67 F. Supp. 626 (E.D. Ill. 1946)," *Justia US Law*, September 21, 1946, https://law.justia.com/cases/federal/district-courts/FSupp/67/626 /2311543/ ; "How the A&P Changed the Way We Shop"; Justin R. Watkins, "Always Low Prices, Always at a Cost: A Call to Arms Against the Wal-Martization of America," *John Marshall Law Review* (Fall 2006): 268, https:// repository.law.uic.edu/cgi/viewcontent.cgi?article=1312&context=lawreview.

24. Richard F. Weingroff, "The Genie in the Bottle: The Interstate System and Urban Problems, 1939–1957," US Department of Transportation, October 2000, www.fhwa.dot.gov/publications/publicroads/00septoct/urban.cfm; "Who We Are," Loblaw, www.loblaw.ca/en/about-us/history.html.

25. Ruth Schwartz Cowan, email to the author.

26. "Supermarket Scanner," Smithsonian National Museum of American History, https://americanhistory.si.edu/collections/search/object/nmah_892778; Michael Ruhlman, *Grocery: The Buying and Selling of Food in America* (New York: Harry N. Adams, 2017), 40.

27. Studs Terkel, *Working: People Talk About What They Do All Day and How They Feel About What They Do* (New York City: New Press, 1974), 374.

28. Isadore Babmash, "The Great Supermarket Battle," *New York Times*, July 16, 1972, www.nytimes.com/1972/07/16/archives/the-great-supermarket -battle-ap-move-to-economy-intensifies.html.

29. "Loblaw Companies Limited—Company Profile, Information, Business Description, History, Background Information on Loblaw Companies Limited," *Reference for Business*, www.referenceforbusiness.com/history2/27 /Loblaw-Companies-Limited.html.

30. Ashley Lutz, "Amazon Is Officially Buying Whole Foods—Here's Everything That Will Change for Customers," *Business Insider*, August 24, 2017, www.businessinsider.com/amazon-buys-whole-foods-changes-2017-8; James F. Peltz, "On the Record: How Whole Foods Has Affected the Grocery Business One Year After the Amazon Deal," *Los Angeles Times*, November 6, 2018, www.latimes.com/business/la-fi-amazon-whole-foods-qa-20181106-story .html.

31. Qu Yunxu and Tang Ziyi, "Alibaba Wants a Hema Supermarket in Every Big Chinese City," *Caixin*, June 25, 2019, www.caixinglobal.com/2019 -06-25/alibaba-wants-a-hema-supermarket-in-every-big-chinese-city -101431387.html; Lauren Hallanan, "Shopping at Hema with Locals: Here's What 'New Retail' Was Really Like," *Forbes*, October 24, 2018, www.forbes

.com/sites/laurenhallanan/2018/10/24/i-shopped-at-hema-with-locals-heres
-what-new-retail-was-really-like/#53465dad3167; Roni Hiranand, "Inside
Hema: A Look into the Cornerstone of Alibaba's New Retail Strategy," *Medium*, October 8, 2018, https://medium.com/@ronihiranand/inside-hema
-a-look-into-the-cornerstone-of-alibabas-new-retail-strategy-bde0368ea992;
Rita Liao, "Alibaba and Amazon Move Over, We Visited JD's Connected Grocery Store in China," *TechCrunch*, November 16, 2018, https://techcrunch
.com/2018/11/15/jd-7fresh-supermarket/.

32. Sylvain Charlebois, "The Rise of the Grocerant," *Canadian Grocer*, November 3, 2017, www.canadiangrocer.com/blog/the-rise-of-the-grocerant-76590.

33. Kate Conger, "Uber Acquires Cornershop, a Grocery Delivery Start-Up,"
New York Times, October 11, 2019, www.nytimes.com/2019/10/11/technology
/uber-cornershop-grocery-delivery.html; "Online and Offline Grocery Market
Share of Leading Food Retailers in the United States in 2017," Statista, November 27, 2020, www.statista.com/statistics/818602/online-and-offline-grocery
-market-share-of-leading-grocery-retailers-us/.

34. "2020 Online Grocery Shopping Statistics: Pre and Post Covid-19,"
Superfood, April 16, 2020, https://superfood.digital/online-grocery-store
-ecommerce-statistics/; "Supermarkets & Grocery Stores in the US—Employment Statistics, 2003–2026," IBISWorld, November 10, 2020, www.ibisworld
.com/industry-statistics/employment/supermarkets-grocery-stores-united
-states/; Michelle Grant, "E-commerce Set for Global Domination—but at Different Speeds," *Forbes*, August 14, 2018, www.forbes.com/sites/michellegrant
/2018/08/14/e-commerce-set-for-global-domination/#49f40fa3bfaf.

35. Alison Griswold, "There's Still One Big Reason Why People Aren't Buying Their Groceries Online," *Quartz*, September 14, 2017, https://
qz.com/1077743/people-dont-buy-groceries-online-because-they-prefer-to
-pick-things-out-in-stores/.

36. Jonathan Bloom, *American Wasteland: How America Throws Away Nearly
Half of Its Food (and What We Can Do About It)* (Boston: Da Capo Press, 2011).

37. Barbara Kafka, *Roasting: A Simple Art* (New York: William Morrow,
1995).

38. "Supermarket Facts," FMI, 2019, www.fmi.org/our-research/supermarket
-facts.

CHAPTER 8: THE VIRTUOUS RESTAURANT

1. Julia Moskin, "Danny Meyer's Restaurants Will End Their No-Tipping
Policy," *New York Times*, July 20, 2020, www.nytimes.com/2020/07/20/dining
/danny-meyer-no-tips.html.

2. Michael Lynn et al., "Consumer Racial Discrimination in Tipping: A Replication and Extension," Online Library, March 19, 2008, https://onlinelibrary
.wiley.com/doi/abs/10.1111/j.1559-1816.2008.00338.x.

3. Joanna Fantozzi, "Why Daniel Patterson's Restaurant Group Is Losing Chefs of Color," *Restaurant Hospitality*, May 24, 2019, www.restaurant-hospitality .com/operations/why-daniel-patterson-s-restaurant-group-losing-chefs -color; Eve Batey, "Kaya Chef Nigel Jones Drops Lawsuit Against Former Partner Daniel Patterson," *Eater*, December 23, 2019, https://sf.eater.com/2019 /12/23/21035585/kaya-daniel-patterson-lawsuit-coi-alta-nigel-jones -dismissed.

4. Kenneth P. Vogel, "New America, a Google-Funded Think Tank, Faces Backlash for Firing a Google Critic," *New York Times*, September 1, 2017, www .nytimes.com/2017/09/01/us/politics/anne-marie-slaughter-new-america -google.html.

5. "2014 Farm Act," Economic Research Service, US Department of Agriculture, February 11, 2019, www.ers.usda.gov/agricultural-act-of-2014-highlights -and-implications/nutrition/.

6. Tunde Wey, "Don't Bail Out the Restaurant Industry, Part 1," Instagram, March 24, 2020, www.instagram.com/p/B-HwhutDaOJ/.

7. Brett Martin, "The Provocations of Chef Tunde Wey," *GQ*, March 6, 2019, www.gq.com/story/chef-tunde-wey-profile.

8. "Modern Monetary Theory," *NPR Planet Money*, NPR, September 26, 2018, www.npr.org/transcripts/652001941.

JAIME HOGGE

COREY MINTZ is a freelance food reporter (*New York Times, Globe and Mail, Eater,* and others) focusing on the intersection between food and labor, politics, farming, ethics, and culture. He has been a cook and a restaurant critic and is the author of *How to Host a Dinner Party,* which chronicled 192 dinner parties he hosted with fascinating people, including politicians, refugees, criminals, artists, academics, acupuncturists, high-rise window washers, competitive barbecuers, and one monkey.

He lives in Winnipeg with his family.

PublicAffairs is a publishing house founded in 1997. It is a tribute to the standards, values, and flair of three persons who have served as mentors to countless reporters, writers, editors, and book people of all kinds, including me.

I. F. STONE, proprietor of *I. F. Stone's Weekly*, combined a commitment to the First Amendment with entrepreneurial zeal and reporting skill and became one of the great independent journalists in American history. At the age of eighty, Izzy published *The Trial of Socrates*, which was a national bestseller. He wrote the book after he taught himself ancient Greek.

BENJAMIN C. BRADLEE was for nearly thirty years the charismatic editorial leader of *The Washington Post*. It was Ben who gave the *Post* the range and courage to pursue such historic issues as Watergate. He supported his reporters with a tenacity that made them fearless and it is no accident that so many became authors of influential, best-selling books.

ROBERT L. BERNSTEIN, the chief executive of Random House for more than a quarter century, guided one of the nation's premier publishing houses. Bob was personally responsible for many books of political dissent and argument that challenged tyranny around the globe. He is also the founder and longtime chair of Human Rights Watch, one of the most respected human rights organizations in the world.

•   •   •

For fifty years, the banner of Public Affairs Press was carried by its owner Morris B. Schnapper, who published Gandhi, Nasser, Toynbee, Truman, and about 1,500 other authors. In 1983, Schnapper was described by *The Washington Post* as "a redoubtable gadfly." His legacy will endure in the books to come.

Peter Osnos, *Founder*